Heirloom Doll Clothes For Götz

By Martha Campbell Pullen, Ph. D.

May God Bless You

Martha Pullen

Martha Pullen

"*Joanna*"

DOLL NO.

289

MARTHA PULLEN COMPANY

Dedication

To Elizabeth Travis Johnson

Elizabeth Johnson is one of the true heroes in my life. Just a few times in a lifetime, if one is very fortunate indeed, does a person meet and call friend an individual such as Elizabeth Travis Johnson. I first met her not in person but rather through her patterns which I bought one after one when making heirloom clothing for Joanna when she was a little girl. I always looked for the Children's Corner patterns which read, "designed by Elizabeth Travis Johnson." Little did I realize when I was sewing those adorable clothes that the author would become one of my close friends and business colleagues. I met Elizabeth for the first time at a Smocking Arts Guild of America national convention. She and I were both teaching and I felt like I should bow when I was introduced to her. (I didn't let her know that because she would have been mortified that I or anyone else considered her royalty.) How could I ever tell her what she had meant to me in my sewing hobby? Were there words to express how much she meant to my customers in my retail store? How could I begin to tell her that it was under her guidance and enthusiasm that heirloom sewing is being enjoyed all over the world like it is today? Should I just tell her that it really is "her industry?" Does she have any concept what she has meant and still means to the thousands, perhaps millions, of women and children who have sewn with her instruction or who have received garments made with her designs? Does she know that she, through her teaching, designs, and books will live forever?

She was at the convention with her adorable husband Glenn who was one of the models for the fashion show. Elizabeth had smocked him a beautiful tuxedo shirt and he looked so handsome walking down the runway. During that meeting and later on I was to learn of the wonderful marriage which they enjoyed for 49 years. When one of them spoke, the other just looked adoringly at the other. Some people might call theirs a storybook romance but I think they would prefer to call their marriage the kind of relationship that all people would love for theirs to be.

Elizabeth is a native of Tennessee and attended David Lipscomb High School. She graduated with a degree in Home Economics from Harding University. She was inducted into the Alpha Honor Society at Harding, and was listed in Who's Who in American Colleges and Universities. For 37 years she taught Sewing for Children and Pattern Drafting at Watkins Institute, an adult school in Nashville. At the time most people consider retirement, she was invited to teach for the Smocking Arts Guild of America, for Martha Pullen's Schools of Art Fashion, for the School of Needle Arts, and at shops and seminars throughout the United States. She has drafted many patterns for The Children's Corner in Nashville, and has written several of their published books.

SAGA produced 3 one-hour tapes featuring Elizabeth teaching on collars, and along with Florence Roberson and Kathryn Kastama, Elizabeth appeared in four more SAGA tapes. She was presented with an Honorary Masters in the Artisan Program by SAGA in 1983.

Elizabeth is a member of the Church of Christ, where she taught Bible classes for children until her hearing loss made it impossible to hear the small voices of children. Almost totally deaf, she "gets by" with her lip reading and the help of her hearing ear dog, Muffy. She has the one type of hearing loss which cannot be helped with hearing aids or surgery.

Elizabeth and Glenn have one daughter, Gwendolyn Ann (Mrs. John) Stephens of Kingston, Tennessee. Elizabeth has literally hundreds of "adopted" daughters in the sewing kingdom and at least a million friends. I consider it one of my life's greatest privileges to be an "adopted" daughter of Elizabeth Johnson. Don't ever forget, Miss Elizabeth, that you are a hero not only to me but to thousands of women the world over. We love you and it is with the greatest amount of respect and admiration that I dedicate this doll book to you.

Acknowledgments

Psalm 23:1   *"The Lord is my shepherd, I shall not want."*

Writing books has been a passion of mine for a number of years; without the help of God, my family, friends and staff, it would never have happened. I am forever grateful to the following people:

My mother and father, Anna Ruth Dicus Campbell and the late Paul Jones Campbell, were my first and greatest teachers. Their example of living a Godly, decent, and hard-working life certainly formed my attitude toward life and what should and could be accomplished. I love them and I thank them.

My Aunt Christine Montrose Jenkins, helped me make my first doll clothes before I started to school. I can still see the scraps of cloth, the needles and thread and the scissors waiting for me each time I visited her house. Sometimes we just tied on the doll clothes rather than sewed them and I thought they were gorgeous. So did she.

My mother made me the most fabulous Christmas present that I ever received when I was in the third grade. She purchased a new Toni doll and made a whole wardrobe of clothing to fit her. She had a wedding dress, a bathing suit, a beach coat, dance clothing, a coat, lots of dresses, an evening dress, an evening wrap, a brownie uniform, a beach towel and many other things.

The birth of my daughter, Joanna, after having four half grown boys, brought back the absolute passion for dolls and doll dressing. Joanna loved dolls from the minute she was able to hold a toy and she still loves them. She has slept with Mary every night since my mother gave her to Joanna for her Christmas present when she was 22 months old. For Christmas this year, she asked for a new, GORGEOUS dress for Mary and she sits in her college room right beside her bed during the day. At night, she still snuggles with Joanna.

My children, Camp and Charisse, John and Suzanne, Mark and Sherry Ann, Jeff and Angela and Joanna have always loved me and believed in me. I love them all, and I am so proud of them.

My grandchildren have to be the most beautiful, the smartest, the cutest, and the most creative in the world! Isn't that spoken like a true grandmother? To Campbell, Morgan Ross, Sarah Joy, Rebekah, Marshall and Bradley—I love you dearly, and I thank you for coming into my life bringing such pure joy! My little granddaughters love their dolls and are almost big enough to begin making doll

clothing themselves. I have to admit that the boys aren't too interested in dolls and their clothing. Oh, well!

My business could not be a reality without the talents of many people. I have dedicated staff; I love them and I appreciate them.

Kathy Brower, Lakanjala Campbell, Camp Crocker, Angie Daniel, Toni Duggar, Amy Duggar, Kathy Pearce, and Leighann Simmons, have kept the business running while others worked on this book!

Camp Crocker, my son who is in business with me, thought we should write a book with Götz. He, like me, loves the beautiful dolls which were designed to be played with for years to come.

Elda Bratager's doll clothing is absolutely fabulous. She designs, cuts, sews with the greatest of ease, it seems. Her doll coat and bonnet is spectacular as well as the rest of her creations. It was my good fortune when on a teaching trip to Minnesota, to meet Elda and to have her become one of our doll designers.

Chery Williams donated the beautiful bishop playsuit and bishop dress. She has been for many years one of my favorite designers in the children's heirloom industry. The bishop dress and smocked jumpsuit have matching children's patterns which I am sure some of you will want to make also. Her address is P.O. Box 190234, Birmingham, AL 35219 (205-290-2700).

Pat Holden, my friend from Australia, fell in love with our Götz dolls while she was here teaching at our School of Art Fashion in Huntsville. She has long been one of Australia's foremost designers of children's wear. I suggested that she might want to design for these dolls and she jumped at the opportunity and within several months mailed me the most glorious box of doll fashions.

Claudia Newton is one of those talented designers who can "do anything" literally. She is such a vital cog in this business and her designing skills as well as her sewing skills are pretty unbelievable. Not only did she design and make doll clothes, but also she wrote many of the directions accompanying them. Claudia was one of our photo stylists for the cute photographs of these dolls.

Patti Smith has been one of my chief engineers of the whole business since I first opened my retail shop. She has stitched some of the doll dresses not only for this book but also for many other doll endeavors that I have done. Her artistry, accuracy and speed are constant sources of amazement to me. I have no idea how she sews so fast and with such beauty.

Sue Pennington has become like a second person to me. She is an incredible designer and she sews tirelessly to meet deadlines for all of our books and our television show. We just say, "Sue, what do you want to do?" and she sends in boxes of the most incredible garments both for dolls and people. Her doll dresses are gorgeous and I know you will enjoy making them.

Craig Sharp has been one of our designers for a number of years. His ideas are creative, fresh and brilliantly executed. He first started heirloom sewing and designing for his niece; then for the magazine, Sew Beautiful. After people all over the world began to enjoy Craig's designs, we thought you who love to sew for dolls would enjoy his talented thinking also.

Jack Cooper's photography is professional and creative. He is always there for all aspects of our business. I think these dolls were a little easier to photograph than our little children.

Paul Hager's photography is on the front cover of this book. He is a creative photographer as well as book designer since it was he that designed and laid out most of this book.

Cynthia Handy-Quintella is much appreciated for the lovely illustrations on lace shaping.

Angela Pullen's drawings add life and magic to all of our books. Her illustrations have great depth, detail, and creativity. She always meets deadlines and never complains about the boxes of work that we send her.

Paul Hager's book design is creative and lends a professional touch to all of the sections. It is not an easy task to take hundreds of drawings and computer disks of information and create a book out of it. To have an element of style and beauty in addition to correctness of directions and pictures is quite a feat. It overwhelms me to think of all the decisions which he had to make concerning the layout of this book.

Ann LeRoy finished the book layout and design that Paul had started. Ann always knows how to create style and beauty from a box of stuff and she never minds having more work to do.

Margaret Taylor was involved in almost every aspect of this book from photo styling to helping with the direction writing. She worked hours gathering up the props and the "stuff" for the photography in this book. I am amazed at her design ability and at all of her other talents.

Kathy McMakin's pattern drafting, construction ideas, technical writing skills and designing/sewing ability make her invaluable to every aspect of this business. She literally helped with every part of this book from direction writing to organizing and sewing. She wrote the construction directions for these dresses with great mastery.

Amelia Johanson, formerly the senior editor of Sew Beautiful magazine, illustrated the construction directions for the doll dresses in this book. Not only is she a master journalist, but also an incredibly talented artist.

There is one person to whom I am especially grateful. Next to God, he has been my faithful advisor, my financial partner, my idea person, and my mentor. My husband, Joe Ross Pullen, has always believed in me more than I believe in myself. He is a wonderful dentist and has been one of the worldwide pioneers in implant dentistry. He is a wonderful Christian husband and father, and God blessed me beyond my wildest imaginations the day that Joe asked me to marry him. He is my best friend and my partner; I love him, and I thank him.

A number of years ago, I gave this whole business to God. He took it, figured out what to do next, and has given the guidance for moving in the directions in which we are moving. All the credit and glory for any success that we have had in the sewing industry go to Him and Him alone. The path has not been nor is it now an easy one. I don't think He promised us an easy trip through life. He did promise to be with us always and I can testify that He has never failed me.

Special thanks to TLC Doll for providing us with beautiful and creative photography props—Furniture, jewelry, "food" and accessories.

TLC Doll • P.O. Box 2383, Brentwood, TN 37024-2383 • (615) 661-5454

Table of Contents

Doll Clothing Directory

Doll Dresses

Doll Lingerie

Introduction to Götz Dolls

Designing and sewing doll dresses have been passions of mine since I was six years old. Those early doll dress designs were a little crude; however, they were joyful creations to me then and now. I can remember wrapping a piece of fabric around a little eight-inch doll and tying it at the waist for the skirt. The top was a little strip tied "bathing suit style" around the top. Not much of a doll dress, but the start to a wonderful journey—making doll clothes. When I was a little girl I loved playing with dolls more than anything else. Even after entering my baseball, football, and basketball stage, I would play with my beloved dolls at night after the sporting events.

Are dolls really for little girls or are they for women of all ages? That question has been resoundingly answered by women of all ages! Yes, it is O.K. to be passionately attached to dolls, doll making, and doll dressing for one's entire life. It must have been about eleven years ago that I went to my first doll show in California to teach heirloom sewing. Since that time, I have written two doll dressing books and a teddy bear dressing book. When planning *Sew Beautiful* magazine since 1987, I have included many articles on doll dressing which included patterns for all sizes of dolls. At the very genesis of planning my television series for PBS *Martha's Sewing Room*, I knew for sure that I wanted to feature a beautiful doll and doll dress pattern on each show. I love dolls to this day and I am happy to say that my only daughter, Joanna, loves dolls just like her mommy.

Speaking of Joanna, who is nearly twenty-one years old and a junior in college, I would love to share with you the only two requests that she has made for her Christmas list. She wants a Götz 19 $1/2$" doll with some beautiful clothes and a new dress for Mary, her baby doll she began sleeping with when she was 18 months old. Mary is in very bad condition to put it mildly. Her fingers are missing, her hair looks like a cone head sticking straight up on top, her legs are hanging by a torn piece of fabric, and her eyes don't open and close very well. She is Joanna's most prized possession; she wouldn't take her to college for her freshman dorm year because of the fear that someone would "steal" Mary. Now that she has an apartment, she says Mary needs a new dress since once again she is with Joanna. I have suggested that we send Mary back to the factory for repair and she replies each time, "Mom, you know that something might happen to Mary if we send her far away to New York. You'll have to find a doll hospital in Huntsville so we won't have to ship her." Well, meanwhile,

we'll just make a beautiful dress for Mary, about christening dress length, so she will be covered.

Her second request for the Götz 19 $1/2$" doll is one that can be easily fixed! I not only have bought her the Götz dress up doll but also one of the newly made Sasha dolls. Joanna had one of the original dolls; then, they weren't made anymore. Götz has begun making them again and we have one in the Christmas closet.

I have loved Götz dolls for many years. They are so beautifully made and last through years of playing with. I love their larger body because it makes it easy to dress and undress. Another wonderful fact about these bodies is the ease of sewing if one is inclined to dress them.

The idea for a Götz doll dressing book occurred to me about a year ago. When I called the sales office, they referred me to the marketing department where I received a warm reception. Upon sending them all of my books so that they could see the quality, I received a delighted phone call telling me that the books would be forwarded to Germany for the owners to make the final decision. Imagine my delight when I received my go ahead to design dresses for three sizes of Götz dolls. These dresses, for 17 $1/2$, 18 $1/2$, 19 $1/2$ and 21 $1/2$" dolls, are fun to make.

After receiving the go ahead for this book, I called some of the country's (not only the country's but also the world's) top designers to ask them to design dresses for these gorgeous dolls. I wanted these dolls to have a wardrobe superb representing all aspects of our beloved heirloom sewing industry. Chery Williams, Pat Holden (Australia), Sue Pennington, Craig Sharp, Elda Bratager and Patti Smith accepted our challenge. With this kind of talent, I know you are in for a surprise when you see "properly designed" heirloom clothing.

As I began working with the Götz company, the idea came to me to ask them to design a doll especially for Martha Pullen Company. In December, 1996, our first doll to be designed by Götz for Martha Pullen will be available. Her name is *Joanna*. She is 19 $1/2$" tall and has blue eyes and blonde hair. Her dress is white and she carries the most adorable white shoulder purse with JOANNA embroidered on the purse. The edition will be limited to 2500 worldwide and I will personally sign and number 1996 (one thousand nine hundred ninety six) dolls. If you want one of these dolls ($170 plus shipping), please call immediately because we expect them to go very quickly (1-800-547-4176).

About The Götz Company

The Götz Company was founded 45 years ago based on the philosophy that "We can produce high quality play dolls for children to be sold around the world."" From this original concept, there are currently four subsidiaries and Götz products are represented worldwide.

With the use of the first vinyl rotary machine in 1957, the way was paved for high standards of quality product and modern doll manufacturing.

In 1965, we were proud to produce our first designer doll, developed in cooperation with Sasha Morgenthaler.

Currently eight world-famous artists are working closely with us to develop future doll designs and concepts.

Today, our worldwide facilities with over 400 employees also offers exclusive play dolls which encourage imaginative play for children.

As one of the leading German doll manufacturers, we want to commit ourselves to high quality standards, setting a precedent for all European Doll Companies.

Götz Dolls-A Company of Outstanding Quality and Achievement! We thank you for your confidence and hope your business with us continues.

Color Doll Dress Photos

*Angel Sleeves
Pinafore Dress*

Antique
Reproduction
Dress,
Coat &
Bonnet

Fantasy Lace &
Netting Pinafore
Dress

Smocked High Yoke Dress

French Waterfall Dress

Green Linen Madeira Appliqué Border Dress

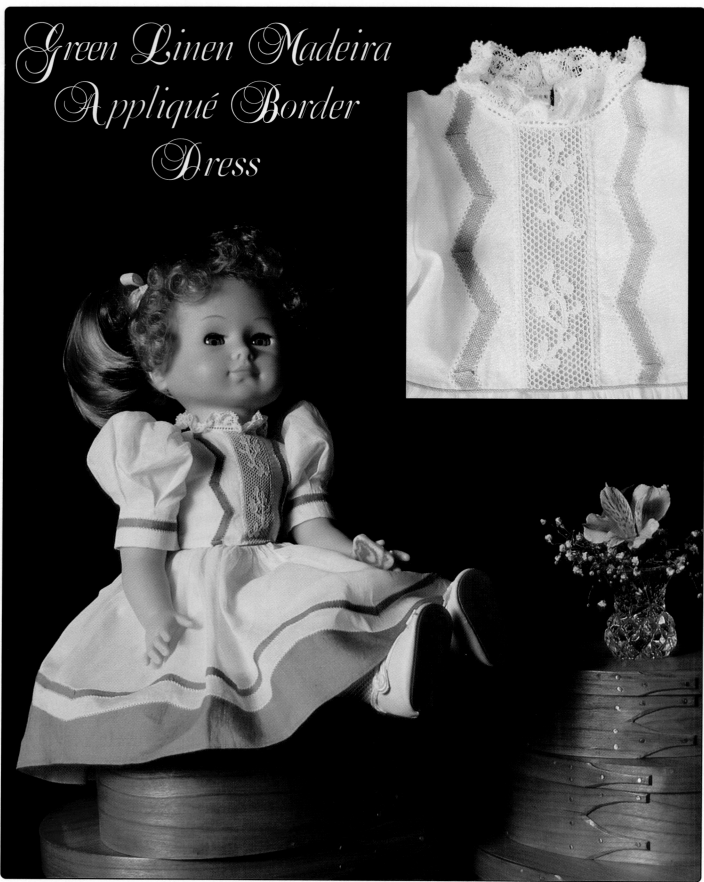

Lace Jabot
Three-Piece Suit

Lace Jabot & Jacket

Lace & Pearl Fantasy Dress

Lavender Leg o' Mutton Dress

Fancy Puffed Camisole & Pantaloons

*Monet's
Garden Of
Flowers Dress*

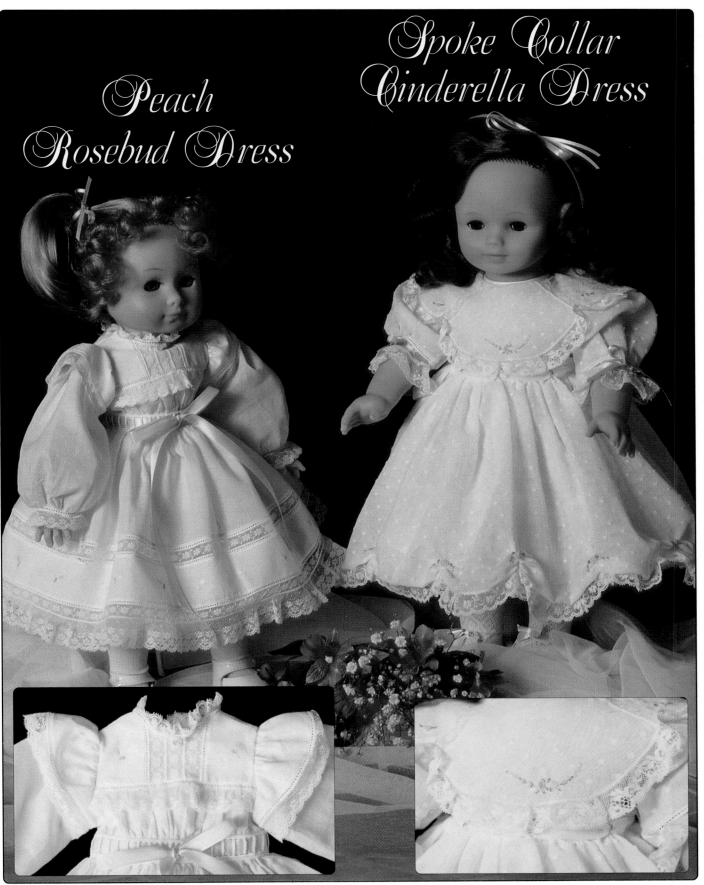

Peach Rosebud Dress

Spoke Collar Cinderella Dress

Pink & Ecru
Heirloom
Party Dress

Pink & Pretty Dress

Masterpiece Ecru Edwardian Dress

Ecru Netting Over Batiste Antique Dress

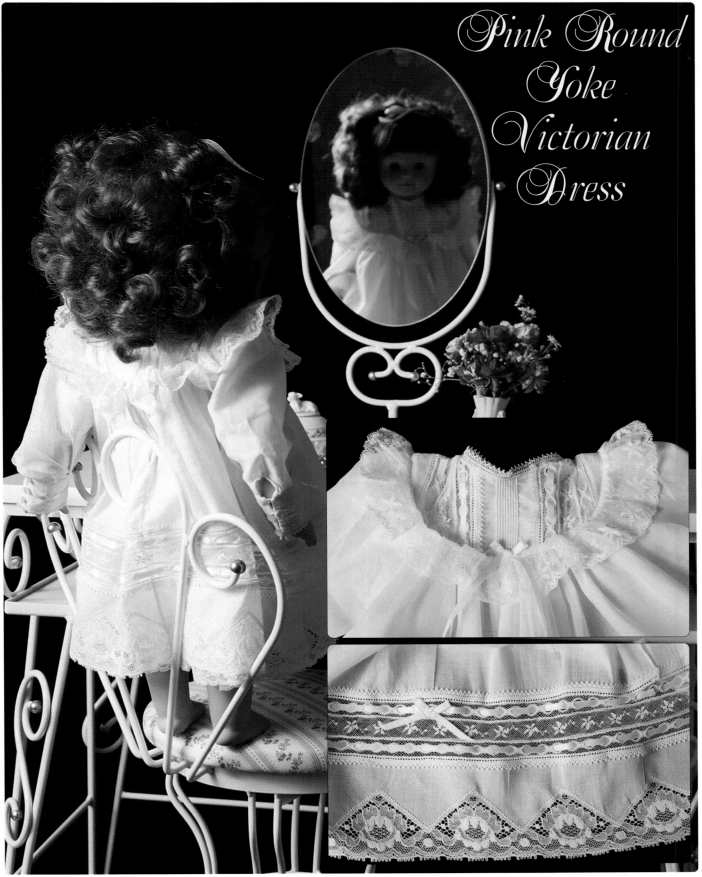

Pink Round Yoke Victorian Dress

Linen Dress With Swiss Trims

Fourth Of July Sailor Dress

White Delicate Antique Dream Dress

Chery's Smocked Purple Party Pants

Flirty Floral Knickers Jumpsuit

Smocked Peasant Blouse

Smocked Skirt With Underslip

Smocked Bishop

Top Left
Peach Slip for Spoke Collar Cinderella Dress

Top Right
A-Line One-Piece Slip

Bottom
White Bloomers & Peplum Camisole

Pink Slip For Victorian Dress

White Cancan Petticoat

Tap Pants & Oval Lace Rosebud Camisole

White Dropped Waist Slip

White Camisole With Pink Ribbon Trim

Sweet French Camisole

Triple Tiered Petticoat

Antique Reproduction Dress

Fantasy Lace & Netting Pinafore

Angel Sleeves Pinafore

Introduction To Dress Section

Just waiting for your sewing machine and hand sewing needles to begin is this collection of wonderful dresses for your doll. A number of styles are included so your doll can be the best dressed girl on the block. From the fanciest of French dresses to adorable party pants to smocked dresses to jumpers and pinafores, the next pages should keep you busy for many wonderful sewing hours.

Perhaps you would like to thrill a special little girl of yours from age 2 to 92 this Christmas with a wardrobe of beautiful doll clothes and a beautiful Götz doll to wear them! Don't think that a doll and a beautiful handmade wardrobe of clothing is only for kids! Far from it! I can almost believe that any woman who loved dolls as a little girl would be thrilled beyond words with a beautiful Götz doll and some heirloom clothing to fit her! Try it and see! Then, of course, you will want to consider making these beautiful garments for your favorite daughter, granddaughter, niece, Godchild or perhaps neighbor child. For the complete joy of a lifetime, make a wardrobe like this for a child who has never had any beautiful doll clothes or a beautiful doll.

In my collection of antique magazines, I ran across this article from *McCall's* magazine, June, 1900. It seemed like the perfect introduction to this doll dress section with all of its frothy and very turn-of-the-century creations. It seems like it could have almost been written to introduce this gorgeous section of clothing to you.

McCall's, June, 1900

Smart Summer Gowns: Attractive Ways of Making Up Washable Materials

Daintiness is the one expressive word that describes the gowns of thin materials which are now being prepared for the hot weather that will surely be with us before many months have passed. Not only are these toilettes dainty in color and materials, but surprisingly dainty in cut and trimming as well.

The idol of the hour is lace which is lavishly used on all these costumes, both in all-over designs, edgings, insertions and in the form of wide or narrow beadings through which ribbons are run.

Sheer cottons such as organdies, lawns, swisses, etc., are made with very dressy and elaborate skirts, while heavier wash fabrics, piques, linens ducks, etc., are plainly finished in tailor fashion. Skirts of sheer materials are to be very much trimmed with lace insertions inset in various forms, for instance a novelty is diamond squares of lace set in a little distance apart or joining corners to form an edge. As the new materials are all so thin and sheer, the elaborate skirts are extremely attractive. Fine tucks in every way that fancy can devise are a great feature of waists as well as skirts, and they are arranged horizontally, vertically and in waved lines, singly and in groups.

Ruffles are extremely popular, in fact ruffled and pleated trimmings are particularly suited to the thin wash fabrics and silks which will be so much worn this summer. Alternate contrasting rows of ruffles, in color and material, are frequently used in various arrangements at the bottom of skirts. Some are set on in points, rising at the middle seam and falling to the side seam, thence proceeding regularly around the bottom of the skirt in three or four rows. There are garnitures which are used on perfectly plain skirts, which, despite the dictates of the fashion artists, will not entirely disappear even with the coming of pleats and fullness.

From very dressy outfits such as the Antique Reproduction Dress, Coat and Bonnet, Fantasy Lace and Netting Pinafore, and French Waterfall Dress to more casual masterpieces such as Sunday School Jumper and Blouse, Flirty Floral Knickers Jumpsuit or Chery's Smocked Purple Party Pants, you should have no trouble outfitting your favorite Götz dolls from head to toe. Speaking of Chery's Smocked Purple Party Pants and Smocked Bishop, both are designed by Chery Williams and have a matching child's pattern to go along with them. Chery Williams' patterns are available at fine smocking shops everywhere or you can write to her at Chery Williams Patterns, P.O. Box 190234, Birmingham, AL 35219 (205-290-2700).

Doll Dress General Directions

Techniques referred to in "quotes" are described in the technique section of this book.

Neck Finishes

a. Entredeux and Gathered Edging

1. Measure the neck of the dress with the facings extended. Cut a strip of entredeux 1/4" longer than this measurement.

2. Cut a piece of edging lace two times the length of the entredeux. Gather the lace to fit the entredeux strip.

3. Trim away one side of the entredeux and attach the gathered edging lace to the trimmed entredeux using the technique "entredeux to gathered lace" **(fig. 1).**

4. If the fabric edge remaining on the entredeux is not already 1/4", trim to 1/4." Clip this fabric so that it will curve along the neck edge of the dress **(fig. 2)**. Place this strip to the neck (facings extended - not folded), right sides together. Attach, using the technique "entredeux to fabric" **(fig. 3)**.

5. Using a tiny zigzag, tack the seam allowance to the dress **(fig. 4)**. This stitching will keep the entredeux/gathered lace standing up at the neck.

b. Entredeux and Flat Swiss Edging

1. Measure the neck of the dress with the facings extended. Cut a strip of entredeux 1/4" longer than this measurement.

2. Cut a piece of Swiss edging the length of the entredeux.

3. Attach the Swiss edging to the entredeux using the technique "entredeux to fabric" **(fig. 5)**.

4. If the fabric edge remaining on the entredeux is not already 1/4", trim to 1/4". Clip this fabric so that it will curve along the neck edge of the dress. Refer to figure 5. Place this strip to the neck

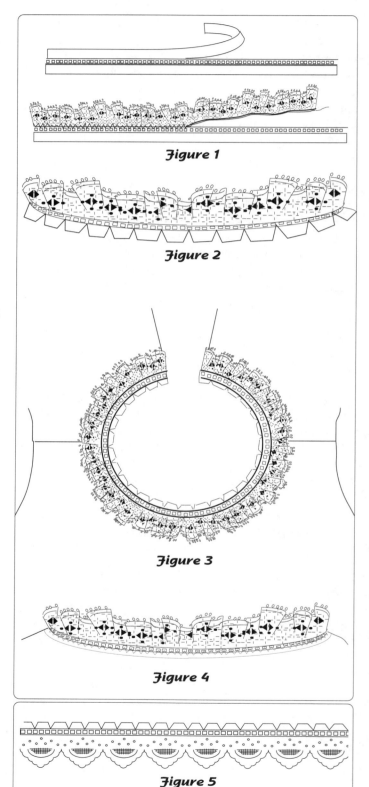

Figure 1

Figure 2

Figure 3

Figure 4

Figure 5

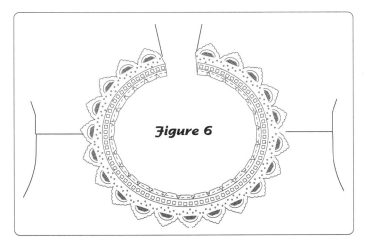

Figure 6

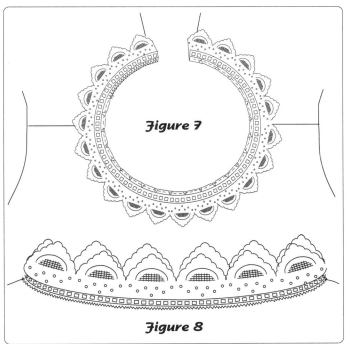

Figure 7

Figure 8

(fig. 6) (facings extended - not folded), right sides together. Attach using the technique "entredeux to fabric" **(fig. 7)**.

5. Using a tiny zigzag, tack the seam allowance to the dress. This stitching will keep the entredeux/ Swiss edging standing up at the neck **(fig. 8)**.

c. Entredeux to Flat Edging Lace or Tatting

1. Measure the neck of the dress with the facings extended. Cut a strip of entredeux 1/4" longer than this measurement.

2. Cut a piece of edging lace or tatting the length of the entredeux.

3. Trim away one side of the entredeux and attach the edging or tatting to the entredeux using the technique "lace to entredeux" **(fig. 9)**.

4. If the fabric edge remaining on the entredeux is not already 1/4", trim to 1/4". Clip this fabric so that it will curve along the neck edge of the dress **(fig. 10)**. Place this strip to the neck (facings extended - not folded), right sides together. Attach, using the technique "entredeux to fabric" **(fig. 11)**.

5. Using a tiny zigzag, tack the seam allowance to the dress. This stitching will keep the entredeux/ lace standing up at the neck **(fig. 12)**.

d. Bias Neck Facing

1. Measure the neck of the dress with the facings folded in place **(fig. 13)**. Cut a bias strip 1" wide by this length. Fold the bias strip in half along the length and press **(fig. 14)**. Place the cut edges of the strip to the neck of the dress and pin. Trim the ends of the strip 1/4" from the fold lines of the garment.

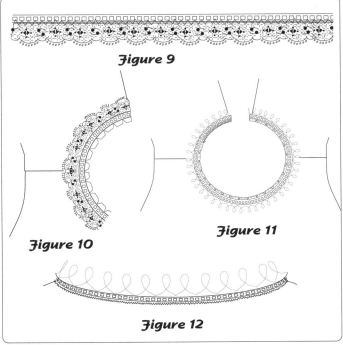

Figure 9

Figure 10

Figure 11

Figure 12

Figure 13

Figure 14

2. Flip the facings to the outside of the garment along the fold lines. Place the facings under the bias strip. Stitch the bias strip to the neck edge using a 1/4" seam **(fig. 15)**. Trim the seam allowance to 1/8". Clip the curves. Flip the bias strip and the facings to the inside of the bodice. Hand stitch the bias strip in place, finishing the neck edge **(fig. 16)**.

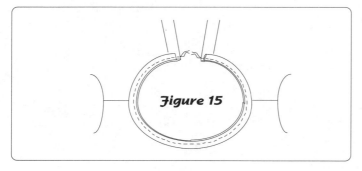

Figure 15

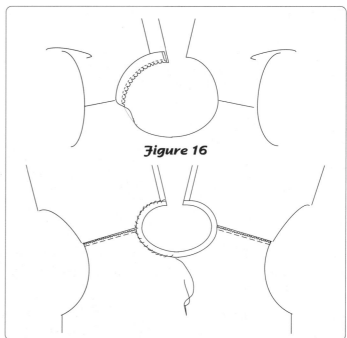

Figure 16

e. Bias Neck Binding

1. Trim away 1/8" from the neck edge of the garment. Fold the facings to the inside of the garment and press **(fig 17)**.

2. Measure around the neck with the facings folded to the inside of the garment. Add 1/2" to this measurement and cut a bias strip 1-1/8" wide by this length.

3. Fold the bias strip in half along the length and press **(fig. 18)**.

4. Place the bias strip to the right side of the garment neck and pin with the cut edges of the bias to the cut edge of the neck. The bias strip will extend 1/4" beyond the folded edges of the facings.

5. Stitch the bias strip in place using a 1/4" seam **(fig. 19)**. Trim the seam allowance to 1/8".

6. Flip the bias up, away from the neck. Fold the 1/4" extensions to the inside **(fig. 20)**. Now place the folded edge of the bias to or just below the

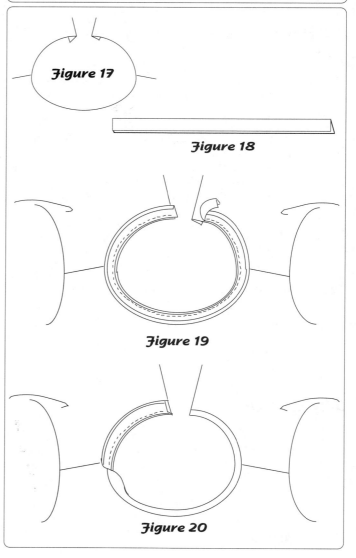

Figure 17

Figure 18

Figure 19

Figure 20

stitching line. This will encase the seam allowance. Hand stitch or machine stitch the bias strip in place **(fig. 21)**.

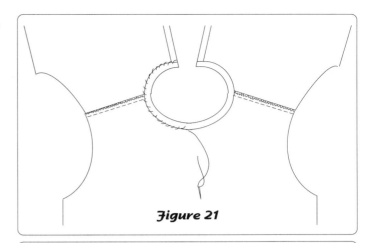

Figure 21

f. Bias Neck Bindings for Bishop Garments

1. Fold one side of the placket to the inside of the garment. The other side of the placket will remain extended **(fig. 22)**. Pull the top pleating thread to gather the neck to the following measurement:

Dolls	17-1/2"	18-1/2"	19-1/2"	21-1/2"
	6-1/2"	7"	7-1/4"	7-7/8"

2. Cut a bias strip 1-1/4" wide by the following measurement:

Dolls	17-1/2"	18-1/2"	19-1/2"	21-1/2"
	7"	7-1/2"	7-3/4"	8-3/8"

3. Fold the bias strip in half along the length and press **(fig. 23)**.

   Place the bias strip to the right side of the garment neck with the cut edges of the bias even with the top pleating thread. The bias strip will extend 1/4" beyond the back opening **(fig. 24)**.

5. Stitch the bias strip in place using a 1/4" seam. Trim the seam allowance to 1/8."

6. Flip the bias up, away from the neck **(fig. 25)**. Fold the 1/4" extensions to the inside and fold the bias to or just below the stitching line of the strip. This will encase the seam allowance. Hand stitch or machine stitch the bias strip in place **(fig. 26)**.

Sleeve Bands and Ruffles

1. Refer to dress directions for cutting and decorating the sleeves.

2. Run two gathering rows 1/8" and 1/4" from the top and bottom edges of each sleeve **(fig. 1)**.

3. Complete the sleeves using one of the sleeve finishing techniques below.

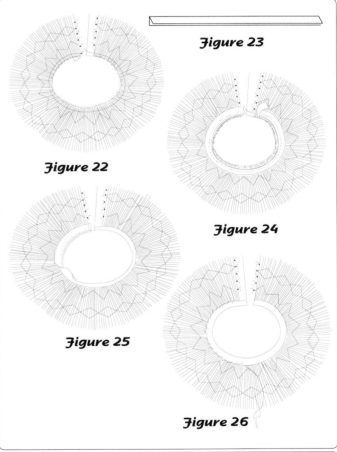

Figure 23

Figure 22

Figure 24

Figure 25

Figure 26

Sleeve Band Chart

Doll Sizes	17-1/2"	18-1/2"	19-1/2"	21-1/2"
Elbow Length Sleeve				
Cutting length	5"	5-1/2"	5-1/2"	6-1/2"
3/4 Length Sleeve				
Cutting length	4"	4-3/4"	4-3/4"	5-1/4"
Long Sleeve				
Cutting length	4"	4-1/2"	4-5/8"	4-3/4"

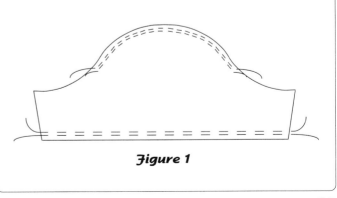

Figure 1

a. Entredeux and Gathered Edging Lace

1. Cut two strips of entredeux to the measurement given in the sleeve band chart for the correct sleeve and doll size. Cut two pieces of edging lace twice the length of the entredeux.

2. Gather the edging lace to fit the entredeux. Stitch together using the technique "entredeux to gathered lace" **(fig. 2)**.

3. Gather the bottom of the sleeve to fit the entredeux/edging lace band **(fig. 2)**. Stitch the band to the sleeve **(fig. 3)**, right sides together, using the technique "entredeux to gathered fabric" **(fig. 4)**.

b. Entredeux, Beading, Entredeux and Gathered Edging Lace

1. Cut four pieces of entredeux and two pieces of beading to the measurement given in the sleeve band chart for the correct sleeve and doll size. Cut two pieces of edging lace twice the length of the measurement given in the sleeve band chart for the correct sleeve and doll size.

2. Stitch one piece of entredeux to each side of the beading **(fig. 5)** using the technique "entredeux to lace." Repeat for remaining entredeux and beading pieces.

3. Gather the edging lace to fit the entredeux/beading/entredeux band. Stitch together using the technique "entredeux to gathered lace" **(fig. 6)**.

4. Gather the bottom of the sleeve to fit the entredeux/edging lace band **(fig. 7)**. Stitch the

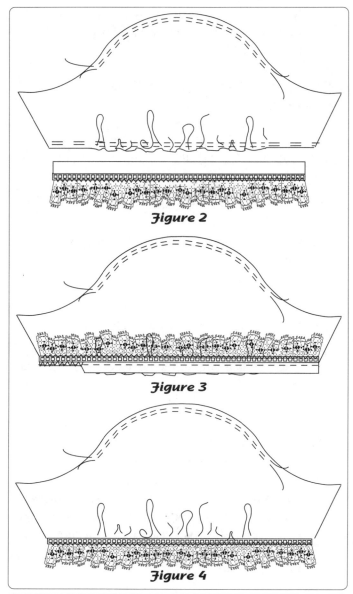

Figure 2

Figure 3

Figure 4

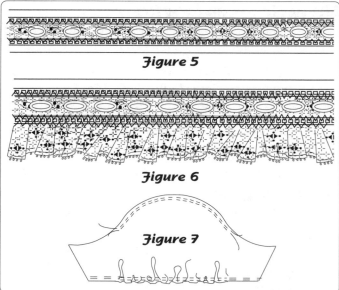

Figure 5

Figure 6

Figure 7

band to the sleeve **(fig. 8)**, right sides together, using the technique "entredeux to gathered fabric" **(fig. 9)**.

c. Entredeux, Beading and Gathered Edging Lace

1. Cut two pieces of entredeux and two pieces of beading to the measurement given in the sleeve band chart for the correct sleeve and doll size. Cut two pieces of edging lace twice the length of the measurement given in the sleeve band chart for the correct sleeve and doll size.

2. Stitch one piece of entredeux to one piece of beading using the technique "entredeux to lace". Repeat for remaining entredeux and beading pieces.

3. Gather the edging lace to fit the entredeux/beading band. Stitch the gathered edging lace to the beading using the technique "lace to lace" **(fig. 10)**.

4. Gather the bottom of the sleeve to fit the entredeux/beading/gathered lace band **(fig. 11)**. Stitch the band to the sleeve, right sides together, using the technique "entredeux to gathered fabric" **(fig. 12)**.

d. Swiss Beading and Gathered Edging Lace

1. Cut two pieces of Swiss beading to the measurement given in the sleeve band chart for the correct sleeve and doll size **(fig. 13)**. Cut two pieces of edging lace twice the length of the measurement given in the sleeve band chart for the correct sleeve and doll size.

2. Gather the edging lace to fit the Swiss beading band. Stitch the gathered edging lace to the beading using the technique "entredeux to gathered lace" **(fig. 14)**.

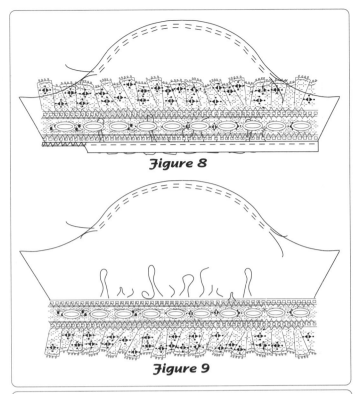

Figure 8

Figure 9

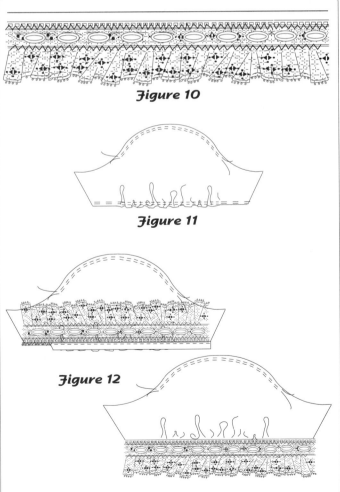

Figure 10

Figure 11

Figure 12

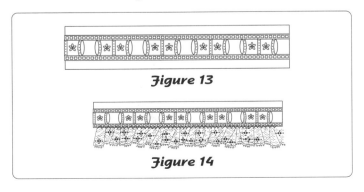

Figure 13

Figure 14

3. Gather the bottom of the sleeve to fit the entre-deux/beading/gathered lace band **(fig. 15)**. Stitch the band to the sleeve **(fig. 16)**, right sides together, using the technique "entredeux to gathered fabric" **(fig. 17)**.

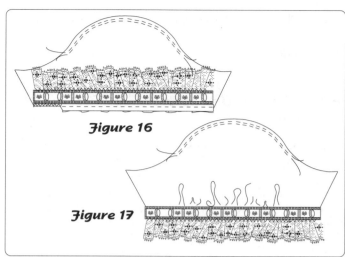

Figure 16

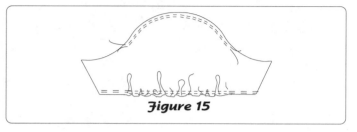

Figure 15

Figure 17

e. Swiss Beading or Insertion and Gathered Swiss Edging

1. Cut two pieces of Swiss beading **(fig. 18)** to the measurement given in the sleeve band chart for the correct sleeve and doll size. Cut two pieces of Swiss edging twice the length of the measurement given in the sleeve band chart for the correct sleeve and doll size.

2. Run two gathering rows in the top edge of the Swiss edging **(fig. 19)**. Gather the edging to fit the Swiss beading band. Stitch the gathered edging to the Swiss beading using the technique "entredeux to gathered fabric" **(fig. 20)**.

3. Gather the bottom of the sleeve to fit the Swiss beading/gathered Swiss edging band **(fig. 21)**. Stitch the band to the sleeve **(fig. 22)**, right sides together, using the technique "entredeux to gathered fabric" **(fig. 23)**.

f. Bias Sleeve Bindings

1. Cut two bias strips of fabric 3/4" wide by the measurement given in the sleeve band chart for the correct sleeve and doll size **(fig. 24)**.

2. Gather the bottom of the sleeve to fit the bias band. Stitch the band to the sleeve, right sides together, using a 1/4" seam. Trim the seam to 1/8" **(fig. 25)**.

3. Fold the lower edge of the band to the inside 1/8."

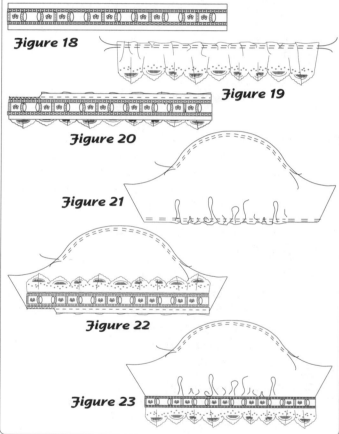

Figure 18

Figure 19

Figure 20

Figure 21

Figure 22

Figure 23

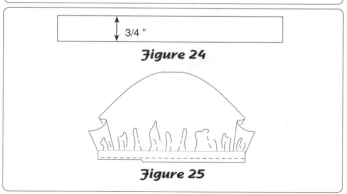

3/4 "

Figure 24

Figure 25

4. Place the folded edge just over the seam line on the inside of the sleeve creating a 1/8" band **(fig. 26)**. Hand stitch or machine stitch in place **(fig. 27)**.

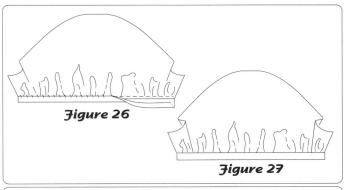

Figure 26

Figure 27

g. Gathered Sleeve with Elastic and Lace

1. Measure the bottom of the sleeves. Cut two pieces of edging lace to this measurement. Stitch a strip of edging lace along the bottom of each sleeve using the technique "lace to fabric" **(fig. 28)**. Press the lace away from the sleeves.

2. Measuring 1" to 1-1/4" from the finished edge of the lace on the wrong side of the sleeves, draw a line with a fabric marker **(fig. 29)**.

3. Cut two pieces of 1/8" elastic 1" longer than the measurement given in the sleeve band chart. The longer measurement will aid in attaching the elastic. Place a dot 3/4" from each end of the elastic **(fig. 30)**.

4. Place an elastic piece on the drawn line of one sleeve with the dot 1/4" from the side edge of the sleeve. Stitch elastic in place with several tiny straight stitches. Continue stitching with a loose zigzag that encloses the elastic but does not catch the elastic **(fig. 31)**. Pull the elastic until the second dot is 1/4" from the side edge **(fig. 32)**. Tack in place with several tiny straight stitches. Trim elastic even with the sides of the sleeve. Repeat for other sleeve.

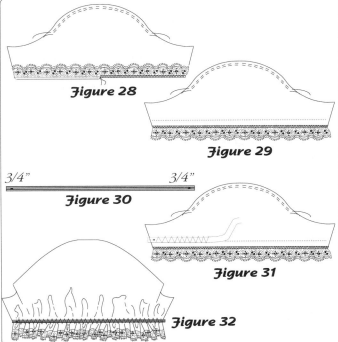

Figure 28

Figure 29

3/4"   3/4"

Figure 30

Figure 31

Figure 32

h. Gathered Sleeve with Elastic and Ribbon

1. Cut sleeves 1/2" longer for this technique.

2. Cut two pieces of 1/4" ribbon the length of the sleeve bottom.

3. Place the ribbon on the wrong side of the sleeve across the bottom edge. The ribbon can be stitched in place along the top edge of the ribbon or held in place with wash away basting tape **(fig. 33)**.

4. Flip the ribbon to the right side of the sleeve **(fig. 34)**. Stitch along the top and bottom edges of the ribbon to hold in place **(fig. 35)**.

5. Refer to steps 2 to 4 above for attaching elastic to the sleeves.

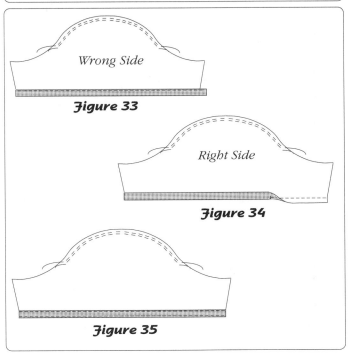

Wrong Side

Figure 33

Right Side

Figure 34

Figure 35

Plackets

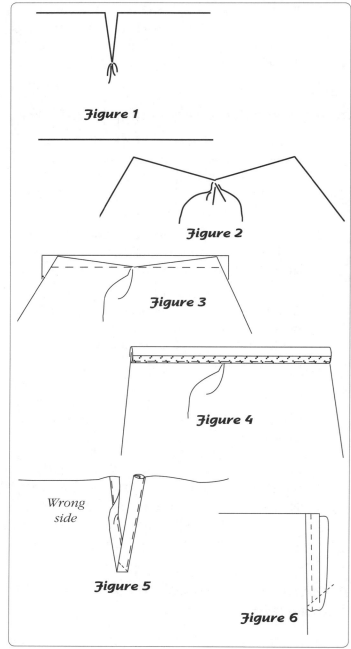

a. Continuous Lap Placket

1. Cut a slit in the garment for the placket. Refer to the garment directions for length and placement of the slit **(fig. 1)**.

2. Cut a strip of fabric from the selvage 3/4" wide by twice the length of the slit.

3. Pull the slit in the garment apart to form a "V" **(fig. 2)**. Place right side of the strip to right side of the garment slit. The stitching will be made from the wrong side with the garment on top and the placket strip on the bottom. The placket strip will be straight and the garment will form a "V." The point of the "V" will fall 1/4" from the cut edge of the placket. Stitch, using a 1/4" seam. As you stitch, you will just catch the tip (a few fibers) at the point of the "V" **(fig. 3)**.

4. Press the seam toward the selvage edge of the placket strip. Turn the selvage edge to the inside of the dress, enclosing the seam allowance. Whip by hand or stitch in place by machine **(fig. 4)**.

5. The garment will lap right over left. Fold the right side of the placket to the inside of the garment and pin. Leave the left back placket open **(fig. 5)**.

6. Match the top edges of the garment and find the center of the placket. Stitch the lower edges of the placket together in a dart, starting about 1/4" above the end of the placket **(fig. 6)**.

Figure 1

Figure 2

Figure 3

Figure 4

Wrong side

Figure 5

Figure 6

b. Continuous Lap Placket with Lace Insertion

1. Cut a slit in the garment for the placket **(fig. 7)**. Refer to the garment directions for length and placement of the slit.

2. Cut a piece of 3/8" to 5/8" insertion lace twice the length of the placket slit. 3. Pull the slit in the skirt apart to form a "V." Place lace insertion to the right side of the skirt slit. Stitch the lace in place using the technique "lace to fabric" **(fig. 8)**.

4. Press the seam toward the lace.

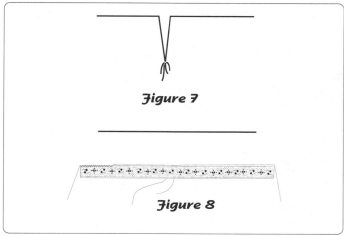

Figure 7

Figure 8

5. The garment will lap right over left **(fig. 9)**. Fold the right side of the lace placket to the inside of the garment and pin. Leave the left side of the placket open **(fig. 10)**.

6. Match the top edges of the garment and find the center of the placket. Stitch the lower edges of the placket together in a dart, starting about 1/4" above the end of the placket **(fig. 11)**.

c. Continuous Placket in a Seam

1. Stitch the seam to a point given in the garment directions, backstitch **(fig. 12)**. Place a clip straight across the seam allowance at the top of the stitching. Overcast the seam allowance below the clip **(fig. 13)**.

2. Cut a strip of fabric from the selvage 3/4" wide by twice the length of the opening (top of garment to the clip).

3. Pull the opening in the garment apart with the clipped edges together. Place the right side of the strip to the right side of the opening with the cut edges of the placket meeting the edge of the opening. The stitching will be made from the wrong side with the garment on top and the placket strip on the bottom **(fig. 14)**. Stitch, using a 1/4" seam. As you stitch, you will just catch a few fibers at the seam line. Refer to figure 3.

4. Press the seam toward the selvage edge of the placket strip. Turn the selvage edge to the inside of the dress, enclosing the seam allowance. Whip by hand or stitch in place by machine **(fig. 15)**.

5. The garment will lap right over left. Fold the right side of the placket to the inside of the garment and pin. Leave the left back placket open **(fig. 16)**.

6. Match the top edges of the garment and find the center of the placket. Stitch the lower edges of the placket together in a dart, starting about 1/4" above the end of the placket **(fig. 17)**.

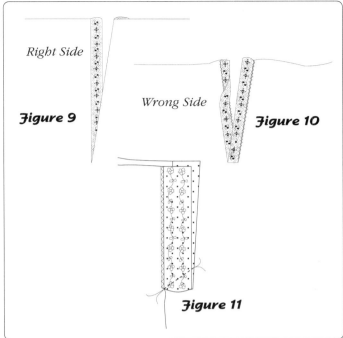

Right Side

Figure 9

Wrong Side

Figure 10

Figure 11

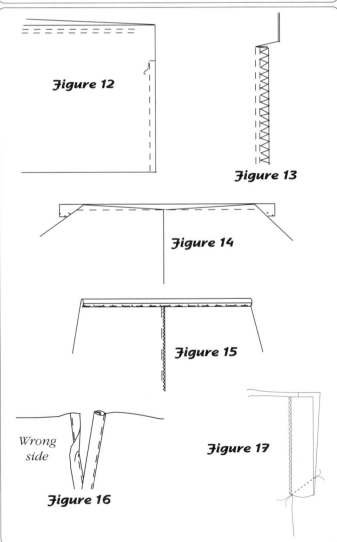

Figure 12

Figure 13

Figure 14

Figure 15

Wrong side

Figure 16

Figure 17

d. Easy Placket in a Seam

1. Stitch the seam to a point given in the garment directions, backstitch. Place a clip straight across the seam allowance at the top of the stitching. Overcast the seam allowance below the clip **(fig. 18)**.

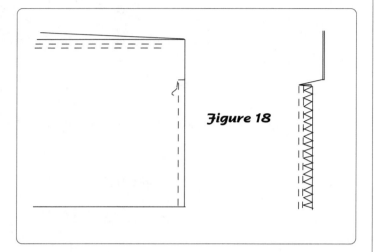

Figure 18

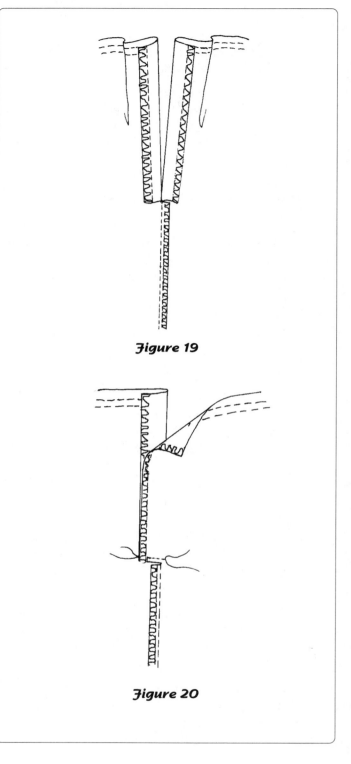

Figure 19

2. Overcast the edges of each side of the garment above the clip **(fig. 19)**.

3. Fold the right side of the opening to the inside of the garment 1/4" and press. Pin in place. The left side of the opening will remain extended and should be placed on top of the right folded edge. Press. This creates a placket.

4. Stitch across the lower edge of the opening just above the clip through all three layers (two placket layers and the skirt). The garment will lap right over left **(fig. 20)**.

Figure 20

Angel Sleeves Pinafore Dress

Details galore make this high yoke dress a stitcher's delight. The blue Nelona Swiss batiste underdress is stitched at the hemline with machine scallops in a pretty, medium-color, rayon thread. The collar is a pretty wide lace, bound at the neck with bias binding in the blue Nelona. The angel sleeves are white organdy with a scalloped hem and delicate embroidery in the center. The long under sleeves are finished at the bottom with a 5/8 inch wide fabric cuff. The Swiss organdy pinafore has a scalloped hem stitched down with a machine pin stitch. A beautiful hand embroidery design with lazy daisy leaves, stem stitch vines and a blue bullion rosebud in the center is found in the center of each scallop. If you love machine embroidery, then feel free to use your machine stitches to create your own designs in each scallop. The organdy pinafore and the blue dress have a skirt fullness of 42 inches. The back is closed with a placket and two buttons and loops. Snaps or Velcro™ would be equally suitable.

- **All pattern pieces and templates found in pull-out section**
- **Color photograph on page 10**

Supplies

Fabric -

Blue Batiste	3/4 yd.
Organdy - White	5/8 yd.
Lace Edging (1/2")	1/4 yd.
Lace Edging (2")	1 yd.

Notions: Lightweight sewing thread, blue and white; Velcro™, snaps or tiny buttons for closure; DMC floss 3013 green and 3755 blue; blue machine embroidery thread; #100 wing needle, or #110 needle (optional)

Pattern Pieces Required: High Yoke Front, High Yoke Back, 3/4-Length Sleeve, Sleeve Cap Ruffle

Templates Required: 4" Scallop, 2-3/4" Scallop, Armhole Guide, Blue Rosebud Embroidery Template

All seams 1/4" unless otherwise indicated. Stitch seam in place and overcast the seam allowances with a zigzag or serge, unless otherwise indicated.

A. Cutting

1. From the batiste, cut one front yoke on the fold, two back yokes on the selvage and two sleeves on the fold. Also cut two cuffs, 2" wide by the following length **(fig. 1)**:

Doll Sizes	17-1/2"	18-1/2"	19-1/2"	21-1/2"
Cuff Length	4-1/2"	5"	5"	4-3/4"

2. Cut two skirt pieces, 21" wide by the following length:

Doll Sizes	17-1/2"	18-1/2"	19-1/2"	21-1/2"
Skirt Length	11"	11-1/2"	12-1/2"	13-3/4"

3. From the organdy, cut one front yoke on the fold, two back yokes on the selvage and two rectangles 4" x 9" for the angel sleeves.

4. Transfer pattern markings to the fabric. Also mark the centers of the skirt pieces at the top and bottom edges, and use the armhole guide to cut the armholes **(fig. 2)**.

5. Finish the bottom edge of each batiste skirt piece with a small machine scallop; use a stabilizer. Stitch 1/2" from the cut edge and trim away the excess fabric. A tiny rolled edge may be used instead of the scallops **(fig. 3)**.

B. Yokes and Neck Edge

1. Place the organdy yoke pieces over the batiste yoke pieces and baste together. The organdy side is the right side **(fig. 4)**.

2. Place the front yoke to the back yokes at the shoulders, right sides together, and stitch **(fig. 5)**.

3. Gather the wide lace edging to fit the neck edge **(fig. 6)**. If the lace is too full for the doll size, trim from the ends until it is right. Finish the cut edges of the lace with a zigzag, or turn under the ends and stitch.

4. Pin the lace to the neck edge **(fig. 7)**, stopping the lace at the center back lines of the back yokes. Baste the lace to the dress.

5. Refer to "Neck Finishes - e. Bias Neck Binding" on page 36 and apply the binding to the neck edge.

6. Trim the narrow lace edging to fit the neck and hand-whip the lace to the inside of the binding, so that it extends above the neck edge **(fig. 8)**.

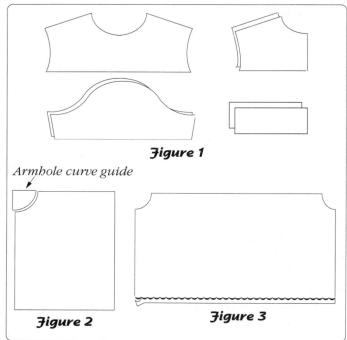

Figure 1

Armhole curve guide

Figure 2

Figure 3

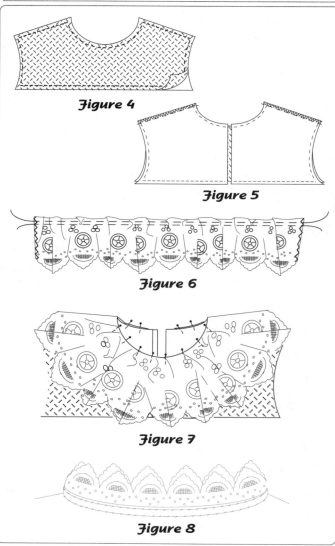

Figure 4

Figure 5

Figure 6

Figure 7

Figure 8

C. Pinafore Skirt and Angel Sleeves

1. Mark the center of the angel sleeve rectangles on the 9" edges. Trace the 2-3/4" scallop template onto the rectangles, matching the centers and placing the scallop points 1/4" from the bottom edges of the rectangles (**fig. 9**).

2. Press a 1" hem to the wrong side, turning the scallops up. Make sure that the scalloped lines show through to the right side (**fig. 10**).

3. Use white thread and the wing needle (or #110 needle) to stitch along the scallops with a narrow pin stitch. Or use a regular needle and a small, close zigzag, but not a satin stitch See figure 10.

4. After the scallops are stitched, trim away the excess organdy on the wrong side (**fig. 11**).

5. Use the sleeve cap ruffle pattern piece to cut the angel sleeves (**fig. 12**), centering the scallops along the bottom edge and letting the bottom edge of the hemmed fabric touch the bottom cutting line of the pattern piece. Baste the organdy pieces over the sleeves and treat as one layer.

6. Finish the bottom edges of the pinafore skirt pieces the same as the angel sleeves, steps 1 through 4, making the following changes: mark the centers along the 21" edges, use the 4" scallop template, and turn up a 2" hem.

D. Skirts to Yokes

1. Place the organdy skirts over the batiste skirts, with the bottom edge of the organdy placed 1/2" above the scalloped batiste edge (**fig. 13**). Trim the top edges so that they are even. Baste the layers together and treat as one (**fig. 14**).

2. Choose one skirt piece to be the back and apply a placket, referring to "Plackets - a. Continuous Lap Placket" found on page 42. Cut the back slit 4-1/2" long. The skirt will lap right over left.

8. Run two rows of gathering stitches across the top edges, 1/8" and 1/4" from the edges. Stop the stitching at the armholes and the placket edges. (**fig. 15 and refer to figure 14**).

9. Pin the front skirt piece to the front yoke, right sides together. Adjust the gathers in the skirt top to fit the bottom edge of the yoke and stitch in place (**fig. 16**).

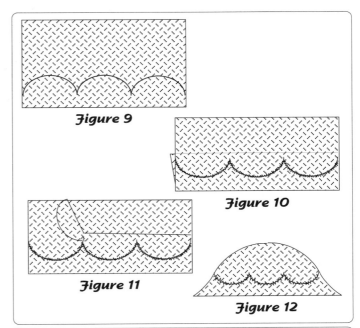

Figure 9

Figure 10

Figure 11

Figure 12

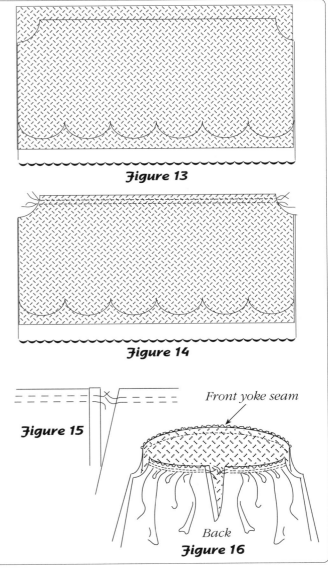

Figure 13

Figure 14

Figure 15

Front yoke seam

Back

Figure 16

10. Place the back skirt to the back yokes, right sides together. The placket edges should meet the back fold line of the yokes. Wrap the back facings to the outside along the fold line, sandwiching the skirt between the yoke and the facing. Stitch in place and press the yokes up, flipping the facings to the inside **(fig. 17)**.

E. Finishing the Dress

1. Run two rows of gathering stitches across the top and bottom edges of the sleeves, 1/8" and 1/4" from the edges **(fig. 18)**.

2. Pin the sleeves to the armholes and adjust the gathers to fit, stopping the gathers and the bottom edges of the angel sleeves at the yoke seam lines **(fig. 19)**. Stitch the sleeves in place.

3. Place one cuff piece to the bottom edge of each sleeve, adjusting the gathers to fit the cuff. Stitch the cuff in place. Refer to figure 19. Press the gathers flat in the seam allowance and trim the seam. Press under 1/4" along the unfinished edge of the cuff.

4. Place the sleeve/side seams with right sides together. Match the sleeve edges and the skirt bottom edges and stitch **(fig. 20)**. The scallops should meet at the side seams.

5. Turn the cuff to the inside of the sleeve, letting the folded edge of the cuff meet the stitching line. Hand-whip the cuff in place **(fig. 21)**.

6. Apply Velcro™, snaps or tiny buttons and button-holes to the back opening, with the right side lapping over the left side.

7. Embroider green leaves and blue bullion roses or other flowers at the center of each scallop on the pinafore hem, and the center scallop on the angel sleeves **(fig. 22)**.

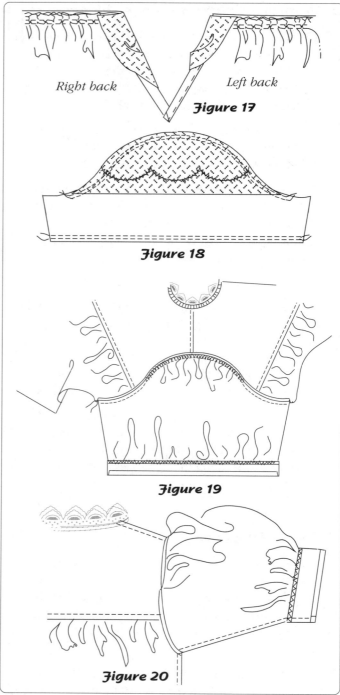

Right back   *Left back*

Figure 17

Figure 18

Figure 19

Figure 20

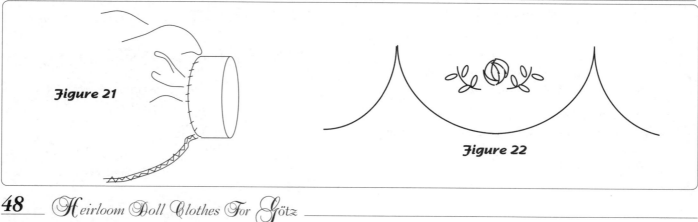

Figure 21

Figure 22

Antique Reproduction Dress

Made of ecru silk batiste this ecru beauty features many different French and English lace patterns. The large collar which extends past the raised waistline in both the front and the back, is composed of alternating strips of ecru insertion and beading. Entredeux is stitched around the edge of the flat collar and gathered ecru French edging goes around the outside edges of the collar. Entredeux and gathered lace finish the neckline also. Pale mint green silk ribbon is run through the beading and pink flowerettes are found at the center front and at all four outside corners of the collar. A green bow it tied at the bottom of the collar and green silk ribbon is run through the beading at the bottom of the sleeve sand on the skirt. The tops of the sleeves have five rows of French insertion and two rows of beading on the top of the sleeve. The bottom of the sleeve is silk. The bottom of the sleeve is finished with entredeux, beading, and flat lace edging. The skirt of the dress has a fancy band of nine rows of French insertion and two rows of French beading. Ecru entredeux is found at both the top and bottom of this fancy band and a double hem of silk finishes the bottom the dress. The dress back is closed with snaps but you could also use buttons and button-holes or beauty pins.

- **All pattern pieces and templates found in pull-out section**
- **Color photograph on page 11**

Supplies

Fabric Requirements: All Sizes		Lace Insertion (3/4")	1 yd.	Silk ribbon (7mm, green)	1-1/2 yds.
Fabric - Silk Batiste	2/3 yd.	Lace Edging (1-1/4")	1-1/4 yds.	Silk Ribbon (7mm, pink)	2 yds. or 1
Entredeux	5 yds.	Lace Edging (5/8")	1/2 yd.	large and 4 small purchased ribbon	
Lace Insertion (5/8")	8-1/2 yds.	Lace Beading (3/8")	5-1/2 yds.	roses.	
Lace Insertion (1-1/4")	1-1/4 yds.	Silk Ribbon (4mm, green)	6 yds.		

Notions: Lightweight sewing thread; Velcro™, snaps or tiny buttons for closure

Pattern Pieces Required: Mid-Yoke Front, Mid-Yoke Back, 3/4-Length Sleeve, Square Collar Front and Back

All seams 1/4" unless otherwise indicated. Stitch seam in place and overcast the seam allowances with a zigzag or serge, unless otherwise indicated.

A. Cutting

1. From the fabric, cut two back yokes on the selvage and one front yoke on the fold **(figs. 1)**.

2. From the fabric, cut one skirt piece, 44" wide by the following length **(fig. 2)**:

Doll Sizes	17-1/2"	18-1/2"	19-1/2"	21-1/2"
Skirt Length	4"	4-1/2"	5-1/2"	16-3/4"

3. For all sizes, also cut a band from the fabric, 2-1/2" wide by 45" long.

4. Mark the centers of the skirt pieces at the top and bottom edges.

5. The collar and sleeves will be cut from rectangles of pieced lace and fabric, described in the following section.

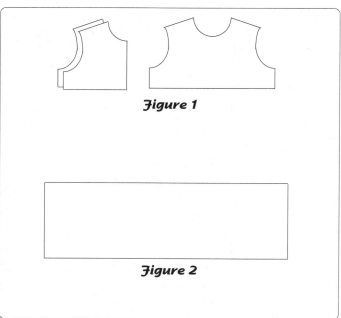

Figure 1

Figure 2

B. Yokes and Collar

1. Place the front yoke to the back yokes at the shoulders and stitch **(figs. 3)**.

2. For the collar front, cut lace insertion and beading to the following sizes:

   a. Cut four strips of 5/8" lace insertion, each 5" long.

   b. Cut one strip of 3/4" lace insertion, 5" long.

   c. Cut four strips of 3/8" lace beading, each 5" long.

2. Piece the rectangle as follows **(fig. 4)**, keeping the lace patterns running in the same direction. Use the technique "lace to lace".

   a. Sew a strip of beading to each side of the 3/4" lace insertion strip.

   b. Sew a strip of 5/8" lace insertion to the beading on each side.

   c. Sew a strip of lace beading to each side of the band.

   d. Sew a strip of 5/8" lace insertion to each side of the band.

   e. From one side of the rectangle to the other, the order is 5/8" insertion, beading, 5/8" insertion, beading, 3/4" insertion, beading, 5/8" insertion, beading, 5/8" insertion.

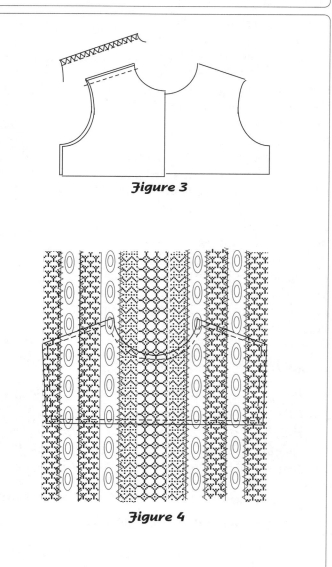

Figure 3

Figure 4

3. Fold the rectangle in half, with the fold running from top to bottom through the center of the 3/4" insertion. Place the collar pattern over the rectangle and trace the collar outline. Stitch along the drawn line, then cut out the collar front. Refer to figure 4.

4. After the collar has been cut, thread 4mm green silk ribbon through the beading, trim the ribbon to the correct length and tack the ends to the collar edges by hand or machine.

5. For each collar back (there will be two), cut lace insertion and beading to the following sizes:

   a. Cut two strips of 5/8" lace insertion, 5" long.

   b. Cut one strip of 3/4" lace insertion, 5" long.

   c. Cut two strips of 3/8" lace beading, each 5" long.

   d. Be sure to cut two sets of strips. Place each set in a separate pile to work from.

6. Piece the rectangle for one collar back as follows **(fig. 5)**, keeping the lace patterns running in the same direction. Use the technique "lace to lace".

   a. Stitch beading to each side of one strip of the 5/8" lace insertion.

   b. Sew a strip of 5/8" insertion to one side of the band.

   c. Sew the 3/4" lace insertion to the remaining edge of the beading.

   d. Repeat steps a - c to create the rectangle for the second collar back piece. Remember that the two rectangles need to be mirror images since they will be right and left collars, with the lace patterns running in the same direction.

7. Place one rectangle over the other with the patterns matched and right sides together. Place the pattern over the rectangles and trace the pattern onto one piece, with the 3/4" insertion along the back edge. Refer to figure 5. Turn the rectangles over and trace the pattern onto the other piece. Stitch along the drawn lines and cut out the collar backs.

8. Thread 4mm green silk ribbon through the beading. Trim the ribbon to fit and tack the ends to the collar edges.

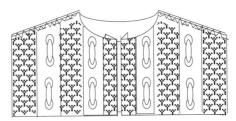

Figure 5

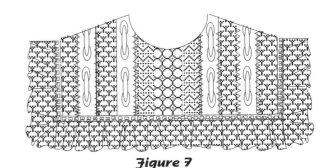

Figure 6

Figure 7

9. Place the collar front to the collar backs at the shoulder seams, right sides together, and stitch the seams **(fig. 6)**.

10. Attach entredeux to the collar side and bottom edges, cutting and overlapping the entredeux at the corners **(fig. 7)**.

11. Cut a piece of 1-1/4" edging 45" long. Beginning at one back edge, pull the heading threads to gather the lace, then attach the lace edging to the entredeux, using the technique "entredeux to lace". Adjust the gathers to a pleasing fullness and trim off any excess at the back neck edges. Remember to add a little extra fullness around the corners to prevent the wide lace from "cupping" around the corners. Refer to figure 7.

12. Place the collar over the dress yokes and baste the two layers together at the neck edge.

13. Finish the neck edge, referring to "Neck Finishes - a. Entredeux and Gathered Edging" found on page 34, and using the 5/8" lace edging **(fig. 8)**.

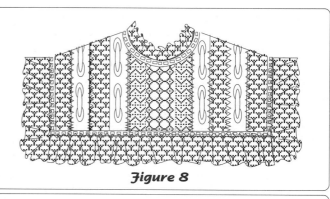

Figure 8

C. Sleeves

1. For the sleeves, cut lace insertion and beading to the following sizes:

    a. Cut eight strips of 5/8" lace insertion, each 9" long.

    b. Cut four pieces of beading, each 9" long.

    c. Cut two pieces of 3/4" lace insertion, each 9" long.

    d. Cut four pieces of fabric, each 5" wide by 9" long.

2. Lay aside four pieces of the 5/8" insertion, one strip of 3/4" insertion and two pieces of the beading. Use the remaining strips to piece a rectangle for one of the sleeves. Keep the lace patterns running in the same direction and use the technique "lace to lace" **(fig. 9)**.

    a. Sew 5/8" insertion to each side of the 3/4" insertion.

    b. Sew the beading to each side of the band.

    c. Sew the remaining pieces of 5/8" insertion to each side of the band.

    d. Attach a strip of fabric to each side of the band, using the technique "entredeux to fabric".

    e. Repeat steps a - c to piece the band for the second sleeve.

3. Mark the top edges of the rectangles and fold the pieces in half, with the fold running down the middle of the 3/4" insertion. Place the pattern over

Figure 9

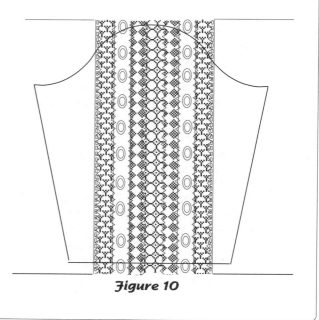

Figure 10

each rectangle and trace the sleeve onto the fabric. Be sure that the top of the pattern is matched to the top edge of the rectangle if the lace design has a definite top and bottom. Stitch along the drawn lines, then cut out the sleeves **(fig. 10)**.

4. Thread 4mm green silk ribbon through the beading. Trim the ribbon and tack the ends to the sleeve edges **(fig. 11)**.

5. Run two rows of gathering threads across the top and bottom edges of the sleeves, 1/8" and 1/4" from the edges (refer to fig. 11).

6. Refer to "Sleeve Bands and Ruffles - a. Entredeux and Gathered Edging Lace" on page 38 to finish the bottom edges of the sleeves, using 3/8" beading and 1-1/4" lace edging **(fig. 12)**.

7. Pin the sleeves to the armholes and adjust the gathers to fit, letting the gathers fall 1-1/2" on each side of the shoulder seam. Stitch the sleeves in place. Do not catch the collar in the stitching **(fig. 13)**.

8. Place the sleeve/side seams with right sides together. Match the sleeve edges and the bottom edges and stitch. Do not catch the collar in the side seams **(fig. 14)**.

D. Skirt

1. Create the fancy band as follows:

   a. Cut four pieces of 5/8" lace insertion, two pieces of lace beading and one piece of 1-1/4" insertion, each 45" long. Cut two pieces of entredeux, each 45" long.

   b. Sew a piece of the 5/8" insertion to each side of the 1-1/4" insertion, using the technique "lace to lace".

   c. Attach a strip of beading to each edge, using the technique "lace to lace".

   d. Attach the remaining 5/8" insertion to the outer edges, using the technique "lace to lace".

   e. Sew a strip of entredeux to each edge of the band, using the technique "entredeux to lace".

2. Mark the center of the fancy band at the top and bottom edges. Place one entredeux edge of the fancy band to the bottom edge of the skirt piece, right sides together and stitch, using the technique "entredeux to fabric". Trim the fancy band to make it fit the skirt **(fig. 15)**.

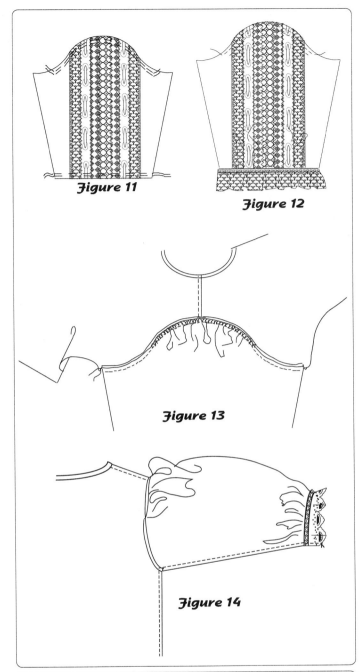

Figure 11

Figure 12

Figure 13

Figure 14

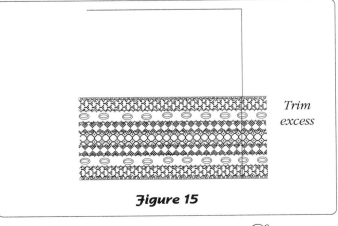

Trim excess

Figure 15

3. Finish the back edges of the skirt piece with a serge or zigzag. Press under 1/2" along the back right edge. **Refer to figure 16.**

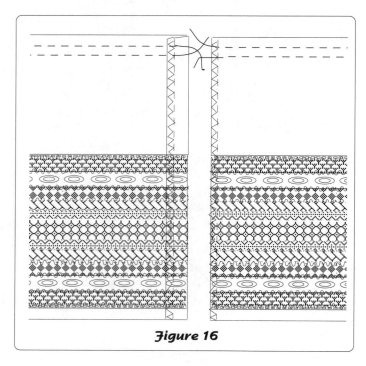

Figure 16

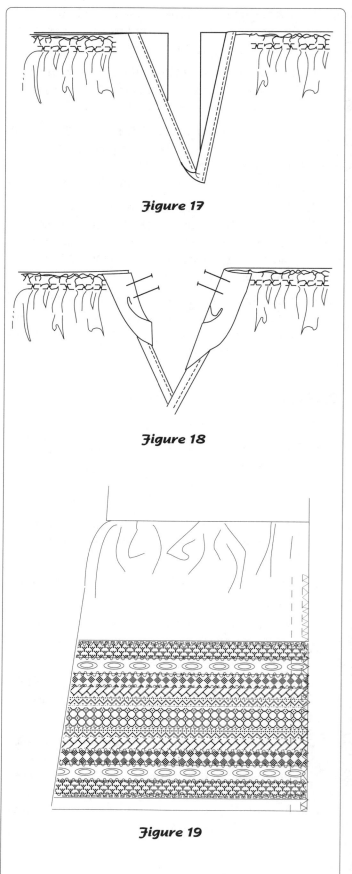

Figure 17

Figure 18

4. Run two rows of gathering threads across the top of the skirt piece, 1/8" and 1/4" from the edge. Stop the stitching 1/2" from the back edges.

5. Pin the skirt piece to the bodice, right sides together. Adjust the gathers in the skirt top to fit the bottom edge of the bodice **(fig. 17)**.

6. The pressed back edges should meet the back fold line of the yokes. Wrap the back facings to the outside along the fold line, sandwiching the skirt between the yoke and the facing. Stitch in place and press the yokes up, flipping the facings to the inside **(fig. 18)**.

7. Starting at the bottom edge of the skirt, stitch the 1/2" center back seam, stopping 4-1/2" below the waistline seam **(fig. 19)**.

8. Refer to "Plackets - c. Continuous Placket in a Seam or d. Easy Placket in a Seam" on page 43 and apply a placket to the back of the skirt.

Figure 19

E. Finishing the Dress

1. Trim the 2-1/2" fabric band to fit the bottom edge of the skirt, allowing a 1/4" seam allowance at each end. Stitch the two short ends of the band with right sides together, forming a circle **(fig. 20)**.

2. Fold the band in half with the long edges meeting and press **(fig. 21)**.

3. Attach the band to the bottom edge of the skirt, using the technique "entredeux to fabric" **(fig. 22)**.

4. Apply Velcro™, snaps or tiny buttons and button-holes to the back opening, with the right side lapping over the left side.

5. Run 4mm green silk ribbon through the beading at the sleeve bottoms, starting at the outside of the sleeve, and tie the ends into a bow. Also run 4mm green silk ribbon through the beading in the fancy band, starting to the left of center front, and tie the ends into bows. **Refer to figure 23.**

6. Cut an 18" piece of 7mm green silk ribbon. Tie the ribbon into a bow and trim the streamers. Tack the bow to the center front of the collar, above the ruffle **(fig. 24)**.

7. Optional: From the 7mm pink silk ribbon, make one large and four small wrapped roses. Use the remaining 7mm ribbon to make a ruffle behind the large rose and leaves for the small roses.

8. Tack the large rose to the center front of the neck, and tack the four small roses to the corners of the collar, front and back. Refer to figure 24.

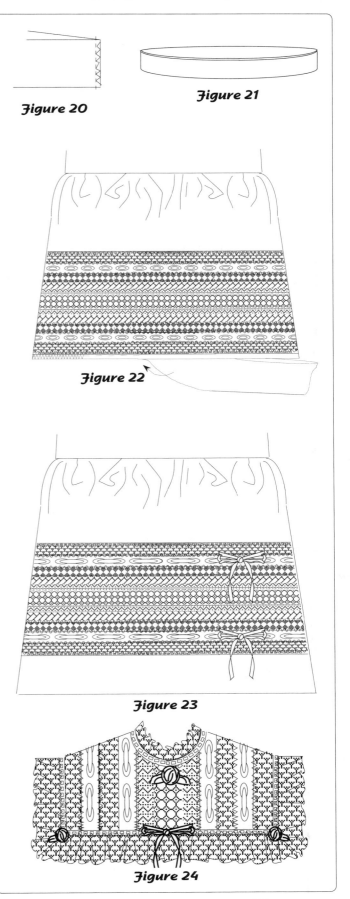

Figure 20

Figure 21

Figure 22

Figure 23

Figure 24

Antique Reproduction Coat

Exquisite describes this gorgeous ecru silk coat which is fully lined and has such elegant details. The round one-piece collar has lace edging shaped on the outside of the collar; it is stitched down with a machine featherstitch on both sides and a perky pink and green silk ribbon flowerette is stitched in the front points. Gathered ecru lace edging is stitched around the collar and is found again where the bodice of the coat joins the skirt on both the front and back of the coat. A puffed sleeve is finished with a beautiful cuff which makes a very tailored finish for this coat. Ecru loops and round buttons close the front of the coat in the bodice area only. I cannot think of a more beautiful garment for a doll than an elegant coat and bonnet. This one should make any one on your gift list happy. I also believe that it would make judges in a doll show really take notice of your costuming ability also. Enjoy!

- **All pattern pieces and templates found in pull-out section**
- **Color photograph on page 11**

Supplies

Fabric Requirements: All Sizes

Fabric - Silk Batiste	3/4 yd.
Lining - Cotton Batiste	3/4 yd.
Lace Insertion (3/4")	3/4 yd.
Lace Edging (1-1/4")	1 yd.
Lace Edging (5/8")	1 yd.
Silk Ribbon (7mm, green)	1/4 yd.
Silk Ribbon (7mm, pink)	1/2 yd. or 2 puurchased ribbon roses

Notions: Lightweight sewing thread, five 1/4" ball buttons with shanks for closure, decorative machine embroidery thread

Pattern Pieces Required: Coat Front Yoke, Coat Back Yoke, Coat Sleeve, Coat Collar, Coat Cuff.

All seams 1/4" unless otherwise indicated. Stitch seam in place and overcast the seam allowances with a zigzag or serge, unless otherwise indicated.

A. Cutting

1. From the silk batiste fabric, cut four front yokes and one back yoke on the fold. Cut two collars and two sleeves **(fig. 1)**. Also cut two cuffs, 2-1/2" wide by the following length **(fig. 2)**:

Doll Sizes	17-1/2"	18-1/2"	19-1/2"	21-1/2"
Cuff Length	4-1/2"	5"	5"	4-3/4"

2. From the silk batiste fabric, cut one skirt piece, 44" wide by the following length:

Doll Sizes	17-1/2"	18-1/2"	19-1/2"	21-1/2"
Skirt Length	12-1/2"	13"	14"	15-1/4"

3. Mark the center of the skirt piece at the top and bottom edges **(fig. 3)**.

4. From the cotton batiste lining fabric, cut one back yoke on the fold, two sleeves and one skirt piece, the same width but 3/4" shorter than the length of the silk skirt piece.

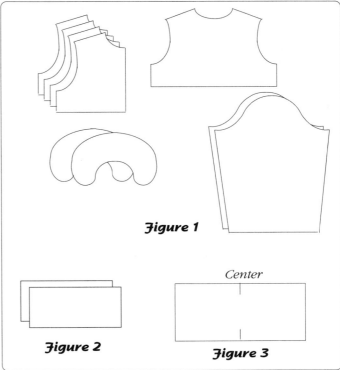

Figure 1

Figure 2

Center

Figure 3

B. Collar and Yokes

1. Shape the 3/4" insertion lace around the outer edge of one collar piece. Place the outer edge of the lace along the 1/4" seam line and stitch both edges in place with a small feather stitch or zigzag. Refer to "Lace Shaping" on page 244 **(fig. 4)**.

2. Place the collar pieces with right sides together, having the piece with lace attached on top **(fig. 5)**.

3. Stitch the two collars together, stitching just outside of the featherstitching that attached the insertion.

4. Trim the seam and turn the collar to the right side. Press the seam well.

5. Gather the 5/8" lace edging and place it around the outer edge of the collar piece. Whip the the edging in place by hand, or butt the two edges and zigzag **(fig. 6)**.

6. Sew two silk front yokes to the silk back yoke at the shoulders, right sides together. This will be the outer bodice **(fig. 7)**.

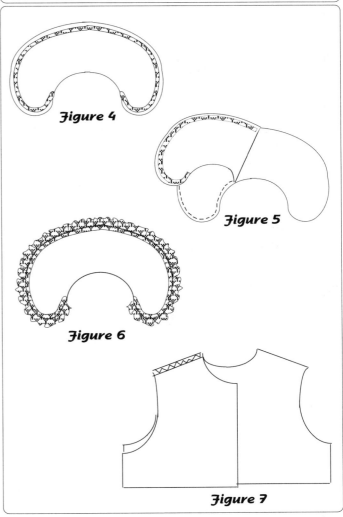

Figure 4

Figure 5

Figure 6

Figure 7

7. Place the collar to the outer bodice at the neck edges, with the wrong side of the collar to the right side of the bodice. The edge of the ruffle should stop at the center front seam lines. Baste along the neck edge **(fig. 8)**.

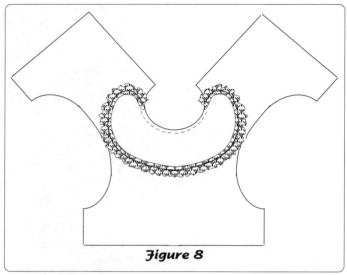

Figure 8

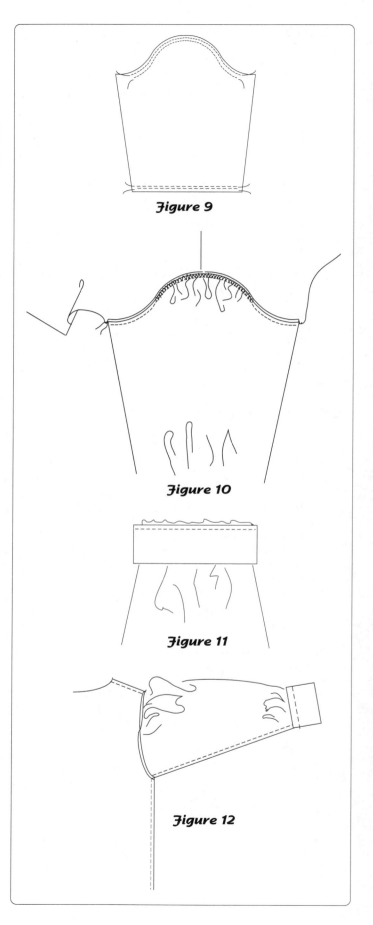

Figure 9

Figure 10

Figure 11

Figure 12

C. Sleeves

1. Run two rows of gathering stitches across the top and bottom edges of the sleeve, 1/8" and 1/4" from the edge **(fig. 9)**.

2. Place the sleeves to the bodice with right sides together. Adjust the sleeve gathers so that the sleeves fit the armholes, letting the gathers fall 1-1/2" to each side of the shoulder seam. Stitch the seam and trim **(fig. 10)**.

3. Place the cuff to the bottom edge of the sleeve, with right sides together, and stitch **(fig. 11)**.

4. Place the side/sleeve seams right sides together and stitch **(fig. 12)**.

D. Bodice Lining

1. Sew the remaining silk front yokes to the cotton back yoke at the shoulders, right sides together.

2. Refer to "C. Sleeves, Steps 1, 2 and 4" above to attach the lining sleeves to the lining bodice.

3. Place the lining to the outer bodice, right sides together.

4. Stitch the lining to the bodice along the front and neck edges **(fig. 13)**. Trim and clip the seam allowance.

5. Turn the lining to the inside and tack the bodice and the lining together at the shoulder seam.

6. Push the sleeve lining into the outer sleeve. Adjust the gathers of the lining to fit the outer sleeve. Pin or baste the sleeve lining to the sleeve at the gathered seam **(fig. 14)**.

7. Turn the cuff to the inside. Turn under 1/4" at the raw edge of the cuff and stitch the fold to the cuff seam by hand **(fig. 15)**.

8. Cut a piece of 1-1/4" edging twice as long as the waistline edge of the bodice. Turn under 1/8", then 1/8" again at each end. Pull the heading thread to gather the lace.

9. Place the gathered edge of the lace along the seam line of the outer bodice, right sides together, adjust the gathers to fit and pin or baste in place. The hemmed edges of the lace should stop at the fold lines of the bodice **(fig. 16)**.

E. Skirt

1. Turn up 1/4" along the bottom edge of the skirt, then turn up a 1-1/4" hem and press. Blind-hem by hand or machine **(fig. 17)**.

2. Repeat step 1 for the lining.

3. Place the lining to the skirt, right sides together, and with the top edges even. The lining will be 3/4" shorter than the outer skirt at the hem edge. The lining will also be shorter than the skirt at the front edges. Match the centers so that the excess is the same on each front edge **(fig. 18)**.

4. Stitch the lining to the outer skirt at the front edges (the two short ends), forming a tube. Turn to the right side.

5. Flatten the tube and press with centers matched, so that the skirt fabric turns to the inside by 1" on each end to form facings.

6. Run two rows of gathering threads along the top edge of the skirt section, stitching through both layers. Place the gathering rows 1/8" and 1/4" from the edge **(fig. 19)**.

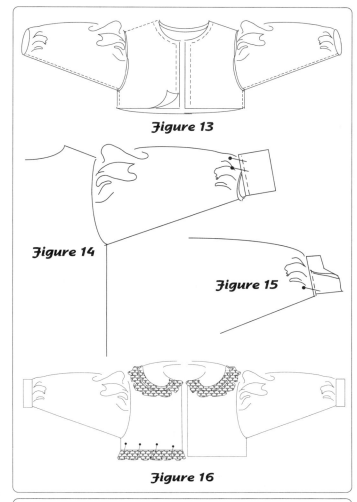

Figure 13

Figure 14

Figure 15

Figure 16

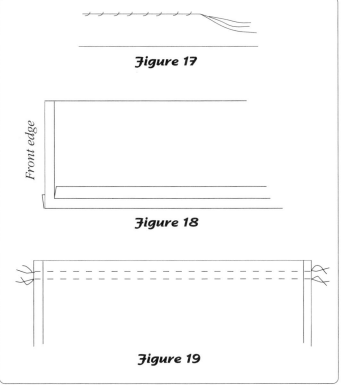

Figure 17

Front edge

Figure 18

Figure 19

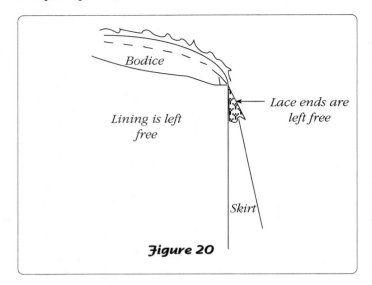

Bodice

Lining is left free

Lace ends are left free

Skirt

Figure 20

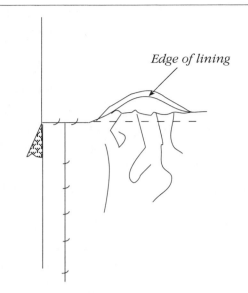

Edge of lining

Figure 21

7. Pull up the gathers to fit the bodice and pin or baste, meeting the front edge of the skirt to the fold line of the bodice **(fig. 20)**. Pin the skirt to the outer bodice only, through the lace, leaving the lining free. Stitch the seam. Do not catch the hemmed edges of the lace in the seam.

8. Fold under the seam allowance of the lining at the waistline seam and meet the folded edge to the seam. Stitch the lining in place by hand **(fig. 21)**.

F. Finishing the Coat

1. Make button loops on the edge of the right front bodice and attach the shank buttons to the left bodice **(fig. 22)**.

2. Optional: Make two small hand-wrapped roses from the pink silk ribbon. Also make two hand-folded leaves from the green silk ribbon.

3. Attach the leaves and roses to the front edges of the collar, in the top edge of the curve in the lace insertion. Refer to figure 22.

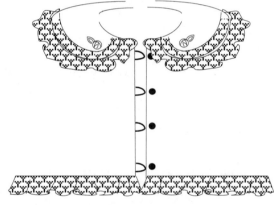

Figure 22

Antique Reproduction Bonnet

Simple to make and beautiful to wear is this antique reproduction silk bonnet made of ecru silk, ecru laces and pale green silk ribbon trims. The bonnet is embellished over the head portion with three strips of ecru French insertion and two rows of ecru French beading. The lace strip is stitched down on both sides with machine featherstitching. Five silk ribbon flowers in pink and green are found across the head. Gathered ecru French edging goes all the way around the outside of the bonnet and green silk ribbon rosettes with two long streamers for tying the bonnet underneath the chin are found on each side.

- **All pattern pieces and templates found in pull-out section**
- **Color photograph on page 11**

Supplies

Fabric Requirements: All Sizes

Fabric - Silk Batiste	1/8 yd.
Lace Insertion (3/4")	1/2 yd.
Lace Insertion (5/8")	1 yd.
Lace Beading (3/8")	1 yd.
Lace Edging (1-1/4")	3-1/2 yds.
Silk Ribbon (4mm, green)	1 yd.
Silk Ribbon (7mm, green)	5 yds.
Silk Ribbon (7mm, pink)	2 yds.

or 3 large and 2 small purchased ribbon roses

Notions: Lightweight sewing thread, decorative machine embroidery thread

Pattern Pieces Required: Bonnet, Bonnet Lining

All seams 1/4" unless otherwise indicated. Stitch seam in place and overcast the seam allowances with a zigzag or serge, unless otherwise indicated.

A. Cutting

1. Cut one bonnet piece and two bonnet lining pieces **(fig. 1)**.

2. Mark the dots on the lining pieces. Refer to figure 1.

3. Press a crease along the length of the bonnet piece and mark the gathering line at each end **(fig. 2)**.

B. Decorating the Bonnet

1. Center the 3/4" lace insertion over the center crease of the bonnet piece. Let the lace extend past the ends of the bonnet piece. Straight stitch the lace in place along both edges **(fig. 3)**.

2. Cut the 3/8" lace beading in half and place a strip along each side of the 3/4" insertion. Butt the headings together and zigzag. Straight stitch along the free edges **(fig. 4)**.

3. Thread the 4mm green silk ribbon through the beading and tack in place at each end **(fig. 5)**.

4. Cut the 5/8" lace insertion in half and butt a strip to each piece of the beading. Refer to figure 5. Zigzag the insertion in place along the butted edges. Feather stitch along the remaining edge of each strip.

5. Trim the ends of the lace to the shape of the bonnet ends **(fig. 6)**.

6. Optional: Using the pink silk ribbon, make three large and two small hand-wrapped roses.

7. Optional: Use the 7mm green silk ribbon to make leaves for the roses.

   a. Make gathered ruffle leaves for each large rose. Cut a piece of ribbon 1-1/2" long. Gather one edge of one ribbon piece by hand, pulling the cut ends together and tacking them. Make two leaves for each large rose **(fig. 7)**.

   b. Make one hand-folded leaf for each small rose. Cut a piece of ribbon 1-1/2" long. Fold both cut ends to the back, lapping one end over the other to form a loop, not a circle. Make one leaf for each small rose **(fig. 8)**.

8. Mark the placement for the roses along the center of the bonnet. Sew the leaves in place first, then attach the roses. Place the three large roses in the center. Let the leaves of the small roses point to the end of the bonnet. Refer to figure 6.

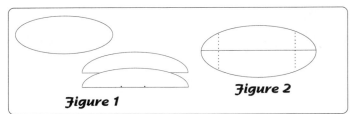

Figure 1

Figure 2

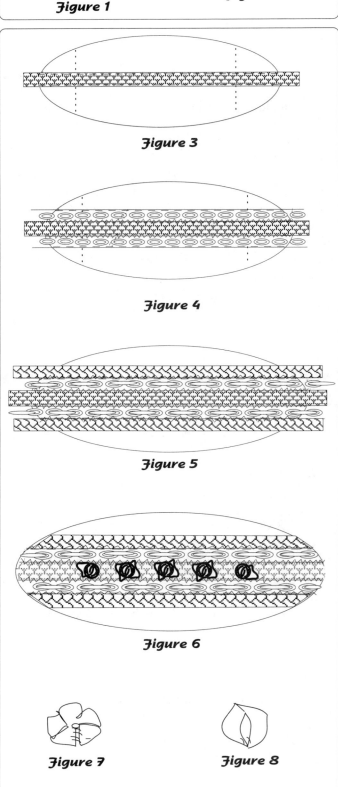

Figure 3

Figure 4

Figure 5

Figure 6

Figure 7

Figure 8

C. Construction

1. Sew the ends of the lace edging into a circle. Pull the heading thread to gather the lace to fit around the outer edge of the bonnet piece **(fig. 9)**.

2. Baste the lace edging to the bonnet piece with the heading of the lace along the seam line, right sides together **(fig. 10)**.

3. Sew the lining pieces together along the center seam, leaving an opening between the dots **(fig. 11)**.

4. Place the bonnet over the lining, right sides together **(fig. 12)**.

5. Stitch the bonnet and lining together around the outer edge. Refer to figure 12. Stitch with the bonnet piece on top and use the basting line for the edging as a guide for the seam line.

6. Turn the bonnet to the right side through the opening in the lining. Close the opening with hand stitching **(fig. 13)**.

D. Finishing the Bonnet

1. Run a row of hand stitches to gather the bonnet along the gathering lines at each end of the bonnet. Pull the gathers up tightly to form a ruffle at the ends of the bonnet **(fig. 14)**.

2. Cut the 7mm green silk ribbon into four pieces. Fold two of the pieces in half to make long streamers and tack the streamers to each end of the bonnet over the gathers. Tie a knot in the end of each streamer about 1" from the end **(fig. 15)**.

3. Use the remaining two pieces of ribbon to make two ribbon rosettes. Leave short streamers on the rosettes. Tack the rosettes over the streamers at the ends of the bonnet.

4. Use the long streamers to tie the bonnet. Refer to figure 15.

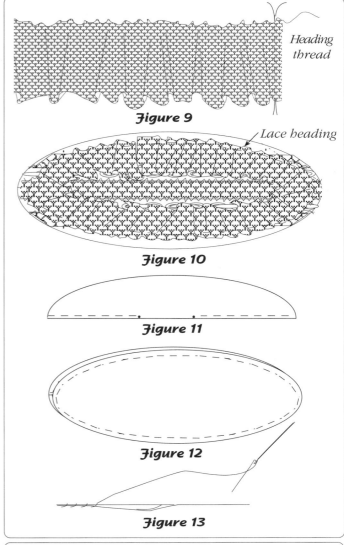

Heading thread

Figure 9

Lace heading

Figure 10

Figure 11

Figure 12

Figure 13

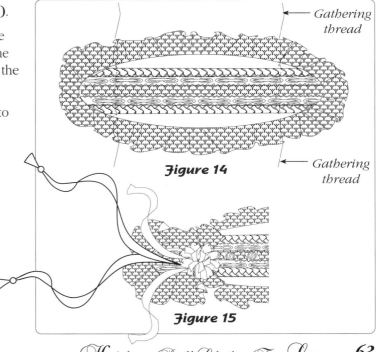

Gathering thread

Figure 14

Gathering thread

Figure 15

Chery's Smocked Purple Party Pants

Chery Williams designed this doll party pants outfit to match her pattern for a little girl! What a precious way to celebrate smocking! Who wouldn't love to make matching smocked outfits for both their Götz and living dolls? This cute play outfit is made of purple Imperial broadcloth smocked with white geometric smocking. Tiny white bows are stitched in-between the smocked rows. White 1/4-inch ribbon is stitched on to trim the sleeves and the legs. Elastic gathers in the fullness of the sleeves and the legs. Velcro™ strips close the legs of this garment as well as the back, making it easy to get into and out of. The neckline is bound with a bias binding. These party pants would be adorable in almost every type of fabric from broadcloth to corduroy to silk dupioni.

Chery Williams, P.O. Box 190234, Birmingham, AL 35219 (205-290-2700)

Supplies

Fabric - Broadcloth	1 yd.
Ribbon - 1/4" wide	2 yds.

- **All pattern pieces and templates found in pull-out section**
- **Color photograph on page 27**

Other Notions: Lightweight sewing thread; Velcro™, snaps or tiny buttons for back closure; 1/8" elastic for sleeves; embroidery floss and #7 or #8 crewel needle for smocking

Pattern Pieces Required: Bishop Jumpsuit Front (long length); Bishop Jumpsuit Back (long length); Bishop Sleeve, long or short; smocking graph and instructions for "Bishop Bows" on page 66

All seams 1/4" unless otherwise indicated. Stitch seam in place and overcast the seam allowances with a zigzag or serge, unless otherwise indicated.

A. Cutting and Pleating

1. Cut two jumpsuit fronts, two jumpsuit backs, and two sleeves **(fig. 1)**. A bias neck strip and placket strip will be cut later. Refer to the layout diagram.

2. Transfer the notches to the front, backs and sleeves. Also transfer the placket marking to the backs. Mark the center front at the top edge to aid in centering smocking.

3. Sew the center front seam **(fig. 2)**. Sew the sleeves to the jumpsuit front and backs, matching the notches and having right sides together **(fig. 3)**. Use a three-thread serge or pressed open seams, no French seams.

4. Refer to the pleating instructions on page 216 and pleat the following number of rows for each size **(fig. 4)**:

Doll Sizes	17-1/2"	18-1/2"	19-1/2"	21-1/2"
Pleated Rows	6	6	6	7
Smocked Rows	4	4	4	5

5. Tie-off the top two pleating threads **(fig. 5)** to the measurement given in "Neck Finishes - f. Bias Neck Bindings for Bishop Garments, Step 1" (omitting the reference to the placket) found on page 37. Shape the garment as shown on page 37.

B. Shaping and Smocking

1. Smock the jumpsuit **(fig. 6)**, using the graph and instructions for the design " Bishop Bows", found on page 66.

2. Shape and block the jumpsuit according to the instructions in "Blocking" found on page 215.

C. Placket and Neck Binding

1. To apply the placket **(fig. 7 inside view)** to the center back seam, refer to "Plackets - c. Continuous Placket in a Seam" on page 43.

2. To apply the bias neck binding **(fig. 8)**, refer to "Neck Finishes - f. Bias Neck Bindings for Bishop Garments" on page 37. If necessary, adjust the top two pleating threads to the measurements given.

D. Sleeves and Side Seams

1. Finish the bottom edges of the sleeves **(fig. 9)**, referring to "Sleeve Bands and Ruffles - h. Gathered Sleeve with Elastic and Ribbon" on page 41.

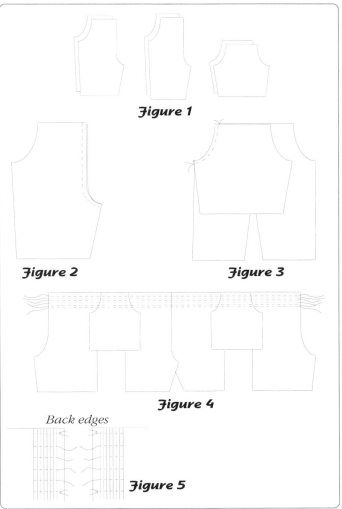

Figure 1

Figure 2

Figure 3

Figure 4

Back edges

Figure 5

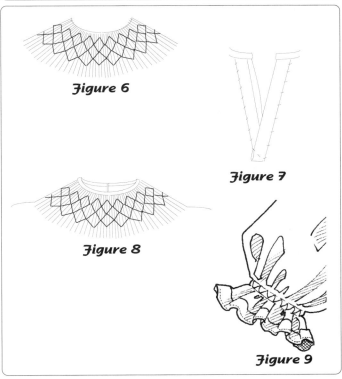

Figure 6

Figure 7

Figure 8

Figure 9

2. Meet the sleeve/side seams of the jumpsuit with right sides together and match the sleeve edges and underarm seams **(fig. 10)**; stitch in place and overcast.

E. Finishing the Jumpsuit

1. Finish the bottom edges of the legs, referring to "Sleeve Bands and Ruffles - h. Gathered Sleeve with Elastic and Ribbon" on page 41. Cut two pieces of elastic to the following length:

Doll Sizes	17-1/2"	18-1/2"	19-1/2"	21-1/2"
Leg Elastic	4-1/4"	5"	5"	5-1/2

2. Place the inner leg seam with right sides together, matching the bottom edges and the center front and back seam **(fig. 11)**; sitch in place and overcast.

3. Attach Velcro™, buttons and buttonholes or snaps to the back placket to close the jumpsuit.

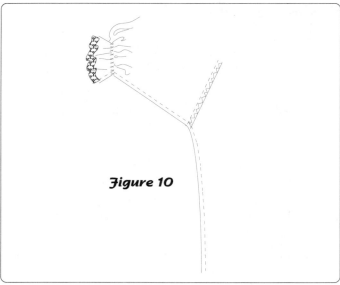

Figure 10

Bishop Bows

(This smocking graph is for Chery's Smocked Purple Party Pants)

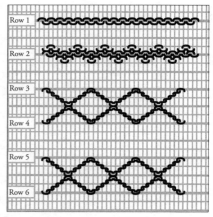

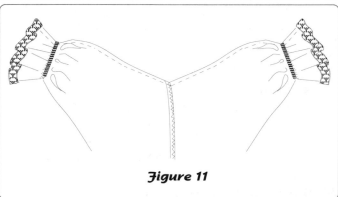

Figure 11

Supplies: DMC floss - white; #8 crewel needle; 9" of 1/8" ribbon. Smock with 3 strand of floss.

Follow the graph closely while smocking.

Pleat 7 rows; smock 6.

Step 1. On Row 1, cable across in the same color floss as the fabric. This row will be used in construction and will not show.

Step 2. Cable across Row 2, starting with an up cable.

Step 3. Work sections of three cable stitches along the top of cable Row 2, skipping two pleats between each section.

Step 4. Work sections of three cable stitches along the bottom of cable Row 2, skipping two pleats between each section.

Step 5. Between Rows 3 and 3-1/2, work four step waves.

Step 6. Between Rows 3-1/2 and 4, work four step waves forming diamonds.

Step 7. Repeat step 5 between Rows 5 and 5-1/2.

Step 8. Repeat step 6 between Rows 5-1/2 and 6.

Step 9. Using about 3" of ribbon for each bow, tie three small bows. Tack a bow at the center seam and each front sleeve seam.

Ecru Netting Over Batiste Antique Dress

Embroidered netting brings an overall elegance to this to-the-waist ecru dress. It seems almost criminal that the batiste underlayer, which was enhanced with pintucks and lace work, is hidden beneath the netting. Rayon edging at the sleeve, neckline and collar edges plays a heavy contrast to the airy netting, and adds to the rich detail. All dolls should be dressed so beautifully.

- *All pattern pieces and templates found in pull-out section*
- *Color photograph on page 22*

Supplies

Fabric

Batiste	3/4 yd.
Netting	3/4 yd.

Netting Lace

Edging (6")	2 yds.
Insertion(1-3/4")	1 yd.

Rayon Edging (1/2")	3 yds.
Lace Insertion A (3/8")	2-1/2 yds.
Lace Beading (1/2")	2-1/2 yds.
Lace Insertion B (1-1/4")	1-1/4 yds.
Lace Insertion C (5/8")	2-3/4 yds.
Lace Edging (1-1/4")	1-1/4 yds.
Ribbon (to fit beading)	2-1/2 yds.
Entredeux	7-1/2 yds.

Ribbon for sash (1" double faced satin)	1 yd.

Notions: Two spools of lightweight sewing thread; Velcro™, snaps or tiny buttons for back closure; 2.0/80 double needle and optional-pearl beads

Pattern Pieces Required: To-The-Waist Front Bodice, To-The-Waist Back Bodice, 3/4-Length Sleeve, 3/4 Sleeve Overlay and Barrel Cuff

All seams 1/4" unless otherwise indicated. Stitch seam in place and overcast the seam allowances with a zigzag or serge.

A. Cutting

1. From the fabric, cut the following: two back bodices from the selvages, two sleeves, two cuffs from a fold, and one skirt piece 45" wide by the following length **(fig. 1)**:

Doll Sizes	17-1/2"	18-1/2"	19-1/2"	21-1/2"
Skirt	4"	4-3/4"	5-1/4"	6-1/4"

   Cut the following from the netting: two back bodices and one front bodice from the fold **(fig. 2)**. The netting overlay on the skirt will be cut later.

2. Cut one fabric rectangle to the following measurement for the front bodice (the length is listed first, the width follows):

Doll Sizes	17-1/2"	18-1/2"	19-1/2"	21-1/2"
Skirt	5" x 7"	6" x 8"	6" x 8"	6" x 9"

3. Cut two sleeve overlays from the wide netting edging lace by placing the scalloped edge of the lace to the overlay line on the sleeve **(fig. 3)**.

4. Transfer fold line markings from the back bodice pattern to the back bodice pieces.

B. Constructing The Bodice

1. Attach entredeux to each side of the lace insertion using the technique "lace to entredeux." This entredeux/lace strip will be used to decorate the bodice, sleeves and skirt.

2. Cut the width of the bodice rectangle in half. (For example - the 17-1/2" doll bodice rectangle is 5" x 7". When cut in half, the two rectangles will measure 5" x 3-1/2"). Cut a piece from the entredeux/lace strip to the length of the rectangle. Stitch one fabric rectangle to each side of the entredeux/lace strip **(fig. 4)**.

3. Stitch three double needle pintucks 1/8" apart starting 3/4" from the entredeux/lace strip **(fig. 5)**. Refer to page 276. Press the pintucks away from the center.

4. Fold the created fabric in half matching the entredeux strips and pintucks. Place the bodice front pattern on the fold and cut out **(fig. 6)**.

5. Place the netting bodices over the fabric bodice pieces, matching all sides. Pin netting pieces to fabric pieces and treat as one layer of fabric **(fig. 7)**.

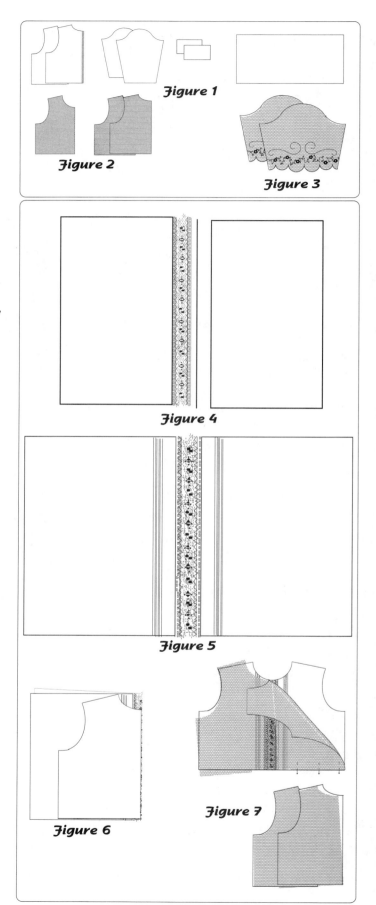

Figure 1

Figure 2

Figure 3

Figure 4

Figure 5

Figure 6

Figure 7

6. Place the front bodice to the back bodice right sides together at the shoulders. Stitch in place using a 1/4" seam **(fig. 8)**.

7. Cut an 18" piece of netting insertion lace and rayon edging. Butt the edge of the rayon edging to the netting insertion lace. Zigzag together **(fig. 9)**.

8. Place two gathering rows in the top edge of the netting insertion lace at 1/8" and 3/8". With the back folds of the bodice extended, gather the insertion to fit the neck of the dress. Baste in place at 1/4" **(fig. 10)**.

9. Finish the neck with entredeux and rayon edging. Refer to "Neck Finishes - c. Entredeux to Flat Lace" found on page 35.

10. Cut two pieces of entredeux/insertion lace the length of the sleeve. Cut each sleeve in half, top to bottom. Stitch a sleeve half to each entredeux/insertion lace strip creating two whole sleeves **(fig. 11)**. Cut away any excess entredeux/insertion lace following the shape of the sleeve.

11. Fold and press cuffs with cut edges matching **(fig. 12)**. Cut two pieces of netting lace insertion and two pieces of rayon edging the length of the cuff. Butt the edging to the insertion and zigzag together. Place the insertion/edging over the cuff with the edging extending beyond the fold. Pin in place and trim the sides of the insertion to fit the cuff **(fig. 13)**.

12. Gather the sleeve to fit the cut, long edges of the cuff. Place the insertion side of the cuff to the right side of the sleeve and stitch in place with a 1/4" seam **(fig. 14)**.

13. Place a sleeve overlay to the top of each sleeve. Pin in place and treat as one layer.

14. Run two gathering rows at 1/8" and 1/4" in the top of each sleeve **(fig. 15)**.

15. Gather the top of the sleeves to fit the arm opening of the bodice, matching the center of the sleeve with the shoulder seam of the bodice.

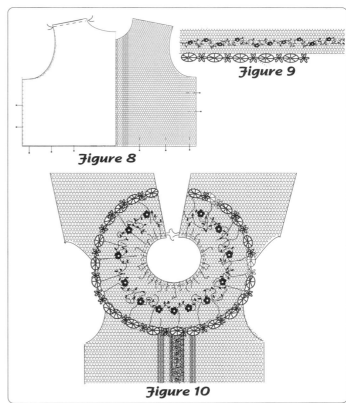

Figure 9

Figure 8

Figure 10

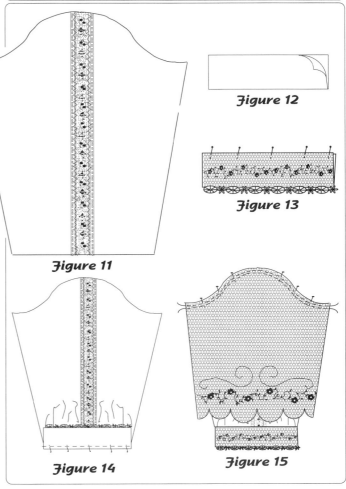

Figure 12

Figure 13

Figure 11

Figure 14

Figure 15

Adjust the gathers in the top of the sleeve to fall 1-1/4" to 1-1/2" on either side of the shoulder seam **(fig. 16)**.

16. Stitch the sleeve to the bodice, right sides together, using a 1/4" seam.

17. Place the sides/sleeves of the bodice, right sides together. Stitch using a 1/4" seam **(fig. 17)**.

C. Skirt

1. Cut the following panels from the skirt piece: eight panels 4-3/4" wide and two panels 2-3/4" wide. Cut nine pieces of entredeux/insertion created in Step B. 1 to the length of the panels. Create a long strip by stitching the entredeux/ insertion strip to each side of the 4-3/4" panels using the technique "entredeux to fabric". End each side of the strip with the 2-3/4" panels **(fig. 18)**.

2. Stitch three double needle pintucks in the center of each of the wider panels. Stitch one pintuck 3/8" from the back edges of the skirt **(fig. 19)**. Press.

3. Measure the width of the skirt. Create a fancy band 2" longer than the skirt width. Cut and stitch the laces together in the following order, using the technique "lace to lace": lace insertion 1/2", lace beading, lace insertion (wide), lace beading, lace insertion 1/2" and lace edging. Cut a piece of entredeux the length of the fancy band and attach to the upper piece of lace using the technique "lace to entredeux" **(fig. 20)**.

4. Stitch the entredeux side of the fancy band to the skirt using the technique "entredeux to fabric."

5. The skirt length should be

> 8" *for the 17-1/2" doll;*
> 8-3/4" *for the 18-1/2" doll;*
> 9-1/4" *for the 19-1/2" doll or*
> 10-1/4" *for the 21-1/2" doll.*

If necessary, trim away any excess from the top edge of the skirt to achieve this measurement.

6. To find the length and width to cut the skirt netting overlay, measure the skirt width and the skirt length from the top edge of the skirt to the entredeux of the fancy band. Cut a piece of netting to this width but 1/4" longer than the measured length.

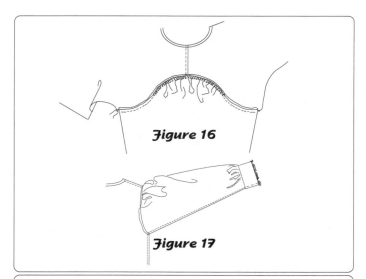

Figure 16

Figure 17

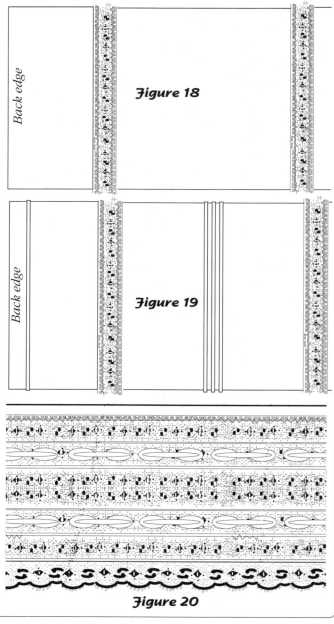

Back edge

Figure 18

Back edge

Figure 19

Figure 20

7. Now, measure the depth of the skirt fancy band from the entredeux to the end of the edging. Cut a piece of netting lace edging the length of the fancy band but 1/4" wider than the depth measurement.

8. Stitch the netting edging lace to the netting using a 1/4" seam. Trim the seam allowance to 1/8" and overcast the seam allowance with a zigzag **(fig. 21)**.

9. Cut a piece of rayon edging to the width of the skirt. Place the edging over the netting/edging seam. Stitch the rayon edging in place with a small zigzag.

10. Place the netting overlay on top of the skirt, matching the top and back edges. Pin in place and treat as one layer of fabric **(fig. 22)**.

11. Place the back edges of the skirt together and stitch from the bottom, stopping 3-1/2" from top of the skirt. Backstitch **(fig. 23)**.

12. Place a placket in the seam opening. Refer to "Placket - c. Continuous Placket or d. Easy Placket" found on page 43.

13. Run two gathering rows 1/8" and 1/4" from the top edge of the skirt. Remember that one side of the placket is folded to the inside of the skirt and the other side is left extended **(fig. 24)**.

D. Finishing the Dress

1. Place the right side of the bodice to the right side of the skirt, matching the center of the bodice with the center of the skirt. Pin in place. Gather the skirt to fit the bodice. Distribute the gathers evenly **(fig. 25)**.

2. At the back edges of the skirt opening wrap the back facings of the bodice to the outside over the placket opening of the skirt. Pin in place **(fig. 26)**.

3. Stitch the skirt to the bodice using a 1/4" seam. Overcast the seam allowance.

4. Attach Velcro™, buttons and buttonholes or snaps to the back of the bodice to close the dress.

5. Optional: Stitch pearls to the edging netting lace of the sleeve and skirt to accent the lace pattern.

6. Place the wide ribbon around the waist of the dress and tie in a bow at the center back.

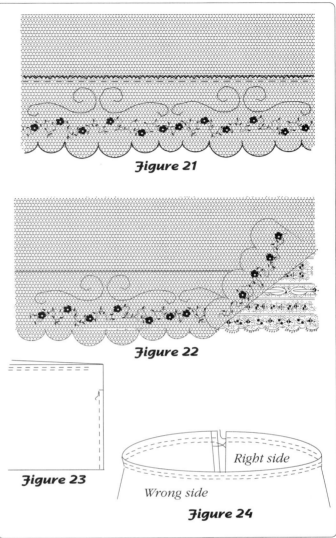

Figure 21

Figure 22

Figure 23

Right side

Wrong side

Figure 24

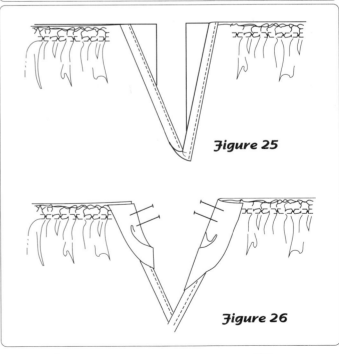

Figure 25

Figure 26

Fantasy Lace And Netting Pinafore Dress

This pinafore dress is a pure dream, combining white cotton netting, Swiss embroidered half moon motifs, scalloped lace, pink Swiss batiste, and of course, creativity and love. A row of French white lace insertion and a row of narrow French lace edging make up the yoke of the pinafore. A scalloped netting/lace, insertion/gathered lace edging ruffle frames this pinafore yoke. The body of the pinafore is a series of 11 panels, each consisting of lace insertion on each side ending in a curve on the bottom; a Swiss embroidered netting motif is tucked away inside each curve. 1-1/4 inch wide French edging is gathered all the way around to the back of the pinafore. Narrow French edging is stitched on flat around the underarm curves. The pinafore closes in back with Velcro™.

The pink Swiss Nelona batiste dress underneath the pinafore is simply elegant. Scalloped French insertion finishes the bottom of the skirt. Gathered 1-1/4 inch wide white French edging trims these scallops. Entredeux and gathered lace edging finish both the bottom of the sleeves and the neckline. The dress is a high yoke style, which is closed in the back with Velcro™. This doll dress is a competition winner for sure as well as a little girl pleaser.

- **All pattern pieces and templates found in pull-out section**
- **Color photograph on page 12**

Dress Supplies

Fabric Requirements: All Sizes	
Fabric - Batiste	3/4 yd.
Entredeux	5/8 yd.
Lace Edging (3/8")	3/8 yd.
Lace Edging (1")	2-2/3 yds.
Lace Insertion (1/2")	1-1/2 yds.

Notions: Lightweight sewing thread and Velcro™, snaps or tiny buttons for closure

Pattern Pieces Required: High Yoke Front, High Yoke Back, Elbow-Length Sleeve

Templates Required: 2-3/4" Scallop for Collar, Fantasy Lace Pinafore Template, Armhole Guide

All seams 1/4" unless otherwise indicated. Stitch seam in place and overcast the seam allowances with a zigzag or serge, unless otherwise indicated.

A. Cutting

1. Cut one front yoke on the fold, two back yokes on the selvage and two sleeves on the fold **(fig. 1)**. Also cut two skirt pieces, 21" wide by the following length:

Doll Sizes	*17-1/2"*	*18-1/2"*	*19-1/2"*	*21-1/2"*
Skirt Length	10"	10-1/2"	11-1/2"	12-3/4"

2. Transfer pattern markings to the fabric. Also mark the centers of the skirt pieces at the top and bottom edges, and use the armhole guide to cut the armholes **(fig. 2)**.

B. Constructing the Yokes and Sleeves

1. With right sides together, sew the front yoke to the back yokes at the shoulder seams **(fig. 3)**.

2. Finish the neck edge, referring to "Neck Finishes - a. Entredeux and Gathered Edging" found on page 34, and using 3/8" lace edging **(fig. 4)**.

3. Run two rows of gathering threads across the top and bottom edges of the sleeves, 1/8" and 1/4" from the edges **(fig. 5)**.

4. Refer to "Sleeve Bands and Ruffles - a. Entredeux and Gathered Edging Lace" on page 38 to finish the bottom edges of the sleeves, using 1" lace edging **(fig. 6)**.

C. Skirt

1. Match the center of the scallop template to the center of the skirt piece, with the bottom edges of the scallops approximately 1/4" above the bottom edge **(fig. 7)**.

2. Trace the scallops onto the fabric, using a washable pen or pencil. Be sure to include the miter lines.

3. Use 1/2" lace insertion to shape the scallops, referring to "Shaping Lace Scallops" on page 242. Let the lace extend off the edge of the fabric at the sides of the skirt. After the scallops are shaped, trim the sides of the skirt so that a 1/4" seam allowance extends past the last miter on each side. Stitch along the top edge only of the scallops **(fig. 8)**.

4. Trim the excess fabric from behind the scallops and stitch the miters.

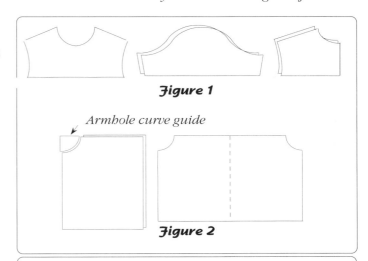

Figure 1

Armhole curve guide

Figure 2

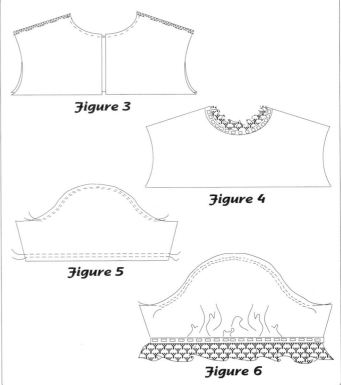

Figure 3

Figure 4

Figure 5

Figure 6

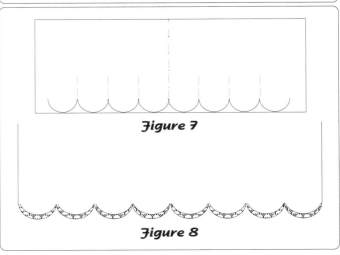

Figure 7

Figure 8

5. Choose one skirt piece to be the skirt back. Cut a 4-1/2" slit at the center on the top edge of the piece and apply a placket **(fig. 9)**. Refer to "Plackets - a. Continuous Lap Placket" found on page 42.

6. Run two rows of gathering threads across the top of each skirt piece, 1/8" and 1/4" from the edge. Stop the stitching at the placket seam line on the back pieces. Refer to figure 9.

7. Pin the front skirt piece to the yoke, right sides together. Adjust the gathers in the skirt top to fit the bottom edge of the yoke and stitch in place **(fig. 10)**.

8. Place the back skirts to the back yokes, right sides together. The placket edges should meet the back fold line of the yoke. Wrap the back facings to the outside along the fold line, sandwiching the skirt between the yoke and the facing **(fig. 11)**. Stitch in place and press the yokes up, flipping the facings to the inside **(fig. 12)**.

D. Finishing the Dress

1. Pin the sleeves to the armholes and adjust the gathers to fit, stopping the gathers at the yoke seam lines. Stitch the sleeves in place **(fig. 13)**.

2. Place only one of the sleeve/side seams with right sides together. Match the sleeve edges and the bottom edges and stitch. The seam should fall at the miter points of the scallops on each side edge of the skirt pieces **(fig. 14)**.

3. Pull the heading thread to gather the 1" lace edging and attach the ruffled lace to the bottom edge of the scallops, using the technique "lace to lace" **(fig. 15)**.

4. Stitch the second side seam as described in step 2 above.

5. Apply Velcro™, snaps or tiny buttons and button-holes to the back opening, with the right side lapping over the left side.

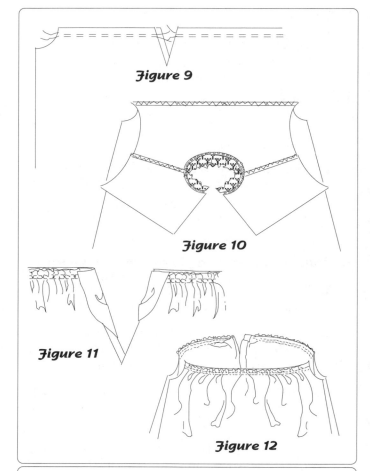

Figure 9

Figure 10

Figure 11

Figure 12

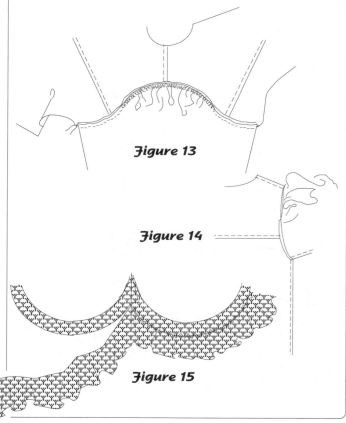

Figure 13

Figure 14

Figure 15

Netting Pinafore

Supplies

Fabric Requirements: All Sizes

Fabric - Netting	3/4 yd.
Lace Edging (3/8")	1/2 yd.
Lace Edging (1")	7 yds.
Lace Insertion (1/2")	10 yds.

Optional: Motifs (3" half circle) 11

Notions: Lightweight sewing thread, Velcro™, snaps or tiny buttons for closure, water soluble stabilizer (WSS)

Pattern Pieces Required: Round Yoke Front and Round Yoke Back

Templates Required: Round Yoke Dress Template, Netting Pinafore Lace Templates - Skirt and Collar

All seams 1/4" unless otherwise indicated. Stitch seam in place and overcast the seam allowances with a zigzag or serge, unless otherwise indicated.

A. Cutting

1. From the netting, cut one front yoke and two back yokes on the selvage. Cut one collar strip from the netting 2" wide by 30" long. Cut one skirt piece, 45" wide by the following length:

Doll Sizes	17-1/2"	18-1/2"	19-1/2"	21-1/2"
Skirt Length	11"	11-1/2"	12-1/2"	13-3/4"

B. Construction

1. Place a piece of water-soluble stabilizer (WSS) to the wrong side of the netting skirt piece. Press in place with a warm iron. Place a piece of WSS to the wrong side of the netting collar strip. Trace the lace shaping template on both the skirt piece and the collar piece with the lower edge of the scallop template to the edge of the fabric, matching the center of the template to the center of the netting **(fig. 1)**.

2. Fold the skirt in half and mark the center. Fold again to get the quarter points **(fig. 2)**. The fold of the netting and the back cut edges of the skirt will line up. Place the upper skirt template with the side of the template to the netting quarter points (two folds of fabric) and the top of the template along the top edge of the fabric **(fig. 2)**. Cut away the top of the fabric to form the curves of the front and back skirt pieces. Also cut away the armhole **(fig. 3)**.

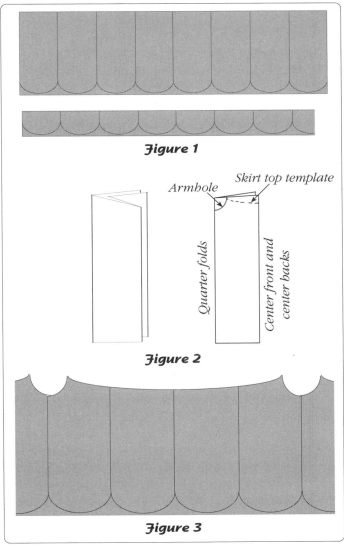

Figure 1

Figure 2

Figure 3

3. Shape the lace along the template lines of the skirt. Pin in place. If motifs are used, place the motifs along the lower part of the template with the edges of the motif to the edges of the lace **(fig. 4)**. Pin in place.

4. Zigzag along the inside edges of each lace panel and across the top of the motif (if used). Also zigzag the lace strips of each panel together starting at the top of the skirt and continuing to the dot. Trim the netting from behind the lace pieces **(fig. 4)**.

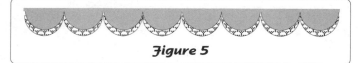

Figure 5

5. Shape the lace along the collar netting strip. Zigzag along the inside edge of the lace. Trim the netting from behind the lace. Zigzag along the miter points. Trim away any excess lace at the miters **(fig. 5)**.

6. Gather two yards of edging lace to fit along the back edges of the collar and around the scallops. Stitch the gathered edging to the lace using the technique lace to lace **(fig. 6)**.

7. Gather the remaining edging to fit along the back edge of the skirt and around the scallops. Stitch the gathered edging to the lace using the technique lace to lace **(fig. 7)**.

8. Place the front yoke to the back yoke at the shoulders and stitch in place using a 1/4" seam **(fig. 8)**. Place a piece of WSS to the wrong side of the round yoke piece. Shape a piece of lace insertion 1/4" from the bottom edge of the yoke. Stitch the lace in place along the lower edge of the lace through the netting using a small zigzag **(fig. 9)**.

9. Shape a piece of small edging just above the insertion lace. Stitch the small edging to the insertion through the netting using a zigzag **(fig. 10)**. Also stitch just under the scalloped edge of the lace using a small zigzag. Transfer the markings for the arm opening to the lower edge of the insertion lace. Carefully trim the netting away above and below the lace piece. Leave the netting behind the lace to give the bodice extra stability **(fig. 11)**.

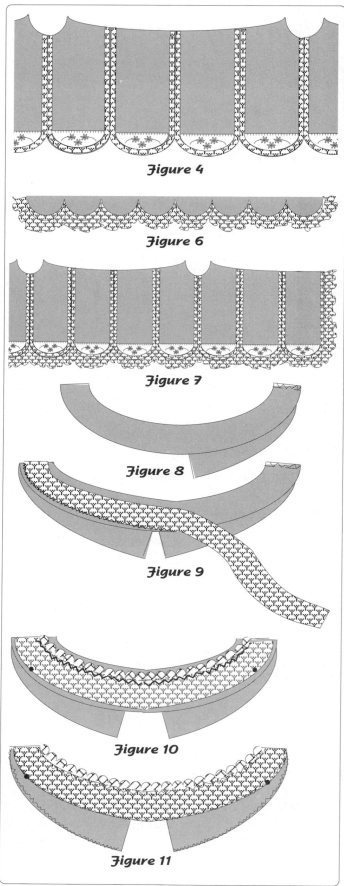

Figure 4

Figure 6

Figure 7

Figure 8

Figure 9

Figure 10

Figure 11

10. Shape 1/2" insertion along the armhole edges and zigzag in place. Run two gathering rows in the skirt front and the skirt backs at 1/8" and 1/4". Gather the front to fit between the armhole marks of the yoke **(fig. 12)**. Tie off the gathering threads to that measurement. Repeat this process for the back skirt pieces, allowing each back skirt lace edge to start on the center back line of the yoke. Tie off the gathering threads to that measurement.

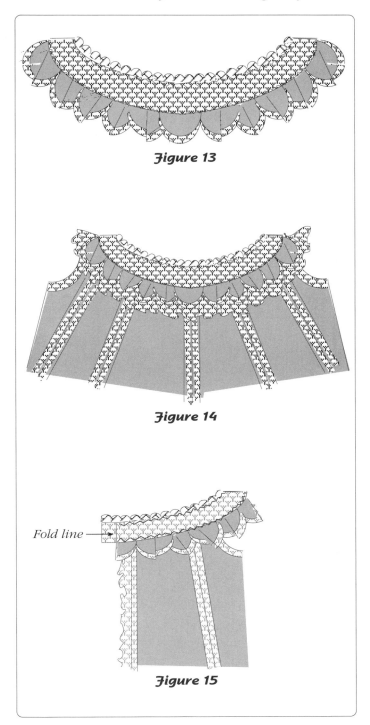

Figure 13

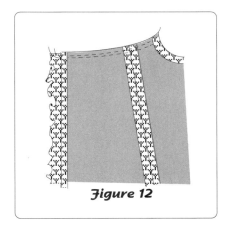

Figure 12

Figure 14

11. Run two gathering rows in the top edge of the collar piece at 1/4" and 1/8". Place the gathered collar edge 1/4" under the edge of the yoke. Distribute the gathers evenly, stopping the collar at the center back lines of the yoke. Pin in place **(fig. 13)**.

12. Place the skirt gathered edge 1/4" under the edge of the yoke even with the gathered edge of the collar. Layering will be in the order, yoke, collar and skirt. Pin in place **(fig. 14)**.

13. Fold the back edges of the yoke to the inside along the fold lines **(fig. 15)**. Pin in place. Stitch all layers together by using a small, tight zigzag along the lower edge of the yoke lace. Trim away the excess seam allowance above the stitching.

14. Place Velcro™ along the back yokes to close.

Fold line

Figure 15

Flirty Smocked Knickers Jumpsuit

What doll wouldn't love this miniature flowers printed jumpsuit which comes to the knicker length? Pretty four-step waves are smocked in dark pink floss and white French edging is stitched to the bottom of the sleeves and pants legs. Elastic gathers in the sleeves as well as the pants. The back is closed with clear snaps and the neckline is finished with a bias neck band. This is a very cute and practical outfit for a doll and one which is easy to take on and off because of the long placket in the back.

Supplies

Fabric - Broadcloth	7/8 yd.
Lace Edging - 1" wide	2 yds.

Other Notions: Lightweight sewing thread; Velcro™, snaps or tiny buttons for back closure; 1/8" elastic for sleeves; embroidery floss and #7 or #8 crewel needle for smocking

Pattern Pieces Required: Bishop Jumpsuit Front (knickers length); Bishop Jumpsuit Back (knickers length); Bishop Sleeve, long or short; smocking graph and instructions on page 79

All seams 1/4" unless otherwise indicated. Stitch seam in place and overcast the seam allowances with a zigzag or serge, unless otherwise indicated.

- **All pattern pieces and templates found in pull-out section**
- **Color photograph on page 27**

Directions

Beginning with "A. Cutting and Pleating", refer to the instructions for the Chery's Smocked Purple Party Pants on page 64, with the following change:

1. Finish the sleeve and leg edges with the method described in "Sleeve Bands and Ruffles - g. Gathered Sleeve with Elastic and Lace" on page 41.

Easy Bishop Design

(Flirty Floral Smocked Knickers Jumpsuit)

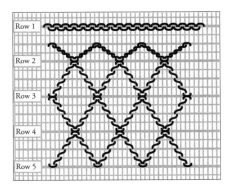

Supplies: DMC floss - rose; #8 crewel needle. Smock with 3 strand of floss.

Follow the graph closely while smocking.

Pleat 6 rows. Smock 5.

Step 1. Beginning on Row 1, cable across starting with a down cable in the same color floss as the fabric. This row will be used in construction and will not show.

Step 2. Between Rows 1-1/2 and 2 work four-step waves.

Step 3. Between Rows 2 and 3 work four-step waves forming diamonds.

Step 4. Between Rows 3 and 4 work four-step waves forming diamonds.

Step 5. Between Rows 4 and 5 work four-step waves forming diamonds.

Fourth Of July Sailor Dress

Any doll is set for Independence Day in this long-sleeve dress made of white batiste and trimmed with Swiss triple-entredeux beading. Three rows of triple-entredeux beading trim the sailor collar, the skirt and the bottom of the sleeves. The detachable, lined sailor collar has three rows of triple-entredeux beading with gathered lace edging all the way around the outside edge. Red, white and navy blue silk ribbons are run through the three rows and then a perky red, white and blue silk ribbon bow is tied to trim the front of the collar. Entredeux and gathered lace edging finish the neckline. The triple-entredeux trimmed sleeve band ends in entredeux and gathered lace edging. A fancy band of the three rows of triple-entredeux beading with red, white and navy blue silk ribbon woven through is positioned about 1-1/2 inches from the bottom of the skirt. Entredeux and flat lace edging finish the bottom of the skirt. The back is closed with snaps. The fullness of this skirt is 35-1/2 inches.

- **All pattern pieces and templates found in pull-out section**
- **Color photograph on page 24**

Supplies

Fabric - Batiste	3/4 yd.
Entredeux	1-5/8 yds.
Insertion Edging (1/2")	2-1/2 yds.
Insertion Edging (3/4")	1-1/4 yds.
Swiss Beading (1/4")	7-1/2 yds.
Silk Ribbon (to fit beading) - All Sizes	
Red	4 yds.
White	4 yds.
Blue	4 yds.

Notions: Lightweight sewing thread, and Velcro™, snaps or tiny buttons for back closure

Pattern Pieces Required: To-the-Waist Front Bodice, To-the-Waist Back Bodice, Long Sleeve and Sailor Collar

All Seams 1/4" unless otherwise indicated. Stitch seam in place and overcast the seam allowances with a zigzag or serge.

A. Cutting

1. Cut one front bodice from the fold **(fig. 1)**, two back bodices from the selvages **(fig. 1)**, two sleeves, two sailor collars **(fig. 1)** (one collar and one lining), one fabric strip for the skirt band 2" long by 45" wide, and one upper skirt piece 45" wide by the following length:

Doll Sizes	17-1/2"	18-1/2"	19-1/2"	21-1/2"
Upper Skirt	5"	5-3/4"	6-1/4"	7-1/4"

2. Transfer fold line markings from the back bodice pattern to the back bodice pieces.

B. Constructing Bodice

1. Place the front bodice to the back bodice right sides together at the shoulders. Stitch in place using a 1/4" seam **(fig. 2)**.

2. Finish the neck with entredeux and gathered 1/2" edging lace **(fig. 3)**. Refer to "Neck Finishes - a. Entredeux to Gathered Edging" found on page 34.

3. Each sleeve band consists of three pieces of Swiss beading and one piece of entredeux. Cut six pieces of Swiss beading and two pieces of entredeux to the measurement given on the Sleeve Band Chart on page for the long sleeve.

4. Stitch three pieces of Swiss beading together by trimming the fabric edges of the beading (leave one fabric edge on one piece), butting the trimmed edges together and zigzagging. The beading with the remaining fabric edge will be the top of the band. Attach trimmed entredeux to the lower edge of the band. Attach gathered edging to the entredeux. Repeat for the remaining three pieces of beading and one piece of entredeux. This entire piece can be treated as Swiss beading **(fig. 4)**.

5. Treat the entire sleeve band created in step 3 and 4 as a piece of Swiss Beading. Complete the sleeve using the directions for "Sleeve Bands and Ruffles - d. Swiss Beading and Gathered Edging Lace" **(fig. 5)** found on page 39.

6. Gather the top of the sleeves to fit the arm opening of the bodice, matching the center of the sleeve with the shoulder seam of the bodice **(fig. 6)**. Adjust the gathers in the top of the sleeve to fall 1-1/4" to 1-1/2" on either side of the shoulder seam.

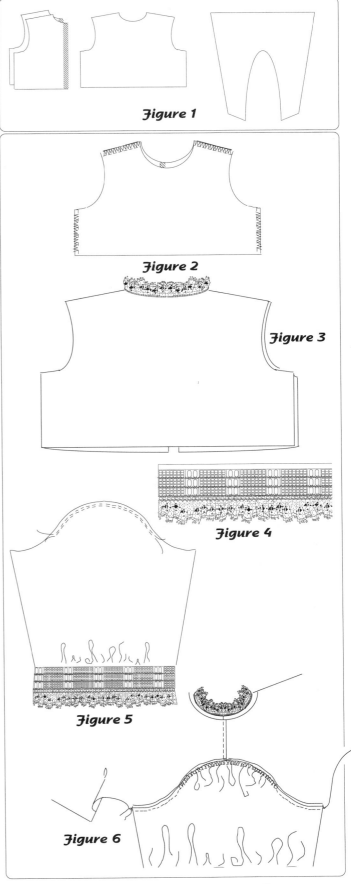

Figure 1

Figure 2

Figure 3

Figure 4

Figure 5

Figure 6

7. Stitch the sleeve to the bodice, right sides together using a 1/4" seam.

8. Weave silk ribbon through the beading, alternating the ribbon colors.

9. Place the sides/sleeves of the bodice right sides together. Stitch together using a 1/4" seam **(fig. 7)**.

C. Skirt

1. Cut three strips of beading 45" long.

2. Create the beading skirt band by stitching three pieces of beading together. Refer to section B - step 4 for stitching directions, but leave one fabric edge on the **upper and lower** edge of the outer beading pieces **(fig. 8)**.

3. Attach the 2" by 45" fabric strip for the skirt band to one side of the beading band using the technique "entredeux to fabric".

4. Cut a piece of entredeux 45" long. Attach the entredeux to the fabric strip using the technique "entredeux to fabric."

5. Attach the 3/4" edging lace to the entredeux using the technique "entredeux to lace." This completes the fancy skirt band **(fig. 9)**.

6. Attach the beading side of the fancy skirt band to the upper skirt piece using the technique "entredeux to fabric" **(fig. 10)**.

7. Weave silk ribbon through the beading, alternating the ribbon colors.

8. Place the back edges of the skirt together and stitch from the bottom edge, stopping 3-1/2" from the skirt top. Backstitch **(fig. 11)**.

9. Place a placket in the 3-1/2" opening. Refer to "Plackets - c. Continuous Placket or d. Easy Placket" found on page 43.

D. Finishing the Dress

1. Stitch two gathering rows in the top edge of the skirt. Remember that one side of the placket is folded to the inside of the skirt and the other side is left extended.

2. Place the right side of the bodice to the right side of the skirt, matching the center of the bodice with the center of the skirt. Pin in place. Gather the skirt to fit the bodice. Distribute the gathers evenly **(fig. 12)**.

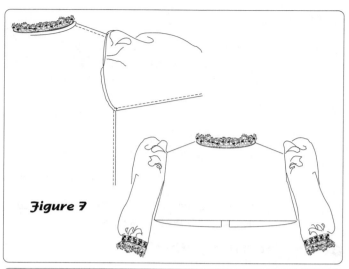

Figure 7

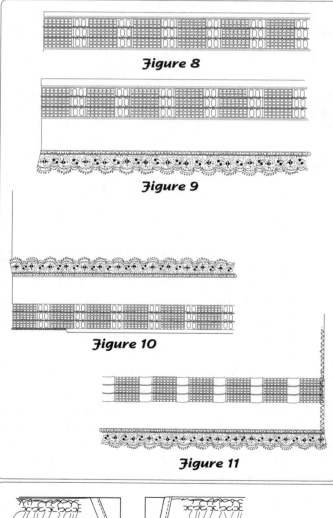

Figure 8

Figure 9

Figure 10

Figure 11

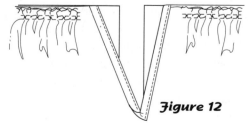

Figure 12

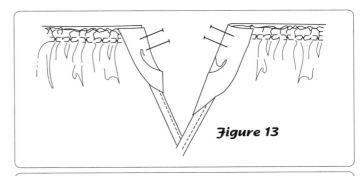

Figure 13

3. At the back edges of the skirt opening, wrap the back facings of the bodice over the open edges of the skirt. Pin in place **(fig. 13)**.

4. Stitch the skirt to the bodice using a 1/4" seam. Overcast the seam allowance.

5. Attach Velcro™, buttons and buttonholes or snaps to the back of the bodice to close the dress.

E. Detachable Sailor Collar

1. Cut three pieces of Swiss beading to the length below:

   17-1/2" dolls to 20";
   18-1/2" and 19-1/2" dolls to 24";
   21-1/2" dolls to 26".

2. Trim both fabric edges from all three beading pieces.

3. Butt the pieces together and stitch with a zigzag.

4. Weave ribbon through the beading, alternating the ribbon colors **(fig. 14)**.

5. Stitch a 1/4" seam around the outer edges of the collar to be used as a guide for the beading placement. Place the outer edge of the beading strip along this seam. Miter the corners of the beading. Zigzag in place along both edges of the beading **(fig. 15)**.

6. Place the collar lining to the collar, right sides together. Pin in place and stitch, using the 1/4" stitching line as a guide. Refer to figure 15. Leave a 3" opening in the back edge of the collar.

7. Clip the curves and corners. Turn the collar through the opening. Fold the 1/4" seam allowance at the opening to the inside and press the entire collar.

8. Cut a piece of 1/2" edging to the following measurement: 17-1/2" dolls to 45"; 18-1/2" and 19-1/2" dolls to 50"; 21-1/2" dolls to 56".

9. Turn the ends of the lace under 1/4" and 1/4" again and gather to fit the outer edge of the collar.

10. Butt the gathered lace to the collar edge and zigzag in place **(fig. 16)**. This zigzag will close the opening.

12. Cut two pieces of each color silk ribbon 24" long. Holding all six ribbon pieces, tie a bow. Tack the bow to the front edge of the collar **(fig. 17)**.

13. Close the collar with one snap.

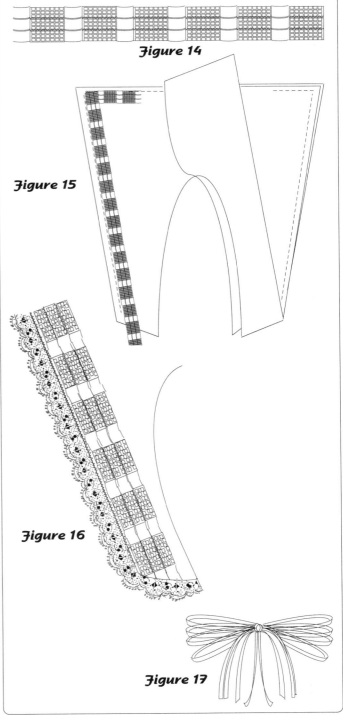

Figure 14

Figure 15

Figure 16

Figure 17

French Waterfall Dress

What could be prettier than this Swiss batiste French waterfall dress in blue and white? The mirror image scallops of white French insertion travel from the neckline down to the skirt, continuing to the back seam. The sleeves have the same delicate French waterfall treatment with double needle pintucking outlining the scallops; the top of the sleeve is white, the bottom is blue. A tiny pintuck follows the scallop on the sleeves. Entredeux and wide French gathered edging finish them. A dusty blue silk ribbon runs through the sleeve entredeux and is tied in a delicate bow. The same entredeux and gathered lace finishes the neckline of the dress. As on the sleeves, double needle pintucks follow the lace scallops down the front of the dress and on the skirt. The fabric section between the lace scallops is cut from a blue Nelona in contrast to the white of the main dress. The sash is also blue and has shaped insertion on the bottom teamed with French edging gathered very full. Scallops on the bottom of the dress are trimmed in this same full French edging. Velcro™ closes the back of this dress.

Supplies

Fabric White Batiste	3/4 yd.
Blue Batiste	3/4 yd.
Entredeux	2/3 yd.
Insertion Lace (3/8")	5 yds.
Edging Lace (1/2")	1/2 yd.
Edging Lace (1")	3-1/4 yds.
Silk Ribbon (2 mm)	2 yds.

- **All pattern pieces and templates found in pull-out section**
- **Color photograph on page 13**

Notions: Two spools of lightweight sewing thread, Velcro™, snaps or tiny buttons for back closure and a double needle (1.6/70 or 2.0/80).

Optional Notions: 7 or 9 groove pintuck foot

Pattern Pieces Required: To-The-Waist Front Bodice, To-The-Waist Back Bodice, and Elbow Length Sleeve

Template Required: French Waterfall Dress Template, Scalloped Sleeve Template and Fancy Sash Tail Template

All seams 1/4" unless otherwise indicated. Stitch seams in place and overcast the seam allowances with a zigzag or serge.

A. Cutting

1. From the white batiste cut one front bodice from the fold, two back bodices from the selvages, two sleeves and one skirt piece 45" wide by the following length **(fig. 1)**:

Doll Sizes	17-1/2"	18-1/2"	19-1/2"	21-1/2"
Skirt	8"	8-3/4"	9-1/4"	10-1/4"

2. Transfer fold line markings from the back bodice pattern to the back bodice pieces.

3. From the blue fabric cut one rectangle 45" wide by the following length:

Doll Sizes	17-1/2"	18-1/2"	19-1/2"	21-1/2"
Front Panel	13"	14"	15"	17"

B. French Waterfall Panel and Sleeves

1. Fold the blue rectangle in half, selvage to selvage. Place the lower scallops of the French waterfall template along the cut edge of the rectangle. Trace the template down the front of the rectangle and across the bottom. Trace seven scallops on each side of the center scallop **(fig. 2)**. Measure 1/2" from the last traced scallops for the seam allowance and trim off the excess. See figure 2.

2. Shape lace along the template lines following the "lace scallops" directions found on page 242 **(fig. 3)**.

3. Stitch the lace scallops to the blue fabric along the inside edges only. Trim the fabric from behind the lace **(fig. 4)**. This will create the waterfall panel which looks like an upside down "T". Two blue fabric rectangles will be left over also. These will be used for the sleeves and sash. Set waterfall panel aside.

4. Trace the sleeve scallops 1-1/2" from the lower edge of the sleeve. Shape insertion lace along the template lines using the directions for "lace scallops" found on page 242. Stitch along the upper edge of the lace scallops only **(fig. 5)**.

5. Trim the fabric from behind the lace, removing the lower part of the sleeve. Place the lower part of the sleeve on one of the blue rectangles. Cut a fabric strip larger than the lower sleeve. Place the blue fabric under the lace scallops of the sleeves, allowing it to extend below the scallops. Stitch the lower edge of the lace scallops to the blue fabric with a zigzag. Re-cut the sleeve to fit the pattern piece. Trim the blue fabric from behind the lace **(fig. 6)**.

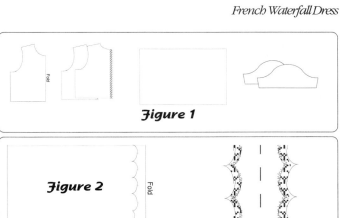

Figure 1

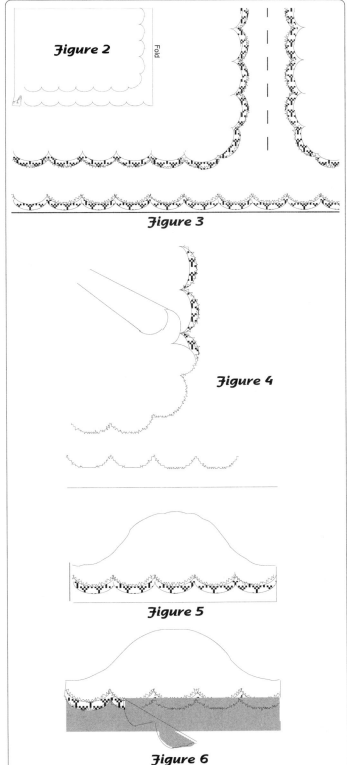

Figure 2

Figure 3

Figure 4

Figure 5

Figure 6

6. Using a double needle and pintuck foot or regular foot stitch a pintuck on the blue fabric 1/4" from the inside edge of the lace scallops **(fig. 7)**. Set sleeves aside. Stitch a pintuck on the blue fabric 1/4" away from the lace scallops of the waterfall panel **(fig. 8)**. Set waterfall panel aside.

7. From the remaining blue rectangle cut two sash strips 2-1/2" wide by 18-1/2" long.

8. Trace the fancy sash template along one short end of each sash piece by placing the point of the template to the cut edge of the sash. Shape insertion along the template lines. Zigzag the lace along the inside edge only **(fig. 9)**. Trim the fabric from behind the lace.

9. Cut two pieces of wide edging lace 6" long. Gather the edging to fit the outer edge of the lace point. Stitch the gathered lace to the lace point using a zigzag **(fig. 10)**.

10. Hem the long sides of the sash strips by turning under each long side 1/8" and 1/8" again. Stitch in place.

11. Run two rows of gathering stitching 1/8" and 1/4" along the remaining short ends of the sash pieces. Gather these ends to 5/8" **(fig. 11)**. Set aside.

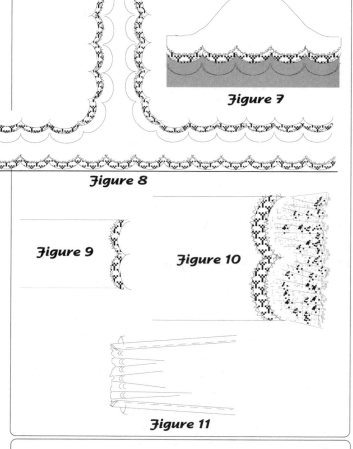

Figure 7

Figure 8

Figure 9

Figure 10

Figure 11

C. Placing the Waterfall Panel and Hem

1. Fold the skirt piece in half and find the center. Place the center of the waterfall panel to the center of the skirt with the edge of the lower scallops even with the cut edge of the skirt. Pin the panel in place along the hem only **(fig. 12)**. Trim the skirt back edges even with the waterfall hem piece. Zigzag or serge along the back edge of the skirt/waterfall hem piece to finish the edges. Fold down the top of the waterfall panel to the waterfall hem so that the skirt top can be gathered without stitching through the fancy panel **(fig. 13)**.

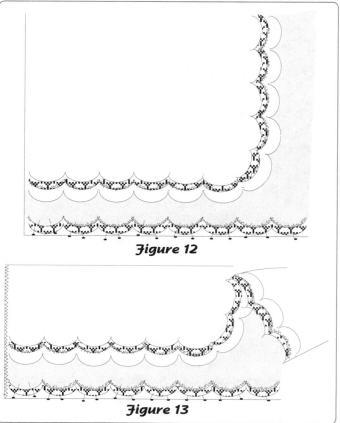

Figure 12

Figure 13

2. Fold one back edge of the skirt top to the inside 1/2" and press. Pin. Run two gathering rows in the top edge of the skirt at 1/8" and 1/4" **(fig. 14)**.

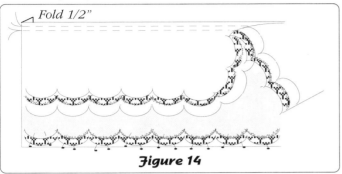

Fold 1/2"

Figure 14

3. Place the front bodice to the back bodice, right sides together, at the sides. Starting at the waist, stitch the sides 3/4", leaving the upper part of the seam open **(fig. 15)**.

4. Gather the skirt to fit the bodice. Leave 1-1/2" ungathered on each side of the center front. This 3" ungathered area will allow for the waterfall panel **(fig. 16)**. At the back edges of the skirt, wrap the back facings of the bodice over the open edges of the skirt (one back edge is turned under 1/2" and the other edge is left extended). Pin in place **(fig. 17)**.

5. Stitch the skirt to the bodice using a 1/4" seam. Overcast the seam allowance.

6. Lay the dress flat and unfold the front waterfall panel. Place the center of the waterfall panel to the center front of the dress. Pin the panel to the dress. Place the gathered sash ends under the waterfall panel, centering the sash along the waist seam. Pin. Trace the neck and shoulders on the waterfall panel **(fig. 18)**.

7. Stitch the panel in place along the outer edge of the lace scallops starting at the shoulder, continuing down the front panel and across the top edge of the waterfall panel at the hem using a small, tight zigzag. Repeat for the other side of the panel. Trim the fabric from behind the lace panel **(fig. 19)**.

8. Gather 2-1/2 yards. of wide lace edging to fit the lace scallops of the hem. Stitch the gathered lace to the lace scallops using the technique "lace to lace" **(fig. 20)**.

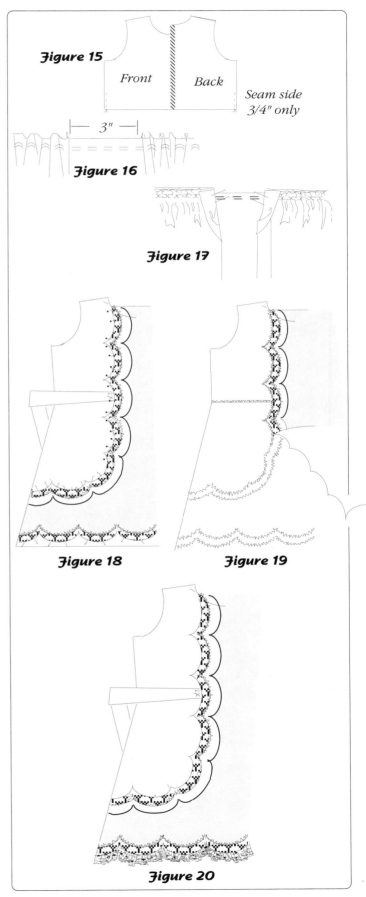

Figure 15

Front   *Back*

Seam side 3/4" only

|— 3" —|

Figure 16

Figure 17

Figure 18

Figure 19

Figure 20

C. Finishing the Dress

1. Re-cut the neck and the shoulder of the bodice front along the drawn lines on the waterfall panel.

2. Place the front bodice to the back bodice right sides together at the shoulders. Stitch in place using a 1/4" seam **(fig. 21)**.

3. Finish the neck with entredeux and gathered 1/2" edging lace. Refer to "Neck Finishes - a. Entredeux to Gathered Edging" found on page 34.

4. Place the backs of the bodice/skirt, right sides together. Pin. Stitch from the bottom edge of the skirt, stopping 3-1/2" from the waist seam. Backstitch. Trim the seam to 1/8" and overcast **(fig. 22)**. Insert a placket referring to "Plackets - d. Easy Placket in a Seam" found on page 44.

5. Run two gathering rows in the top and bottom of the sleeves. Finish the ends of the sleeves with entredeux and gathered 1/2" edging lace **(fig. 23)**. Refer to "Sleeve Bands and Ruffles - a. Entredeux and Gathered Edging Lace" found on page 38.

6. Gather the top of the sleeves to fit the arm opening of the bodice, matching the center of the sleeve with the shoulder seam of the bodice. Adjust the gathers in the top of the sleeve to fall 1-1/4" to 1-1/2" on either side of the shoulder seam **(fig. 24)**.

7. Stitch the sleeve to the bodice, right sides together, using a 1/4" seam.

8. With the sides of the bodice/sleeves, right sides together, complete the stitching of the side seam and sleeve seams **(fig. 25)**.

9. Attach Velcro™, buttons and buttonholes or snaps to the back of the bodice to close the dress.

10. Cut the silk ribbon into four equal pieces (about 18" each). Two pieces of ribbon, treated as one piece, will be woven in each sleeve. Weave the silk ribbon under two entredeux bars and over two bars of the entredeux at the sleeves. Tie the excess ribbon into bows.

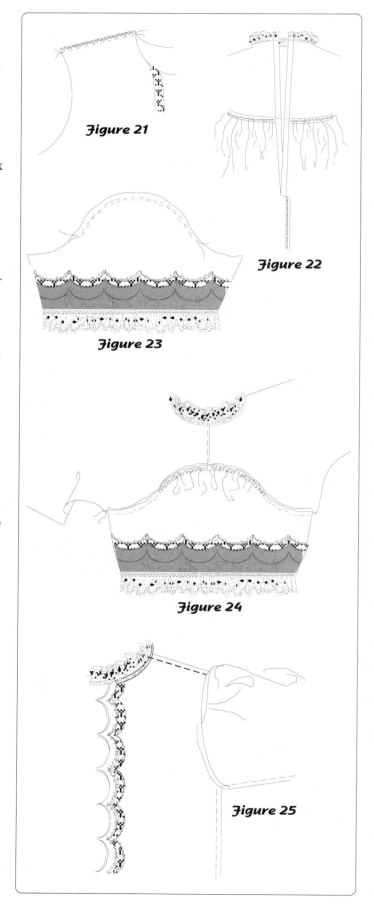

Figure 21

Figure 22

Figure 23

Figure 24

Figure 25

Green Linen Madeira Appliqué Border Dress

Unique in its special detailing, this precious little dress combines ecru Nelona Swiss batiste with green linen trims. The Madeira appliqué border is of green linen as well as the Madeira appliqué zigzag strips on the sleeves, the bodice and the skirt. Wing needle Madeira appliqué machine stitching attaches all of the Madeira green linen trims to the dress. Entredeux and gathered ecru French lace edging finish the neckline. The front bodice is embellished with a green linen strip down the center front covered with antique ecru French lace and attached with wing needle, machine entredeux stitching. The fullness of the puffed sleeves is captured at the bottom by pleats. Tiny green linen piping trims the waistline. The back is closed with Velcro™. The fullness of the skirt is 41 inches.

Supplies

Fabric - Ecru Batiste	3/4 yd.
Fabric - Green Linen	1/4 yd.
Entredeux 1/3 yd.	
Lace Insertion (3/4")	1/6 yd.
Lace Edging (1/2")	1/2 yd.

- **All pattern pieces and templates found in pull-out section**
- **Color photograph on page 14**

Notions: Lightweight sewing thread, 1/4" Bias Tape Maker, and Velcro™ or tiny buttons for back closure.

Optional Notions: Size 100 or 110 regular needle; No-Pin Basting Fabric Adhesive

Pattern Pieces Required: To-The-Waist Front Bodice, To-The-Waist Back Bodice and Short Tucked Sleeve

Templates Required: Madeira Appliqué Hem Template, Zigzag Bodice Template and Zigzag Hem Template

All Seams 1/4" unless otherwise indicated. Stitch seam in place and overcast the seam allowances with a zigzag or serge.

A. Cutting

1. Cut two back bodices from the selvages, two sleeves, and one skirt piece 45" wide by the following length **(fig. 1)**:

Doll Sizes	17-1/2"	18-1/2"	19-1/2"	21-1/2"
Skirt	8-1/4"	9"	9-1/2"	10-1/2"

2. Transfer fold line markings to the back bodice pieces, and the pleating lines to the sleeves **(fig. 2)**.

B. Decorating the Bodice

1. Cut two linen fabric strips about 5/8" wide by 45" long . Stitch the strips together to form one long strip **(fig. 3)**. Press the seam open. Run the strip through the bias tape maker following the directions on the package **(fig. 4)**. Note: These strips are not cut on the bias but running straight strips through the bias tape maker is much easier than pressing both of the long edges under to create 1/4" tape. Press well. Set aside. This 1/4" strip of folded and pressed fabric will be referred to as "linen tape."

2. Cut a rectangle of batiste 6" long by 8" wide for the front bodice.

3. Cut a strip of green linen 1-1/4" wide by 6" long. Fold each of the long sides to the inside 1/4" and press. Now the strip is 3/4" wide by 6" long **(fig. 5)**.

4. Center the linen strip to the center of the batiste rectangle, wrong side of strip to right side of rectangle **(fig. 6)**. Pin. Place the lace insertion on top of the strip. Pin in place through all layers. Stitch along each side of the lace using a small zigzag **(fig. 7)**, blind hem stitch or a large, regular needle (size 100 or 110) with a pin stitch.

5. Center the bodice pattern on the created rectangle with the center front of the pattern matching the center of the lace. Draw the pattern on the created rectangle **(fig. 8)**.

6. Trace the "zigzag" template 1/4" from the lace lining up the points along each side. Refer to figure 8.

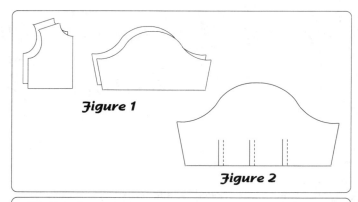

Figure 1

Figure 2

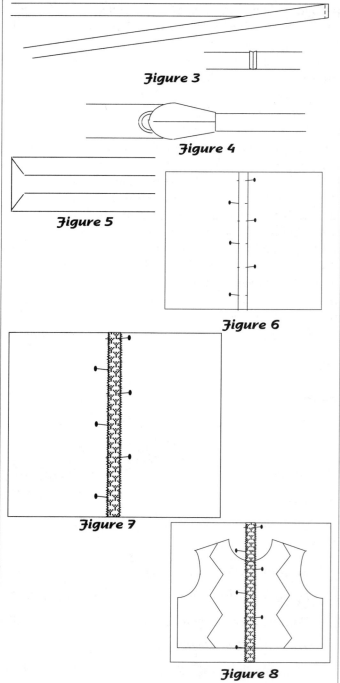

Figure 3

Figure 4

Figure 5

Figure 6

Figure 7

Figure 8

7. Shape the linen tape along the template lines using fabric adhesive or pins to hold the tape in place. Place a small fold at each point to create the miter **(fig. 9)**.

8. Stitch the tape in place along each side using a small zigzag, blind hem stitch or a large regular needle (size 100 or 110) with a pin stitch. Press well.

9. Cut out the front bodice **(fig. 10)**.

C. Constructing the Bodice

1. Place the front bodice to the back bodice right sides together at the shoulders. Stitch in place using a 1/4" seam **(fig. 11)**.

2. Finish the neck with entredeux and gathered 1/2" edging lace. Refer to "Neck Finishes - a. Entredeux to Gathered Edging" found on page 34.

3. Place three tucks in the bottom of each sleeve by folding the sleeve bottom, right sides together, along the tuck dotted line and stitching along the solid lines **(fig. 12)**. Repeat for all sleeve tucks. Press the tucks to form box pleats **(fig. 13)** (the dotted line will fall behind the stitching line).

4. Fold the bottom of the sleeve to the inside 1" and press.

5. Place a piece of linen tape 1/2" from the fold on the right side. Stitch in place as described in Step 8 above **(fig. 14)**.

6. Run two gathering rows at the top of the sleeve at 1/4" and 1/8". Refer to figure 14. Gather the top of the sleeves to fit the arm opening of the bodice, matching the center of the sleeve with the shoulder seam of the bodice **(fig. 15)**. Adjust the gathers in the top of the sleeve to fall 1-1/4" to 1-1/2" on either side of the shoulder seam **(fig. 16)**.

7. Stitch the sleeve to the bodice, right sides together using a 1/4" seam.

8. Place the sides/sleeves of the bodice, right sides together, and stitch using a 1/4" seam.

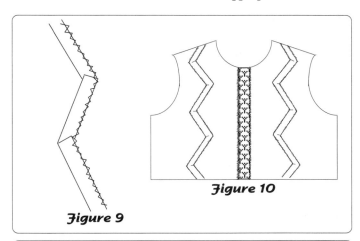

Figure 9

Figure 10

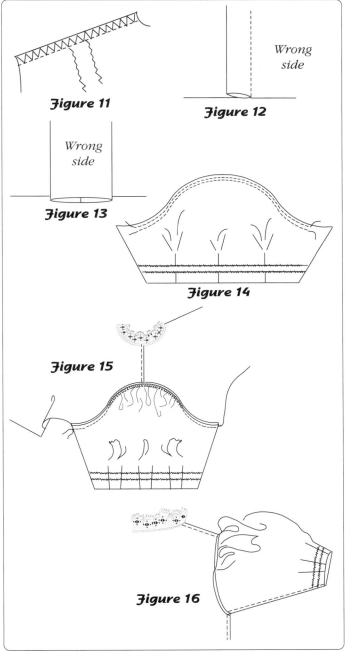

Figure 11

Figure 12

Figure 13

Figure 14

Figure 15

Figure 16

9. Measure across the bottom of the bodice with the back folds extended. Add 1" to this measurement and cut a strip of linen fabric to this length by 5/8" wide. Place piping cord in the center of the strip, fold the strip over the cord and stitch close to the cord with a zipper foot or pintuck foot **(fig. 17)**.

10. Place the piping along the lower edge of the bodice with the cut edges of the piping to the cut edge of the bodice. Stitch in place **(fig. 18)**.

D. Decorating the Skirt

1. Cut a strip of linen and a piece of WSS 2-1/2" wide by 45" long for the Madeira border hem. Trace the Madeira Hem Template on the wrong side of the linen strip **(fig. 19)**. Place the WSS on the **right** side of the border strip. Pin the WSS in place **(fig. 20)**. Straight stitch the WSS to the border strip along the pointed template line (wrong side of the strip on top, so that you can see the template lines) **(fig. 21)**. Trim the seam allowance to 1/8" **(fig. 22)**. Clip the points. The lower edge, straight edge, is not stitched.

2. Flip the WSS to the wrong side of the border, treating the WSS like a facing **(fig. 23)**. Use a point turner to ensure sharp points. Press.

3. Place the right side of the border fabric to the wrong side of the skirt, straight edge to straight edge. Stitch in place using a 1/4" seam **(fig. 24)**.

4. Flip the border to the right side of the skirt and press.

5. Pin in place. Stitch using a small zigzag, blind hem stitch or a large regular needle (size 100 or 110) with a pin stitch. Press well **(fig. 25)**.

6. Trace the zigzag skirt template above the Madeira hem (refer to fig. 26).

7. Shape and stitch the linen tape along the template lines. Refer to section B. Decorating the Bodice, Steps 7 & 8 and figure 26.

8. Place the back edges of the skirt together so that the Madeira hem and the zigzag linen tape design are continuous **(fig. 26)**. Trim away any excess skirt beyond the 1/4" seam allowance. Stitch the back seam in place from the bottom edge, stopping 3-1/2" from the skirt top. Backstitch.

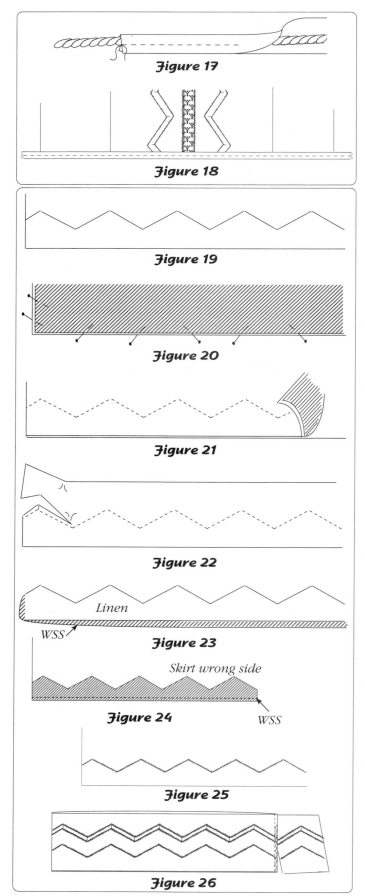

Figure 17

Figure 18

Figure 19

Figure 20

Figure 21

Figure 22

Figure 23

Linen

WSS

Figure 24

Skirt wrong side

WSS

Figure 25

Figure 26

9. Place a placket in the 3-1/2" opening. Refer to "Plackets - c. Continuous Placket or d. Easy Placket" found on page 43.

E. Finishing the Dress

1. Mark the center of the skirt. Stitch two gathering rows in the top edge of the skirt. Remember that one side of the placket is folded to the inside of the skirt and the other side is left extended **(fig. 27)**.

2. Place the right side of the bodice/piping to the right side of the skirt, matching the center of the bodice with the center of the skirt. Pin in place. Gather the skirt to fit the bodice. Distribute the gathers evenly **(fig. 28)**.

3. At the back edges of the skirt opening, wrap the back facings of the bodice over the open edges of the skirt. Pin in place **(fig. 29)**.

4. Stitch the skirt to the bodice using a 1/4" seam. Overcast the seam allowance.

5. Attach Velcro™, buttons and buttonholes or snaps to the back of the bodice to close the dress.

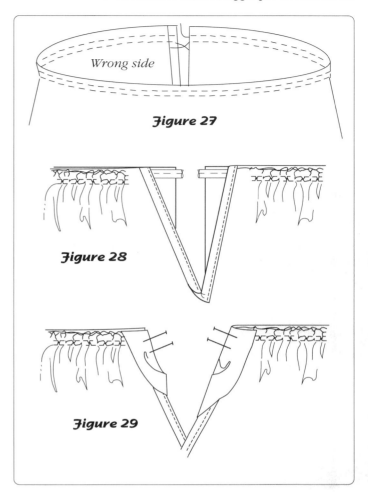

Wrong side

Figure 27

Figure 28

Figure 29

Lace Jabot Three-Piece Suit

Modified leg o' mutton sleeves, diamond- pointed shadow shapes, and a magnificent ecru lace jabot are just some of the highlights on this doll suit. The bottom of the jacket sleeves as well as the edge of the jacket are finished with the diamond-pointed shadow shapes. The leg o' mutton sleeves have a center seam and the bottom has the same shadow shaped points as the hem of the skirt. The jacket comes to a V-shape in the front and then the shadow shapes form a hem from the shoulder all the way around the bottom of the jacket. The back of the jacket is most unusual and features a dropped bustle with the shadow shaped hem.

The blouse could stand alone in detail, which includes tiny double needle pintucks stitched in a "V" on the front, then up and back down near the armholes. The full, puffed sleeves echo this V- shaped detailing in a series of double needle pintucks at the bottom where the bias binding finishes the bottom of the sleeve. The blouse closes in the back with tiny snaps. The waistband of the skirt closes with a snap also. The skirt has a "V" shadow shaped band about the waist with a similar wider treatment as a band for the hem. The ecru lace jabot is of French lace, which was designed to go all the way around the neckline. An antique cameo pin is placed at the center front of the jabot.

The crowing glory, an elastic headband, is made of matching fabric and finished on top with a fabric bow.

- *All pattern pieces and templates found in pull-out section*
- *Color photograph on page 15*

Supplies

Fabric Requirements: The amounts listed here will make all three garments. Individual fabric requirements are listed in the specific instructions for each item.

Fabric - Batiste   1-1/2 yds.

Other Notions: Lightweight sewing thread; five clear plastic snaps; water-soluble stabilizer (WSS); 1.6/70 or 2.0/80 double needle; (optional) 7-groove pintuck foot

Pattern Pieces Required: Blouse Front Bodice, Blouse Back Bodice, Elbow Length Sleeve, Jacket Front, Jacket Back, Leg o' Mutton Sleeve, Jabot

Templates Required: Sleeve Cuff Template, Jacket Hem Templates (marked on pattern pieces), Skirt Hem Template, Skirt Trim Template, Tuck Templates for Blouse Front and Blouse Back, Blouse Sleeve Tuck Template

All seams 1/4" unless otherwise indicated. Stitch seam in place and overcast the seam allowances with a zigzag or serge, unless otherwise indicated.

I. The Tucked Blouse

Fabric Requirement: Batiste, all sizes, 1/4 yd.

Notions: Lightweight sewing thread, three plastic snaps for back closure, 1.6/70 or 2.0/80 double needle, (optional: 7-groove pintuck foot)

Pattern Pieces Required: Blouse Front, Blouse Back, Elbow Length Sleeve

Templates Required: Tuck Templates for blouse front, back and sleeve

A. Cutting

1. Use the chart below to cut rectangles of fabric, which will be pintucked before the pieces are cut out. The two back rectangles should each be cut with one "length" edge along the selvage.

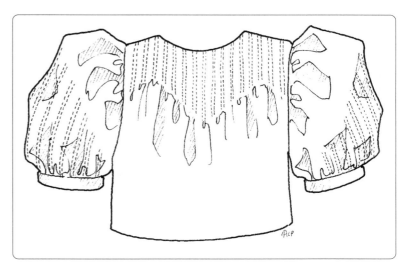

- **All pattern pieces and templates found in pull-out section**
- **Color photograph on page 15**

Doll Sizes	17-1/2"	18-1/2"	19-1/2"	21-1/2"
Front (cut 1)	7L x 11W	7L x 11W	7L x 11W	8L x 11W
Backs (cut 2)	7L x 7W	7L x 7W	7L x 7W	8L x 7W
Sleeves (cut 2)	6-1/2L x 12W	6-1/2L x 12W	7L x 12W	7-1/2L x 12W

2. Trace the tuck template lines onto the rectangles **(fig. 1)**. Use a double needle and pintuck foot (optional) to make pintucks in the template areas. The pintucks for the blouse front and backs will be approximately 1/8" apart; the pintucks for the sleeves will be approximately 1/4" apart.

3. After the tucks are sewn, place the pattern pieces over the rectangles and cut the following pieces: one blouse front, two blouse backs and two elbow-length sleeves **(fig. 2)**.

4. Transfer pattern markings to the pieces, using a washable pen or pencil.

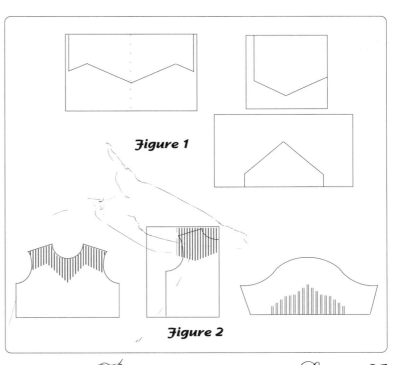

Figure 1

Figure 2

B. Shoulder Seams and Neck Edge

1. Place the blouse front to the blouse backs at the shoulders, right sides together. Stitch the seam and press it toward the back **(fig. 3)**.

2. Press the back selvage edges to the inside along the fold line to form facings **(fig. 4)**.

3. Finish the neck edge according to the instructions in "Neck Finishes - . Bias Neck Facing" on page 35 **(fig. 5)**.

C. Sleeves

1. Run two rows of gathering threads across the top and bottom edges of the sleeves, 1/8" and 1/4" from the edges **(fig. 6)**.

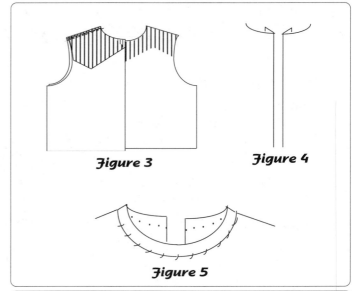

Figure 3   **Figure 4**

Figure 5

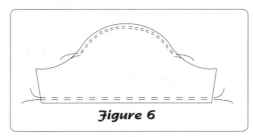

Figure 6

2. Apply a bias binding to the bottom edges of the sleeves, referring to the sleeve band chart on page 37 and the instructions in "Sleeve Bands and Ruffles - f. Bias Sleeve Bindings" on page 40, working only through Steps 1 and 2 **(fig. 7)**.

3. Pin the sleeves to the blouse armholes, adjust the gathers to fit, and stitch in place **(fig. 8)**.

4. Place the side/sleeve seams right sides together and stitch from the sleeve edge to the blouse bottom edge **(fig. 9)**.

5. Refer to "Sleeve Bands and Ruffles - f. Bias Sleeve Bindings" on page 40 and finish the sleeve bottoms, following Steps 3 and 4 **(fig. 10)**.

D. Finishing

1. Attach three snaps to the back opening, lapping right side over left side **(fig. 11)**.

2. Press 1/4" to the inside along the bottom edge, then press another 1/4". Stitch the hem in place by hand or machine **(fig. 12)**.

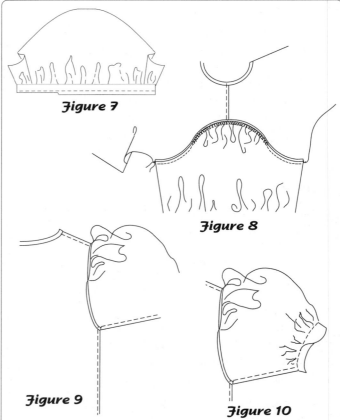

Figure 7

Figure 8

Figure 9   **Figure 10**

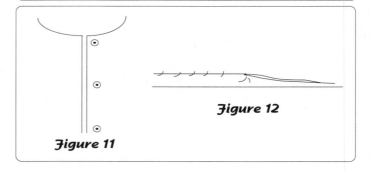

Figure 11   **Figure 12**

II. The Zigzag Skirt

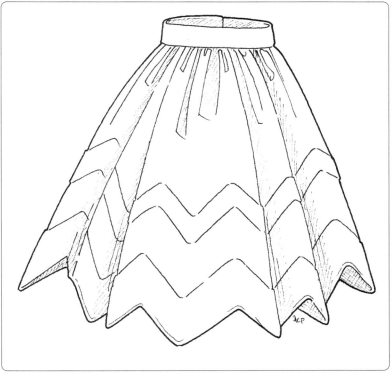

Fabric Requirement: Batiste, all sizes, 1/2 yd.

Notions: Lightweight sewing thread, one plastic snap, water-soluble stabilizer (WSS)

Templates Required: Skirt Hem Template and Skirt Trim Template, found on pattern pull-out

All seams 1/4" unless otherwise indicated. Stitch seam in place and overcast the seam allowances with a zigzag or serge, unless otherwise indicated.

A. Cutting

1. Cut two rectangles 20-1/2" wide by the following lengths:

Doll Sizes	17-1/2"	18-1/2"	19-1/2"	21-1/2"
Skirt Length	8-1/2"	9-1/4"	9-3/4"	10-3/4"

2. Cut one waistband 1-1/4" wide by the following lengths:

Doll Sizes	17-1/2"	18-1/2"	19-1/2"	21-1/2"
Cut Waistband	9-3/4"	11-1/4"	10-3/4"	12-3/4"

3. Cut two bands 4" x 20-1/2" for the hem facing, and two strips 2-1/2" x 20-1/2" for the skirt trim. Also cut pieces of WSS the same sizes as the bands and strips.

B. Hem Facings and Skirt Trim

1. Working with the two skirt rectangles, draw a line across each skirt 4" above the bottom edge, using a washable pen or pencil **(fig. 1)**.

2. Trace the hem template onto the hem facing bands, and trace the skirt trim template onto the skirt trim strips, using a washable pen or pencil **(figs. 2)**.

- ***All pattern pieces and templates found in pull-out section***
- ***Color photograph on page 15***

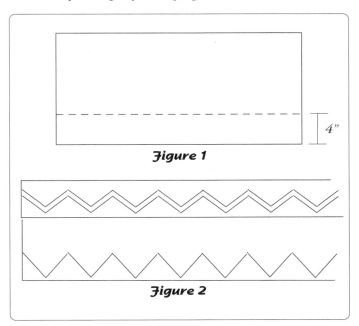

Figure 1

Figure 2

3. Apply the skirt hem facings to the skirt pieces according to the instructions for Madeira appliqué hems found on page 292. Make the following change: The hem facing and the skirt will be sewn with right sides together and the facing will turn to the inside of the skirt. The facing may be hand-whipped or pinstitched by hand or machine.

4. To make the skirt trim, sew the strip to the WSS, this time sewing along both edges of the trim template. Trim as for Madeira appliqué and turn the WSS to the wrong side of the fabric along both edges of the strip.

5. Apply the trim to the skirt by placing the bottom edge of the points along the line drawn on the skirt pieces. Pin the trim and attach the same way as the hem facing **(fig. 3)**.

C. Skirt Construction

1. Cut a 3-1/2" slit along the skirt back at the top edge and apply a placket, referring to "Plackets - a. Continuous Lap Plackets" on page 42. The skirt will lap right over left **(fig. 4)**.

2. Sew the side seams together. Try to match the pattern of the hem facings.

3. Run two rows of gathering threads along the top edge of the skirt, starting and stopping at the placket seams **(fig. 5)**.

4. Pin the waistband to the top edge of the skirt with the edges even and right sides together. Let the placket edges stop 1/4" from the ends of the waistband **(fig. 6)**.

5. Adjust the skirt gathers to fit the waistband and stitch in place. Press the gathers flat in the seam allowance and trim the seam to neaten the edges. Press the seam toward the waistband.

6. Press 1/4" to the wrong side along the long unsewn edge of the waistband. Fold the band with right sides together so that the fold meets the stitching line on the outside of the skirt **(fig. 7)**.

7. Stitch across the ends of the waistband with a 1/4" seam. Stitch right next to but not through the placket edges **(fig. 8)**.

8. Turn the unsewn edge of the band to the inside and pin, so that the fold meets the seam line on the inside of the skirt. Whip in place by hand or stitch- in-the-ditch from the right side.

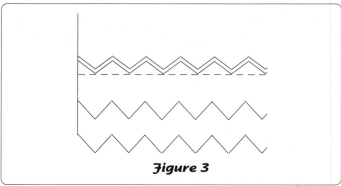

Figure 3

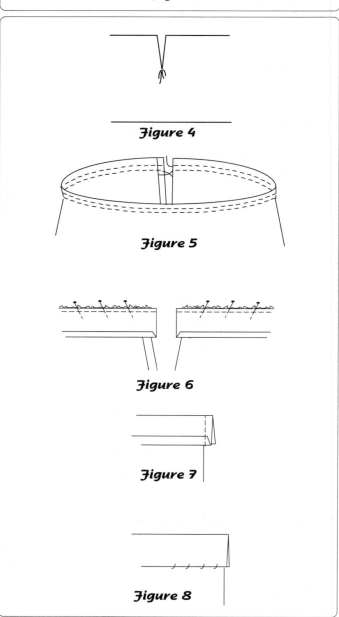

Figure 4

Figure 5

Figure 6

Figure 7

Figure 8

9. Attach a plastic snap to the back edges of the waistband, with the right side lapped over the left.

III. *The Leg o' Mutton and Peplum Jacket*

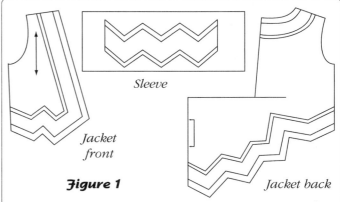

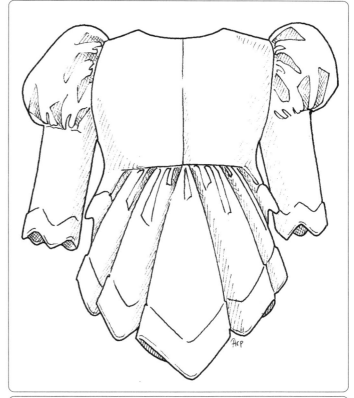

Supplies

Fabric Requirements:

Doll Sizes	17-1/2"	18-1/2"	19-1/2"	21-1/2"
Batiste	1/2 yd.	1/2 yd.	5/8 yd.	2/3 yd.

Notions: Lightweight sewing thread, one plastic snap, water-soluble stabilizer (WSS)

Pattern Pieces Required: Jacket Front, Jacket Back, Leg o' Mutton Sleeve

Templates Required: Jacket Front and Back Hem Templates (on pattern pieces), Sleeve Cuff Template

All seams 1/4" unless otherwise indicated. Stitch seam in place and overcast the seam allowances with a zigzag or serge, unless otherwise indicated.

A. Cutting

1. Cut the following pieces: four jacket fronts; two jacket backs, cut on the fold; two sleeves, cut on the fold.

2. Transfer pattern markings to fabric, using a washable pen or pencil.

3. Trace the jacket hem templates onto two jacket fronts (right and left), one jacket back, and two 2-1/4" x 6" strips of fabric for the sleeve cuffs **(fig. 1)**.

B. Jacket Front and Back

1. Run two rows of gathering stitches along the long slashed line of the back piece, 1/8" and 1/4" from the cut edge, refer to the pattern piece **(fig. 2)**.

Figure 1

Sleeve

Jacket front

Jacket back

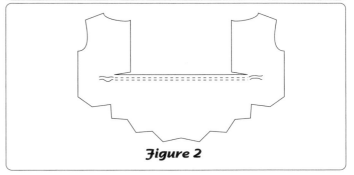

Figure 2

2. Sew the center back seam **(fig. 3)**.

3. Adjust the gathers to fit the slashed edge, pin in place and stitch **(fig. 4)**.

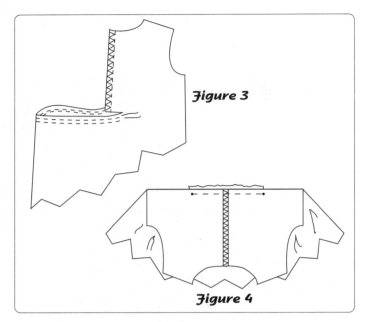

Figure 3

Figure 4

4. Sew the fronts and back together at the shoulders **(fig. 5)**.

5. Sew the center back seam of the remaining jacket back piece, do not gather the lower part of the jacket. Sew the remaining fronts to the back at the shoulders. These pieces will be used to make the Madeira appliqué facings **(refer to figs. 3 and 5)**.

6. Apply the jacket hem facings to the jacket pieces according to the instructions for Madeira appliqué collars found on page 291. Make the following change: The hem facing and the jacket will be sewn with right sides together and the facing will turn to the inside of the jacket. The facing may be hand-whipped or pinstitched by hand or machine. The front edges, front hems and neck facing will all be in one piece. The back hem will be a separate piece **(fig. 6)**.

C. Sleeves

1. Run two gathering rows, 1/8" and 1/4" from the edges, across the top of the sleeve and across the long slashed edge **(fig. 7)**.

2. Sew the outer cuff seam **(fig. 8)**.

3. Adjust the gathers to fit the slashed edge of the sleeve, pin in place and stitch **(fig. 9)**.

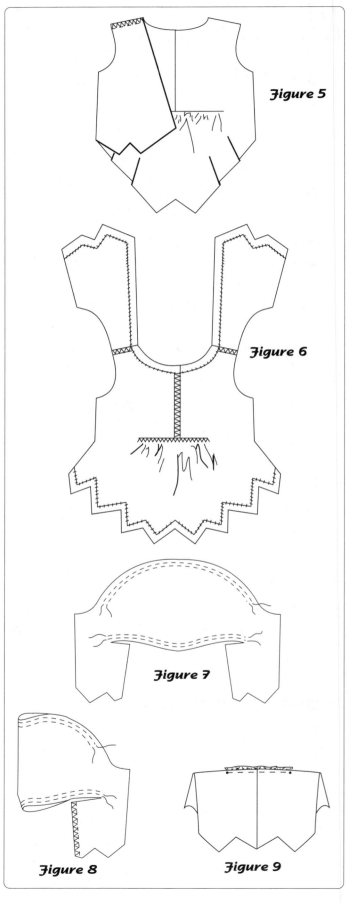

Figure 5

Figure 6

Figure 7

Figure 8

Figure 9

4. Following the Madeira appliqué hem instructions on page 292, apply the sleeve facings to the bottom edges of the sleeves. Make the following change: The hem facing and the sleeve will be sewn with right sides together and the facing will turn to the inside of the sleeve. The facing may be hand-whipped or pinstitched by hand or machine **(refer to fig. 6)**.

5. Pin the sleeves to the armholes, right sides together, and adjust the gathers to fit. Stitch the sleeve in place **(fig. 10)**.

6. Sew the sleeve/side seams. Try to match the facings at the sleeve and hem edges **(fig. 11)**.

7. Sew a plastic snap to the front edge of the jacket.

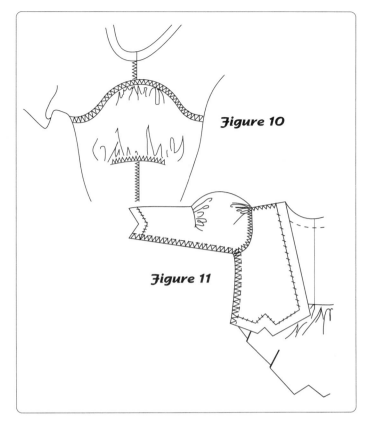

Figure 10

Figure 11

IV. The Jabot

Supplies

Lace Requirements: all sizes

Lace insertion, 1/2" wide: 1-1/4 yds.

Lace edging, 1" wide: 2-1/2 yds.

Notions: Lightweight sewing thread, one plastic snap, water-soluble stabilizer (WSS)

Pattern Pieces Required: Jabot

Seam allowances will be defined in the instructions.

1. Trace the jabot pattern onto a piece of WSS **(fig. 1)**.

2. Beginning at the bottom edge, place strips of lace insertion across the traced outline, right sides up and with the edges butted together. Let the cut ends extend 1/4" beyond the edges of the traced pattern. Sew the first two strips together using the method "lace to lace".

3. Add the third strip and sew it to the second strip, using the method "lace to lace" **(fig. 2)**. Repeat

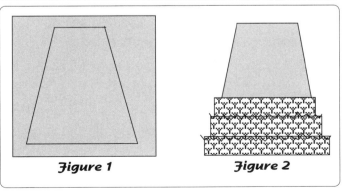

Figure 1   **Figure 2**

until the traced design is covered. Mark the center front at the top edge (**fig. 3**).

4. Pull the heading thread of the lace edging to gather the lace. Beginning at the bottom edge, place the heading of the lace over the bottom edge of the bottom insertion piece and zigzag the edging to the insertion. Cut the edging 1/4" wider than the pattern. Place the next piece of edging over the butted seam of the lace insertion and zigzag the edging over the seam. Continue up the rows until the piece is covered with ruffled edging (**fig. 4**).

5. Place a strip of insertion on each side of the jabot, along the side seam lines, with right sides together (**fig. 5**). Stitch the insertion over the edges of the edging, trim the seam and turn the insertion to the inside to form side hems. Hand-whip the insertion to the back side of the jabot (**fig. 6**).

6. Cut two strips of the insertion for the neck edge. Cut to the following measurement: 21-1/2" dolls to 8"; all others to 7". Mark the centers.

7. Place the strips with wrong side together, matching the pattern of the lace if possible. Slip the top edge of the jabot between the bottom edges of the two insertion pieces, matching the center marks (**fig. 7**).

8. Straight stitch the bottom edges of the insertions together. Trim any excess at the top of the jabot between the insertion pieces (**fig. 8**).

9. Straight stitch the top edges of the insertion pieces together.

10. Beginning at the right back neck edge, place the heading of the ruffled edging over the top edge of the insertion strip and zigzag the two together. Stitch across the top edge, curve around the left end of the neck piece and stitch along the bottom edge, catching the top edge of the jabot (**fig. 9**). Cut the lace when the right back edge is met.

11. Turn 1/4" to the wrong side at the right back neck edge, stitch in place (**fig. 10**).

12. Attach a plastic snap to the neck edges of the jabot. A doll-sized brooch may be pinned at the front of the neck.

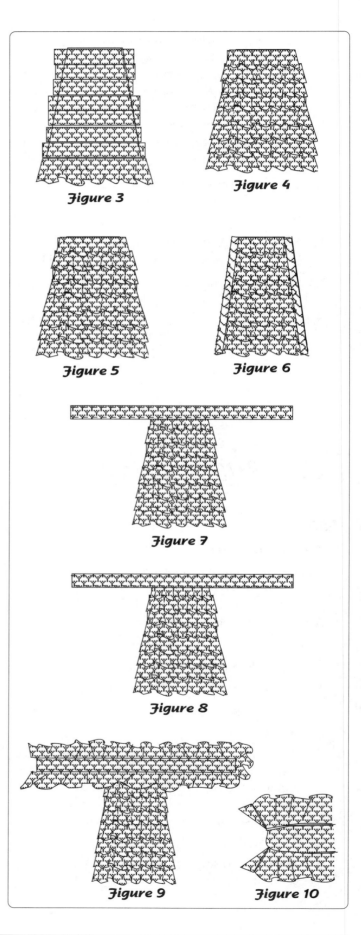

Figure 3

Figure 4

Figure 5

Figure 6

Figure 7

Figure 8

Figure 9

Figure 10

V. The Headband

Supplies

Fabric, all sizes: one strip 35" x 2-1/2", or scraps to be cut as directed in Step 1 below

Elastic, 1/4" wide, all sizes: 10-1/2"

1. Cut the following pieces:
   21" x 2-1/4" for the band,
   2-1/4" x 2-1/4" for the knot,
   10" x 2-1/2" for the bow.

2. Fold the bow piece so that the short ends are folded to the middle and overlapped by 1/4", with right sides together **(fig. 1)**. Pin the overlap.

3. Stitch along the two long sides, using a 1/4" seam. Trim the corners.

4. Turn the bow right side out and press. The opening may be slip-stitched or left as is, it will be hidden by the knot **(fig. 2)**.

5. Fold the band pieces in half with the long edges meeting, right sides together. Stitch the long seam and turn to the right side through one end. Press the band flat with the seam along one edge **(fig. 3)**.

5. Topstitch 1/4" from each long edge **(fig. 4)**.

6. Insert the elastic into the band and stitch the ends of the band together, through the elastic **(fig. 5)**.

7. Fold the knot square in half and stitch the long edges. Turn right side out and press with the seam along one edge **(fig. 6)**.

8. Place the bow over the band seam and tack in place.

9. Wrap the knot around the bow and band, hiding the band seam. Turn one edge under 1/4" and hand-stitch the edge at the back of the knot. Also tack the knot to the band at the back. **(fig. 7)**

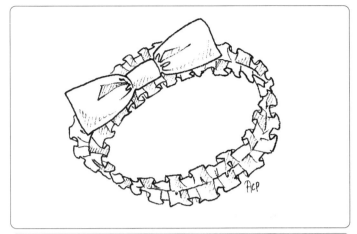

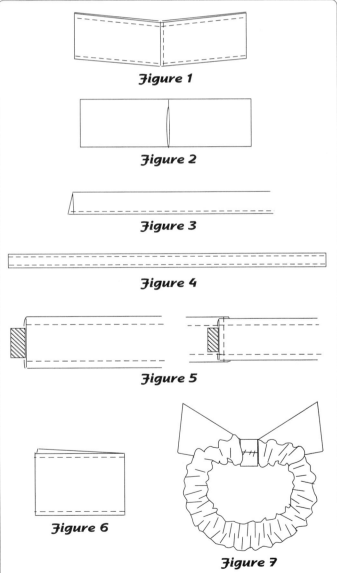

Figure 1

Figure 2

Figure 3

Figure 4

Figure 5

Figure 6

Figure 7

Lace and Pearls Fantasy

Frilly white lace edging, beading, blue ribbons and pearls make this a dress to tickle any doll's fancy! The base fabric of the dress is white Nelona Swiss batiste. Lace edging is used to create ruffles on the bodice, the sleeves and the skirt.

Blue ribbon covered by narrow lace insertion is mitered about halfway down the full, puffed sleeve. Narrow lace edging is gathered along this V and tiny white pearls are stitched down on top of it. The sleeves are finished with entredeux, beading and gathered lace edging.

The same insertion and blue satin ribbon treatment flanked by two rows of gathered lace narrow edging embellish the center front of this dress. Two more rows of ribbon/insertion/pearls enhance each side of the to-the-waist bodice, with wider lace edging gathered on the outside of these pieces. Tiny pearls are stitched down in the middle of the ribbon/insertion strips. The ribbon/insertion strips on the side go over the shoulder to the back waist. Gathered lace/entredeux finishes the neckline of this dress.

The skirt is trimmed with two rows of wide gathered lace edging. On the top row of this gathered lace edging is a row of beading with blue ribbon run through it. At the top of this row of beading is gathered lace edging.

- **All pattern pieces and templates found in pull-out section**
- **Color photograph on page 16**

Other Notions: Lightweight sewing thread; Velcro™, snaps or tiny buttons for back closure; small pearls (approximately 50)

Pattern Pieces Required: To-The-Waist Front Bodice, To-The-Waist Back Bodice, Elbow Length Sleeve

Template: Lace "V" template for the sleeves

All Seams 1/4" unless otherwise indicated. Stitch seam in place and overcast the seam allowances with a zigzag or serge.

Supplies

Fabric Requirements:

Fabric - Batiste	3/4 yd.
Lace Edging (2-1/4")	8 yds.
Lace Edging (3/4")	1-1/2 yds.
Lace Edging (1/2")	8-2/3 yds.
Lace Insertion (3/8")	1-3/4 yds.
Lace Beading	1-3/4 yds.
Ribbon (3/8")	1-3/4 yds.
Ribbon (to fit beading)	3 yds.
Ribbon (1")	1 yd.
Entredeux	1 yd.

A. Cutting

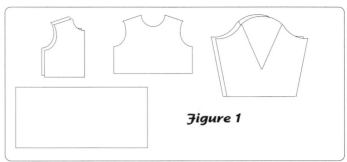

1. Cut one front bodice from the fold, two back bodices from the selvages, two sleeves, and one skirt piece 45" wide by the following length **(fig. 1)**:

Doll Sizes	17-1/2"	18-1/2"	19-1/2"	21-1/2"
Skirt	9-3/4"	11"	11-1/2"	12-1/2"

2. Transfer fold line markings from the back bodice pattern to the back bodice pieces.

3. Transfer the "V" lace shaping template onto each sleeve. Refer to figure 1.

B. Constructing Bodice

1. Place the front bodice to the back bodice, right sides together at the shoulders. Stitch in place using a 1/4" seam **(fig. 2)**.

2. Center a strip of 3/8" ribbon along the center front of the bodice **(fig. 3)**. Pin in place. Center a piece of 3/8" lace insertion on top of the ribbon. Stitch the lace in place with a zigzag or straight stitch **(fig. 4)**.

3. Cut two pieces of edging lace twice the length of the insertion. Gather each piece to fit each side of the lace. Butt the gathered lace to each side of the insertion and zigzag **(fig. 5)**.

4. Place ribbon along the sides of the bodice starting 1/2" from the neck edge at the shoulder seam and angling slightly to the waist of the front and back. Place a small fold in the ribbon at the shoulder seam, if needed. Pin the ribbon in place **(fig. 6)**.

5. Center a piece of 3/8" lace insertion on top of the ribbon. Pin. Stitch the lace/ribbon in place with a small, tight zigzag. Refer to figure 5.

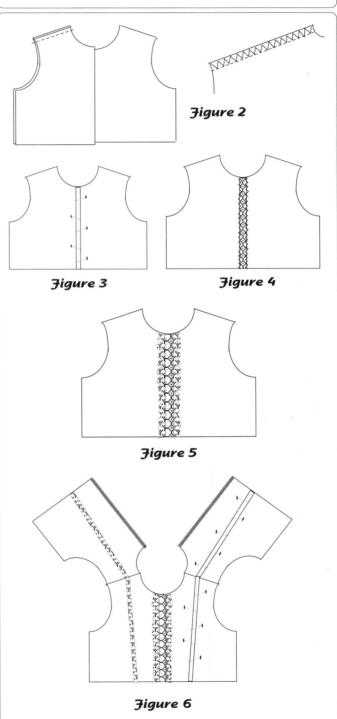

Figure 1

Figure 2

Figure 3

Figure 4

Figure 5

Figure 6

6. Cut two pieces of the 3/4" edging lace twice the length of the ribbon/lace insertion. Gather each lace piece to fit the outer edge of the ribbon/lace insertion. Zigzag the gathered edging in place **(fig. 7)**.

7. Finish the neck with entredeux and gathered 1/2" edging lace. Refer to "Neck Finishes - a. Entredeux to Gathered Lace" found on page 34 **(fig. 8)**.

8. Shape ribbon on each sleeve following the "V" template. Pin in place. Shape the lace insertion on top of each ribbon piece **(fig. 9)**. The mitering instructions for lace can be found on page 257. Ribbon is mitered in the same manner. Stitch the lace/ribbon in place with a small, tight zigzag.

9. Cut two pieces of 1/2" lace edging twice the measurement of the lace "V". Gather each edging piece to fit the outer and inner edge of the lace insertion. Butt the gathered edging to the insertion and zigzag. Repeat for the other sleeve **(fig. 10)**.

10. Finish the sleeves with entredeux, beading and gathered 1/2" edging lace. Refer to "Sleeve Bands and Ruffles - c. Entredeux, Beading and Gathered Edging Lace" found on page 39. Refer to figure 10.

11. Gather the top of the sleeves to fit the arm opening of the bodice, matching the center of the sleeve with the shoulder seam of the bodice. Adjust the gathers in the top of the sleeve to fall 1-1/4" to 1-1/2" on either side of the shoulder seam **(fig. 11)**.

12. Stitch the sleeve to the bodice, right sides together, using a 1/4" seam.

13. Place the sides/sleeves of the bodice right sides together. Stitch together using a 1/4" seam **(fig. 12)**.

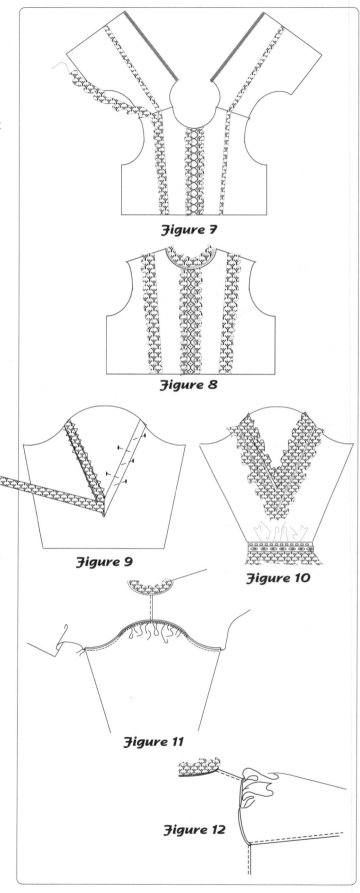

Figure 7

Figure 8

Figure 9

Figure 10

Figure 11

Figure 12

C. Skirt

1. Place the back edges of the skirt together and stitch from the bottom, stopping 3-1/2" from top of the skirt. Backstitch **(fig. 13)**.

2. Place a placket in the seam opening. Refer to "Placket - c. Continuous Placket or d. Easy Placket" found on page 43 **(fig. 14)**.

3. To hem the skirt, turn the bottom edge of the skirt to the inside 1/4" and again 2". Press in place. Stitch along the top edge of the 1/4" fold. This stitching line will be hidden by the lace **(fig. 15)**.

4. Draw a line with a fabric marker 1" above the stitching line of the hem **(fig. 16)**.

5. Gather 4 yards of 2-1/4" edging to 45". Stitch the short ends of the lace right sides together to form a circle **(fig. 17)**. Place the gathered edging on the skirt with the top edge of the lace on the stitching line of the hem. Zigzag the top edge of the lace in place **(fig. 18)**.

6. Gather the remaining 4 yard piece of 2-1/4" edging to 45". Stitch the short ends of the lace right sides together to form a circle. Refer to figure 17. Place the gathered edging on the skirt with the top edge of the lace on the drawn line. Zigzag the top edge of the lace in place **(fig. 19)**.

7. Place beading just above the top piece of edging. Butt the beading to the edging. Pin. Zigzag along both edges of the beading. Refer to figure 19.

8. Cut a 4 yard piece of 1/2" edging lace. Gather to 45". Stitch the short ends of the lace right sides together to form a circle. Refer to figure 17. Butt the gathered lace to the top edge of the beading and stitch in place with a zigzag. Refer to figure 19.

9. Weave 1-3/4 yds. of ribbon through the beading, starting and stopping about 5" from the center front on the left side of the skirt. Tie the excess ribbon in a bow. Trim the tails of the ribbon if necessary **(fig. 20)**.

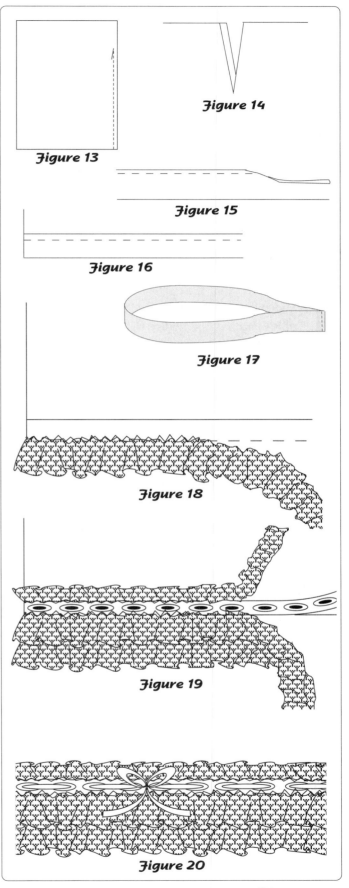

Figure 13

Figure 14

Figure 15

Figure 16

Figure 17

Figure 18

Figure 19

Figure 20

D. Finishing the Dress

1. Stitch two gathering rows in the top edge of the skirt. Remember that one side of the placket is folded to the inside of the skirt and the other side is left extended **(fig. 21)**.

2. Place the right side of the bodice to the right side of the skirt, matching the center of the bodice with the center of the skirt. Pin in place. Gather the skirt to fit the bodice. Distrubute the gathers evenly **(fig. 22)**.

3. At the back edges of the skirt opening, wrap the back facings of the bodice over the placket opening of the skirt. Pin in place **(fig. 23)**.

4. Stitch the skirt to the bodice using a 1/4" seam. Overcast the seam allowance.

5. Attach Velcro™, buttons and buttonholes or snaps to the back of the bodice to close the dress.

6. Stitch pearls, 3/8" apart, in the center of the three lace/ribbon strips on the front bodice **(fig. 24)**.

7. Stitch a three-pearl cluster at the lace/ribbon point of each sleeve. Stitch two pearls on each side of the cluster in the center of the lace ribbon strip **(fig. 25)**.

8. Cut the remaining ribbon in half and weave through the beading of the sleeves. Tie the excess ribbon in bows.

9. Place the wide ribbon around the waist of the dress and tie in a bow at the center back.

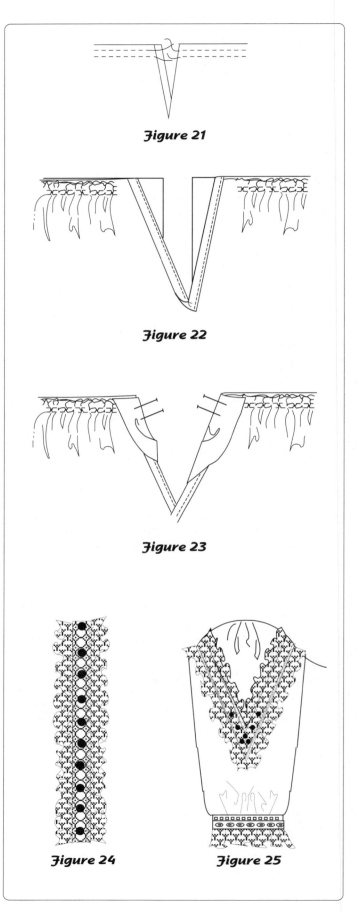

Figure 21

Figure 22

Figure 23

Figure 24   **Figure 25**

Lavender Leg o' Mutton Dress

White Victorian embroideries and batiste are dyed lavender to give this old-fashioned dress a look of its own. Note: For best results, restrict dyes to all natural fibers. Embroidered fabric is used for the high yokes on this particular style. Three tucks trim the collar, which is also finished with entredeux/flat embroidered trim mitered at the corners. This same trim combination completes the neckline. The sleeve and extended cuff of the leg o' mutton sleeve are cut from a wide eyelet embroidered trim. The full skirt features three folded tucks on the bottom of the skirt and the ruffle is wide eyelet edging, which is gathered to the skirt with entredeux.

A colored ribbon in shades ranging from white to dark rose is tied in a pretty bow on the front of the dress. This ribbon has wiring which facilitates shaping. The dress closes with a placket and snaps in the center back of the dress.

- **All pattern pieces and templates found in pull-out section**
- **Color photograph on page 17**

Supplies

Fabric - Broadcloth	2/3 yd.
Entredeux	1-1/2 yds.
Eyelet Edging with Entredeux (5/8")	1 yd.
Eyelet Edging (6")	4 yds.
Wired Ribbon (1")	1 yd.

Notions: Lightweight sewing thread, Velcro™, snaps or tiny buttons for closure

Pattern Pieces Required: Mid-Yoke Front, Mid-Yoke Back, 3/4-Length Sleeve, Barrel Cuff, Straight Collar

All seams 1/4" unless otherwise indicated. Stitch seam in place and overcast the seam allowances with a zigzag or serge, unless otherwise indicated.

A. Cutting

1. From the 6" wide eyelet, cut one front yoke on the fold, two back yokes, and two sleeves on the fold. Cut two single-layer barrel cuffs with the fold line along the decorative edge of the eyelet **(fig. 1)**.

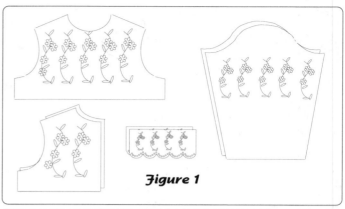

Figure 1

2. From the broadcloth, cut two collars, and cut two skirt pieces, 22" wide by the following length:

Doll Sizes	17-1/2"	18-1/2"	19-1/2"	21-1/2"
Skirt Length	8"	8-1/2"	9-1/2"	10-3/4"

3. Transfer pattern markings to the fabric. Also mark the centers of the skirt pieces at the top and bottom edges, and mark the center front of the yoke at the waistline edge.

B. Constructing the Yokes and Collars

1. With right sides together, sew the front yoke to the back yokes at the shoulder seams **(fig. 2)**.

2. Finish the neck edge, referring to "Neck finishes - b. Entredeux and Flat Swiss Edging" found on page 34, and using 5/8" lace edging **(fig. 3)**. The entredeux and Swiss edging are already attached, so omit Steps 2 and 3.

3. Fold the collar pieces along the tuck lines, with wrong sides together, and press a crease along each line **(fig. 4)**.

4. Stitch the tucks 1/8" from the folded edge. Press the tucks toward the fold line of the collar. (See figure 4).

5. Fold the collar along the fold line, with right sides together. Stitch across the short ends, trim and clip the corners **(fig. 5)**. Turn right side out and press.

6. Using the Swiss edging with entredeux, trim the seam allowance away from the entredeux edge. Attach the edging to the short ends and long outer edge of the collar, butting the edges together and mitering around the corners **(fig. 6)**.

7. Finish the raw edges with a zigzag or serge. The collar will be attached later.

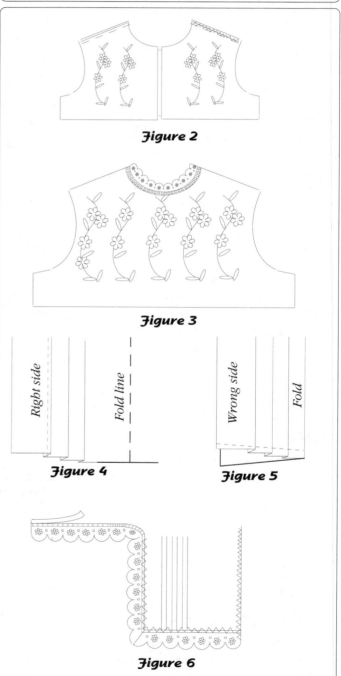

Figure 2

Figure 3

Right side   Fold line

Wrong side   Fold

Figure 4   **Figure 5**

Figure 6

C. Sleeves and Collars

1. Run two rows of gathering threads across the top and bottom edges of the sleeves, 1/8" and 1/4" from the edges **(fig. 7)**.

2. Gather the sleeve bottom edge to fit the top edge of the barrel cuff. Stitch the cuff to the sleeve right sides together. **(fig. 8)**.

3. Pin the sleeve to the bodice, right sides together, matching the center top of the sleeve to the shoulder seam **(fig. 9)**. Adjust the gathers to fit, letting the gathers fall 1-1/2" on each side of the shoulder seam. Stitch the seam.

D. Skirt

1. Choose one skirt piece to be the skirt back. Cut a 4-1/2" slit at the center on the top edge of the piece and apply a placket **(fig. 10)**. Refer to "Plackets - a. Continuous Lap Placket" found on page 42.

2. Run two rows of gathering threads across the top of each skirt piece, 1/8" and 1/4" from the edge. Stop the stitching at the placket seam line on the back pieces.

3. Pin the front skirt piece to the yoke, right sides together. Adjust the gathers in the skirt top to fit the bottom edge of the yoke and stitch in place **(fig. 11)**.

4. Place the back skirts to the back yokes, right sides together. The placket edges should meet the back fold line of the yoke. Wrap the back facings to the outside along the fold line, sandwiching the skirt between the yoke and the facing. Stitch in place and press the yokes up, flipping the facings to the inside **(fig. 12)**.

D. Attaching the Collars

1. Use a wash-out pencil to make a mark on the shoulder seam, 3/8" away from the neck edge for 17-1/2 and 19-1/2 dolls and 1/2" away for 21-1/2 and 18-1/2 dolls. Make a mark at the center front waistline edge. Also make marks at the back waistline, on the folded edge of the right yoke, and 3/4" away from the edge of the back yoke **(fig. 13)**.

2. Draw lines to connect the shoulder marks to the waistline marks (refer to figure 13).

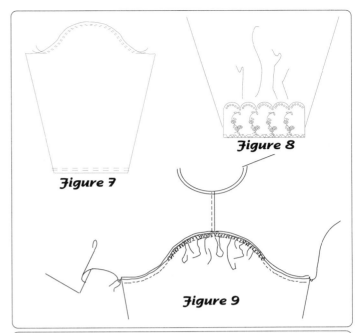

Figure 7

Figure 8

Figure 9

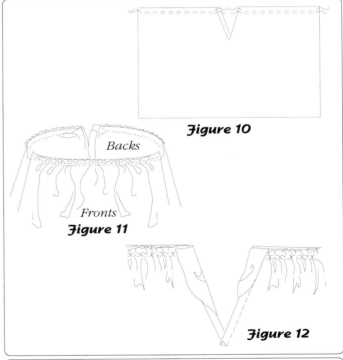

Figure 10

Backs

Fronts
Figure 11

Figure 12

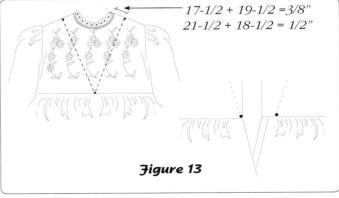

17-1/2 + 19-1/2 =3/8"
21-1/2 + 18-1/2 = 1/2"

Figure 13

3. Place the collar pieces to the bodice, right sides together, with the zigzagged edge along the line. The collar will extend over the neck edge during attachment **(fig. 14)**.

4. Sew the collar to the bodice with a 1/4" seam. Press the collar pieces toward the shoulder seams. The collar pieces will meet at the center front and back to form a point.

E. Finishing the Dress

1. Place only one of the sleeve/side seams with right sides together. Match the sleeve edges and the bottom edges and stitch **(fig. 15)**.

2. Press three creases around the bottom of the skirt, 1/2" apart, with the first crease 1" above the bottom edge. Stitch tucks by topstitching 1/8" from each crease. Press the creases toward the bottom of the skirt **(fig. 16)**.

3. Attach a piece of entredeux to the bottom edge of the skirt, using the technique "entredeux to fabric" **(fig. 17)**.

4. Cut a ruffle strip 3-1/2" wide by 45" long, along the decorative edge of the eyelet. Mark the center of the ruffle. Run two rows of gathering threads along the long raw edge **(fig. 18)**.

5. Pin the ruffle to the entredeux at the bottom skirt edge, matching centers. Adjust the gathers to fit and stitch the ruffle to the skirt.

6. Stitch the second side seam as described in step 1 above.

7. Apply Velcro™, snaps or tiny buttons and button holes to the back opening, with the right side lapping over the left side.

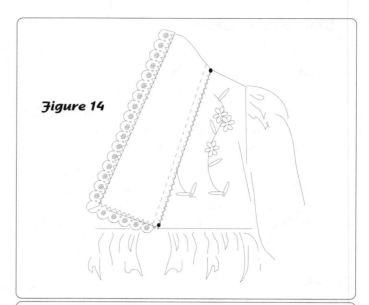

Figure 14

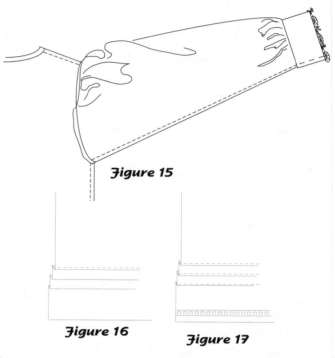

Figure 15

Figure 16

Figure 17

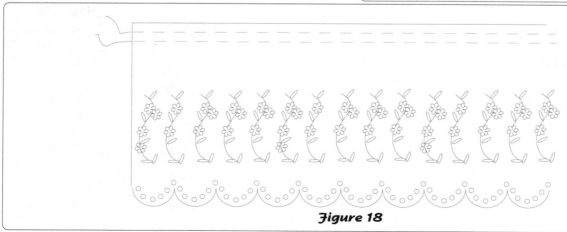

Figure 18

Linen Dress With Swiss Trims

This dress is the ideal Christmas or Valentine's day dress, if for no other reason, the color scheme! The white linen dress fabric is the perfect showcase for the lady bug Swiss trim. Or, create your own designs using the embroidery capabilities on your sewing machine. The dress bodice is simply decorated with four red buttons down the center of two sets of four double needle pintucks. The neckline is finished with a bias binding and the back is closed with buttons and buttonholes. The full, puffed sleeves are gathered at the bottom with a narrow Swiss trim and a 1-1/4 inch wide, gathered Swiss edging. The skirt fullness is 42 inches. The skirt makes use of the pintuck treatment applied to the bodice, sporting three rows, then a row of 3/8 inch wide Swiss entredeux-like trim, a 1-1/4 inch wide strip of Swiss handloom with lady bugs, a row of 3/8 inch wide Swiss entredeux-like trim, and a 2 inch wide piece of Swiss handloom stitched flat for the bottom. A 1 inch wide satin ribbon is tied at the waist for the sash.

Supplies

Fabric - Batiste	3/4 yd.
Swiss Edging (2-1/4")	2 yds.
Embroidered Insertion (1-3/4")	1-1/4 yds.
Swiss Insertion (1/4")	3 yds.
Ribbon (1") All Sizes	1 yd.

- **All pattern pieces and templates found in pull-out section**
- **Color photograph on page 24**

Notions: Two spools of lightweight sewing thread; Velcro™, snaps or tiny buttons for back closure; three 1/4" shank buttons; double needle (2.0/80)

Pattern Pieces Required: To-the-Waist Front Bodice, To-the-Waist Back Bodice and Elbow Length Puffed Sleeve

All seams 1/4" unless otherwise indicated. Stitch seam in place and overcast the seam allowances with a zigzag or serge.

A. Cutting

1. Cut two back bodices from the selvages, two sleeves, and one skirt piece 45" wide by the following length:

Doll Sizes	17-1/2"	18-1/2"	19-1/2"	21-1/2"
Upper Skirt	4-1/4"	5"	5-1/2"	6-1/2"

2. Transfer fold line markings from the back bodice pattern to the back bodice pieces.

3. Cut one fabric rectangle for the bodice front. For 17-1/2" and 18-1/2" dolls, cut the rectangle to 6" long by 8" wide; for 19-1/2" and 21-1/2" dolls, cut rectangle to 7" long by 9" wide.

B. Constructing Bodice

1. Find the center of the fabric rectangle for the bodice front. Starting 1/8" from each side of center, stitch five double needle pintucks about 1/16" apart **(fig. 1)**. The pintucks should run parallel to the 6" or 7" side of the rectangle. This spacing will leave a 1/4" space in the center of the rectangle.

2. Fold the rectangle in the center and cut the bodice front **(fig. 2)**.

3. Place the front bodice to the back bodice right sides together at the shoulders **(fig. 3)**. Stitch in place using a 1/4" seam.

4. Finish the neck with a bias binding **(fig. 4)**. Refer to "Neck Finishes - e. Bias Neck Binding" found on page 36.

5. Finish the sleeves with 1/4" Swiss insertion and Swiss edging lace **(fig. 5)**. Cut the width of the Swiss edging to 1-3/4". Refer to "Sleeve Band and Ruffles - e. Swiss Beading or Insertion and Gathered Swiss Edging" found on page 40.

6. Gather the top of the sleeves to fit the arm opening of the bodice, matching the center of the sleeve with the shoulder seam of the bodice. Adjust the gathers in the top of the sleeve to fall 1-1/4" to 1-1/2" on either side of the shoulder seam **(fig. 6)**.

7. Stitch the sleeve to the bodice, right sides together, using a 1/4" seam.

8. Place the sides/sleeves of the bodice right sides together. Stitch together using a 1/4" seam **(fig. 7)**.

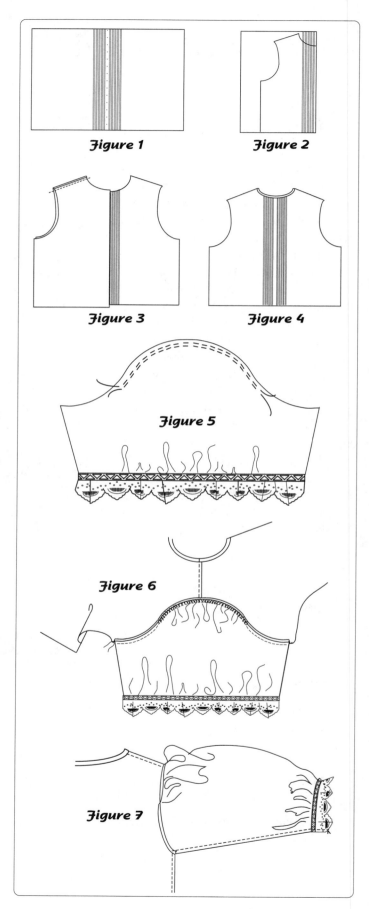

Figure 1

Figure 2

Figure 3

Figure 4

Figure 5

Figure 6

Figure 7

C. Skirt

1. Cut two strips of 1/4" Swiss insertion, one piece of embroidered insertion and one piece of Swiss edging each 45" long.

2. Attach the Swiss insertion to each side of the embroidered insertion using the technique "entredeux to fabric." Attach Swiss edging to one side of the Swiss insertion. This creates a fancy band of Swiss insertion, embroidered insertion, Swiss insertion and Swiss edging **(fig. 8)**.

3. Attach the fancy band to the skirt piece using the technique "entredeux to fabric."

4. Starting 1/4" above the fancy band, stitch three double needle pintucks 1/8" apart **(fig. 9)**.

5. Place the back edges of the skirt together and stitch from the bottom, stopping 1/8" above the top pintuck **(fig. 10)**. Backstitch.

6. Place a placket in the seam opening. Refer to "Plackets - c. Continuous Placket or d. Easy Placket" found on page 43.

D. Finishing the Dress

1. Stitch two gathering rows in the top edge of the skirt. Remember that one side of the placket is folded to the inside of the skirt and the other side is left extended **(fig. 11)**.

2. Place the right side of the bodice to the right side of the skirt, matching the center of the bodice with the center of the skirt. Pin in place. Gather the skirt to fit the bodice. Distribute the gathers evenly.

3. At the back edges of the skirt opening, wrap the back facings of the bodice over the open edges of the skirt. Pin in place **(fig. 12)**.

4. Stitch the skirt to the bodice using a 1/4" seam. Overcast the seam allowance.

5. Attach Velcro™, buttons and buttonholes or snaps to the back of the bodice to close the dress.

6. Add three buttons to the center front of the bodice for embellishment **(fig. 13)**.

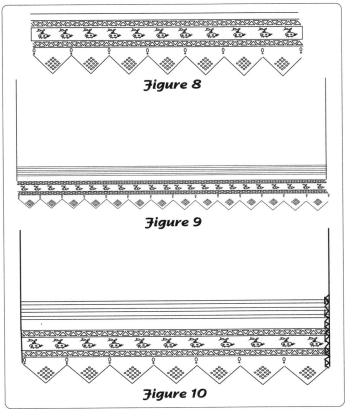

Figure 8

Figure 9

Figure 10

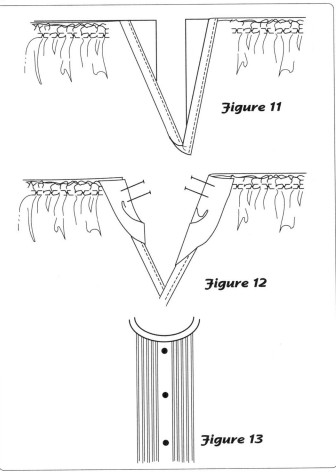

Figure 11

Figure 12

Figure 13

Masterpiece Ecru Edwardian Dress

Fit for a doll in the Victoria and Albert Museum, this dress with its Edwardian type collar offers magnificent styling. The underdress or lining is just as elaborate as the outerdress, which is made of ecru cotton netting. Using English laces and antique styling, the design could have appeared in the 1905 Butterick pattern book for doll dresses. The antique shaped collar is lined with ecru Swiss batiste with an ecru netting overlay. The overlay has English cotton edging in ecru mitered at the corners of the collar. Gathered English ecru edging finishes this lined collar. Ecru entredeux with narrow English edging gathered to entredeux finish the neckline; a pretty silk ribbon rose in pale yellow and pale green is stitched at the center front. Two silk ribbon ecru rosettes are stitched at both sides of the front of the collar. Snaps close the back of the dress.

The long sleeves are batiste with ecru netting on top. The center of the netting portion of the sleeves has been slit and finished with flat ecru narrow edging down both sides. Batiste pintucked fabric is found in-between this butterfly sleeve effect. Entredeux, beading and wide ecru edging finish the bottom of the sleeve. This sleeve is designed for ribbon to pull in the fullness, a typical treatment for a French sewn dress. The top portion of the skirt of the dress is English netting with a wide fancy band of English laces at the bottom. The fancy band consists of edging, beading, insertion, wider insertion, insertion, beading and wide edging. Ribbons are run through the beading. The Swiss batiste underskirt is made elaborate with a section of seven pintucks, entredeux, insertion, entredeux, seven more pintucks, entredeux, wider insertion, narrow insertion, and French wide edging for the bottom. This elaborate underskirt peeks through the ecru netting for a beautiful effect.

- **All pattern pieces and templates found in pull-out section**
- **Color photograph on page 22**

Supplies

Fabric Requirements: All Sizes

Fabric - Batiste	3/4 yd.
Cotton Netting	5/8 yd.
Entredeux	4 yds.
Lace Beading (3/8")	3-1/2 yds.
Lace Insertion (5/8")	4 yds.
Lace Edging (1-1/4")	4-1/2 yds.
Lace Edging (3/8")	3 yds.
Lace Insertion (1-1/2")	1-1/8 yds.
Lace Insertion (7/8")	1-1/8 yds.
Silk Ribbon (4mm)	5 yds.

Notions: Lightweight sewing thread; Velcro™, snaps or tiny buttons for closure; one small ribbon rose; 1.6/70 or 2.0/80 double needle; (optional: 7-groove pintuck foot)

Pattern Pieces Required: High Yoke Front, High Yoke Back, 3/4-Length Sleeve, Six-Point Collar

Templates Required: Armhole Guide

All seams 1/4" unless otherwise indicated. Stitch seam in place and overcast the seam allowances with a zigzag or serge, unless otherwise indicated.

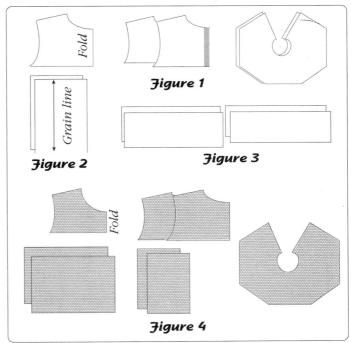

Figure 1

Figure 2

Figure 3

Figure 4

A. Cutting

1. From the batiste, cut one front yoke on the fold, two back yokes on the selvage and two collars **(fig. 1)**. Transfer pattern markings to the fabric.

2. Cut two 9" x 12" rectangles for the sleeves, with the 12" sides on the lengthwise grain of the fabric. Do not cut out the sleeves **(fig. 2)**.

3. Cut two rectangles of batiste for the lower skirt pieces, each 20" wide by 5" long. Also cut two rectangles for the upper skirt pieces, each 20" wide by the following length **(fig. 3)**:

Doll Sizes	17-1/2"	18-1/2"	19-1/2"	21-1/2"
Upper Skirt	4-3/4"	5-1/4"	6-1/4"	7-1/2"

4. From the cotton netting, cut one front yoke on the fold, two yoke backs, one collar and two 9" x 12" rectangles for the sleeves **(fig. 4)**. Also cut two rectangles for the skirt, each 20" wide by the following length:

Doll Sizes	17-1/2"	18-1/2"	19-1/2"	21-1/2"
Skirt Length	7-1/2"	8"	9"	10-1/4"

B. Yokes and Collar

1. Place the netting yoke pieces over the batiste yoke pieces and baste the two layers together along all edges **(fig. 5)**.

2. Place the front yoke to the back yokes at the shoulder seams, right sides together, and stitch **(fig. 6)**.

3. Place 5/8" lace insertion around the netting collar with the edge of the lace 1/2" from the edge. Miter the corners and stitch the lace along both edges **(fig. 7)**.

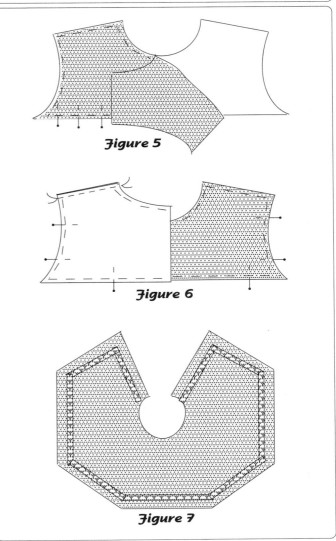

Figure 5

Figure 6

Figure 7

4. Place the netting collar over one of the batiste collars, with the wrong side of the netting collar to the right side of the batiste. Baste the layers together around the edges **(fig. 8)**.

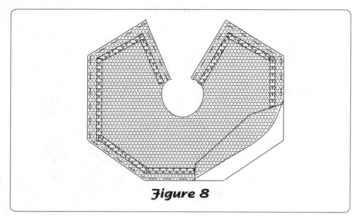

Figure 8

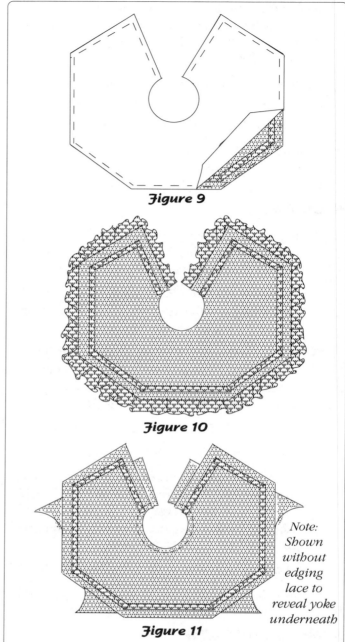

Figure 9

Figure 10

Figure 11

Note: Shown without edging lace to reveal yoke underneath

5. Place the remaining batiste collar over the netting/batiste collar, right sides together, and stitch through all layers, leaving the neck edge open **(fig. 9)**.

6. Trim the seam and turn the collar right side out. Press the seamed edge.

7. Cut a 36" piece of the 1-1/4" lace edging. Pull the heading thread to gather the edging.

8. Place the edging around the outer edge of the collar and up the back edges, with the heading just under the edge. Adjust the gathers to fit, leaving 1/2" extended at the neck edges. Whip the lace to the collar by hand or butt the edges and zigzag **(fig. 10)**.

9. Place the collar to the yoke neck edge, with the wrong side of the collar to the right side of the yoke. Let the edges of the lace meet the back fold lines. Baste through all layers **(fig. 11)**.

10. Finish the neck edge according to the directions for "Neck Finishes - a. Entredeux and Gathered Edging" found on page 34.

C. Sleeves

1. Fold the 9" x 12" batiste rectangles in half along the length, so that the folded pieces measure 4-1/2" x 12". Mark the fold with a washable pencil or pen.

2. Use the double needle and pintuck foot (optional) to make seven pintucks in the batiste, making the center pintuck first, along the marked fold line **(fig. 12)**. The tucks should be 1/8" to 1/4" apart. Refer to "Pintucks" on page 276. Press all of the tucks in one direction.

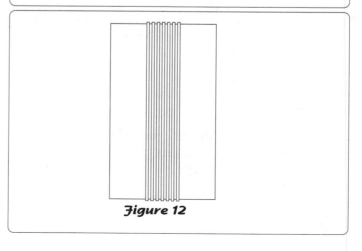

Figure 12

3. Fold the netting rectangles in half like the batiste rectangles, then cut in half along the fold to create 4-1/2" x 12" pieces **(fig. 13)**.

4. Along one 12" side of each netting piece, attach a strip of 3/8" edging lace, letting the lace heading overlap the edge of the netting by 1/4". Zigzag the lace in place along the heading, then trim away the excess netting behind the lace **(fig. 14)**.

5. Place the netting pieces over the tucked batiste pieces, letting the lace edge lie on top of the last two tucks on each side. The three center tucks will show.

6. Baste the netting to the batiste on all sides **(fig. 15)** and trace the sleeve pattern onto each batiste/netting rectangle. Baste along the traced lines and cut out the sleeves **(fig. 16)**.

7. Finish the bottom edge of each sleeve, referring to "Sleeve Bands and Ruffles - c. Entredeux, Beading and Gathered Edging Lace" found on page 39. Use 3/8" beading and 1-1/4" edging **(fig. 17)**.

8. Run two gathering rows across the top of the sleeve, 1/8" and 1/4" from the edge.

C. Underskirt

1. Working with the fabric rectangles for the skirts, draw a line 1-1/4" from one long edge of each piece.

2. Using the double needle and pintuck foot (optional), make seven pintucks on each piece, with the first tuck on the drawn line. The other tucks will all go on the same side, leaving the 1-14" edge un-tucked. In other words, the tucks will not be centered as they were on the sleeves. The tucks should be 1/8" to 1/4" apart **(fig. 18)**. Refer to "Pintucks" on page 276.

3. The 5" wide pieces will be the lower skirts. Attach a strip of entredeux to the 1-1/4" un-tucked edge of the lower skirts, using the technique "entredeux to fabric".

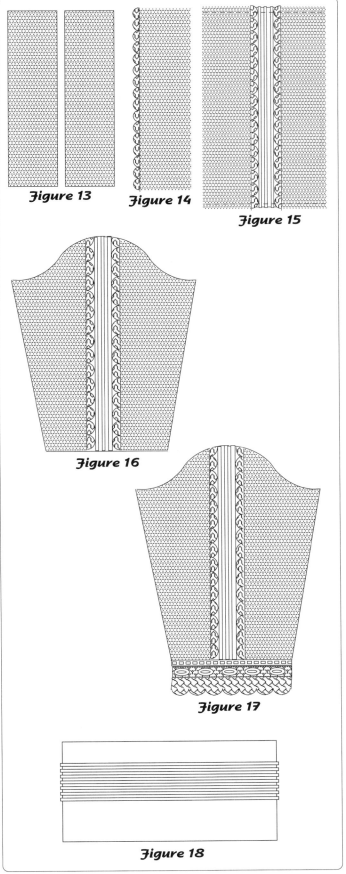

Figure 13   *Figure 14*

Figure 15

Figure 16

Figure 17

Figure 18

4. Trim the remaining edge of the entredeux and attach a strip of 5/8" insertion to the entredeux, using the technique "entredeux to lace" **(fig. 19)**.

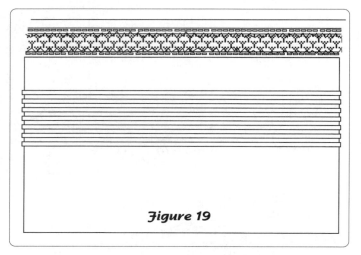

Figure 19

5. Attach another strip of entredeux to the free edge of the insertion, using the technique "entredeux to lace".

6. Attach the remaining strips of tucked fabric (the upper skirts) to the entredeux strips, stitching along the 1/14" un-tucked edge. Press all of the tucks toward the bottom **(fig. 20)**.

7. At the bottom edge of the skirts, attach entredeux, using the technique "entredeux to fabric".

8. Cut two 20" pieces of the following laces and sew them together in the order given, using the technique "lace to lace": 7/8" lace insertion, 5/8" lace insertion, 1-1/4" lace edging **(fig. 21)**.

9. Attach the flat edge of the lace strips to the entredeux at the bottom of the skirts, using the technique "entredeux to lace". See fig. 21.

10. Trace the armholes onto the top edges of the skirt pieces, but do not cut out **(fig. 22)**.

D. Netting Overskirt

1. Cut two 20" pieces of the following laces: 1-1/2" insertion, 1-1/4" edging; cut four 20" strips of 3/8" beading. Separate the laces into two piles, each having one 20" strip of 1-1/2" insertion and 1-1/4" edging, and two strips of 3/8" beading.

2. Make two lace bands, attaching laces together in the following order, using the technique "lace to lace": 3/8" beading, 1-1/2" insertion, 3/8" beading, 1-1/4" edging **(fig. 23)**.

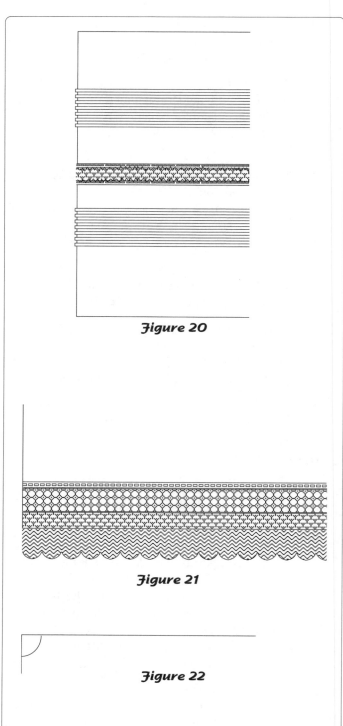

Figure 20

Figure 21

Figure 22

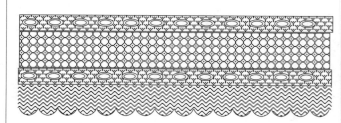

Figure 23

3. Place the top beading strip of one lace band over the 20" edge of one netting rectangle, letting the heading of the lace overlap the netting by 1/4". Straight stitch the lace in place **(fig. 24)**.

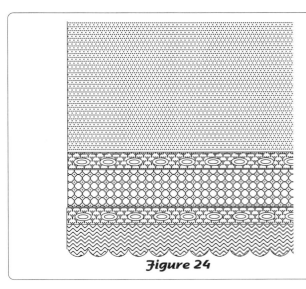

Figure 24

Figure 25

4. Butt a 20" strip of 3/8" edging to the top edge of the beading, on top of the netting. Use a tiny zigzag to attach the edging to the beading and the netting. Trim away any excess netting from behind the lace band. Repeat Steps 3 and 4 for the remaining lace and netting **(fig. 25)**.

5. Place one netting piece over each underskirt piece, with the lace edges even at the bottom **(fig. 26)**. The top edges will probably not be even. Trim the top edges so that the skirt pieces will be the following length:

Doll Sizes	17-1/2"	18-1/2"	19-1/2"	21-1/2"
Skirt Length	10-1/2"	11"	12"	13-1/4"

If the fabric/netting pieces are shorter than this length, trim both pieces to the same size.

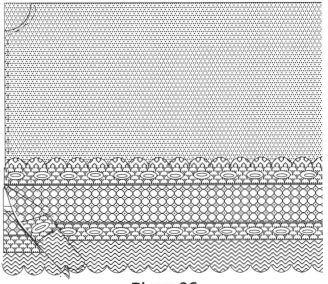

Figure 26

6. Cut out the armholes and baste the edges together at the armholes and down the side seams. Refer to figure 26.

7. Choose one skirt piece to be the back and apply a placket, referring to "Plackets - a. Continuous Lap Placket" found on page 42. Cut the back slit 4-1/2" long. The skirt will lap right over left **(fig. 27)**.

8. Baste the fabric/netting together with two rows of gathering stitches across the top edge, 1/8" and 1/4" from the edges. Stop the stitching at the armholes and the placket edges. Refer to figure 27.

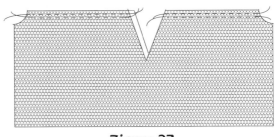

Figure 27

9. Pin the front skirt piece to the yoke, right sides together. Adjust the gathers in the skirt top to fit the bottom edge of the yoke and stitch in place **(fig. 28)**.

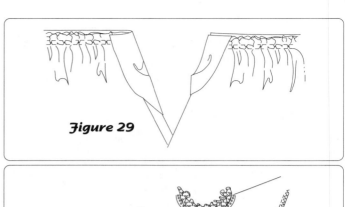

Figure 29

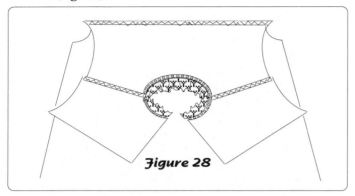

Figure 28

10. Place the back skirt to the back yokes, right sides together. The placket edges should meet the back fold line of the yokes. Wrap the back facings to the outside along the fold line, sandwiching the skirt between the yoke and the facing. Stitch in place and press the yokes up, flipping the facings to the inside **(fig. 29)**.

E. Finishing the Dress

1. Pin the sleeves to the armholes and adjust the gathers to fit, stopping the gathers at the yoke seam lines. Stitch the sleeves in place **(fig. 30)**.

2. Place the sleeve/side seams with right sides together. Match the sleeve edges and the bottom edges and stitch **(fig. 31)**.

3. Apply Velcro™, snaps or tiny buttons and buttonholes to the back opening, with the right side lapping over the left side.

4. Cut two 18" pieces of the 4mm silk ribbon and thread one piece through the beading, starting below the center tuck of each sleeve. Tie the ribbon into a bow and trim the streamers.

5. Cut two 36" pieces of the 4mm silk ribbon and make two ribbon rosettes, referring to **(fig. 32)**. Leave long streamers and tack one rosette to each of the two front collar points **(fig. 33)**.

6. Cut the remaining 4mm silk ribbon in half and thread one piece through each of the beading strips in the skirt fancy band. Begin and end the ribbons so that the bows will be somewhere on the front of the skirt.

7. Tack the small ribbon rose at the center front neck edge, just below the entredeux.

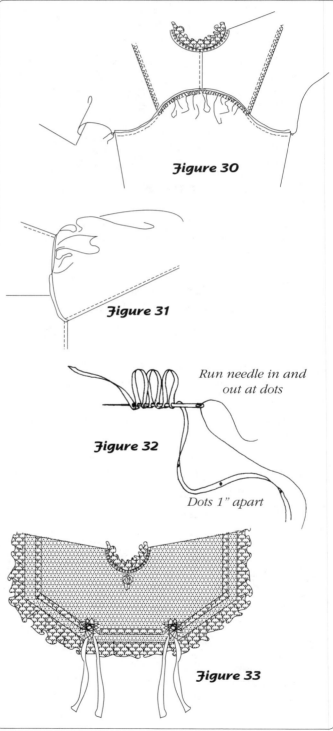

Figure 30

Figure 31

Run needle in and out at dots

Figure 32

Dots 1" apart

Figure 33

Monet's Garden Of Flowers Dress

It is hard to find a place to begin when describing this unusual dress. What a masterpiece of machine embroidery on the front scalloped organdy panel. The flower stems and leaves are embroidered in three shades of green; the flowers are white, peach, medium blue, pale blue, lavender, yellow and dusty rose. Two double needle pintucked bows hold the bouquets of flowers on the bottom of the skirt. This organdy panel features scalloped laces from the neckline to the bottom of the skirt; narrow white French insertion forms the scallop. The basic lavender, Swiss batiste, Nelona dress is a to-the-waist style. A white organdy sash is tied at the waist and is joined at the side of the French insertion treatment. Scallops follow all the way around the rest of the skirt; gathered French edging finishes the bottom of the scallops. The full, puffed sleeves are finished at the bottom with entredeux and gathered lace edging. The same treatment of entredeux/gathered lace edging is on the neckline. The dress closes in the back with three buttonholes and tiny buttons.

- **All pattern pieces and templates found in pull-out section**
- **Color photograph on page 18**

Supplies

Fabric	
Batiste	3/4 yd.
Organdy	1/3 yd.
Entredeux	2/3 yd.
Insertion Lace (3/8")	3 yds.
Edging Lace (1/2")	2 yds.
Edging Lace (1-1/4")	3 yds.

Notions: Lightweight sewing thread, Velcro™, snaps or tiny buttons for back closure and several colors of silk ribbon, embroidery floss or machine embroidery thread for the flowers. The flower colors on the dress are light blue, medium blue, lavender, medium pink, yellow and peach. Leaves and vines are stitched in three shades of green.

Pattern Pieces Required: To-The-Waist Front Bodice, To-The-Waist Back Bodice and Long Sleeve

Templates Required: Monet's Garden Front Panel Template, Scalloped Skirt Template

All seams 1/4" unless otherwise indicated. Stitch seams in place and overcast the seam allowances with a zigzag or serge.

A. Cutting

1. From the batiste, cut one front bodice from the fold, two back bodices from the selvages, two sleeves and one skirt piece 45" wide by the following length **(fig. 1)**.

Doll Sizes	*17-1/2"*	*18-1/2"*	*19-1/2"*	*21-1/2"*
Skirt	8"	8-3/4"	9-1/4"	10-1/4"

2. Transfer fold line markings from the back bodice pattern to the back bodice pieces.

3. Cut two rectangles of organdy for the front panel 7" wide by the following length:

Doll Sizes	*17-1/2"*	*18-1/2"*	*19-1/2"*	*21-1/2"*
Front Panel	13"	14"	15"	17"

   Pin the two layers of organdy together and treat as one layer **(fig. 2)**. This adds stability to the panel and will keep it from being so sheer.

4. Cut two organdy sash strips 3" wide by 21" long.

B. Constructing the Dress Front

1. Finish one long side of the sash strips with a zigzag (zig on the fabric and zag off the fabric. This is called a rolled and whipped edge) **(fig. 3)**. Fold one of the short cut ends to the unfinished edge of the side creating a point. Refer to figure 3. Pin in place. Zigzag the remaining side of the sash. Run two gathering rows 1/4" and 1/8" in the remaining short cut ends of the sash and gather the ends to 1-1/4" **(fig. 4)**. Set aside.

2. Place the front bodice to the back bodice, right sides together, at the sides. Starting at the waist, stitch the sides 3/4" leaving the upper part of the seam open **(fig. 5)**.

3. Fold the skirt piece in half to find the center front. Trace the skirt template along the skirt bottom with the lower edge of the scallop to the cut edge of the skirt **(fig. 6)**. Trace eight scallops on each side of the center front fold. Refer to figure 6. Trim the back edges of the skirt 1/2" from the last scallop **(fig. 7)**. Overcast the cut edge with a zigzag or serge. Refer to figure 8.

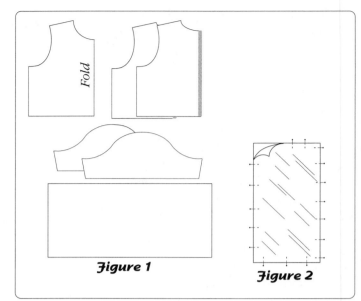

Fold

Figure 1

Figure 2

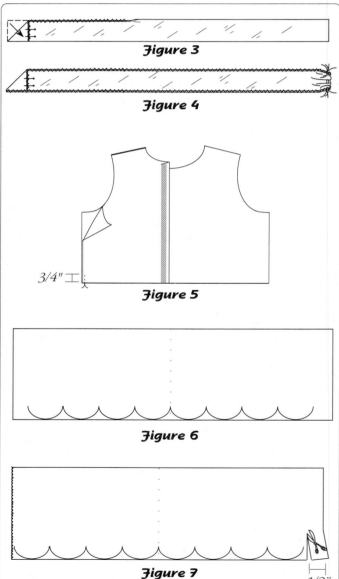

Figure 3

Figure 4

3/4" ⊥

Figure 5

Figure 6

Figure 7

⊢⊣ 1/2"

4. Shape insertion lace along the scallops using the directions for shaping lace scallops found on page 242. ***Do not shape lace on the two center scallops***, simply leave 1/2" lace tabs extending into these scallops **(fig. 8)**. Stitch the scallops in place along the inside edge of the lace only! Wait until the center panel is in place before cutting the fabric from behind the lace insertion.

5. Fold one back edge of the skirt to the inside 1/2" and press. Pin **(fig. 9)**. Run two gathering rows in the top edge of the skirt at 1/8" and 1/4 **(fig. 10)**. Gather the skirt to fit the bodice. Leave 1-3/4" ungathered on each side of the center front. This 3-1/2" ungathered area will allow for the organdy panel. At the back edges of the skirt, wrap the back facings of the bodice over the edges of the skirt. Remember one side has been turned back 1/2" **(fig. 11)**. Pin in place.

6. Stitch the skirt to the bodice using a 1/4" seam. Overcast the seam allowance.

7. Fold the organdy rectangle in half long ways to find the center. Lay the dress flat and place the center of the organdy rectangle to the center front of the dress. Trace the neck, shoulders and skirt cut edge on the organdy **(fig. 12)**.

8. Remove the organdy panel and place the panel on the Monet's Garden Front Panel Template, matching the lower edge of the template with the skirt cut edge line. Trace the scalloped template along the side and across the bottom **(fig. 13)**.

9. Work the flowers, stems and leaves either using machine embroidery, hand embroidery or decorate the panel as desired **(fig. 14)**.

10. Shape lace insertion along the template lines, starting at the shoulder, moving around the panel and stopping at the opposite shoulder **(fig. 15)**. Refer to shaping lace scallops found on page __ for lace shaping directions.

11. Stitch the lace in place using a small, tight zigzag, along the inside edge of the lace only! Trim the fabric from behind the lace **(fig. 16)**.

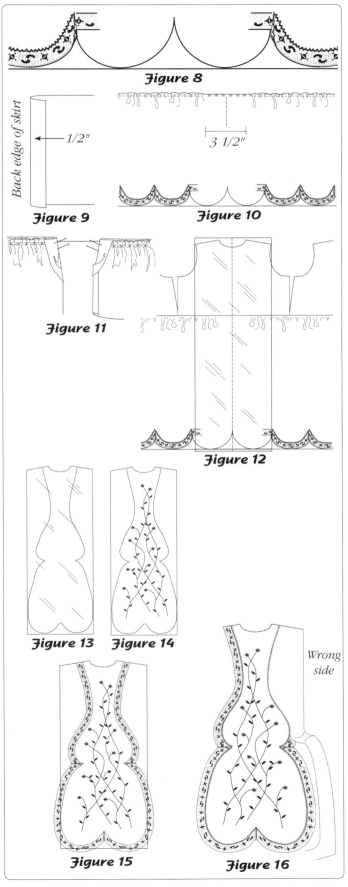

12. Place the organdy/lace panel on the dress front matching the shoulders, neck and lace hem. Pin the front panel in place. Trim the neck and shoulders of the front panel to fit the dress. Slip the gathered ends of the sash under the front panel allowing 1" to fall above the waist line seam and 1/4" to fall below. Pin in place **(fig. 17)**.

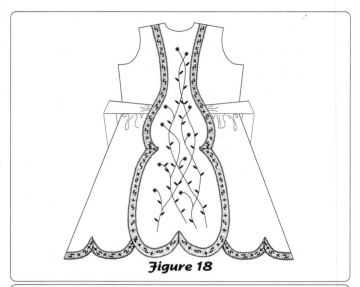

Figure 18

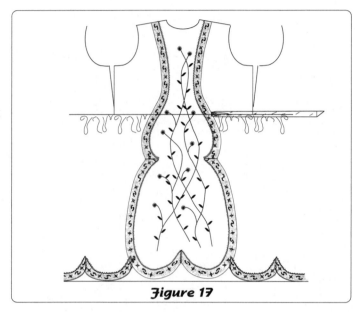

Figure 17

13. Stitch the front panel to the dress along the outer edge of the lace scallops starting at the shoulder and stitching through the lace insertion along the bottom. Begin again on the opposite shoulder and stitch through the lace insertion at the bottom. The sashes will be stitched in place in the stitching **(fig. 18)**.

14. Trim the fabric from behind the center panel and from the lace scallops along the bottom of the skirt.

C. Finishing the Dress

1. Gather wide lace edging and stitch to the lace scallops at the dress bottom using the technique lace to lace **(fig. 19)**.

2. Place the backs of the bodice/skirt, right sides together. Pin. Stitch from the bottom edge of the skirt, stopping 3-1/2" from the waist seam. Backstitch. Trim the seam to 1/8" and overcast **(fig. 20)**.

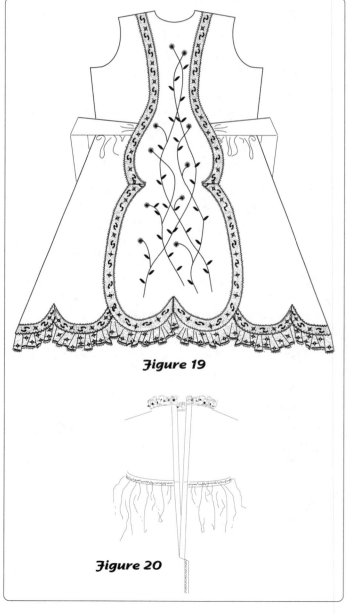

Figure 19

Figure 20

3. Place the front bodice to the back bodice right sides together at the shoulders. Stitch in place using a 1/4" seam.

4. Finish the neck with entredeux and gathered 1/2" edging lace. Refer to "Neck Finishes - a. Entredeux to Gathered Edging" found on page 34.

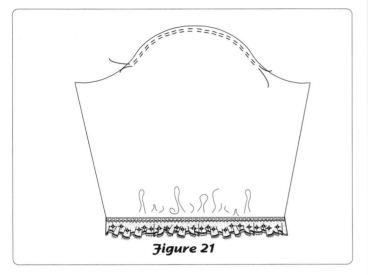

Figure 21

5. Run two gathering rows in the top and bottom of the sleeves. Finish the ends of the sleeves with entredeux and gathered 1/2" edging lace **(fig. 21)**. Refer to "Sleeve Bands and Ruffles - a. Entredeux and Gathered Edging Lace" found on page 38.

6. Gather the top of the sleeves to fit the arm opening of the bodice, matching the center of the sleeve with the shoulder seam of the bodice. Adjust the gathers in the top of the sleeve to fall 1-1/4" to 1-1/2" on either side of the shoulder seam.

7. Stitch the sleeve to the bodice, right sides together, using a 1/4" seam **(fig. 22)**.

8. With the sides of the bodice/sleeves, right sides together, complete the stitching of the side seams and sleeve seams **(fig. 23)**.

9. Attach Velcro™, buttons and buttonholes or snaps to the back of the bodice to close the dress.

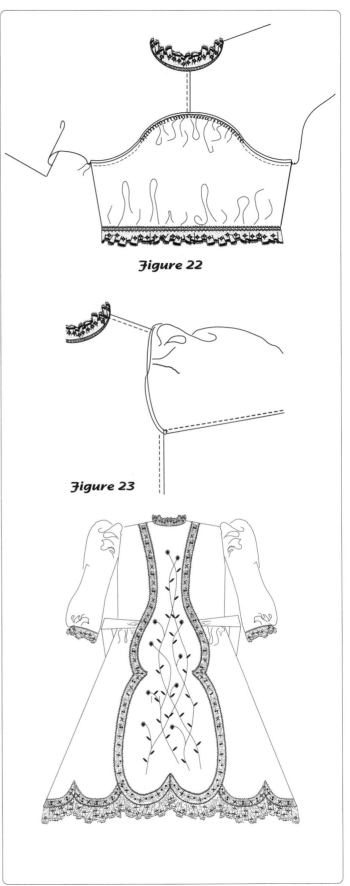

Figure 22

Figure 23

Peach Rosebud Dress

Using the basic to-the-waist styling, this dress incorporates lots of pleasing detail. The high yoke has an overlay of Swiss handloom with peach roses embroidered every 2 inches. On either side of the handloom is entredeux and three strips of white French insertion butted together. Entredeux and gathered lace are apparent at the bottom of this high yoke overlay. Entredeux and gathered lace edging finish the neckline; a tiny peach rosebud is stitched in the center front of the bodice. Gathered peach Swiss batiste is stitched from the bottom of the fancy, high yoke to the waistline. Wide faggoting in peach serves as beading for peach ribbon, which goes around the waistline. Angel sleeves made of the peach rosebud handloom are found on top of the peach batiste sleeves. Entredeux and flat white French lace edging embellish the angel sleeves. At the bottom of each sleeve is entredeux and slightly gathered French edging. The skirt is peach batiste with a fancy band on the bottom, which calls for entredeux, white French insertion, entredeux, peach handloom, entredeux, white French insertion, and gathered French edging. The back yokes of the dress mirror the front, and the dress closes with snaps.

- **All pattern pieces and templates found in pull-out section**
- **Color photograph on page 19**

Supplies

Fabric - Peach Batiste	5/8 yd.	*Peach Rosebud Insertion (2")*	5/8 yd.
Faggoting (1/2")	3/8 yd.	*Lace Edging (1/2")*	1/2 yd.
Lace Edging (5/8")	1-3/4 yds.	*Lace Edging (1")*	2 yds.
Lace Insertion (1/2")	3 yds.	*Satin Ribbon (3/8")*	1 yd.

Notions: Lightweight sewing thread; Velcro™, snaps or tiny buttons for closure

Pattern Pieces Required: High Yoke Front, High Yoke Back, Midriff Front Template, Midriff Back Template, Long Sleeve, Sleeve Cap Ruffle

All seams 1/4" unless otherwise indicated. Stitch seam in place and overcast the seam allowances with a zigzag or serge, unless otherwise indicated.

A. Cutting

1. From the batiste, cut one front yoke on the fold, two back yokes on the selvage, two midriff backs on the selvage, one midriff front on the fold and two sleeves on the fold **(fig. 1)**.

2. Cut one skirt piece, 45" wide by the following length:

Doll Sizes	17-1/2"	18-1/2"	19-1/2"	21-1/2"
Skirt Length	5-1/2"	6"	6-1/2"	7-1/2"

3. Sleeve cap ruffles and yoke overlays will be cut later.

4. Transfer pattern markings to the fabric. Also mark the centers of the skirt pieces and the midriff front at the top and bottom edges.

B. Yokes and Neck Finish

1. Create the lace rectangles for the back yoke overlays as follows **(fig. 2)**:

   a. Cut two 9" strips of the lace insertion and sew them together, using the method "lace to lace".

   b. Attach entredeux to one side of the lace strip, using the method "entredeux to lace". Do not trim the second side of the entredeux.

   c. Cut the 9" lace/entredeux strip in half, and attach embroidered edging to the entredeux edge of each piece, using the method "entredeux to fabric". Be sure that the pattern of the embroidered insertion matches and is centered on the two pieces, since these will form the back yokes.

2. Place the two created rectangles over the batiste back yoke pieces, with the lace trims running from top to bottom. The edge of the insertion lace should be placed on the back fold line. If the rectangles are not large enough to cover the batiste yokes, add lace insertion to the outer edges of the embroidered insertion pieces to add enough width **(fig. 3)**.

3. Stitch the lace along the back fold line. Baste the overlays to the yokes along the neck, shoulder, bottom and armhole edges. Trim away the excess of the overlay pieces.

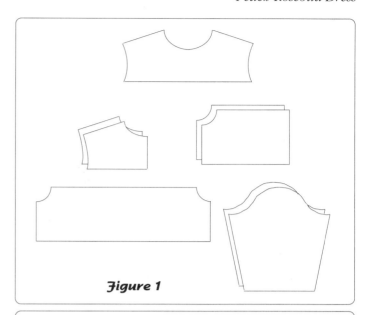

Figure 1

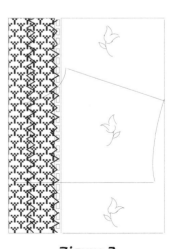

Figure 2

Figure 3

4. Create a rectangle for the front yoke overlay as follows:

   a. Sew three 4-1/2" strips of the lace insertion together, using the method "lace to lace".

   b. Add a piece of entredeux to each side of the lace strip, using the method "entredeux to lace".

   c. Attach embroidered insertion to the entredeux edge on each side of the piece, using the method "entredeux to fabric". Be sure that the embroidery pattern matches on the two sides and is centered, since this will form the front yoke.

5. Place the created rectangle over the batiste front yoke piece, with the lace trims running from top to bottom. The middle piece of lace should be centered over the yoke front center. If the rectangle is not large enough to cover the batiste yoke, add lace insertion to the outer edges of the embroidered insertion pieces to add enough width **(fig. 4)**.

6. Baste the overlay to the yoke along the neck, shoulder, bottom and armhole edges. Trim away the excess of the overlay piece. Refer to figure 4.

7. Place the front yoke to the back yokes at the shoulders, right sides together, and stitch **(fig. 5)**.

8. Finish the neck edge with entredeux and 1/2" lace edging, referring to "Neck Finishes - a. Entredeux and Gathered Edging" found on page 34.

C. Midriff

1. Run two rows of gathering threads along the top and bottom edges of the midriff pieces, stopping 1/4" from the sides and armholes **(fig. 6)**.

2. Cut a strip of entredeux 14" long and cut a strip of 5/8" lace edging 21" long. Pull the heading thread of the lace, gathering it to fit the entredeux **(fig. 7)**. Sew the two strips together, using the method "entredeux to lace". If the remaining tape edge of the entredeux is wider than 1/4", trim the edge to 1/4".

3. Gather the top edges of the midriff pieces to fit the bottom edges of the yokes, with the facings extended in the back, stopping the gathers 1/4" from the edges and at the back fold line **(fig. 8)**.

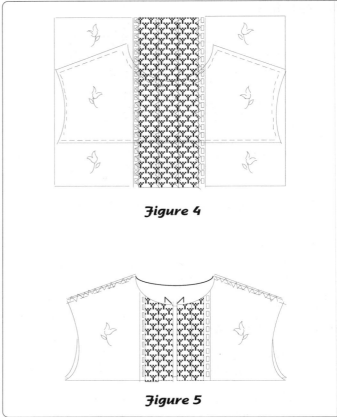

Figure 4

Figure 5

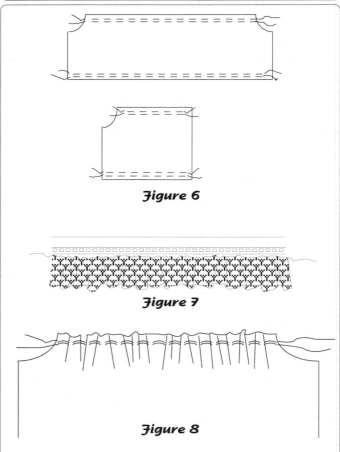

Figure 6

Figure 7

Figure 8

4. Place the entredeux/edging strip to the bottom edges of the yoke pieces, right sides together **(fig. 9)**, then place the yokes over the midriff pieces, right sides together, having the bottom edges of the yokes even with the top edges of the midriffs **(fig. 10)**.

5. Stitch the yokes to the midriffs, using the method "entredeux to fabric", with the entredeux sandwiched between the fabric layers **(fig. 11)**.

D. Sleeves

1. Create rectangles for the sleeve cap ruffles as follows **(refer to fig. 12)**:

   a. Cut a strip of entredeux 22" long and attach a 22" strip of 5/8" lace edging to the entredeux.

   b. Trim the remaining edge of the entredeux to 1/4" and cut the strip in half.

   c. Attach the entredeux to strips of embroidered insertion. Make sure that the pattern matches on the two pieces and the design is centered, since these will become the sleeve cap ruffles.

   d. Place the entredeux of the sleeve cap ruffle pieces along the sleeve cap line on the sleeve pieces and baste along the top and side edges. Trim the sleeve cap ruffles to fit the tops of the sleeves **(fig. 13)**.

2. Run two rows of gathering threads along the top and bottom edges of the sleeves, 1/8" and 1/4" from the edges **(fig. 14)**.

3. Finish the bottom edges of the sleeves, referring to "Sleeve Bands and Ruffles - a. Entredeux and Gathered Lace Edging" found on page 38. Use 5/8" edging **(fig. 15)**.

4. Place the sleeves to the armholes, right sides together, and stitch in place **(fig. 16)**.

5. Place the sleeve/side seams of the dress with right sides together and stitch **(fig. 16a)**.

E. Skirt

1. Cut three 45" strips of entredeux, two 45" strips of lace insertion, one 45" strip of embroidered insertion and one 72" strip of 1" lace edging. Piece the fancy band as follows, working from top to bottom **(fig. 17)**.

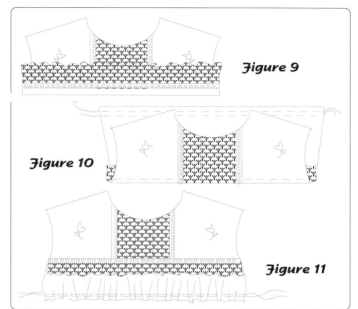

Figure 9

Figure 10

Figure 11

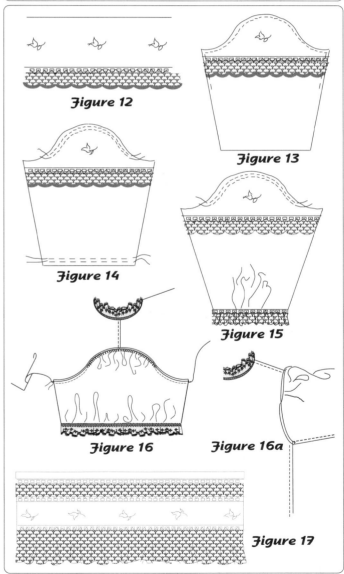

Figure 12

Figure 13

Figure 14

Figure 15

Figure 16

Figure 16a

Figure 17

a. Attach entredeux to each side of one lace insertion strip, using the method "entredeux to lace". Trim the remaining tape edges of the entredeux to 1/4".

b. Attach one entredeux edge of the lace/entredeux strip to the embroidered insertion, using the method "entredeux to fabric". Also attach entredeux to the remaining edge of the embroidered insertion.

d. Attach lace insertion to the bottom piece of entredeux, using the method "entredeux to lace".

e. Pull the heading thread in the top edge of the lace edging and gather it to fit the entredeux. Attach the edging to the bottom strip of lace insertion, using the method "lace to lace".

2. Attach the fancy band to the skirt piece **(fig. 18)**, using the method "entredeux to fabric".

3. Run two rows of gathering threads across the top edge of the skirt, 1/8" and 1/4" from the edge. Refer to figure 18.

4. Cut a piece of faggoting to the following size:

Doll Sizes	17-1/2"	18-1/2"	19-1/2"	21-1/2"
	10-1/2"	12"	11-1/2"	13-1/2"

5. Place the skirt to the faggotting, right sides together **(fig. 19)**, and gather the top edge of the skirt to fit the faggoting, stopping the gathers at the back fold line. Stitch the seam, using the method "entredeux to fabric".

F. Finishing the Dress

1. Place the top edge of the faggotting to the midriff, with right sides together, and with the back facings opened out **(fig. 20)**. Adjust the gathers to fit the faggotting and stitch the seam, using the method "entredeux to fabric".

2. Cut the ribbon into two pieces. Run ribbon through the faggotting, beginning at center front and working toward the back on each side. Tack the ends of the ribbon at the back edges of the midriff. Tie a bow at center front.

3. Press the back facings to the inside and hand-tack in place **(fig. 21)**.

4. Begin at the bottom edge and stitch the back skirt seam, stopping 3-1/2" below the waist. Refer to "Plackets - d. Easy Placket in a Seam" on page 44 to apply a placket for the back opening.

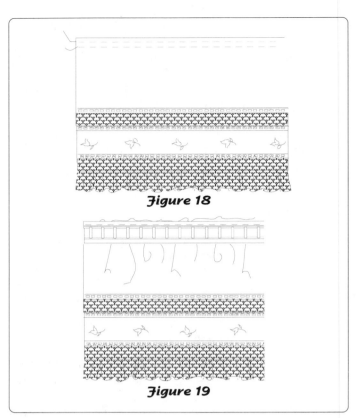

Figure 18

Figure 19

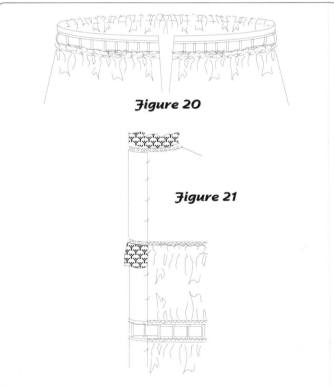

Figure 20

Figure 21

5. Attach Velcro™, snaps or tiny buttons and buttonholes for the back closure.

6. Hand-tack the small ribbon rose at the center front of the neck edge.

Pink & Ecru Heirloom Party Dress

From day one in this business, I have loved the heirloom party dress. This style dress has a high yoke, puffed sleeves, a fancy band and a ruffle on the bottom. I must have made 10 of these dresses for Joanna before I attempted another style. Dolls will look almost as precious as children do in a party dress made of pink Swiss batiste and ecru trims. The high yoke has an insert of entredeux, insertion, beading, insertion, beading, insertion, and entredeux. Entredeux travels around the high yoke sections in both the front and back of the dress. The neckline is entredeux/gathered lace trim. Gathered lace edging is stitched to the entredeux around the yokes. The sleeves have a slit down the middle, which is filled with the same sequence of entredeux and laces as is found in the bodice front. Entredeux and gathered lace trim finish the edges of the sleeves and silk ribbon is run through the sleeves to gather in the fullness.

- *All pattern pieces and templates found in pull-out section*
- *Color photograph on page 20*

Supplies

Fabric - Batiste	5/8 yd.
Entredeux	3-1/2 yds.
Satin Ribbon (1/8")	4 yds.
Lace Insertion (5/8")	6 yds.
Lace Beading (3/4")	4 yds.
Lace Edging (1")	3-1/4 yds.
Lace Edging (3/4")	1 yd.
Silk Ribbon (7mm)	1 yd.

Notions: Lightweight sewing thread; Velcro™, snaps or tiny buttons for closure

Pattern Pieces Required: High Yoke Front, High Yoke Back, Elbow-Length Sleeve

Templates Required: Armhole Guide

All seams 1/4" unless otherwise indicated. Stitch seam in place and overcast the seam allowances with a zigzag or serge, unless otherwise indicated.

A. Cutting

1. Cut two back yokes on the selvage **(fig. 1)**.

2. Cut two skirt pieces, 19" wide by the following length:

Doll Sizes	17-1/2"	18-1/2"	19-1/2"	21-1/2"
Skirt Length	5"	5-1/2"	6-1/2"	7-3/4"

3. Cut two ruffle strips across the width of the fabric, 2" wide by 38" long.

4. Mark the centers of the skirt pieces and the ruffle pieces at the top and bottom edges, and use the armhole guide to cut the armholes **(fig. 2)**.

5. The front yoke and sleeves will be cut from pieced lace and fabric, described in the following section.

B. Piecing Lace Bands for Sleeves, Fancy Band and Front Yoke

1. Cut lace and entredeux to the following sizes: **(fig. 3)**

   a. Cut three strips of 5/8" lace insertion, each 72" long.

   b. Cut two strips of 3/4" lace beading, each 72" long.

   c. Cut two strips of entredeux, each 72" long.

2. Piece the lace band as follows:

   a. Sew a strip of beading to each side of one insertion strip, using the "lace to lace" technique.

   b. Sew a strip of insertion to each strip of the beading, using the "lace to lace" technique.

   c. Sew a strip of entredeux to each side of the band, using the "entredeux to lace" technique.

   d. From the top to the bottom, the band is composed in this order: Entredeux - insertion - beading - insertion - beading - insertion - entredeux.

   e. Thread 1/8" satin ribbon through the beading. **Note:** *Illustrations do not show ribbon.*

3. Neaten one end of the lace band and cut a strip 38" long for the fancy band.

4. Add the skirt ruffle to the bottom of the 38" fancy band as follows:

   a. Sew the two ruffle strips together to make one long strip **(fig. 4)**.

   b. Attach 1" edging lace along one long edge of the ruffle strip, using the "lace to fabric" technique. See figure 4.

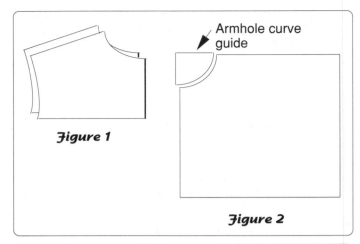

Figure 1

Armhole curve guide

Figure 2

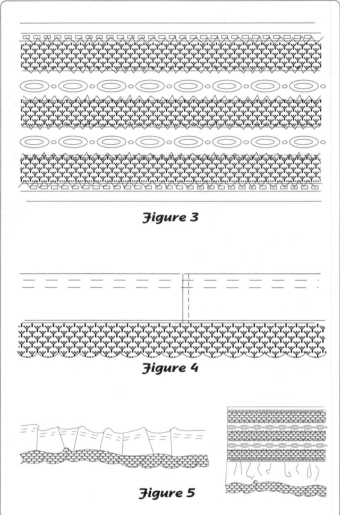

Figure 3

Figure 4

Figure 5

c. Run two rows of gathering threads across the unfinished long edge of the ruffle strip, 1/8" and 1/4" from the edge. See figure 4.

d. Gather the ruffle strip to fit the entredeux on one edge of the fancy band and stitch, using the "entredeux to fabric" technique **(fig. 5)**.

4. Cut two strips of batiste across the width of the fabric, 4" wide by 36" long. Sew one strip to each side of the lace band that is left after cutting the fancy band, using the "lace to fabric" technique **(fig. 6)**.

5. Fold the new band in half, lengthwise, with the center piece of insertion on the fold. Trace two sleeves on the fold, and trace one yoke front on the fold, opening the fabric flat to trace the second half of each piece. Stitch across the lace on the drawn lines, then cut out the yoke and sleeves **(fig. 7)**.

C. Yokes, Neck and Sleeve Construction

1. Place the front yoke to the back yokes at the shoulder seams, right sides together, and stitch **(fig. 8)**.

2. Finish the neck edge, referring to "Neck finishes - a. Entredeux and Gathered Edging" found on page 34, and using 3/4" lace edging **(fig. 9)**.

3. Run two rows of gathering threads across the top and bottom edges of the sleeves, 1/8" and 1/4" from the edges **(fig. 10)**.

4. Refer to "Sleeve Bands and Ruffles - a. Entredeux and Gathered Edging Lace" on page 38 to finish the bottom edges of the sleeves, using 3/4" lace edging **(fig. 11)**.

D. Skirt

1. Choose one skirt piece to be the skirt back. Cut a 4-1/2" slit at the center on the top edge of the piece and apply a placket. Refer to "Plackets - a. Continuous Lap Placket" found on page 42 **(fig. 12)**.

2. Run two rows of gathering threads across the top of each skirt piece, 1/8" and 1/4" from the edge. Stop the stitching at the placket seam line on the back pieces. See figure 12.

3. Pin the front skirt piece to the yoke, right sides together. Adjust the gathers in the skirt top to fit the bottom edge of the yoke and stitch in place **(fig. 13)**.

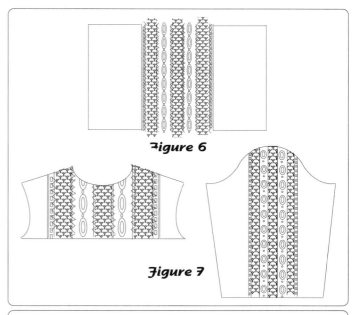

Figure 6

Figure 7

Figure 8

Figure 9

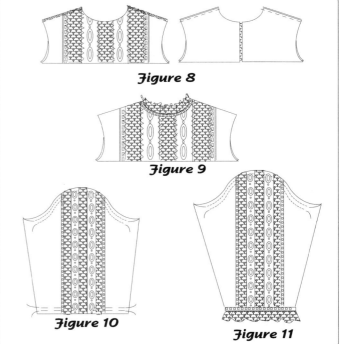

Figure 10

Figure 11

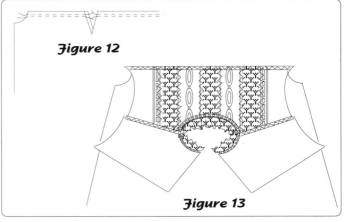

Figure 12

Figure 13

4. Place the back skirt to the back yokes, right sides together. The placket edges should meet the back fold line of the yokes. Wrap the back facings to the outside along the fold line, sandwiching the skirt between the yoke and the facing. Stitch in place and press the yokes up, flipping the facings to the inside **(fig. 14)**.

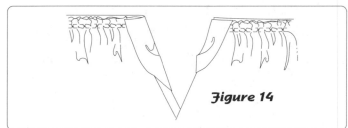

Figure 14

E. Finishing the Dress

1. Pin the sleeves to the armholes and adjust the gathers to fit, stopping the gathers at the yoke seam lines. Stitch the sleeves in place **(fig. 15)**.

2. Pull the heading thread in the remaining 1" lace edging and fit the edging to the remaining entredeux. Attach the two pieces, using the "entredeux to lace" technique.

3. Beginning at the back edge, place the lace/entredeux strip along the seam lines of the yoke. Let the strip extend 1/2" beyond the back edge, run across the back, over the shoulder, across the front and over the second shoulder, then across the back to extend 1/2" past the back edge, folding the strip in place around the corners **(fig. 16)**.

4. Use a small zigzag to stitch the lace/entredeux strip in place, stitching in every hole of the entredeux. Refer to figure 16. Turn the back extensions to the inside and stitch in place by hand or machine.

5. Place only one of the sleeve/side seams with right sides together. Match the sleeve edges and the bottom edges and stitch. Do not catch the lace edging around the yoke in the side seam **(fig. 17)**.

6. Place the entredeux edge of the fancy band to the bottom edge of the skirt, right sides together and stitch, using the technique "entredeux to fabric". Trim the fancy band to make it fit the skirt **(fig. 18)**.

7. Stitch the second side seam as described in Step 5 above.

8. Apply Velcro™, snaps or tiny buttons and button holes to the back opening, with the right side lapping over the left side. Cut the 7mm silk ribbon in half and thread one piece through the entredeux at the bottom of each sleeve, beginning and ending at the outside of the sleeve. Tie a bow and trim the streamers.

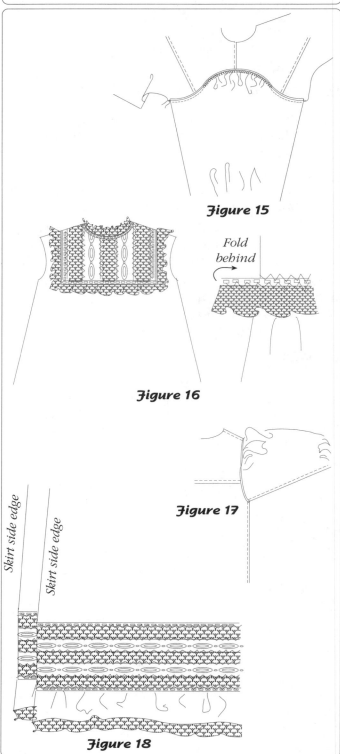

Figure 15

Fold behind

Figure 16

Figure 17

Skirt side edge

Skirt side edge

Figure 18

Pink & Pretty Dress

Looking somewhat like an ice cream cone, this pink dress has yummy details. The collar is made from a pink, green and pale blue Swiss. Two strips of French insertion, surrounded by entredeux fit between the three strips of handloom. The square collar extends nearly to the waist of the doll dress in both the front and the back. Little white silk ribbon bows are tied at all four corners of the collar. The long sleeves have a fancy band down the middle with entredeux, French insertion, and more entredeux. The bottom of the sleeves and the neckline are finished with entredeux and gathered lace edging. Entredeux, lace insertion, entredeux, Swiss handloom, entredeux and flat lace French edging combine for the fancy band. The back closes with snaps.

- **All pattern pieces and templates found in pull-out section**
- **Color photograph on page 21**

Supplies

Fabric - Batiste	2/3 yd.
Entredeux	9 yds.
Embroidered Insertion	3 yds.
Lace Insertion (5/8")	3 yds.
Lace Edging (1-1/4")	1-1/4 yds.
Lace Edging (5/8")	3 yds.
Silk Ribbon (7mm white)	2 yds.

Notions: Lightweight sewing thread; Velcro™, snaps or tiny buttons for closure

Pattern Pieces Required: High-Yoke Front, High-Yoke Back, 3/4-Length Sleeve, Square Collar Front and Back

Template Required: Armhole Guide

All seams 1/4" unless otherwise indicated. Stitch seam in place and overcast the seam allowances with a zigzag or serge, unless otherwise indicated.

A. Cutting

1. Cut two back yokes on the selvage and one front yoke on the fold **(fig. 1)**.

2. Cut two skirt pieces, 22" wide by the following length:

Doll Sizes	*17-1/2"*	*18-1/2"*	*19-1/2"*	*21-1/2"*
Skirt Length	8"	8-1/2"	9-1/2"	10-3/4"

3. Mark the centers of the skirt pieces top and bottom edges and use the armhole guide to cut the armholes **(fig. 2)**.

4. The collar and sleeves will be cut from rectangles of pieced lace and fabric, described in the following section.

B. Yokes and Collar

1. Place the front yoke to the back yokes at the shoulders and stitch **(fig. 3)**.

2. For the collar front, cut lace insertion, embroidered insertion and entredeux to the following sizes:

   a. Cut two strips of 5/8" lace insertion, each 5" long.

   b. Cut three strips of embroidered insertion, each 5" long. If the embroidered design has a very definite repeat pattern, match the pieces as closely as possible.

   c. Cut six strips of entredeux, each 5" long.

2. Piece the rectangle as follows, working from the center out **(fig. 4)**:

   a. Sew a strip of entredeux to each side of one embroidered insertion strip, using the technique "entredeux to fabric."

   b. Sew a strip of lace insertion to each strip of the entredeux, using the technique "entredeux to lace."

   c. Sew a strip of entredeux to each side of the band, using the technique "entredeux to lace."

   d. Sew a strip of embroidered insertion to each side of the band, using the technique "entredeux to fabric."

   e. Sew entredeux to each side of the rectangle, using the technique "entredeux to fabric."

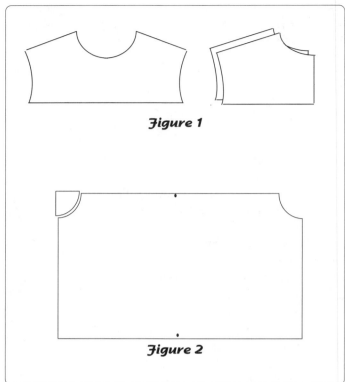

Figure 1

Figure 2

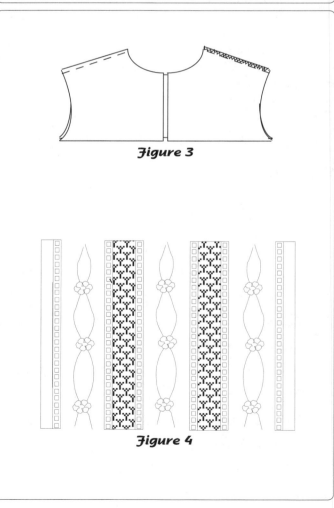

Figure 3

Figure 4

f. From one side to the other, the rectangle is composed of entredeux, embroidered insertion, entredeux, lace insertion, entredeux, embroidered insertion, entredeux, lace insertion, entredeux, embroidered insertion, entredeux.

3. Fold the rectangle in half from top to bottom, with the fold running through the center of the center strip of embroidered insertion. Place the collar pattern over the rectangle and trace the collar outline. Stitch along the drawn line, then cut out the collar front **(fig. 5)**.

4. For the collar backs, cut lace insertion, embroidered insertion and entredeux to the following sizes:

    a. Cut two strips of 5/8" lace insertion, each 5" long.

    b. Cut four strips of embroidered insertion, each 5" long. If the embroidered design has a very definite repeat pattern, match the pieces as closely as possible.

    c. Cut eight strips of entredeux, each 5" long.

5. Put aside one strip of 5/8" lace insertion, two strips of embroidered insertion and four strips of entredeux. Use the remaining pieces and piece a rectangle for one collar back as follows **(fig. 6)**:

    a. Stitch entredeux to each side of the lace insertion, using the technique "entredeux to lace".

    b. Sew a strip of embroidered insertion to each side of the band, using the technique "entredeux to fabric."

    c. Sew entredeux to the remaining edges of the embroidered insertions, using the technique "entredeux to fabric".

    d. Repeat Steps a - c to create the second rectangle, using the strips that were laid aside earlier.

6. Place one rectangle over the other with the patterns matched and right sides together. Place the pattern over the rectangles and trace the pattern onto one piece **(fig. 7)**. Turn the rectangles over and trace the pattern onto the other piece. Stitch along the drawn lines and cut out the collar backs **(fig. 8)**.

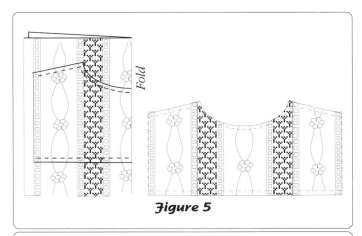

Figure 5

Figure 6

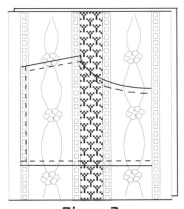

Figure 7

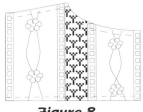

Figure 8

7. Trim the fabric away from the entredeux at the side and back edges of all collar pieces. Attach a strip of entredeux across the bottom edges of the collar front and backs, using the technique "entredeux to fabric." Trim the fabric away from the bottom entredeux on the collar front and backs.

8. Place the collar front to the collar backs at the shoulder seams, right sides together, and stitch the seams.

9. Cut a piece of 5/8" lace edging 45" long. Beginning at one back edge, attach the lace edging to the entredeux. Keep the lace flat along the back edges, then gather the lace along the sides and front edge. Adjust the gathers to a pleasing fullness and trim off any excess at the back neck edges **(fig. 9)**.

10. Place the collar over the dress yokes and baste the two layers together at the neck edge, then treat as one .

11. Finish the neck edge **(fig. 10)**, referring to "Neck Finishes - a. Entredeux and Gathered Edging" found on page 34.

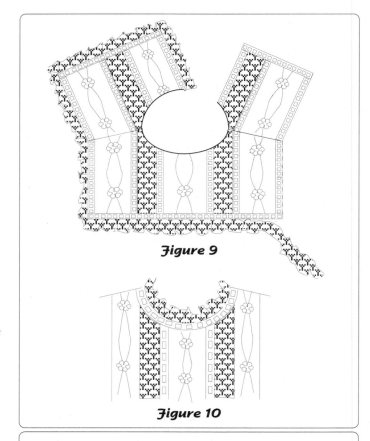

Figure 9

Figure 10

C. Skirt

1. Choose one skirt piece to be the skirt back. Cut a 4-1/2" slit at the center on the top edge of the piece and apply a placket. Refer to "Plackets - a. Continuous Lap Placket" found on page 42.

2. Run two rows of gathering threads across the top of the skirt, 1/8" and 1/4" from the edge. Stop the stitching at the placket seam line on the back edges **(fig. 11 and 12)**.

3. Pin the front skirt piece to the yoke, right sides together. Adjust the gathers in the skirt top to fit the bottom edge of the yoke and stitch in place **(fig. 13)**.

4. Place the back skirt to the back yokes, right sides together. The placket edges should meet the back fold line of the yokes. Wrap the back facings to the outside along the fold line, sandwiching the skirt between the yoke and the facing. Stitch in place and press the yokes up, flipping the facings to the inside **(fig. 14)**.

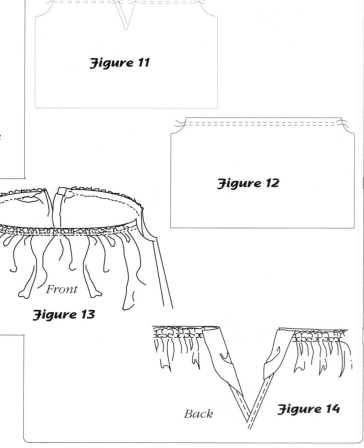

Figure 11

Figure 12

Front

Figure 13

Back

Figure 14

D. Sleeves

1. For the sleeves, cut lace insertion, embroidered insertion and entredeux to the following sizes:

    a. Cut two strips of embroidered insertion, each 9" long, with the patterns matched and centered.

    b. Cut eight pieces of entredeux, each 9" long.

    c. Cut four pieces of lace insertion, each 9" long.

    d. Cut four pieces of fabric, each 5" wide by 9" long.

2. Lay aside one piece of the embroidered insertion, four strips of entredeux and two pieces of the lace insertion. Use the remaining strips to piece a rectangle for one of the sleeves **(fig. 15)**:

    a. Sew entredeux to each side of the embroidered insertion, using the technique "entredeux to fabric."

    b. Sew lace insertion to each side, using the technique "entredeux to lace."

    c. Sew the remaining pieces of entredeux to each side of the band.

    d. Attach a strip of fabric to each side of the band, using the technique "entredeux to fabric."

    e. Repeat Steps a - c to piece the band for the second sleeve.

3. Mark the top edges of the rectangles and fold the pieces in half, with the fold running down the middle of the embroidered insertion. Place the pattern over each rectangle and trace the sleeve onto the fabric. Be sure that the top of the pattern is matched to the top edge of the rectangle, and that the designs are matched on the two pieces. Stitch along the drawn lines, then cut out the sleeves **(fig. 16)**.

4. Run two rows of gathering threads across the top and bottom edges of the sleeves, 1/8" and 1/4" from the edges **(fig. 17)**.

5. Refer to "Sleeve Bands and Ruffles - a. Entredeux and Gathered Edging Lace" on page 38 to finish the bottom edges of the sleeves, using 5/8" lace edging **(fig. 18)**.

6. Pin the sleeves to the armholes and adjust the gathers to fit, letting the gathers fall 1-1/2" on each side of the shoulder seam. Stitch the sleeves in place. Do not catch the collar in the stitching **(fig. 19)**.

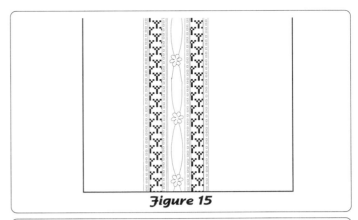

Figure 15

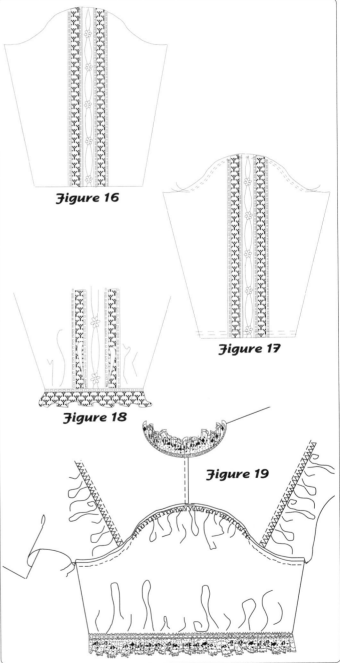

Figure 16

Figure 17

Figure 18

Figure 19

7. Place one sleeve/side seam with right sides together. Match the sleeve edges and the bottom edges and stitch **(fig. 20)**. Do not catch the collar in the side seam.

D. Fancy Band

1. Press three creases around the bottom edge of the skirt. The creases should be 1/2" apart, with the first crease 3/4" above the bottom edge **(fig. 21)**.

2. Stitch 1/8" from the folded edges to make tucks. Press the tucks toward the bottom edge of the skirt (See figure 21).

3. Create the fancy band as follows **(fig. 22)**:

   a. Cut one piece each of 5/8" lace insertion, embroidered insertion, and 1-1/4" edging, each 45" long. Cut three pieces of entredeux, each 45" long.

   b. Sew a piece of the entredeux to each side of the embroidered insertion, using the technique "entredeux to fabric."

   c. Attach the strip of lace insertion to one edge, using the technique "entredeux to lace."

   d. Attach the wide edging lace to the other edge, using the technique "entredeux to lace." This will be the bottom edge of the skirt.

   e. Sew a strip of entredeux to the remaining edge of the lace insertion. This will be the top edge of the fancy band.

   f. Measure the skirt bottom edge and cut the band to that measurement plus a 1/2" seam allowance. Sew the short ends of the fancy band together to make a circle **(fig. 23)**.

4. Place the entredeux edge of the fancy band to the bottom edge of the skirt, right sides together and stitch, using the technique "entredeux to fabric."

5. Stitch the remaining side seam.

E. Finishing the Dress

1. Apply Velcro™, snaps or tiny buttons and button-holes to the back opening, with the right side lapping over the left side.

2. Cut the 7mm silk ribbon into four pieces. Tie each piece into a bow and trim the streamers. Tack the four bows to the corners of the collar.

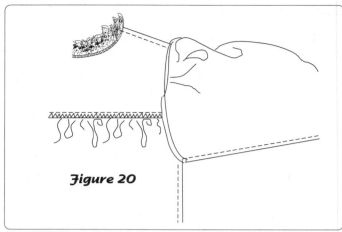

Figure 20

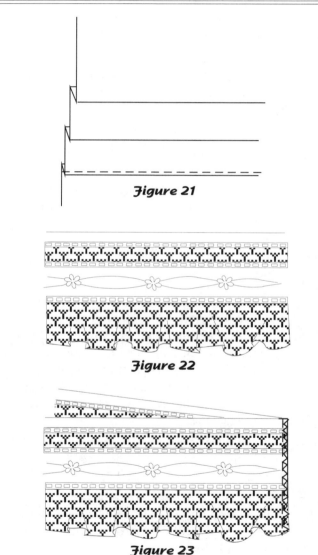

Figure 21

Figure 22

Figure 23

Pink Round Yoke Victorian Dress

Aptly named "Victoria" by the designer, this dress appears to have stepped from the pages of a Victorian history book. Pink Nelona Swiss batiste is used for both the dress and the slip. The historically correct, round yoke is a combination of trims. In the center are nine tiny pintucks made with a 1.6 double needle, that's the smallest made. Next comes entredeux, beading insertion, beading, entredeux and fabric. A tiny lace trim is stitched to the side of the entredeux between the entredeux and the pintucks. These trims travel over the shoulder to the back of the round yoke. Entredeux and tiny lace edging finish the neckline of the dress. Entredeux is also used to join the round yoke to the body of the dress. The back of the dress is closed with three tiny pink buttons and button loops. The long sleeves end in a wide, lace trimmed cuff. The cuff features a row of insertion, beading and insertion lined with the pink batiste. A row of tiny edging finishes the bottom of the sleeve. The fancy band is a repeat of the side portions of the round yoke with entredeux, beading, insertion, beading, and entredeux. Tiny lace edging is stitched at the top and the bottom of the entredeux. The bottom of the fancy band is made of pink batiste with pyramid French lace wing needle pin stitched to the batiste making an inverted, half diamond on this interesting skirt treatment. Pink ribbons are run through all of the beading on this dress and a pink bow is stitched below the double needle pintucks in the center front of the round yoke.

- **All pattern pieces and templates found in pull-out section**
- **Color photograph on page 23**

Supplies

Fabric - Batiste	1 yd.
Lace Insertion (5/8")	2-1/2 yds.
Tatted Edging (3/8")	4 yds.
Lace Edging (1-1/2")	1-1/4 yds.
Lace Galloon (2")	1-1/4 yds.
Entredeux	6 yds.
Lace Beading	5 yds.
Ribbon (to fit beading)	5-1/2 yds.

Notions: Two spools of lightweight sewing thread; 2.0/80 or 1.6/70 double needle; Velcro™, snaps or tiny buttons for back closure

Optional Notions: Seven or nine groove pintuck foot and a 100 wing needle for hemstitching

Pattern Pieces Required: Front Round Yoke, Back Round Yoke, Round Yoke Sleeve and Barrel Cuff

Template Required: Round Yoke Skirt Template

All seams 1/4" unless otherwise indicated. Stitch seam in place and overcast the seam allowances with a zigzag or serge.

A. Cutting

1. Cut two sleeves and two barrel cuffs. Cut two fabric rectangles 22" wide by the following lengths **(fig. 1)**:

Doll Sizes	17-1/2"	18-1/2"	19-1/2"	21-1/2"
Skirt	8-1/4"	8-3/4"	10-1/4"	11"

   (These length are to be used with a 4-1/2" fancy band.)

2. Transfer back facing markings and X's on the back yoke pieces.

B. Constructing Bodice

1. Cut two pieces of beading 72" long and one piece of insertion lace 72" long. Attach the beading on each side of the insertion using the technique lace to lace **(fig. 2)**.

2. Cut two pieces of entredeux 72" long. Trim the fabric edge from one side of the entredeux. Attach the trimmed entredeux to the beading using the technique "entredeux to lace" **(fig. 3)**. Weave ribbon through the beading. The excess ribbon will be used later. This created lace strip will be used on each side of the pintucked panel of the front yoke, on each side of the back yoke and for the skirt fancy band.

3. Cut a strip of fabric 2-1/2" by 6" to be pintucked. Using a double needle, start the pintucks in the center of the fabric, parallel to the 6" side. Stitch a total of nine pintucks about 1/16" apart. The total width of the nine pintucks is about 5/8". Trim the fabric on each side of the outer pintuck to 5/8" **(fig. 4)**.

4. Cut two 6" pieces from the created lace strip stitched in step 2. Attach the 6" strips to each side of the pintucked fabric using the technique "entredeux to fabric" **(fig. 5)**.

5. Place tatted edging next to the pintucks, butted to the entredeux. Stitch in place with a small zigzag **(fig. 6)**.

6. Cut two pieces of fabric 3" wide by 6" long. Attach a fabric piece to each side of the created rectangle using the technique "entredeux to fabric". Press **(fig. 7)**.

7. Trace the front yoke on the created rectangle with the center pintuck along the center front of the yoke. Stitch 1/8" inside the drawn lines **(fig. 8)**. Cut out the yoke on the lines. Transfer the X's for sleeve placements. Set aside **(fig. 9)**.

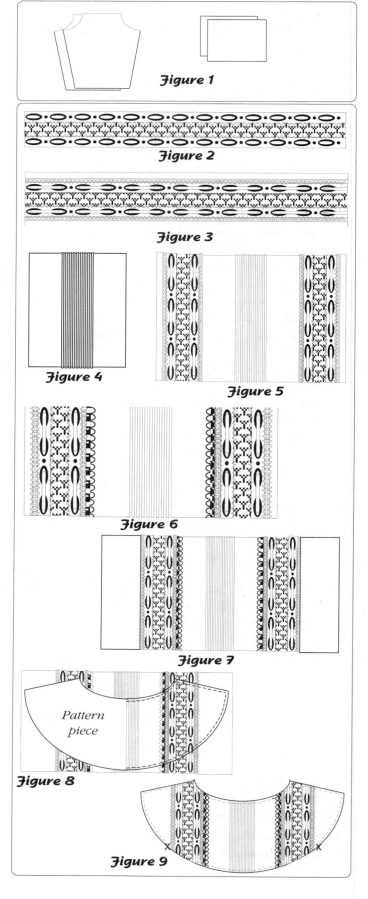

Figure 1

Figure 2

Figure 3

Figure 4

Figure 5

Figure 6

Figure 7

Pattern piece

Figure 8

Figure 9

8. Cut two 6" pieces from the created lace strip stitched in Step 2 for the back yokes. Cut two pieces of fabric 1" wide by 6" long. Fold the strip in half and press **(fig. 10)**. Now the strips are 1/2" by 6". Place the cut edges of the fabric piece to the lace strip and attach using the technique "entredeux to fabric." Cut two fabric strips 3" by 6". Attach to the other side of the lace strip using the technique "entredeux to fabric." Place the two created pieces right sides together, matching the corresponding fabric pieces. Place the folded fabric edge along the back fold line on the back yoke pattern **(fig. 11)**. Trace the yoke on the created rectangles. Stitch 1/8" inside the drawn lines. Cut out the back yokes on the lines **(fig. 12)**. Transfer the X's for sleeve placements. Set aside.

9. Attach a strip of entredeux to each back yoke shoulder using the technique "entredeux to fabric," using a 1/4" seam. Press away from the yoke **(fig. 13)**.

10. Place the front bodice to the back bodice, right sides together, at the shoulders. Stitch in place using the technique "entredeux to fabric" and a 1/4" seam **(fig. 14)**.

11. Cut a piece of entredeux 1" larger than the measurement around the lower, outer edge of the yokes (back facings extended). If one fabric edge of the entredeux does not measure 1/4", trim to 1/4". Place clips in the 1/4" fabric edge to allow the entredeux to curve. Attach the entredeux to the yokes using the technique entredeux to fabric **(fig. 15)**.

12. Finish the neck with entredeux and tatting. Refer to "Neck Finishes - c. Entredeux to Flat Lace or Tatting" found on page 35.

B. Sleeves

1. Cut two pieces of insertion lace, one piece of beading and one piece of ribbon 12" long. Stitch the insertion on each side of the beading using the technique lace to lace. Weave the ribbon through the beading.

2. Cut the lace strip in half. Fold the barrel cuff in half and place the edge of the lace strip along the fold line of each barrel cuff. Stitch in place along each side of the lace with a small zigzag **(fig. 16)**.

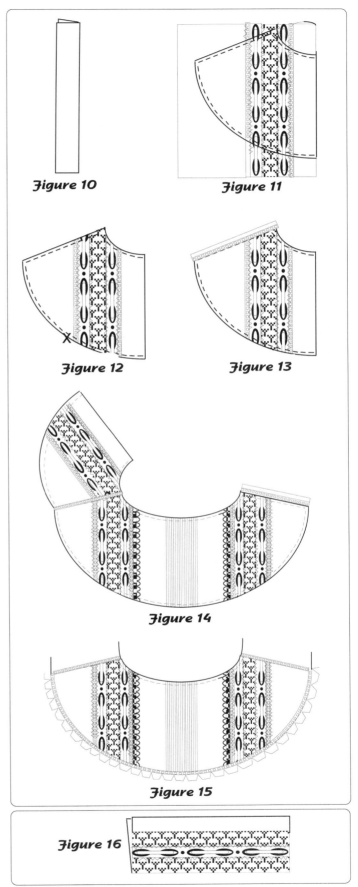

Figure 10

Figure 11

Figure 12

Figure 13

Figure 14

Figure 15

Figure 16

3. Stitch tatting to the fold of each cuff piece using a small zigzag. Trim the upper part of the cuff 1/4" from the top edge of the lace strip **(fig. 17)**.

4. Run two gathering rows in the lower edge of each sleeve **(fig. 18)**.

5. Gather the sleeve to fit the cuff. Stitch the cuff to the sleeve using a 1/4" seam **(fig. 19)**.

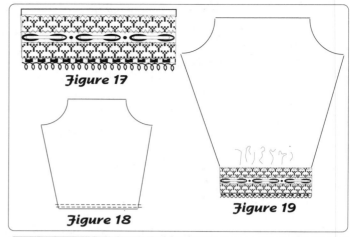

Figure 17

Figure 18

Figure 19

C. Fancy Skirt Band

1. Cut a strip of fabric 45" wide by 2-1/2".

2. Attach the fancy band created in section B - Step 2 to the fabric strip using the technique "entredeux to fabric."

3. Cut a strip of lace galloon 45" long. Galloon lace is attached in the following manner:

a) Place the lace on the fabric strip, wrong side of lace to right side of fabric overlapping the lace and fabric so that the total width from the top of the fabric to the end of the lace is 3-1/4" **(fig. 20)**.

b) Stitch the top edge of the lace in place with a small zigzag. Optional: A wing needle hem stitch can be used to stitch the lace in place.

c) Trim the excess fabric from behind the lace. This completes the fancy band.

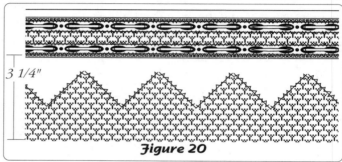

3 1/4"

Figure 20

D. Finishing the Dress

1. Fold the skirt rectangles in half. Place the skirt pattern along the top edge of the skirt pieces matching the fold of the fabric with the fold of the pattern. Cut away the top to create the curve and the armhole **(fig. 21)**.

2. Place the sleeves to the skirt right sides together with the armhole of the sleeves to the armhole of the skirt. Stitch in place using a 1/4" seam **(fig. 22)**.

3. Cut a 3-1/2" slit down the center back of the skirt. Place a placket in the slit. Refer to "Placket - a. Continuous Lap Placket or b. Continuous Lap Placket with Lace Insertion" found on page 42.

4. Run two gathering rows in the top of the skirt/ sleeves at 1/4" and 1/8". Remember that one side of the placket is folded to the inside of the skirt and the other side is left extended **(fig. 23)**.

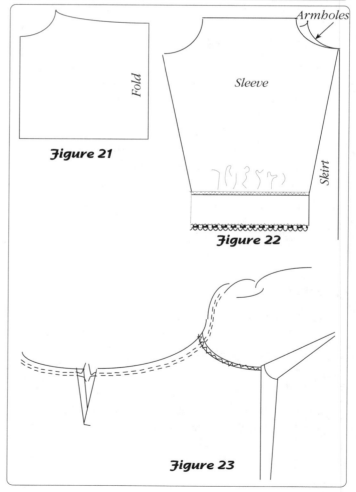

Fold

Figure 21

Armholes

Sleeve

Skirt

Figure 22

Figure 23

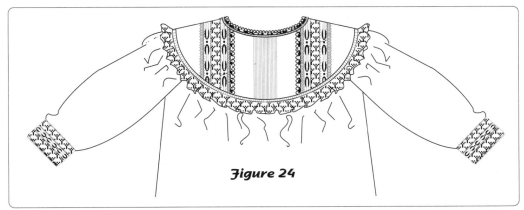

Figure 24

Gather the skirt to fit the bodice matching the sleeve seam markings on the yoke with the sleeve seams.

5. Stitch the yoke to the skirt/sleeves using a 1/4" seam and the technique "entredeux to gathered fabric."

6. Gather 1-1/2" wide edging to fit around yoke. Attach along yoke to skirt/sleeve seam **(fig. 24)** with a narrow zigzag. Turn edges to inside at yoke backs. Stitch one side seam in place.

7. Stitch the fancy band to the bottom of the skirt using the technique "entredeux to fabric" **(fig. 25)**.

8. Place the tatted edging on both sides of the fancy band against the entredeux **(fig. 26)**. Stitch in place using a small zigzag.

9. Stitch the second side seam in place.

10. Attach Velcro™, buttons and button-holes or snaps to the back of the bodice to close the dress.

11. Cut two pieces of ribbon 7" long. Tie each piece of ribbon in a bow and stitch in place by hand along the beading of the fancy band. The bows are placed 9" apart, 4-1/2" on each side of the center front. Tie the remaining ribbon into a bow and stitch in place by hand at the center front along the yoke seam. Trim the ribbon tails to fall just below the fancy band.

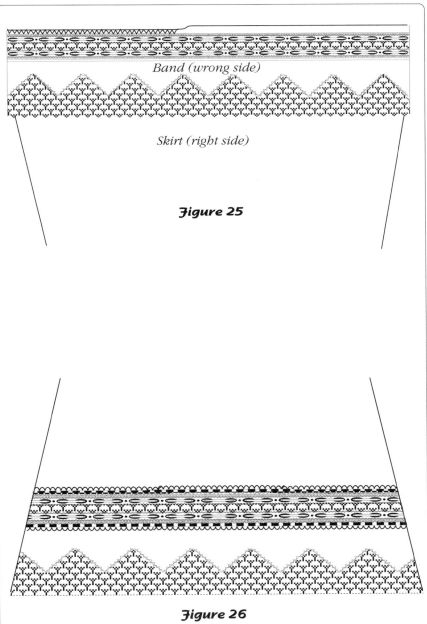

Band (wrong side)

Skirt (right side)

Figure 25

Figure 26

Smocked Bishop Dress

We asked designer Chery Williams who is noted for her bishop designs to design a matching doll dress to go along with her adorable children's patterns. What could be sweeter than making matching doll/daughter or doll/grand-daughter dresses? This precious long sleeved bishop is very easy to make with its pale green smocking design which has simple smocking with two-step waves. The sleeves are gathered with elastic and the open back has Velcro for its closing. A bias binding finishes the top of the neck and the sleeves are simply hemmed with a straight stitch from the sewing machine. Even though Velcro isn't usually used when making dresses for competition, it is certainly handy for little hands to dress and undress a doll. Of course you could use beauty pins, snaps or buttonholes and buttons to close the back of this elegant and classic style. For more information on Chery Williams patterns which match this dress contact Chery Williams Patterns, P.O. Box 190234, Birmingham, AL 35219, (205-290-2700).

Supplies

Fabric - Broadcloth 1 yd.

- **All pattern pieces and templates found in pull-out section**
- **Color photograph on page 28**

Notions: Lightweight sewing thread; Velcro™, snaps or tiny buttons for back closure; 1/8" elastic for sleeves; embroidery floss and #7 or #8 crewel needle for smocking

Pattern Pieces Required: Bishop Dress Front; Bishop Dress Back; Bishop Sleeve, long or short (add 1/2" to the sleeve length before cutting); smocking graph and instructions on page 151

All seams 1/4" unless otherwise indicated. Stitch seam in place and overcast the seam allowances with a zigzag or serge, unless otherwise indicated.

A. Cutting and Pleating

1. Cut one dress front on the fold, two dress backs on the selvage, and two sleeves **(fig. 1)**. A bias neck strip and a placket strip will be cut later.

2. Transfer the notches to the front, backs and sleeves. Also transfer the placket marking to the backs. Mark the center front at the top edge to aid in centering smocking.

3. Sew the sleeves to the dress front and backs **(fig. 2)**, matching the notches and having right sides together. Use a three-thread serge or a pressed open seam, no French seams.

4. Refer to the pleating **(fig. 3)** instructions on page 217 and pleat the following number of rows for each size:

Doll Sizes	17-1/2"	18-1/2"	19-1/2"	21-1/2"
Pleated Rows	6	6	6	7
Smocked Rows	4	4	4	5

5. Tie-off the top two pleating threads **(fig. 4)** to the measurement given in "Neck Finishes - f. Bias Neck Bindings for Bishop Garments, step 1" (omitting the reference to the placket) found on page 37.

B. Shaping and Smocking

1. Shape and block the dress **(fig. 5)** according to the instructions in "Blocking" found on page 215.

2. Smock the dress **(fig. 6)**, using the graph and instructions for the design "Sara's Simple Smocking" found on page 151.

C. Placket and Neck Binding

1. To apply the placket **(fig. 7)** to the center back seam, refer to "Plackets - c. Continuous Placket in a Seam or d. Easy Placket in a Seam" on page 43.

2. To apply the bias neck binding **(fig. 8)**, refer to "Neck Finishes - f. Bias Neck Bindings for Bishop Garments" on page 37. If necessary, adjust the top two pleating threads to the measurements given.

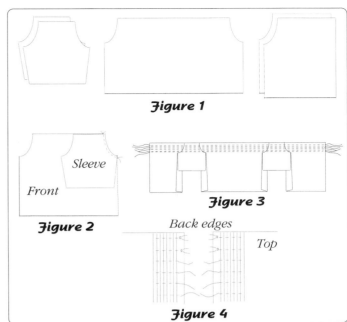

Figure 1

Sleeve

Front

Figure 2

Figure 3

Back edges

Top

Figure 4

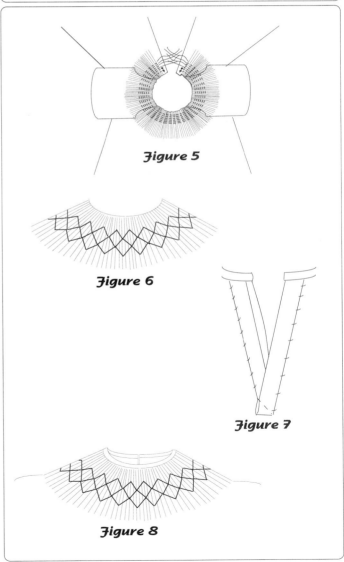

Figure 5

Figure 6

Figure 7

Figure 8

D. Sleeves

1. Narrow-hem the sleeves, using one of the following methods:

   a. Topstitch 1/8" from the bottom edge of the sleeve. Turn up to the inside and press, with the stitches on the fold. Turn up 1/8" again, press and stitch in place with a short straight stitch **(fig. 9)**.

   b. Finish the bottom edge of the sleeve by serging. Turn up the serged edge to the inside, press and stitch in place with a short straight stitch.

2. On the wrong side, use a fabric marker to draw a line across the sleeve, 1" from the finished bottom edge.

3. To apply the elastic to the sleeve **(fig. 10)**, refer to "Sleeve Bands and Ruffles - g. Gathered Sleeve with Elastic and Lace," Steps 3 and 4 on page 41, omitting the lace.

E. Finishing the Dress

1. With right sides together, stitch the sleeve/side seams of the dress, matching the bottom edges of the sleeves and the underarm seams **(fig. 11)**.

2. Finish the bottom edge of the dress by topstitching 1/8" from the edge, or by serging the edge. Turn 1/8" to the inside along the stitched or serged line and press.

3. The pattern allows a 3" hem, or the hem may be adjusted for a specific doll. Turn the hem allowance to the inside, pin and press. Hem the dress by hand, or with a machine blind-hem **(fig. 12)**.

4. Attach velcro™, buttons and buttonholes or snaps to the back placket to close the dress.

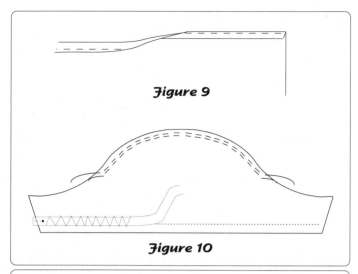

Figure 9

Figure 10

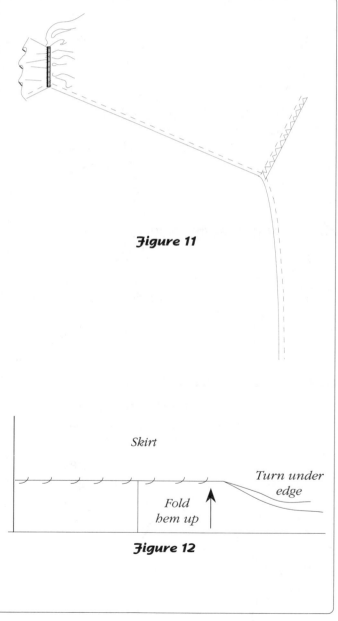

Figure 11

Skirt

Turn under edge

Fold hem up

Figure 12

Sara's Simple Smocking

(Smocked Bishop Dress)

Supplies: DMC floss - aqua; #8 crewel needle. Smock with 3 strands of floss.

Follow the graph closely while smocking.

Pleat 5 rows. Smock 6.

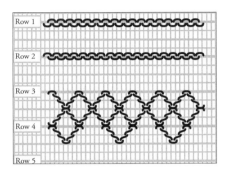

(Smocked Bishop Dress graph)

Step 1. Beginning on Row 1, cable across starting with a down cable in the same color floss as the fabric. This row will be used in construction and will not show.

Step 2. Cable across Row 2, starting with an up cable.

Step 3. Between Rows 3 and 3-1/2, work two-step waves.

Step 4. Between Rows 3-1/2 and 4, work two-step forming diamonds.

Step 5. Between Rows 4 and 4-1/2 work two-step waves. See graph for placement.

Smocked High Yoke Dress

Of all the smocking styles, I think this one is my favorite. I love the high yoke dress with smocking below the front yoke. The back yokes are lower than the front. This precious little white dress would be so cute in a matching doll/daughter or doll/granddaughter outfit. The smocking design is in a deep peach and there are three little hearts in-between two rows of cables. The sleeves are adorable with their two rows of cables and a pink silk ribbon bow tied in the middle. There is white French lace on the bottom of each sleeve and the neckline is finished with a bias binding. The back is closed with Velcro and it has a nice placket in the skirt so little hands can dress and undress the doll very easily. Of course, the back could also be closed with snaps, beauty pins or buttonholes and buttons.

Supplies

Batiste 1 yd.

Lace Edging (5/8") 2/3 yd.

Silk Ribbon (4mm) 1/2 yd.

- **All pattern pieces and templates found in pull-out section**
- **Color photograph on page 13**

Notions: Lightweight sewing thread; Velcro™, snaps or tiny buttons for closure; DMC floss for smocking; baby piping for front yoke; wash-out basting tape

Pattern Pieces Required: High Yoke Front, Mid-Yoke Back, Elbow-Length Sleeve, smocking graph and instructions for "Peach Hearts" found on page 155

Template Required: Armhole Guide

All seams 1/4" unless otherwise indicated. Stitch seam in place and overcast the seam allowances with a zigzag or serge, unless otherwise indicated.

A. Cutting

1. Cut two back yokes on the selvage and one front yoke on the fold **(fig. 1)**.

2. Before cutting the sleeves, trace a whole pattern piece, so that the sleeves will not be cut on the fold. Straighten the bottom edge of the sleeve pattern by drawing a line straight across, from one side edge to the other. Cut two sleeves **(fig. 2)**.

3. Cut one front skirt piece, 36" wide by the following length:

Doll Sizes	17-1/2"	18-1/2"	19-1/2"	21-1/2"
Skirt Length	13-3/4"	14-1/4"	15-1/4"	16-1/2"

4. Cut one back skirt piece, 24" wide by the following length:

Doll Sizes	17-1/2"	18-1/2"	19-1/2"	21-1/2"
Skirt Length	12-3/4"	13-3/8"	14-3/8"	15-5/8"

5. Mark the centers of the skirt pieces at the top and bottom edges, and use the armhole guide to draw the armholes, but do not cut the armholes **(fig. 3)**.

B. Pleating and Smocking

1. For all sizes, pleat four rows across the top of the front skirt piece, using half-spaces if available. Refer to "Pleating and Smocking" found on page 208 for tips and general instructions. On the top pleating row, remove the pleating thread inside the armhole area so that the armhole will not be smocked. Remove the pleating threads on every row below the top row, stopping at the same pleat on each row **(fig. 4)**.

2. For all sizes, pleat four rows across the bottom of each sleeve, with the bottom row 1" from the cut edge **(fig. 5)**. Half spaces are not necessary. Leave long pleating threads so that the sleeves can be flattened after pleating. Remove the pleating threads from 1/2" at each side edge.

3. Flatten the sleeves and run two rows of gathering threads across the top edge, 1/8" and 1/4" from the edge **(fig. 6)**.

4. Attach 5/8" edging to the bottom of each sleeve, using the technique "lace to fabric." Refer to figure 6.

5. Smock the skirt and sleeves, using the graph and instructions for "Peach Hearts" found on page 155. Remember that the top and bottom pleating rows are holding rows and will not be smocked **(fig. 7)**.

C. Yokes and Neck Finish

1. Place the front yoke to the back yokes at the shoulder seams, right sides together, and stitch **(fig. 8)**.

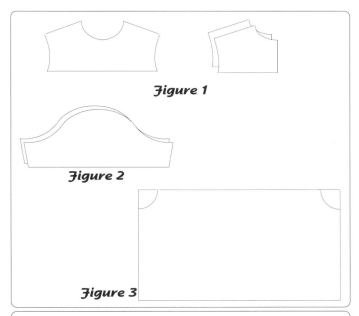

Figure 1

Figure 2

Figure 3

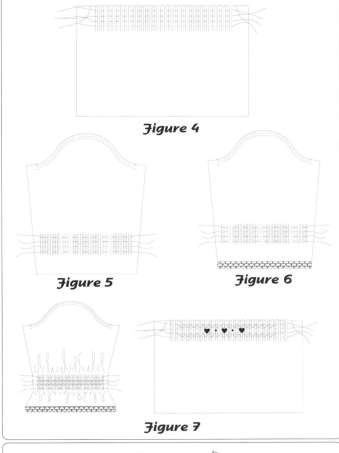

Figure 4

Figure 5

Figure 6

Figure 7

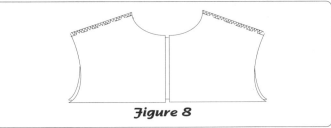

Figure 8

2. Finish the neck edge, referring to "Neck Finishes - e. Bias Neck Binding" found on page 36.

3. Cut a piece of baby piping the length of the front yoke bottom edge. Trim the seam allowance of the piping to 1/4" (**fig. 9**).

4. Place the basting tape to the wrong side of the piping seam allowance (**fig. 10**).

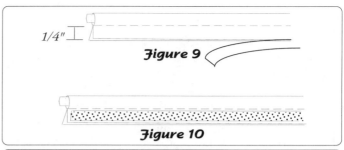

Figure 9

Figure 10

D. Skirt

1. Choose one skirt piece to be the skirt back. Cut a 4-1/2" slit at the center on the top edge of the piece and apply a placket. Refer to "Plackets - a. Continuous Lap Placket" found on page 42.

2. Run two rows of gathering threads across the top of each skirt piece, 1/8" and 1/4" from the edge (**fig. 11**). Stop the stitching at the placket seam line on the back pieces.

3. Turn the bottom seam allowance of the yoke to the inside. Adjust the gathers in the front skirt top to fit the bottom edge of the yoke (**fig. 12**). Remove the paper from the basting tape and stick the yoke to the skirt, placing the piping just above the top row of smocking.

4. Be sure that the piping is straight with the smocking, then use a zipper foot to stitch "in-the- ditch" between the piping and the yoke (refer to fig. 12).

5. Place the back skirt to the back yokes, right sides together. The placket edges should meet the back fold line of the yokes (**fig. 13**). Wrap the back facings to the outside along the fold line, sandwiching the skirt between the yoke and the facing. Stitch in place and press the yokes up, flipping the facings to the inside.

D. Finishing the Dress

1. Pin the sleeves to the armholes and adjust the gathers to fit, stopping the gathers at the yoke seam lines. Stitch the sleeves in place (**fig. 14**).

2. Place the sleeve/side seams with right sides together. Match the sleeve edges and the bottom edges and stitch (**fig. 15**).

3. Press 1/4" to the inside along the bottom edge of the hem. Turn a 3" hem to the inside and press, then pin in place. Stitch the hem in place with a blind-hem, by hand or machine.

4. Cut the silk ribbon in half. Tie a small bow in each piece of ribbon and attach the bows to the outside of each sleeve, between the rows of smocking (**fig. 16**).

5. Apply Velcro™, snaps or tiny buttons and buttonholes to the back opening, with the right side lapping over the left side.

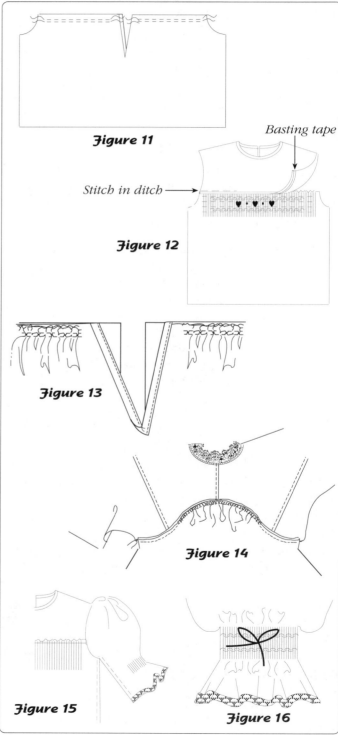

Figure 11

Basting tape

Stitch in ditch

Figure 12

Figure 13

Figure 14

Figure 15

Figure 16

Peach Hearts *(smocking graph for Smocked High-Yoke Dress)*

Supplies: DMC floss - peach; #8 crewel needle; 12" of 2mm silk ribbon to match floss for ties on sleeves. Smock with 3 strands of floss. Follow the graph closely while smocking.

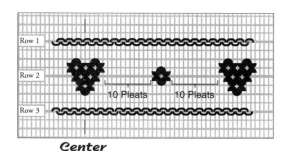

Center

Smocking graph for Smoked High Yoke Dress

Dress

Pleat 7 half rows; smock 3-1/2 full rows.

Step 1. On Row 1/2, cable across in the same color floss as the fabric. This row will be used in construction and will not show.

Step 2. Cable across Row 1 starting with a down cable.

Step 3. Cable across Row 3 starting with an up cable.

Step 4. Start stacking the center heart in the center of the skirt. Count over 10 pleats and work flowerette. Count over 10 pleats and work heart.

Step 5. Hearts - Starting on Row 1-1/2 work the top row of the heart. Continue stitching heart following graph. The hearts are worked between Row 1-1/2 and 2-1/2.

Step 6. Flowerettes - Starting on Row 2 work three cable stitches: down, up, down. Work three cable stitches below these stitches: up, down, up. Refer to graph.

Sleeves

Pleat 4 rows. Smock 2 rows.

Step 1. Starting and stopping 1" from the edge of the sleeve, cable across Row 2 starting with an up cable.

Step 2. Starting and stopping 1" from the edge of the sleeve, cable across Row 3 starting with a down cable.

Step 3. Cut the silk ribbon in half. Thread the ribbon through the four center pleats of the sleeves and tie in a bow.

Smocked Peasant Blouse

This blouse with eye-catching honeycomb smocking sports an unusual color combination taken from its matching skirt. Five rows of smocking grace the sleeves and neckline. A pink scalloped Swiss trim is stitched on around the neckline and the sleeves. An elastic casing nips in the blouse at the waist. Buttons and loops close the back.

- **All pattern pieces and templates found in pull-out section**
- **Color photograph on page 28**

Supplies

Fabric Requirements: batiste, all sizes, 1/4 yd.

Notions: Lightweight sewing thread, four 1/4" shank buttons for back closure, machine embroidery thread to edge the neck and sleeves, DMC embroidery floss in three colors, elastic thread, 1/4" wide elastic

Pattern Pieces Required: Bishop Blouse Front, Bishop Blouse Back and Bishop Short Sleeve, smocking graph and instructions found on page 159

All seams 1/4" unless otherwise indicated. Stitch seam in place and overcast the seam allowances with a zigzag or serge, unless otherwise indicated.

A. Cutting and Pleating

1. Cut one blouse front on the fold, two blouse backs on the selvage, and two sleeves **(fig. 1)**.

2. Transfer the notches to the front, backs and sleeves. Draw a line across each front and back piece, 1-1/2" above the bottom edge, for waistline elastic placement. Mark the center front at the top edge to aid in centering smocking.

3. Sew the sleeves to the blouse front and backs, matching the notches and having right sides together. Use a three-thread serge or a pressed open seam, no French seams **(fig. 2)**.

4. Finish the neck and sleeve edges with machine embroidered scallops, or with a tiny rolled edge made with a wide zigzag (refer to "lace to fabric" on page 230, omitting the reference to the lace). Stitch 1/2" from the fabric edge for scallops (a stabilizer may be necessary) and trim away the excess. For a rolled edge, trim away 1/4" and zigzag along the cut edge. The thread may match the fabric or be a decorative contrast **(fig. 3)**.

5. Refer to the pleating instructions on page 217 and pleat four rows with half-spaces across the bottom edge of each sleeve, letting the finished bottom edge run through the second empty needle groove. The top and bottom rows are stabilizer rows and will not be smocked **(fig. 4)**.

6. Refer to the pleating instructions on page 217 and pleat five rows with half-spaces at the neck edge, using elastic thread in the top pleated row. The finished neck edge should run through the first empty needle groove. The bottom row is the stabilizer row and will not be smocked. Refer to figure 4.

7. Remove the pleating threads from 1/2" at each sleeve edge and from 3/4" at the back neck edges.

8. Tie-off the top two pleating threads **(fig. 5)** to the measurement given in "Neck Finishes - f. Bias Neck Bindings for Bishop Garments, Step 1" (omitting the reference to the placket) found on page 37.

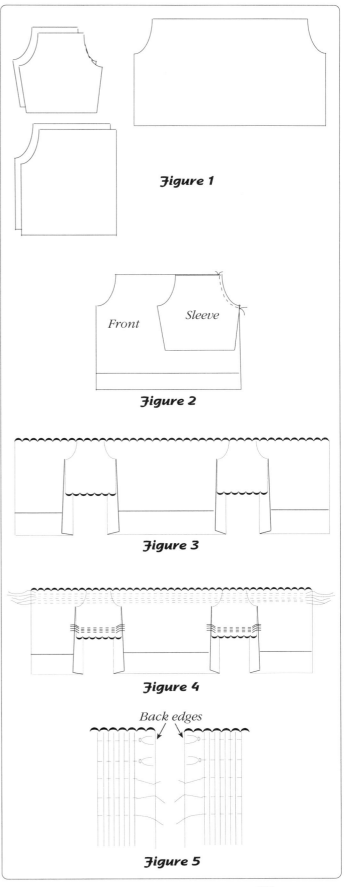

Figure 1

Front   *Sleeve*

Figure 2

Figure 3

Figure 4

Back edges

Figure 5

B. Shaping and Smocking

1. Shape and block **(fig. 6)** the blouse according to the instructions in "Blocking" found on page 215.

2. Smock the blouse **(fig. 7)**, using the graph and instructions found on page 159.

C. Back Facings

1. Press 1/4" to the wrong side at each back edge, then press another 1/2" to form the back facings **(fig. 8)**.

2. Stitch the facings in place close to the first fold.

D. Finishing the Blouse

1. With right sides together, stitch the sleeve/side seams of the blouse, matching the bottom edges of the sleeves and the underarm seams **(fig. 9)**. Finish the bottom with a tiny rolled hem or turn under 1/8" and 1/8" again and hand stitch **(fig. 10)**.

2. Cut a strip of fabric on the lengthwise grain, 7/8" wide and as long as the width of the blouse, plus 2".

3. Press 1/4" to the wrong side along each long edge of the strip **(fig. 11)**. Center the strip over the waistline elastic marking and stitch in place close to both edges **(fig. 12)**.

4. Cut a piece of 1/4" elastic to the following length and thread it through the casing, stitching through the ends at the center back edges. (Refer to figure 12).

Doll Sizes	17-1/2"	18-1/2"	19-1/2"	21-1/2"
Elastic Length	9"	10-1/2"	10"	12"

5. Attach buttons to the left side and make thread loops on the right side of the back edges to close the blouse.

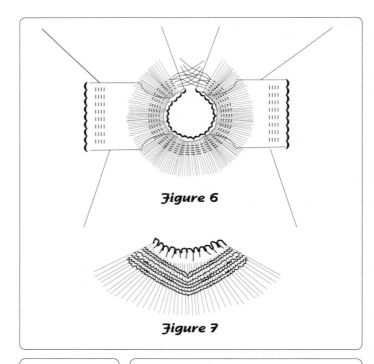

Figure 6

Figure 7

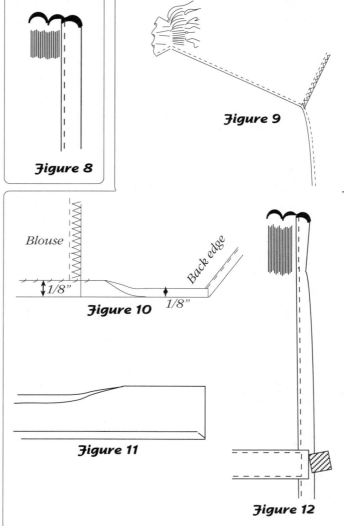

Figure 8

Figure 9

Figure 10

Figure 11

Figure 12

Smocked Peasant Blouse

Supplies: DMC floss - purple, hot pink and black; #8 crewel needle. Smock with 1 strand of floss.

Follow the graph closely while smocking.

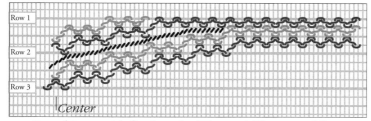

Smocking graph for Smocked Peasant Blouse neckline

Blouse Neckline

Pleat 5 rows; smock 3 rows. Remove the pleats from the back facing allowance.

Step 1. Using hot pink floss, begin at center front with an up cable on Row 1-3/4. Take 1 step down to Row 2, down cable, 2-step trellis up to Row 1-1/2, work a 1/4-space baby wave between Rows 1-1/2 and 1-3/4 (up cable, 1 step down to Row 1-3/4, down cable, 1 step up to Row 1-1/2), up cable, 1 step down to Row 1-3/4, down cable, 2-step trellis up to Row 1-1/4, 1/4-space baby wave between Rows 1-1/4 and 1-1/2, down cable, 2-step trellis up to Row 1, 1/4-space baby waves between Rows 1 and 1-1/4 to finish the row. Turn the work upside down and complete the other end of the row.

Step 2. Using purple floss, begin at center front with a down cable on Row 1-3/4, meeting the up cable of the previous smocking. 2-step trellis up to Row 1-1/4, 1/4 space baby wave between Rows 1-1/4 and 1-1/2, up cable, 1 step down to Row 1-1/2, down cable, 2-step trellis up to Row 1, 2 baby waves between Rows 1 and 1-1/4, end with an up cable on Row 1. Turn the work upside down and complete the other end of the row.

Step 3. Using purple floss, repeat step 2 beginning on Row 2-3/4. Repeat the trellis, baby wave combination for five complete patterns, ending on Row 1-1/4. Work baby waves between Rows 1-1/4 and 1-1/2 to finish the row. The up cables will be 1/4 space below the up cables of the upper smocked row, and the

down cables will be 1/4 space below the down cables of the upper smocked Row. Turn the work upside down and complete the other end of the row.

Step 4. Use hot pink floss and repeat step 1, beginning with an up cable on Row 2-3/4. Take 1 step down to Row 3, then repeat the trellis, baby wave combination for a total of five patterns, then work baby waves between Rows 1-1/2 and 1-3/4 to finish the row. The up cables will met the down cables of the previous row. Turn the work upside down and complete the other end of the row.

Step 5. Using the black floss, work a row of outline stitches between the two center smocking rows. Stop the outline stitch at the point where the baby waves begin to repeat across the rows. Turn the work upside down and complete the other end of the row.

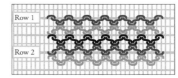

Smocking graph for Smocked Peasant Blouse sleeve

Sleeves

Pleat 4 rows, smock 2-1/4 rows. Remove the pleats at each sleeve edge to leave 1/2" of flat fabric.

Step 1. Work 1/4-space baby waves between Rows 1 and 1-1/4. Repeat between Rows 1-1/4 and 1-1/2, then between Rows 1-1/2 and 1-3/4, until the last row is worked between Rows 2 and 2-1/4. From top to bottom, the colors will be hot pink, purple, black, hot pink and purple.

Smocked Skirt With Underslip

Honeycomb smocking picks up the magnificent range of color in this printed skirt. Smocking, worked in shades of pink, lavender, and black, forms a V in front and is straight across in the back. The skirt incorporates 45 inches of fabric, which accounts for its lovely fullness. The waistband of the skirt is closed with two buttons and loops. The attached underslip is white batiste with a pink scalloped, Swiss trim stitched to the bottom. If your machine has scallop or other decorative finishing capabilities, the bottom of the underslip is an ideal place to make use of them.

- **All pattern pieces and templates found in pull-out section**
- **Color photograph on page 28**

Supplies

Fabric: Print fabric, all sizes, 1/3 yd.; batiste, all sizes, 1/3 yd.

Notions: Lightweight sewing thread, one plastic snap, machine embroidery thread for edging the slip, DMC floss in three colors for smocking the skirt, smocking graph and instructions for found on page 163

All seams 1/4" unless otherwise indicated. Stitch seam in place and overcast the seam allowances with a zigzag or serge, unless otherwise indicated.

A. Cutting

1. Cut one rectangle from the print fabric, 44" wide by the following length **(fig. 1)**:

Doll Sizes	17-1/2"	18-1/2"	19-1/2"	21-1/2"
Skirt Length	10"	10-1/2"	11"	12"

2. Cut one rectangle from the slip fabric, 44" wide by the following length **(fig. 1a)**:

Doll Sizes	17-1/2"	8-1/2"	19-1/2"	21-1/2"
Slip Length	8-1/2"	9"	9-1/2"	10-1/2"

3. Cut one waistband 1-1/4" wide by the following length:

Doll Sizes	17-1/2"	18-1/2"	19-1/2"	21-1/2"
Waistband Length	9-3/4"	11-1/4"	10-3/4"	12-3/4"

B. Pleating and Smocking the Skirt

1. Following the pleating instructions on page 217, roll the skirt rectangle onto a dowel **(fig. 2)** and pleat six rows **(fig. 2a)**. The first pleating row should be 1/4" from the top edge of the fabric.

2. Remove the pleating threads from 1/4" at each back edge and tie off the top two threads **(fig. 3)** to the waistband length given in step 3 of part A above.

3. Smock the skirt with the graph found on page 163 **(fig. 4)**.

C. Slip Construction

1. Finish the bottom edge of the slip with a decorative machine scallop, or a tiny rolled edge made with a wide zigzag (refer to "lace to fabric," omitting the reference to the lace) **(fig. 5)**. Stitch 1/2" from the fabric edge for scallops (a stabilizer may be neccessary) and trim away the excess. For a rolled edge, trim away 1/4" and zigzag along the cut edge.

2. Run two rows of gathering threads along the top edge of the slip, 1/8" and 1/4" from the edge. Refer to figure 5.

3. Finish the back edges of the slip with a tiny rolled edge (refer to "lace to fabric," omitting the reference to the lace) **(fig. 5)**.

4. Stitch the center back seam, beginning at the bottom with right sides together, and stopping 3-1/2" below the top edge **(fig. 6)**. Use a 1/2" seam allowance and press the seam open, allowing the 1/2" allowances to press to the inside above the seam **(fig. 7)**.

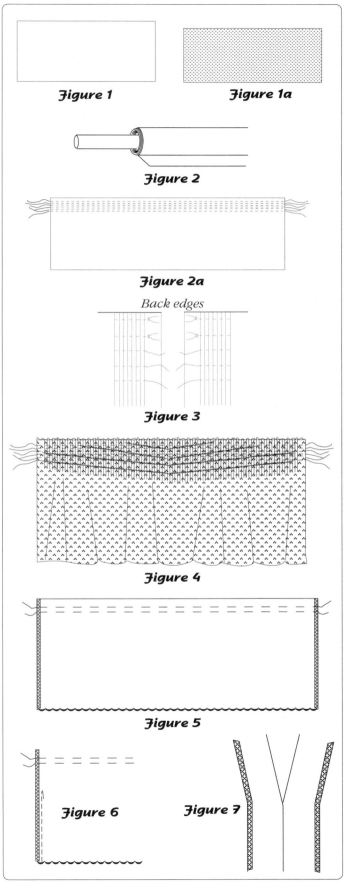

Figure 1

Figure 1a

Figure 2

Figure 2a

Back edges

Figure 3

Figure 4

Figure 5

Figure 6

Figure 7

D. Skirt Construction

1. Begin at the bottom with right sides together and sew the center back seam, stopping 3" below the top edge **(fig. 8)** and apply a placket, referring to "Plackets - c. Continuous Placket in a Seam" on page 43 **(fig. 9)**. The skirt will lap right over left.

2. Press 1/4" to the wrong side along the bottom edge of the skirt piece, then press a 1-1/2" hem to the wrong side. Blind-hem by hand or machine **(fig. 10)**.

3. Slide the slip into the skirt, with the right side of the slip against the wrong side of the skirt. Let the folded edges of the slip meet the placket stitching lines of the skirt. Adjust the gathers of the slip to fit the waist of the skirt, stopping the gathers 1/2" from the slip edges. Baste the two layers together, with the top edges even. The slip will extend approximately 1/4" below the skirt hem **(fig. 11)**.

4. Pin the waistband to the top edge of the skirt/slip with the edges even and right sides together **(fig. 12)**. Let the placket edges stop 1/4" from the ends of the waistband.

5. Adjust the skirt/slip to fit the waistband by adjusting the pleating threads, and stitch in place. Press the gathers flat in the seam allowance and trim the seam to make neat the edges. Press the seam toward the waistband. Refer to figure 12.

6. Press 1/4" to the wrong side along the long unsewn edge of the waistband. Fold the band with right sides together so that the 1/4" fold meets the stitching line on the outside of the skirt.

7. Stitch across the ends of the waistband with a 1/4" seam. Stitch right next to but not through the placket edges **(fig. 13)**.

8. Turn the unsewn edge of the band to the inside and pin, so that the fold meets the seam line on the inside of the skirt. Whip in place by hand or stitch-in-the-ditch from the right side **(fig. 14)**.

9. Attach a button to the back left edge of the waistband and attach a thread loop to the right side, with the right side lapped over the left. Also attach another button and loop at the bottom of the smocked design, on the placket.

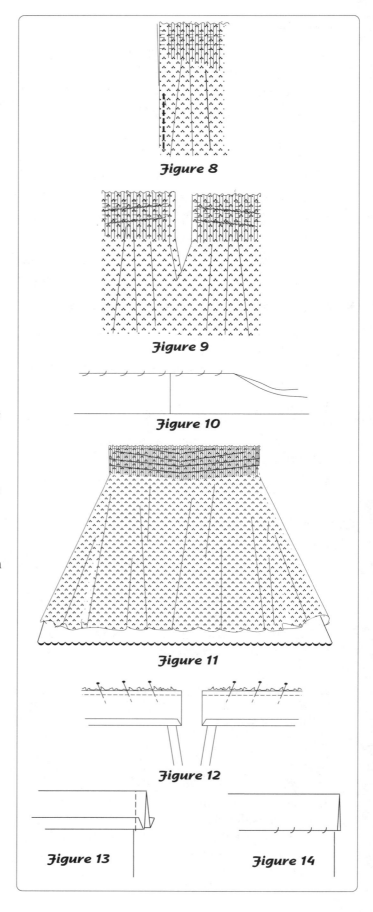

Figure 8

Figure 9

Figure 10

Figure 11

Figure 12

Figure 13

Figure 14

Smocked Skirt with Underslip

Supplies: DMC floss - purple, hot pink and black; #8 crewel needle. Smock with 1 strand of floss.

Follow the graph closely while smocking.

Smocking graph for Smocked Skirt

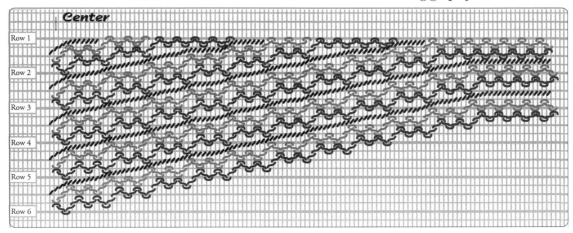

Skirt

Pleat 8 rows, smock 6. Remove the pleats from the center back seam allowance.

Step 1. Using purple floss, begin at center front with a down cable on Row 1-3/4. Repeat the 2-step trellis, 1/4-space baby wave from the blouse neckline instructions, completing two full patterns. Take a step up to Row 1 and end with an up cable. Turn the work upside down and complete the other end of the row.

Step 2. Use hot pink floss and begin at center front with an up cable. Take 1 step down to Row 2, down cable, work three 2-step trellis, 1/4-space baby wave combinations, take a step up to Row 1, up cable, then work three baby waves between Rows 1 and 1-1/4, ending on Row 1 with an up cable. Turn the work upside down and complete the other end of the row.

Step 3. Use purple floss and begin on Row 2-3/4 with a down cable. Work six trellis, baby wave combinations. Work one more baby wave between Rows 1 and 1-1/4, then end on Row 1 with an up cable. Turn the work upside down and complete the other end of the row.

Step 4. Using the hot pink floss, begin on Row 2-3/4 with an up cable. Work 1 step down to Row 3, then work seven trellis, baby wave combinations. Work three additional baby waves between Rows 1 and 1-1/4, then end on Row 1 with an up cable.

Turn the work upside down and complete the other end of the row.

Step 5. Use the purple floss and begin at center front on Row 3-3/4 with a down cable. Work ten trellis, baby wave combinations, then work baby waves between Rows 1 and 1-14 to the end of the row. Turn the work upside down and complete the other end of the row.

Step 6. Use the hot pink floss and begin at center front on Row 3-3/4 with an up cable. Take 1 step down to Row 4, then work ten trellis, baby wave combinations. Work baby waves between Rows 1-1/4 and 1-1/2 to the end of the row. Turn the work upside down and complete the other end of the row.

Step 7. Repeat steps 5 and 6, beginning at center front on Row 4-3/4 and working eleven trellis, baby wave combinations. Baby waves will be worked between Rows 1-3/4 and 2, and between Rows 2 and 2-1/4 to complete the smocking rows. Turn the work upside down and complete the other end of the row.

Step 8. Repeat steps 5 and 6, beginning at center front on row 5-3/4 and working twelve trellis, baby wave combinations. Baby waves will be worked between Rows 2-1/2 and 2-3/4, and between Rows 2-3/4 and 3 to complete the smocking rows. Turn the work upside down and complete the other end of the row.

Spoke Collar Cinderella Dress

Combining embroidery, Swiss dotted fabric, and a spoke collar, this to-the-waist dress is nothing short of spectacular! I can just imagine the squeals from your special little girl when she dresses her Götz dolls in this fantasy dress. Each of the five collar sections created by the lace spokes features embroidery worked in shades of peach, yellow and green. Each section has bullion rosebuds on it; the front panel has an arch of bullion rosebuds and leaves. Gathered French lace trims the collar's scalloped edges.

The 3-1/2 inch wide sash ties into a bow at the back of the dress; the ends are angled and trimmed with flat lace edging. At three places on the front of the dress, the sash has been gathered and secured with a beautiful variegated thread bullion rosebud and bullion leaves. The variegated threads go from shades of peach to yellow. The full, puffed sleeves are trimmed with entredeux, beading, entredeux and gathered lace at the bottom. Peach ribbon is run through the beading and tied in bows on each side. The skirt is gathered up at several points on the bottom and fastened with large bullion rosebuds and bullion leaves. Slightly gathered lace edging is stitched onto the bottom of the skirt. The dress closes in the back with three tiny buttons and loops.

- **All pattern pieces and templates found in pull-out section**
- **Color photograph on page 19**

Supplies

Fabric- Dotted Swiss	1 yd.
Satin	1/4 yd.
Entredeux 3/4 yd.	
Lace Insertion (1/2")	1/2 yd.
Lace Edging (3/4")	5 yds.
Lace Beading (1/2")	1 yd.
Ribbon (to fit beading)	1 yd.

Notions: Lightweight sewing thread, variegated peach/yellow floss, green floss and Velcro™, snaps or tiny buttons for back closure

Pattern Pieces Required: To-The-Waist Front Bodice, To-The-Waist Back Bodice, Elbow-Length Sleeve and Spoke Collar

All Seams 1/4" unless otherwise indicated. Stitch seam in place and overcast the seam allowances with a zigzag or serge.

A. Cutting

1. Cut one front bodice from the fold, two back bodices from the selvages, two sleeves **(fig. 1)**, and one fabric strip for the skirt 44-1/2" wide by the following length:

Doll Sizes	17-1/2"	18-1/2"	19-1/2"	21-1/2"
Skirt	8-1/4"	9"	9-1/2"	10-1/2"

2. Transfer fold line markings from the back bodice pattern to the back bodice pieces.

3. Cut one 10" square for the spoke collar.

4. Cut one sash 42" by 3-1/2".

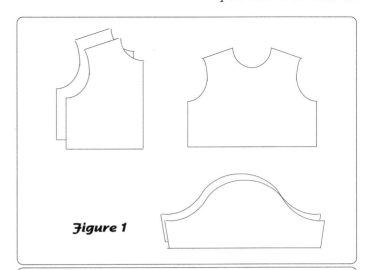

Figure 1

B. Constructing the Collar

1. Trace the collar pattern and lace template on the fabric rectangle **(fig. 2)**.

2. Place lace along the spoke template lines. Pin in place **(fig. 3)**.

3. Stitch along each side of the lace using a small zigzag. Refer to figure 3.

4. Gather 1-1/4 yds. of edging lace to fit the outer edge of the collar starting at the neck edge of the collar back.

5. Place the gathered lace along the template line and zigzag in place **(fig. 4)**.

6. Trim the fabric from behind the insertion and edging lace. Cut out the neck of the collar. Refer to figure 4. Set aside.

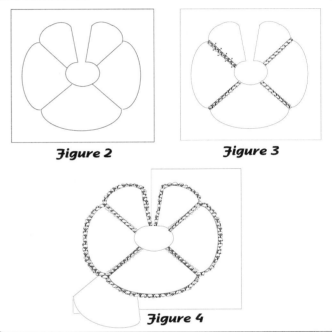

Figure 2   **Figure 3**

Figure 4

C. Constructing the Bodice

1. Place the front bodice to the back bodice right sides together at the shoulders. Stitch in place using a 1/4" seam **(fig. 5)**.

2. Place the wrong side of the collar to the right side of the bodice. Pin in place and treat as one layer of fabric **(fig. 6)**. Finish the neck with a bias binding. Cut the neck binding from the satin. Refer to "Neck Finishes - e. Bias Neck Binding" found on page 36.

3. Run two gathering rows in the top and bottom of each sleeve at 1/4" and 1/8" **(fig. 7)**.

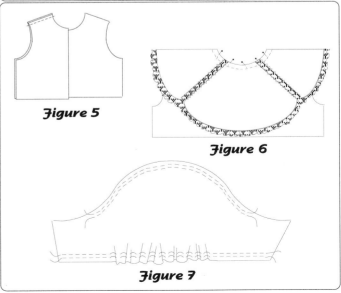

Figure 5

Figure 6

Figure 7

4. To create the sleeve bands **(fig. 8)**, cut two pieces of beading and four pieces of entredeux to the measurement given on the Sleeve Band Chart on page 37 for the elbow length sleeve.

5. Complete the sleeve using the directions for "Sleeve Bands and Ruffles - b. Entredeux, Beading, Entredeux and Gathered Edging Lace" found on page 38 **(fig. 9)**.

6. Gather the top of the sleeves to fit the arm opening of the bodice, matching the center of the sleeve with the shoulder seam of the bodice. Adjust the gathers in the top of the sleeve to fall 1-1/4" to 1-1/2" on either side of the shoulder seam **(fig. 10)**.

7. Stitch the sleeve to the bodice, right sides together using a 1/4" seam.

8. Place the sides/sleeves of the bodice right sides together. Stitch together using a 1/4" seam **(fig. 11)**.

D. Finishing the Skirt and Sash

1. Place a dot 2" from the end along one side of the sash. Cut from the lower edge of the sash to the dot, creating an angle **(fig. 12)**. Stitch flat edging lace along each angled end of the sash **(fig. 13)**. Trim the ends of the lace even with the long sides of the sash.

2. Finish the long sides of the sash and the ends of the lace with a rolled hem on the serger or zigzag (zig on the fabric and zag off the fabric, rolling the fabric edge. This is called a rolled and whipped edge). Set aside.

3. Gather the remaining edging lace to fit the lower edge of the skirt. Attach the gathered lace to the skirt edge using the technique "lace to fabric".

4. Place the back edges of the skirt together and stitch from the bottom edge, stopping 3-1/2" from the skirt top **(fig. 14)**. Backstitch.

5. Place a placket in the 3-1/2" opening. Refer to "Plackets - c. Continuous Placket or d. Easy Placket" found on page 43.

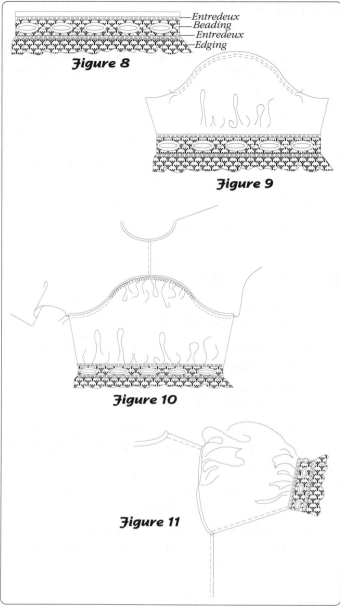

Entredeux
Beading
Entredeux
Edging

Figure 8

Figure 9

Figure 10

Figure 11

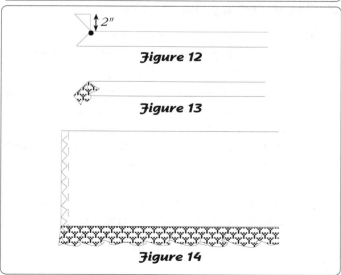

 2"

Figure 12

Figure 13

Figure 14

E. Finishing the Dress

1. Stitch two gathering rows in the top edge of the skirt. Remember that one side of the placket is folded to the inside of the skirt and the other side is left extended **(fig. 15)**.

2. Place the right side of the bodice to the right side of the skirt, matching the center of the bodice with the center of the skirt. Pin in place. Gather the skirt to fit the bodice. Distribute the gathers evenly **(fig. 16)**.

3. At the back edges of the skirt opening, wrap the back facings of the bodice over the open edges of the skirt. Pin in place **(fig. 17)**.

4. Stitch the skirt to the bodice using a 1/4" seam. Overcast the seam allowance.

5. To create the scalloped hem on the skirt, draw 1-1/2" lines with a fabric marker vertically along the skirt bottom starting on the center back seam **(fig. 18)**. Continue drawing the lines spaced 4" from each other. There will be a total of 11 lines around the bottom of the skirt.

6. Stitch along each line in the following manner: Starting at the lace/skirt seam take two stitches and back stitch to "tie off the seam" **(fig. 19)**; continue stitching along the drawn line with a long stitch used for gathering. Gather the line to 3/8" and tie off the gathering thread **(fig. 20)**.

7. Draw three lines across the sash, one in the center and the others 1-1/2" from center **(fig. 21)**. Stitch across the line as described in step 6. Gather to 1/2" and tie off **(fig. 22)**.

8. Cut the ribbon into two pieces and weave it through the beading at the sleeve. Tie the excess ribbon into bows.

9. Attach Velcro™, buttons and buttonholes or snaps to the back of the bodice to close the dress.

F. Embroidery

1. Stitch a bullion rose at the top of each gathered line on the skirt **(fig. 23)**. Each bullion rose consists of 10 bullion stitches with the center three stitches consisting of five wraps each, the middle four stitches consisting of two stitches with eight wraps and two stitches with 10 wraps, and the outer three stitches have 12 wraps each.

2. Stitch two bullion stitches (five wraps each) to form leaves on each side of the rose. Add one bullion stitch (five wraps each) and one French knot below leaves on each side.

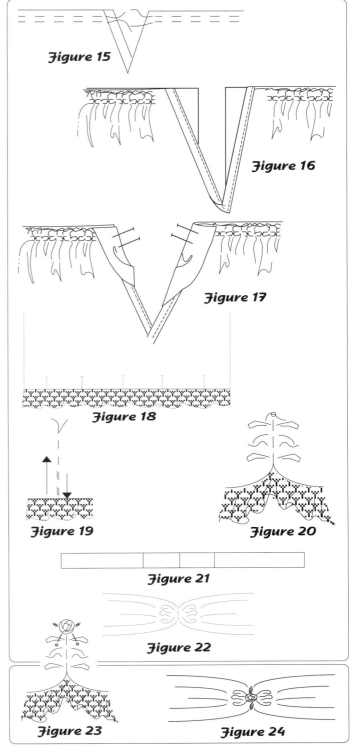

Figure 15

Figure 16

Figure 17

Figure 18

Figure 19

Figure 20

Figure 21

Figure 22

Figure 23

Figure 24

3. Stitch bullion roses along the gathering lines of the sash **(fig. 24)** as described in Step 1 and leaves as described in Step 2.

4. Stitch bullion roses, leaves and French knots using the embroidery template on the collar.

5. Center the sash to the center of the dress and baste in place along the three gathering lines.

Sunday School Blouse & Jumper

This adorable jumper and blouse ensemble is sure to take the prize at any doll show. The blouse is made of white broadcloth and has a Mandarin collar. The front of the blouse has five pleats in the front and a high yoke front and back. A man's shirt cuff finishes the bottom of the sleeves. The round yoke features children in red, yellow, black and white, applied using the technique shadow appliqué by machine. Black piping finishes the bottom of this round yoke. The dress is made of tiny black and white gingham. Madeira appliqué decorates the scalloped white portion of the bottom of the skirt, which is further enhanced by stitched musical notes with a treble clef sign at the left-hand side. The words, "Jesus loves the little children, all the children of the world, red, and yellow, black and white, they are precious in his sight," are stitched in on the bottom of the skirt.

- *All pattern pieces and templates found in pull-out section*
- *Color photograph on page 26*

Pleated-Front High Yoke Blouse

Supplies

Fabric - Broadcloth 1/3 yd.

Notions: Lightweight sewing thread; 3/8" buttons: 7 for back closure and cuffs

Pattern Pieces Required: High Yoke Front, High Yoke Back, Long Sleeve (trace the pattern onto folded paper to create a whole sleeve pattern), Lower Shirt Back, Lower Shirt Front, Band Collar, Band Cuff

All seams 1/4" unless otherwise indicated. Stitch seam in place and overcast the seam allowances with a zigzag or serge, unless otherwise indicated.

A. Cutting

1. Refer to the cutting layout guide to cut the following pieces: two yoke backs, on the fold; two yoke fronts, on the fold; two lower shirt backs, on the selvage; one lower shirt front, on the fold; two sleeves; two collars; four cuffs **(fig. 1)**.

2. Transfer pattern markings to the fabric. Be sure to mark the pleat lines on the front, button and buttonhole markings on the sleeve cuffs and backs, and the back fold lines and center back lines.

B. Lower Front and Front Yokes

1. To make the pleats on the lower front piece, working from the right side, fold the solid lines to meet the dotted lines and press. The pleats will point to the sides of the blouse **(fig. 2)**.

2. Baste across the top edge of the pleats. Refer to figure 2.

3. Place the two front yoke pieces (one will be the lining) with right sides together and sandwich the pleated piece between them, with the upper edge of the pleated piece even with the lower yoke edges **(fig. 3)**.

4. Stitch the yokes to the lower front and press the yokes up, away from the lower front.

5. Baste the yoke to the yoke lining at the shoulders and neck edge **(fig. 4)**.

C. Lower Back and Back Yokes

1. Fold 1/2" along the selvage edges of the lower back to the inside and press **(fig. 5)**.

2. Fold each yoke piece in half, wrong sides together, and press. This creates a self-lining for each yoke piece **(fig. 6)**.

3. Open the yokes out flat. Place one yoke piece together with one lower back, right sides together, with the top edge of the lower back even with the lower edge of the yoke piece **(fig. 7)**. Wrap the lining part of the yoke to the wrong side of the lower back, so that the lower back is sandwiched between the yoke and yoke lining **(fig. 8)**.

4. Stitch the seam and press the yoke and yoke lining up, away from the lower back. This will flip the yoke linings to the inside.

5. Repeat Steps 3 and 4 for the remaining yoke and lower back.

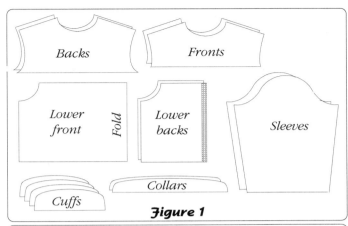

Backs   Fronts

Lower front   Fold   Lower backs   Sleeves

Cuffs   Collars

Figure 1

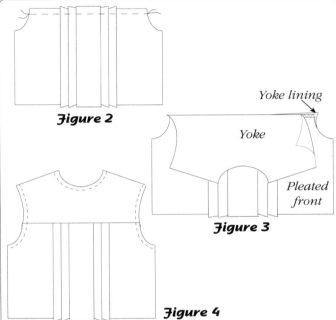

Figure 2

Yoke lining

Yoke

Pleated front

Figure 3

Figure 4

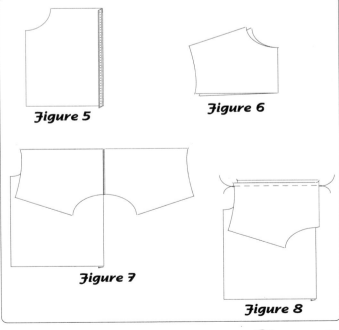

Figure 5

Figure 6

Figure 7

Figure 8

D. Front to Back

1. Press under 1/4" at the shoulder edge of each back yoke lining piece **(fig. 9)**.

2. Place the front to the backs, right sides together, at the shoulder seams.

3. Open out the back yoke linings so that they are not caught in the shoulder seam. Stitch the shoulder seam through the back yoke and both layers of the front yoke and front yoke lining **(fig. 10)**.

4. Press the shoulder seam toward the back. Refold the back yoke linings to the inside and place the folded edge of the back yoke shoulder over the seam, with the folded edge of the yoke meeting the stitching line. Hand-stitch in place **(fig. 11)**.

5. Baste the back neck edges and the armhole edges through both layers.

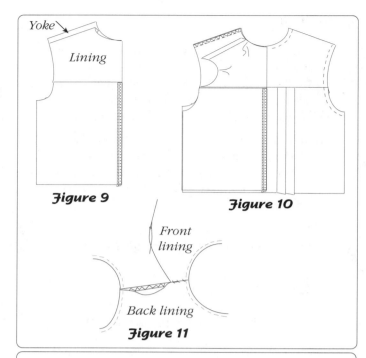

Figure 9

Figure 10

Figure 11

E. Collar and Neck Finish

1. Place the two collar pieces with right sides together and stitch, leaving the neck edge open **(fig. 12)**.

2. Trim and clip the seam allowance.

3. Turn the collar to the right side and press. Baste the neck edges together.

4. Pin the collar to the shirt neck edge, right sides together. The back edges of the collar should meet the center back line of the shirt **(fig. 13)**. Baste the collar to the shirt.

5. Finish the neck edge with a bias facing, referring to "Neck Finishes - d. Bias Neck Facing" found on page 35.

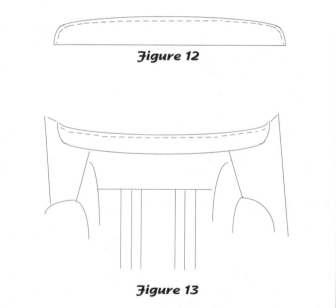

Figure 12

Figure 13

F. Sleeves

1. Cut the placket slit in the lower sleeve edges. Apply a continuous lap placket, referring to "Plackets - a. Continuous Lap Placket" found on page 42. The front edge of the placket will be folded to the inside and the back edge will be left extended.

2. Run two gathering rows across the top and bottom edges of the sleeves, 1/8" and 1/4" from the edges **(fig. 14)**.

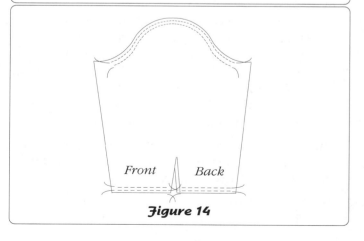

Figure 14

3. Pin the sleeve to the shirt, right sides together, and adjust the gathers to make the sleeve fit the armhole. Stitch in place **(fig. 15)**.

4. Sew the sleeve/side seams **(fig. 16)**.

5. Place the long straight side of one cuff piece to the bottom edge of one sleeve, right sides together, so that the placket edges of the sleeve meet the 1/4" seam line of the cuff side edges. Remember that the front edge of the placket should be folded to the inside **(Fig. 17)**.

6. Adjust the gathers in the sleeve to fit the cuff, pin and stitch. Press the gathers in the seam allowance flat and trim to neaten the edges of the seam. Press the seam toward the cuff.

7. On a second cuff piece, press 1/4" to the inside along the long straight edge. Place the second cuff piece over the stitched cuff, right sides together, matching the edges. Pin and stitch along the curved edges, leaving the long straight edge open **(fig. 18)**.

8. Trim and clip the seam allowance, turn to the inside and press. The folded long edge should meet the stitching line. Hand-stitch the cuff in place.

G. Finishing

1. Mark buttonhole and buttonhole placement on the back edges and the cuffs. Work five buttonholes in the back right side and attach the buttons to the left side **(fig. 19)**. The buttonholes in the cuffs will be worked on the front edges and the buttons will be attached to the back edges **(fig. 20)**.

2. Press 1/4" to the inside along the bottom edge of the shirt, then press another 1/2". Stitch the hem in place by hand or machine.

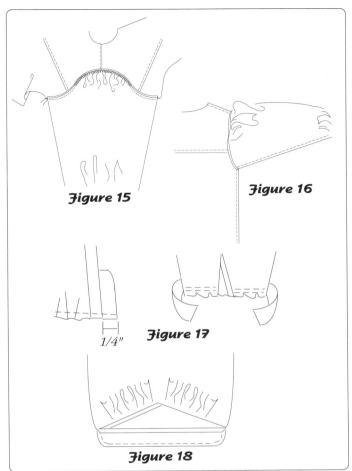

Figure 15

Figure 16

Figure 17

1/4"

Figure 18

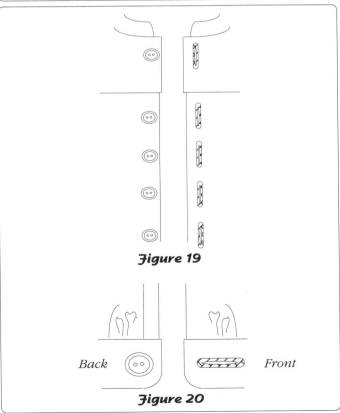

Figure 19

Back

Front

Figure 20

Jesus Loves The Little Children Jumper

Supplies

1/16 gingham	*1/2 yd.*
Batiste - white	*3/8 yd.*
Broadcloth - all sizes:	*3" x 4" scraps of red,*
	yellow, tan, black

Notions: Lightweight sewing thread in white, red, yellow, tan, black; Velcro™, snaps or tiny buttons for closure; black piping; water-soluble stabilizer; wash-out pencil

Pattern Pieces Required: Jumper Round Yoke

Templates Required: Shadow Appliqué Template; Round Yoke Skirt Template and Jumper Hem Template

All seams 1/4" unless otherwise indicated. Stitch seam in place and overcast the seam allowances with a zigzag or serge, unless otherwise indicated.

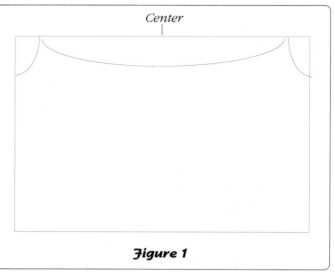

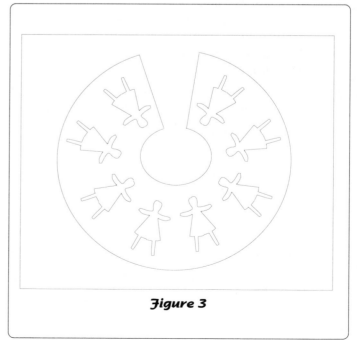

Figure 1

A. Cutting

1. For the skirt, cut two rectangles of the gingham, each 21-1/2" wide by the following length:

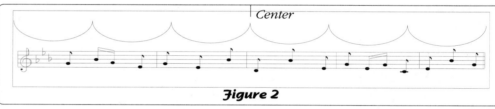

Figure 2

Doll Sizes	17-1/2" 18-1/2" 19-1/2" 21-1/2"
Length	12-3/4" 13-3/4" 14-1/4" 15-3/4"

Place the round yoke skirt template at the top edge of the skirt rectangles and shape the skirt **(fig. 1)**. Mark the center front and back at the top and bottom edges.

2. For the skirt hem, cut two rectangles of the white batiste 21-1/2" wide by 3-3/4". Trace the scallops and the music design from the jumper hem template onto both pieces of batiste **(fig. 2)**. Do not cut the scallops. Mark the center on each piece.

3. From the remaining white batiste, cut one round yoke and one 8" x 8" square. Trace the yoke pattern and shadow applique template onto the square **(fig. 3)**. Transfer yoke markings to both yoke pieces.

Figure 3

B. Skirt

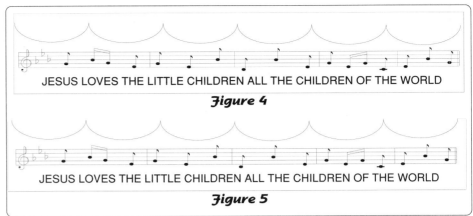

Figure 4

Figure 5

1. Place a piece of water-soluble stabilizer (WSS) under one of the jumper hem pieces. Using black thread, stitch around the music design with a tiny zigzag stitch. Use a wider zigzag to shape the wider areas of the clef symbols and notes. If your machine has a "dot" stitch, it may be used to form the notes. Use the machine alphabet to stitch the words across the bottom line, or embroider the words by hand **(fig. 4)**. Tear away the excess WSS. (Another option is to draw the entire design with a fine-tipped permanent quilt pen.) Repeat for the other skirt hem piece.

2. Following the instructions for "Madeira applique" on page 290, prepare the skirt hem **(fig. 5)**.

3. Place the right side of the skirt hem pieces to the wrong side of the skirt pieces, with the bottom edges even and centers matched **(fig. 6)**. Stitch across the bottom edge with a 1/4" seam. Trim the seam to 1/8".

4. Turn the hem to the outside along the bottom seam line, press the seam and pin the hem in place **(fig. 7)**.

5. Using white thread and the pinstitch on your machine (a tiny zigzag can be used if there is no pinstitch), stitch the hem to the skirt. The straight side of the pinstitch should be on the gingham and the "bite" of the stitch will catch the hem edge.

6. Choose one skirt piece for the back piece. Cut a 3" slit down from the top edge at the center back. Apply a placket at the center back, referring to "Plackets - a. Continuous Lap Placket" on page 42.

7. Run two gathering rows across the top edge of each skirt pieces, 1/8" and 1/4" from the top edge, and stopping 1/2" from the armholes and center back placket **(fig. 8)**.

8. Sew the side seams of the skirt pieces together with French seams **(fig. 9)**.

9. Referring to "Neck Finishes - d. Bias Neck Facing" on page 34, apply bias facings to the armholes **(fig. 10)**, omitting references to the dress facings.

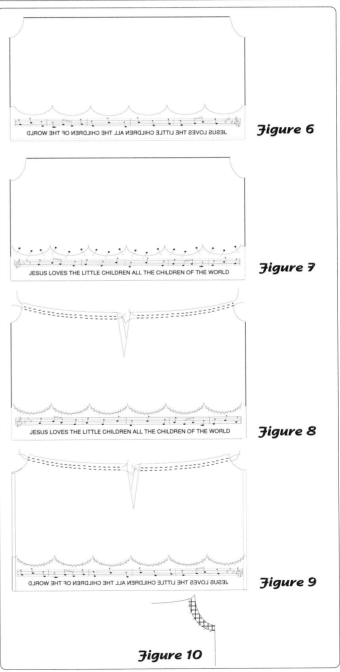

Figure 6

Figure 7

Figure 8

Figure 9

Figure 10

C. Yokes

1. Following the instructions for "shadow applique" on page 286, work the child figures onto the traced yoke, beginning at one back edge and following the sequence black, tan, red and yellow. Cut out the yoke **(fig. 11)**.

2. Trim the seam allowance of the piping to 1/4". Clip the seam allowance of the piping to allow it to lie smoothly around the curves **(fig. 12)**. Place the piping to the bottom edge of the appliqued yoke, with right sides together and raw edges even. At the center back seams, let the ends of the piping extend into the bottom seam allowance. Stitch the piping to the yoke with a 1/4" seam allowance **(fig. 13)**.

3. With right sides together, stitch the two yoke sections together at the center back edges only **(fig. 14)** (the plain yoke will be the lining). Do not catch the piping in this seam. Trim the seam to 1/8", turn right side out and press. Turn back to wrong side out.

D. Yokes to Skirt

1. Sandwich the top edges of the skirt between the bottom edges of the yoke pieces, matching the centers. The right side of the yoke will be against the right side of the skirt, and the right side of the yoke lining will be against the wrong side of the skirt. The raw edges should be even. Place the armhole edges at the yoke marks, and let the back placket edges meet the yoke back seams **(fig. 15)**.

2. Stitch the bottom yoke seam, stitching the yokes to the skirt, using a 1/4" seam allowance. The yokes will be sewn together at the armhole openings, with no skirt fabric between them.

3. Trim and clip the seam. Turn the yokes to the right side.

4. Baste the yoke and the yoke lining together at the neck edge and treat as one layer.

E. Finishing the Jumper

1. Finish the neck edge of the jumper with a bias neck facing, referring to "Neck Finishes - d. Bias Neck Facing" found on page 35.

2. Attach Velcro™, buttons and buttonholes or snaps to the back yokes to close the jumper.

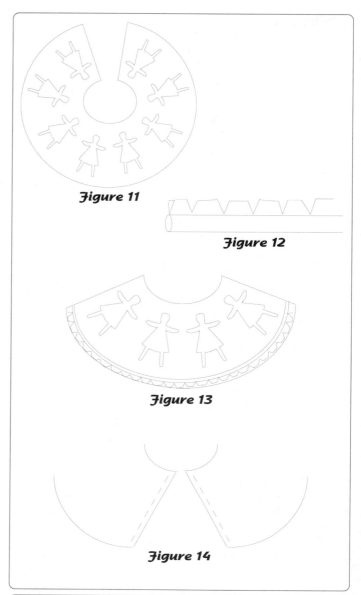

Figure 11

Figure 12

Figure 13

Figure 14

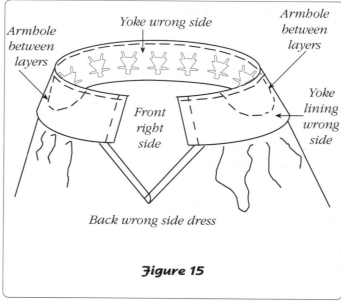

Figure 15

White Delicate Antique Dream Dress

This antique-look dress calls for a combination of seven different materials and trims to make it totally unique. The key to making a doll dress appear antique is to use trims and laces that don't match. This dropped waist style has a tiny entredeux type trim around the waistline and down the front and back of the bodice. This same Swiss entredeux tiny trim is used at the bottom of the gathered sleeve. The puffed sleeves are magnificent with their fancy band of tiny French insertion with three tiny 1/8-inch tucks. Gathered lace edging 1-1/2 inches wide finishes the bottom of the sleeve below the 3/8-inch Swiss entredeux insertion; this gathers in the fullness of the sleeve. Down the center front bodice of the dress is white-on-white Swiss handloom with narrow French insertion going all the way around this edging and being mitered about 1 inch below the waistline of the dress on the bottom of the front panel. Sets of three tucks come next on the front panel, then two strips of the narrow Swiss insertion. Wide French edging is gathered at the edge of this Swiss insertion across the shoulders and about three-quarters of the way down both the front and the back center bodice. The back closes with Velcro™. The skirt, with its 31-1/2 inch fullness, is made from wide Swiss embroidered trim.

- **All pattern pieces and templates found in pull-out section**
- **Color photograph on page 25**

Supplies

Fabric - Batiste	1/2 yd.
Lace Insertion (3/8")	2-1/4 yds.
Swiss Insertion (3/8")	1-1/2 yds.
Lace Edging (3/8")	1/2 yd.
Lace Edging (1-1/4")	2 yds.
Entredeux	1/2 yd.
Swiss Edging	
8" wide (for 19 1/2" and 21 1/2"dollos)	1-1/4 yds.
7" wide (for 18 1/2" dolls)	1-1/4 yds.
6-1/2" wide (for 17 1/2" dolls)	1-1/4 yds.
Embroidered Insertion (1-1/2" wide with an embroidery width of 5/8" or less in the center of the strip)	1/4 yd.

Other Notions: Lightweight sewing thread; Velcro™, snaps or tiny buttons for back closure

Pattern Pieces Required: Dropped Waist Front Bodice, Dropped Waist Back Bodice, Elbow Length Sleeve

Template Needed: Antique Dream Front Bodice Template

All seams 1/4" unless otherwise indicated. Stitch seam in place and overcast the seam allowances with a zigzag or serge.

A. Cutting

1. Cut two back bodices from the selvages and two sleeves **(fig. 1)**.

2. Cut one rectangle to the following measurement for the front bodice (the length is listed first, the width follows):

Doll Sizes	17-1/2"	18-1/2"	19-1/2"	21-1/2"
Bodice	6" x 12"	7" x 13"	7" x 14"	8" x 14"

3. Transfer fold line markings from the back bodice pattern to the back bodice pieces.

4. The skirt piece is the length and width of the Swiss edging listed under the fabric requirements.

B. Constructing The Bodice

1. Cut the strip of embroidered insertion 1-1/2" wide by the following measurement:

Doll Sizes	17-1/2"	18-1/2"	19-1/2"	21-1/2"
	7"	7-1/2"	7-1/2"	8-1/2"

2. Trace the lace template on the embroidered insertion piece **(fig. 2)**.

3. Following the template lines, shape lace insertion around the embroidered strip, mitering at the corners. Stitch the lace in place along the inner edge of the lace only. Trim the fabric from behind the lace. This strip will be used later in decorating the bodice **(fig. 3)**.

4. Place a line down the center front of the bodice rectangle **(fig. 4)** (parallel to the length of the rectangle). Place lines for tucks measuring from each side of the center front line 7/8", 1-3/8" and 1-7/8", mark using a fabric marker. Place the fabric, wrong sides together, and press along each line. Stitch 1/8" from each fold to create tucks. Press tucks away from the center **(fig. 5)**.

5. Fold the bodice rectangle in half along the center front line. Cut out the front bodice on the fold **(fig. 6)**.

6. Place the embroidery/lace strip along the center of the rectangle, between the pintucks, with the lower edge of the strip extended 3/4" below the lower edge of the bodice.

7. Zigzag the embroidery/lace strip to the bodice along the outer edges of the lace, stopping 1-1/2" from the bottom of each side. Trim the strip even with the neck line of the bodice **(fig. 7)**.

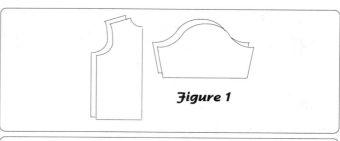

Figure 1

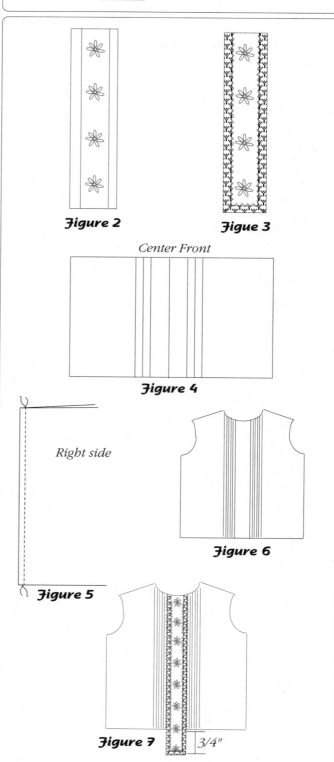

Figure 2   **Figue 3**

Center Front

Figure 4

Right side

Figure 5   **Figure 6**

Figure 7   3/4"

8. Place the front bodice to the back bodice, right sides together, at the shoulders. Stitch in place using a 1/4" seam **(figs. 8 and 8a)**.

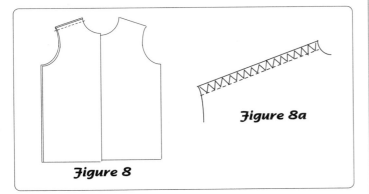

Figure 8a

Figure 8

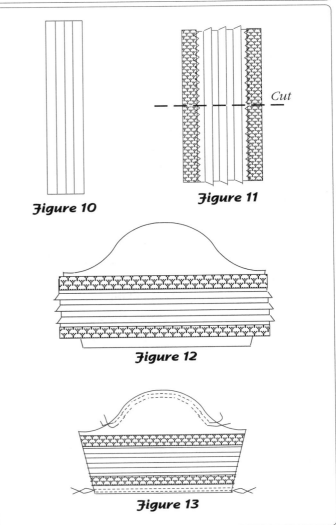

Figure 9

9. Cut two pieces of Swiss insertion 16" long. Trim away the fabric edges of the insertion. Place the insertion next to the pintucks of the bodice front, continue the piece over the shoulder and down the back bodice parallel to the back facing fold lines. A small tuck may be needed at the shoulder. Pin the insertion in place and zigzag along both sides of the insertion. Trim the insertion even with the lower edge of the bodices **(fig. 9)**.

C. Decorating the Sleeves

1. Cut a strip of fabric 24" long by 2" wide for the tucked strip. Draw a line down the center of the strip along the 24" side **(fig. 10)**. Place a line 3/8" on either side of the center line.

2. Fold the strip, wrong sides together, along each line. Stitch 1/8" from the folds to create tucks. Press tucks one way. (Refer to figure 5).

3. Cut two pieces of insertion lace 24" long. Attach the lace to each side of the tucked strip using the technique "lace to fabric". Press. Cut in half **(fig. 11)**.

Figure 10

Figure 11

Cut

4. Place each strip to the right side of the sleeve. The strip should fall 1/2" above the bottom of the sleeve at the under arm edge and continue straight across to the other side. Zigzag in place along the outer lace edges. Trim the fabric from behind the lace **(fig. 12)**.

Figure 12

5. Run two gathering rows at 1/8" and 1/4" in the top and bottom of each sleeve **(fig. 13)**.

Figure 13

6. Finish the bottom of each sleeve using Swiss insertion and gathered edging lace. Refer to "Sleeve Finishes - d. Swiss Beading to Gathered Edging Lace" found on page 39 **(fig. 14)**.

7. Gather the top of the sleeves to fit the arm opening of the bodice, matching the center of the sleeve with the shoulder seam of the bodice. Adjust the gathers in the top of the sleeve to fall 1-1/4" to 1-1/2" on either side of the shoulder seam.

8. Stitch the sleeve to the bodice, right sides together, using a 1/4" seam **(fig. 15)**.

9. Cut two pieces of wide lace edging 16" long for the 17-1/2" doll, 17" for the 18-1/2" and 19-1/2" doll, and 18" for the 21-1/2" doll.

10. Fold (to the wrong side) the cut ends of the lace to the scalloped edge and press. Stitch along each fold with a long stitch for gathering **(fig. 16)**.

11. Place a dot along the outer edge of each Swiss insertion piece 2" from the lower edge for the 17-1/2" to 19-1/2" dolls and 2-1/2" from the lower edge for the 21-1/2" dolls.

12. Gather the edging lace to fit between the dots. Use the stitched gathering thread and the gathering thread in the heading of the lace to gather **(fig. 17)**.

13. Butt the gathered edging to the outer edge of the Swiss insertion and zigzag in place. Trim the excess lace from the fold.

D. Finishing the Dress

1. Shape insertion lace around the neck edge 1/4" from the cut edge. Stitch around the lower edge of the lace using a small, tight zigzag **(fig. 18)**. Press well.

2. Trim the fabric from behind the lace.

3. Finish the neck with entredeux and gathered edging. Refer to "Neck Finishes - a. Entredeux to Gathered Lace, Steps 1-3" found on page 34. Attach the entredeux/gathered lace strip to the neck using the technique "lace to entredeux." Refer to figure 18 .

4. Place the sides/sleeves of the bodice, right sides together. Stitch using a 1/4" seam **(fig. 19)**.

5. Cut a piece of Swiss insertion for the hip band to the following measurement:

Doll Sizes	17-1/2"	18-1/2"	19-1/2"	21-1/2"
Skirt	12-1/4"	14"	13-3/4"	15-1/4"

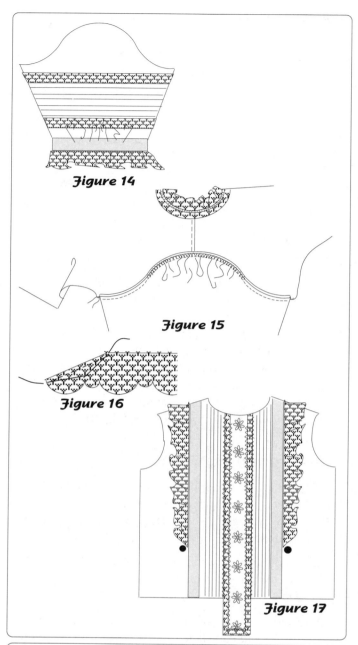

Figure 14

Figure 15

Figure 16

Figure 17

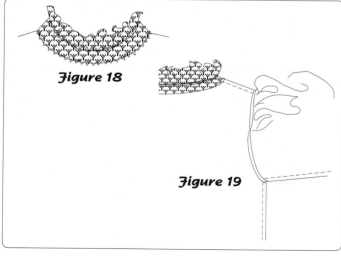

Figure 18

Figure 19

6. Pin the lace/embroidery strip away from the lower edge of the skirt. With the back facings extended, stitch two gathering rows in the lower edge of the bodice at 1/8" and 1/4" and gather to fit the Swiss insertion**(fig 20)**. Distribute the gathers evenly and stitch in place using the technique "entredeux to gathered fabric".

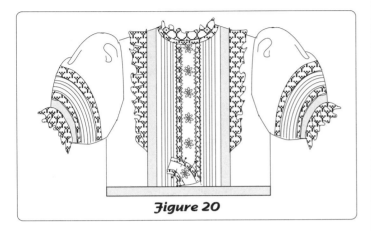

Figure 20

7. Place the back edges of the skirt together and stitch from the bottom, stopping 2" from top of the skirt. Backstitch **(fig. 21)**.

8. Place a placket in the seam opening. Refer to "Placket - c. Continuous Placket or d. Easy Placket" found on page 43.

9. Run two gathering rows 1/8" and 1/4" from the top edge of the skirt **(fig. 22)**. Remember that one side of the placket is folded to the inside of the skirt and the other side is left extended.

10. Place the right side of the bodice to the right side of the skirt, matching the center of the bodice with the center of the skirt. Pin in place. Gather the skirt to fit the bodice. Distribute the gathers evenly but leave 1-1/2" ungathered in the center front of the skirt **(fig. 23)**.

11. At the back edges of the skirt opening wrap the back facings of the bodice to the outside over the placket opening of the skirt **(fig. 24)**. Pin in place.

12. Stitch the skirt to the bodice using a 1/4" seam. Overcast the seam allowance.

13. Place the lace/embroidered strip over the hip band and skirt. Pin in place. Zigzag the unstitched part of the strip to the dress. Carefully trim the fabric from behind the lace embroidered strip **(fig. 25)**.

14. Attach Velcro™, buttons and buttonholes or snaps to the back of the bodice to close the dress.

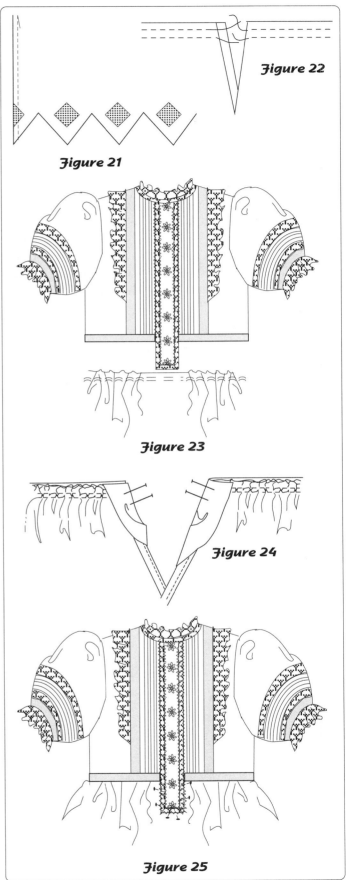

Figure 22

Figure 21

Figure 23

Figure 24

Figure 25

Doll Lingerie

A number of years ago when I, once again, became passionately interested in dolls, I went to a doll show for the first time. I was thrilled with the aisle after aisle of tiny doll products. During the course of that doll show I learned a lot about dressing dolls. One of the most important facts that I learned at that show was that it is very important to put proper underwear on your dolls. I was taught that dolls love elegant lingerie and they don't consider themselves dressed without pantaloons, slips and camisoles. Would you believe that many doll makers make the lingerie with as much handwork, lace, and care as they make the outer garment? Trust me, they do.

When we were planning this book for these beautiful Götz dolls, one of the first things I told our designers was, "We must have gorgeous lingerie for these dolls." Their designs are so fabulous that they make me smile thinking about the fun you are going to have making these wonderful garments for your doll, or for the doll of someone you love very much.

There are several slip patterns, including a beautiful peach one with a to-the-waist design and a lace ruffle on the bottom. Some people love the A-line one piece petticoat which is so fast and easy to make. We have bloomers and a peplum to go with it. There are several more full slips which make the dresses stand out ever so prettily. The cute tap pants have an oval lace rosebud camisole to go with them. For your dropped waist dresses you will find a dropped waist slip. A triple tiered petticoat will be just the thing with the white camisole or the French camisole. If you really want something fancy, try the puffed camisole and pantaloons; they have tiny puffing around each leg and up and down the bodice front.

You can add any trims or lace treatment you wish to any of these basic lingerie patterns. It is fun to embroider lingerie because it is so quick and easy on a garment this small. I love to use the most delicate of fabrics on doll lingerie so they will hang beautifully. You might want to make straps out of a piece of ribbon and tie it on the shoulder. Your imagination is the only limiting factor in what you can do to make these lingerie patterns the world's most beautiful. One thing I am sure of; your doll will be happy that we didn't include a corset among these turn of the century garments. We don't want your Götz doll to be sorry that you bought this book! We have included only comfortable lingerie and I bet you will have fun really embellishing them to the hilt.

The idea of doll lingerie's being included in a doll pattern isn't new to me. When searching through some of my old magazines, I found an adorable doll ensemble pattern in the *McCall's*, December, 1913 magazine. The title of the pattern page is "New Patterns For Old Needs: Practical Apparel for Men, Women and Children and a Doll's Outfit for the Tiny Tots." Pattern number 5640 was a doll wardrobe.

No. 5640, Doll's Set (10 cents).—All the clothes needed by Miss Dolly will be found in this pretty outfit. The pattern comes in five sizes for dolls from fourteen to thirty inches long. The materials needed are given on the pattern envelope.

McCall's, December, 1913

White Camisole With Pink Ribbon Trim

Pink on pink, as in pink featherstitching on pink silk ribbon, dresses up a white camisole with a touch of color. The camisole is Swiss batiste. The straps are made of two pieces of narrow white edging joined together at the heading with a tiny zigzag stitch. Pink silk ribbon secured down the center with a machine featherstitch, hides the lace-to-lace join. The same technique dresses up the lower edge of the camisole where the ribbon is featherstitched over the batiste and lace join. The back closes with two pieces of Velcro® and a pretty pink silk ribbon bow is tacked to the front.

- All pattern pieces and templates found in the pattern section page 294.
- Color photograph on page 31

Supplies

Fabric	1/6 yd.
Lace Edging (3/8")	1-1/4 yds.
Lace Edging (3/4")	1/2 yd.
Silk Ribbon (4mm)	1-1/2 yds.

Notions: Lightweight sewing thread; snaps, buttons or Velcro®

Directions

1. Cut one Basic Camisole Front from the fold. Cut two Basic Camisole Backs from the selvage. If selvages are not available, zigzag or serge the edge of the fabric. Mark the fold lines and strap placement lines along the back of the camisole **(fig. 1)**.

2. Place the backs to the front right sides together at the sides. Stitch in place **(fig. 2)**

3. Place 3/8" edging lace along the top edge of the camisole with the scalloped edge of the lace to the cut edge of the fabric. Miter the lace at the points (refer to mitering lace on page 257). Stitch the lace in place **(fig. 3)** using the technique for extra stable lace finishing (page 238).

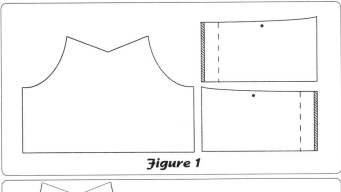

Figure 1

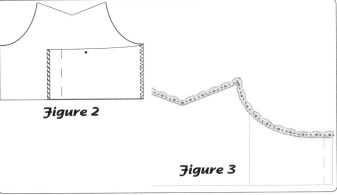

Figure 2

Figure 3

4. Place 3/4" edging lace along the lower edge of the camisole. Stitch the lace in place **(fig. 4)** using the technique for extra stable lace finishing (page 238).

5. Place 4mm silk ribbon just above the edging lace at the bottom of the camisole. Stitch in place with a sewing machine featherstitch or small zigzag **(fig.5)**.

6. Cut two pieces of 3/8" edging 10" long for the straps.

7. Place the edging pieces together, straight edge to straight edge. Stitch together using a small zigzag **(fig. 6)**.

8. Place 4mm silk ribbon in the center of the lace strap piece. The silk ribbon will hide the zigzag stitch made earlier. Stitch the ribbon in place with a sewing machine featherstitch or small zigzag. See **(fig. 6)**. Cut two straps from the strap piece to the following measurement:

17-1/2" dolls	4-1/4"
18-1/2" dolls	5"
19-1/2" dolls	4-7/8"
21-1/2" dolls	5"

9. Place the straps along the placement marks of the back and centering on the lace points of the front. The straps should extend 1/2" to the inside of the camisole **(fig. 7)**. Stitch in place using a small, tight zigzag along the top and bottom edge of the camisole lace. See figure 7. Trim excess strap lace from behind.

10. Fold back edges to the inside of the camisole along the fold lines. See figure 7. Press.

11. Close with Velcro®, snaps or buttonholes and buttons.

12. Tie a small bow with the remaining silk ribbon. Stitch the bow to the center front of the camisole just below the lace.

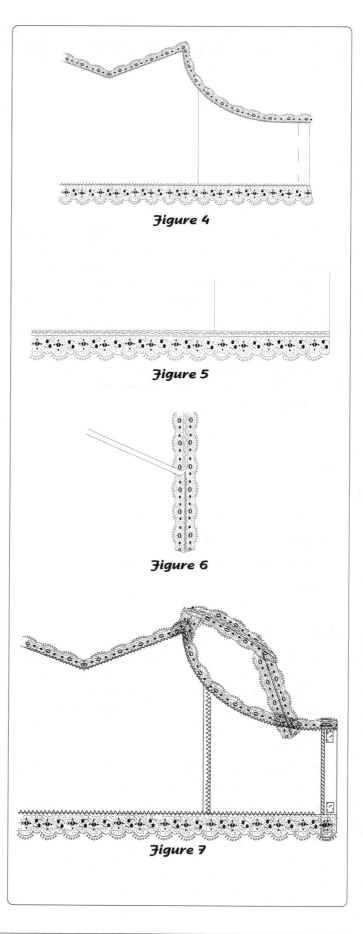

Figure 4

Figure 5

Figure 6

Figure 7

Oval Lace Rosebud Camisole

This camisole is just plain pretty. Made from Swiss batiste, the body of the delicate undergarment is trimmed in narrow French laces. The neckline edging dips and loops into an oval at center front, which frames a bullion rose of pink and green. The straps are formed by two rows of narrow French edging joined to a single strip of pink silk ribbon. Velcro® secures the camisole in back.

- All pattern pieces and templates found in the pattern section page 294.
- Color photograph on page 30

Supplies

Fabric	1/6 yd.
Lace Edging (3/8")	2 yds.
Ribbon (1/8")	2/3 yd.

Notions: DMC embroidery floss (light pink #963, medium pink #776, light green #955), lightweight sewing thread; snaps, buttons or Velcro®.

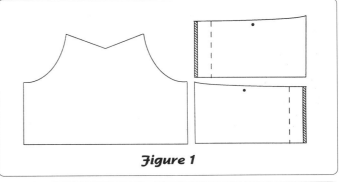

Figure 1

Directions

1. Cut one Basic Camisole Front from the fold. Cut two Basic Camisole Backs from the selvage **(fig.1)**. If selvages are not available, zigzag or serge the edge of the fabric. Mark the fold lines and strap placement lines along the back of the camisole

2. Place the backs to the front right sides together at the sides **(fig. 2)**. Stitch in place.

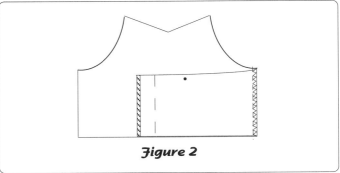

Figure 2

3. Place 3/8" edging lace along the top edge of the camisole, mitering the lace at the points (refer to mitering lace, page 257) and shaping the lace along the template lines of the center loop (refer to lace shaping, page 257). The scalloped edge of the lace should be placed to the cut edge of the fabric. Stitch the lace in place using the technique for extra stable lace finishing (page 239). The outer edge of the lace loop should be stitched just inside the scalloped edge of the lace **(fig. 3)**.

4. Place 3/8" edging lace along the lower edge of the camisole. Stitch the lace in place using the technique for extra stable lace finishing (page 238) **(fig. 4)**.

5. Cut two pieces of 3/8" edging 10" long and one piece of ribbon 10" long for the strap piece. Butt a piece of edging to each side of the ribbon. Stitch each piece in place with a zigzag **(fig. 5)**.

6. Cut two straps from the strap piece to the following measurement:

17-1/2" dolls	4-1/4"
18-1/2" dolls	5"
19-1/2" dolls	4-7/8"
21-1/2" dolls	5"

7. Place the straps along the placement marks of the back and centering on the lace points of the front. The straps should extend 1/2" to the inside of the camisole. Stitch in place using a small, tight zigzag along the top and bottom edge of the camisole lace **(fig. 6)**. Trim excess strap lace from behind.

8. Fold back edges to the inside of the camisole along the fold lines. Press. See figure 6.

9. Close with Velcro®, snaps or buttonholes and buttons. See figure 6.

10. Stitch a bullion rose in the center of the lace loop **(fig. 7)**. The bullion rose consists of the following:

    center, medium pink - three bullion stitches with eight wraps each

    outer, light pink - four bullion stitches with eleven wraps each

    leaves, light green - three lazy daisy stitches with two strands each

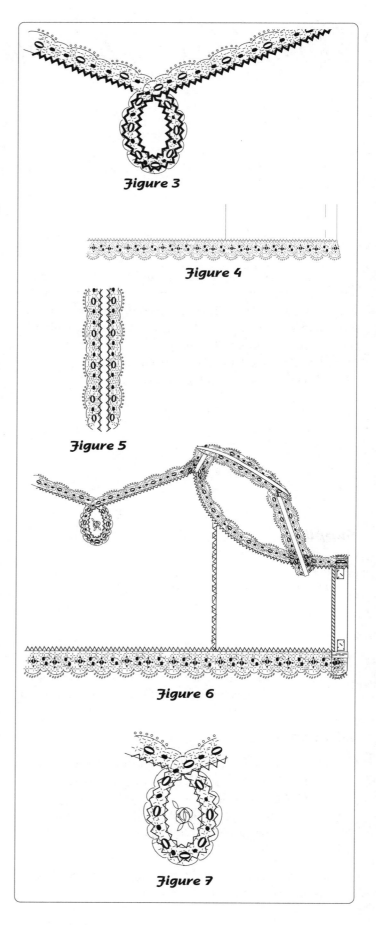

Figure 3

Figure 4

Figure 5

Figure 6

Figure 7

Tap Pants and Sweet French Camisole

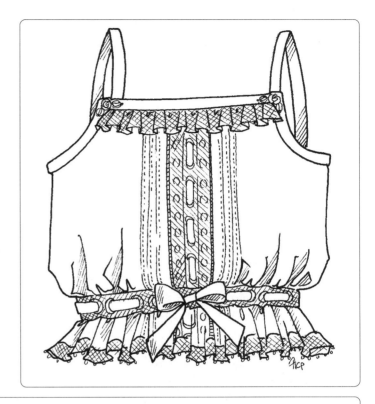

Sometimes even a doll needs to slip into her fancy underthings to feel pretty. This camisole and tap pant combination is rich in heirloom detail. The straight-line camisole becomes a peplum style when ribbon is run through beading around the waist. A fancy lace band runs vertically down the front; three vertical pintucks frame either side. Gathered narrow French edging embellishes the top of the camisole neckline. Three tiny buttons and loops serve as the back closure. The straps are narrow satin ribbon prettied with a tiny pink bullion rosebud on the front where they join the camisole. The top and the armholes of the camisole are bound in a bias binding. Flat French edging trims the bottom of the camisole.

The tap pants are elasticized at the waist. Two bullion rosebuds in pink with green lazy daisy leaves dot the front of each leg. The bottom of the pants have an entredeux/gathered lace edging trim with a tiny bow tacked at the lower side seams.

Supplies

Fabric	1/2 yd.
Lace Insertion (1/2")	1/3 yd.
Lace Edging (3/8")	1 yd.
Lace Edging (3/4")	1-1/2 yds.
Beading	3/4 yd.
Entredeux	1-1/4 yds.
Elastic (1/8")	1/3 yd.
Ribbon (1/8" or 1/16") for bows on tap pants	1/4 yd.
Ribbon (to fit beading)	1-1/2 yds.
Ribbon (for straps)	1/3 yd.

Notions: Two spools lightweight sewing thread, double needle (2.0/80 or 1.6/70), DMC embroidery floss (light pink #963, medium pink #776, light green #3813); 3 buttons, Velcro® or snaps

- **Tap pants pattern pieces found in pull-out section. Camisole found in the pattern section page 295.**
- **Color photographs on page 30 and 31**

Directions

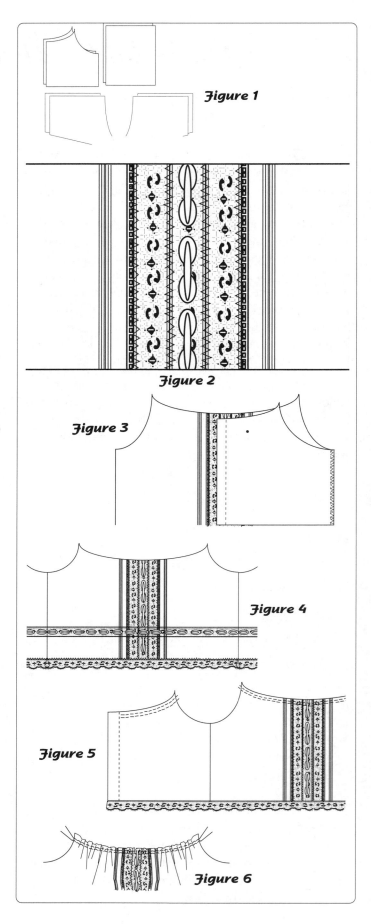

Figure 1

1. Using the Tap Pants and Camisole pattern, cut two camisole backs and two squares to the following measurements **(fig 1)**:

17-1/2" to 19-1/2" dolls	cut pieces 5" square
21-1/2" dolls	cut pieces 7" square

   Cut two tap pants front and two tap pants back and transfer all markings. Set pants aside for later construction.

2. Cut these strip(s): one piece of beading (with ribbon inserted), two pieces of lace insertion and two pieces of entredeux to the following measurement:

17-1/2" to 19-1/2" dolls	cut pieces 5"
21-1/2" dolls	cut pieces 7"

   Figure 2

3. Attach the strips together by stitching the lace insertion on each side of the beading using the technique "lace to lace" (page230). Attach entredeux to each side of the insertion/beading band using the technique "lace to entredeux" (page 234). Attach each fabric rectangle cut in Step 1 to the entredeux on the sides of the band using the technique "entredeux to fabric" (page 234). Place three double needle pintucks on each side of the lace band 1/4" from the entredeux **(fig. 2)**. The pintucks are 1/16" apart. Press. Fold the piece in half and cut out the camisole front.

   Figure 3

4. Place the front camisole to the back camisoles, right sides together. Stitch the sides together using a 1/4" seam **(fig. 3)**. Transfer the waistline marking from the pattern.

   Figure 4

5. Attach 3/8" edging along the bottom of the camisole using the technique "lace to fabric". Center beading along the waist line mark and stitch in place along the outer edges of the beading with a straight stitch **(fig. 4)**.

   Figure 5

6. Run gathering rows 1/4" from the top of the front and back, stopping the stitching at back fold lines **(fig. 5)**. Gather the camisole front and bcks to the following measurement **(fig. 6)**:

	front	each back
17-1/2" dolls	3-1/4"	1-3/4"
18-1/2" dolls	3-3/4"	2"
19-1/2" dolls	3-1/2"	2"
21-1/2" dolls	4"	2-1/2"

   Figure 6

7. The top edge of the camisole will be finished with a bias binding. One bias strip will be needed for the front and two strips will be needed for the back. Cut one bias strip for the front 1-1/8" wide by the measurement given in step 6. Press all strips in half lengthwise. Cut two bias strips for the back 1-1/8" wide by the measurement given in step 6 plus 1/4". Press all strips in half lengthwise (**fig. 7**).

8. Place the cut edges of the strip to the edge of the camisole front. For the camisole backs, press folds in place and allow the strip to extend 1/4" from the back edge. Stitch in place using a 1/4" seam (**fig.8**). Trim the seam allowance to 1/8". Finger press the binding toward the seam allowance. Fold the 1/4" tab at the back edge to the inside of the camisole then fold the binding to enclose the seam allowance (**fig. 9**). Stitch the fold of the binding to the inside of the bodice by hand or machine.

9. Measure around the arm openings. Cut two bias strips 1-1/8" long and 1/2" longer than this measurement. Fold the strips in half lengthwise. Attach bias pieces to the arm opening allowing a 1/4" extension at each end. Follow the directions in Step 8 to complete the binding.

10. Gather the remaining 3/8" lace. Hand stitch the gathered lace below the bindings, turning the cut ends under 1/4" (**fig. 10**).

11. Cut the ribbon that fits the beading in half. Weave each piece through the beading starting at the selvage edge of the backs and stopping at the center front. With the back folds in place, stitch the ribbon 1/4" from the folded edge of the backs (**fig. 11**). Tie ribbon into a bow at the center front, drawing up the waist.

12. Cut strap ribbon to the following measurement:

    17-1/2" and 18-1/2" dolls   cut two pieces 4-3/4"

    19-1/2" and 21-1/2" dolls   cut two pieces 5"

13. Attach straps at the top of the arm opening by turning the ribbon under 1/4" and overlap the camisole 1/4" (**fig. 12**). Stitch in place by hand. Close the camisole with Velcro®, snaps or small buttons and buttonholes.

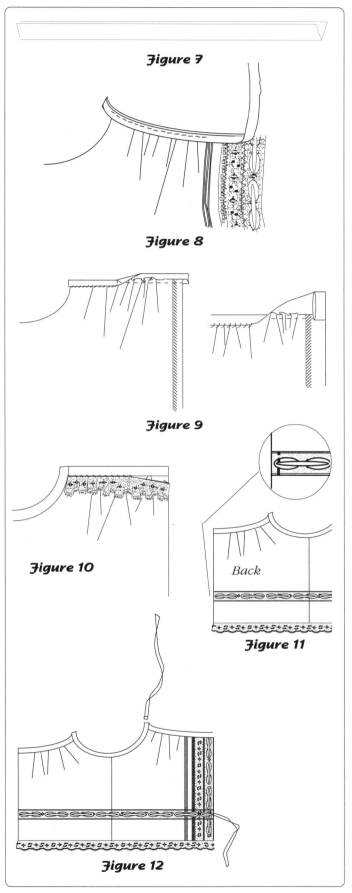

Figure 7

Figure 8

Figure 9

Figure 10

Figure 11

Back

Figure 12

14. To construct the tap pants, place entredeux along the bottom of each leg piece with a 1/4" seam stopping at the side dot **(fig. 13)**. Use the technique "entredeux to fabric" (page 234) and a 1/4" seam to attach.

15. Trim away the remaining fabric edge of the entredeux. Press the entredeux away from the pants (refer to figure 13).

16. Stitch one front piece to one back piece at the sides, stitching through the entredeux at the bottom edge **(fig. 14)**.

17. Cut the edging lace in half and gather it to fit each front/back piece. Stitch in place using the "gathered lace to entredeux" technique (page 248) **(fig .15)**.

18. Place the front to the front and the back to the back, right sides together. Stitch along the center front and center back **(fig. 16)**.

19. Place the crotch (entredeux and lace), right sides together and stitch **(fig. 17)**.

20. Turn the top edge of the pants to the inside 1/8" and then 1/4". Press. To create a casing, stitch along the inside folded edge leaving 1" open **(fig. 18)**.

21. Cut one elastic piece to the following size:

17-1/2" dolls	cut 8-1/2"
18-1/2" dolls	cut 10"
19-1/2" dolls	cut 9-1/2"
21-1/2" dolls	cut 11-1/2"

    Run elastic through the casing, overlapping the elastic 1/4". Stitch the ends of the elastic together with a small zigzag **(fig. 19)**.

22. Stitch the opening closed.

23. Work two bullion flowers and eight lazy daisy leaves along each side of the leg front about 1/2" from the side seam. Work one bullion flower and two leaves on each side of the camisole front just below the strap.

24. Cut the ribbon in half and tie into bows. Stitch to the side seam just above the entredeux.

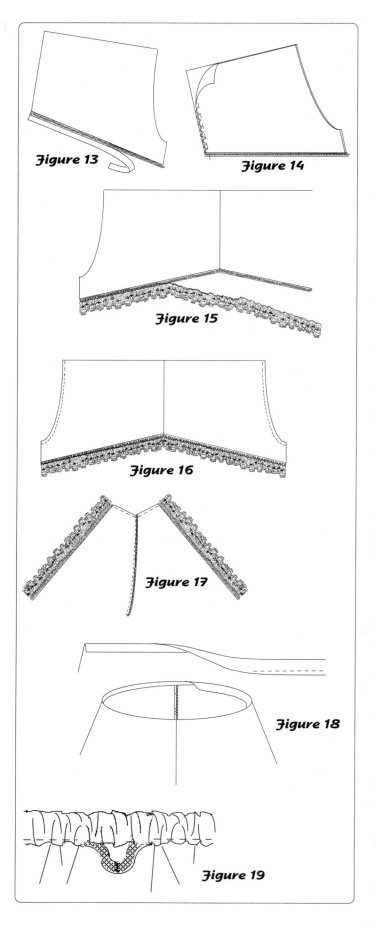

Figure 13

Figure 14

Figure 15

Figure 16

Figure 17

Figure 18

Figure 19

A-Line One-Piece Slip

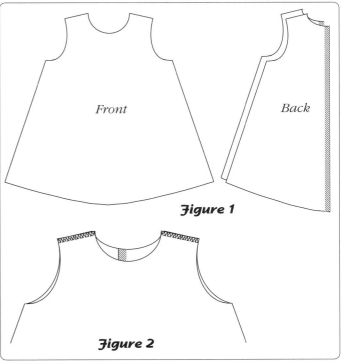

This slip offers the ultimate in simplicity. Trim on the all-white design is limited to flat lace and a single wide ruffle. Narrow lace trims the armholes and neckline, while a wider lace finishes the 3" ruffle at the bottom of the slip. A placket opening in the back closes with Velcro®. Anyone who has sewn heirloom dresses for children has probably made at least one of these slips.

- **All pattern pieces and templates found in the pattern section page 300-301**
- **Color photograph on page 29**

Supplies

Fabric	1/2 yd.
Lace Edging (3/8")	1 yd.
Lace Edging (3/4")	1-5/8 yds.

Notions: Lightweight sewing thread; snaps, buttons or Velcro®

Directions

1. Cut one A-line Slip Front from the fold and two A-line Slip Backs from the selvage **(fig. 1)**

2. Place the shoulders of the slip right sides together and stitch **(fig. 2)**.

Front   *Back*

Figure 1

Figure 2

3. Place edging lace along the neck of the slip, allowing the scalloped edge of the lace to fall on the fabric edge and the lace to extend beyond the selvage edges 1/4" **(fig. 3)**. Stitch along the straight side of the lace using the technique "extra stable lace finishes" (page 238).

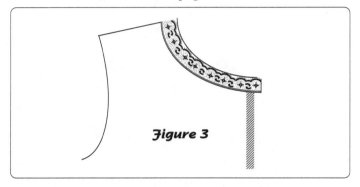

Figure 3

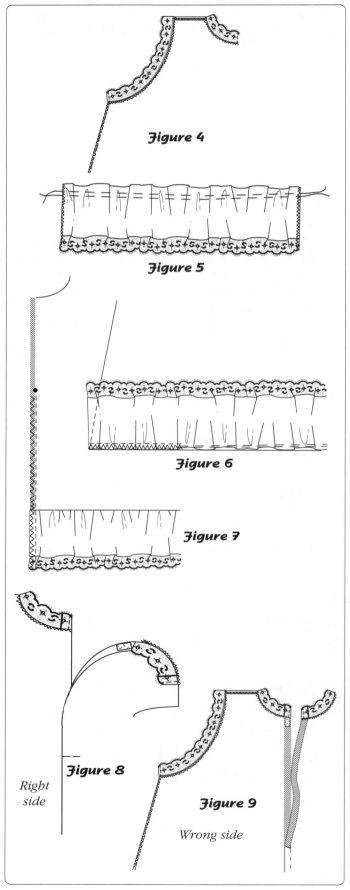

Figure 4

Figure 5

Figure 6

Figure 7

Figure 8

Right side

Figure 9

Wrong side

4. Place lace around the armhole using the same technique.

5. Place the sides of the slip right sides together and stitch **(fig. 4)**.

6. Cut ruffle strip(s) 2-1/2" wide by the following measurements:

   17-1/2" dolls cut one strip 45" long

   18-1/2" to 21-1/2" dolls cut one strip 45" and one strip 12" *(Stitch the two strips together to create one piece about 56".)*

7. Place edging lace along one edge of the ruffle using the technique "lace to fabric" (page 230). Finish the short, raw edge with a zigzag or serger. Stitch two gathering rows at 1/8" and 1/4". Gather the ruffle piece to fit the bottom edge of the slip **(fig. 5)**.

8. Stitch the ruffle to the slip, right sides together **(fig. 6)**.

9. Stitch the backs, right sides together with a 1/4" seam, stopping 5" from the neck edge for the 17-1/2" doll and 6" from the neck edge for other sizes **(fig. 7)**. This will create a placket .

10. Press the seam allowances to the left side of the slip. Turn the slip to the right side and press the right side of the opening to the inside 1/4". Topstitch the seam allowance in place at the bottom of the opening **(fig. 8)**.

11. Fold the lace tabs to the inside of the slip and zigzag in place **(fig. 9)**.

12. Close with small buttons, snaps or Velcro®.

Pink Slip for Round Yoke Victorian Dress

Machine scalloping around the neckline and armholes is the highlight of this pretty pink slip. The to-the-waist design uses additional decorative stitching — a pin stitch — to attach the lace beading and edging at the bottom of the skirt. Pink ribbon is run through the beading and tied in a tiny bow in the front. The back is closed with three buttons and loops and the placket in the skirt extends the back opening for easy dressing.

- **All pattern pieces and templates found in the pattern section page 300-301.**
- **Color photograph on page 30**

Supplies

Fabric	1/2 yd.
Lace Edging (3/4")	1-1/4 yds.
Lace Beading	1-1/4 yds.
Ribbon (to fit beading)	1-1/2 yds.

Notions: Lightweight sewing thread; snaps, buttons or Velcro®. Optional: Stabilizer

Directions

1. Using the To-The-Waist Slip bodice pattern cut one front from the fold and two bodice backs from the selvage **(fig. 1)**.

2. Place the shoulders of the slip bodice right sides together and stitch **(fig. 2)**. Starch and press the neck and arm openings.

3. Stitch around the neck edge and arm openings with a machine satin stitch scallop about 1/4" from the fabric edge. Stabilizer may be required for the scallop stitch **(fig. 3)**. Trim very close to the scallop stitching being careful not to cut into the stitching **(fig. 4)**.

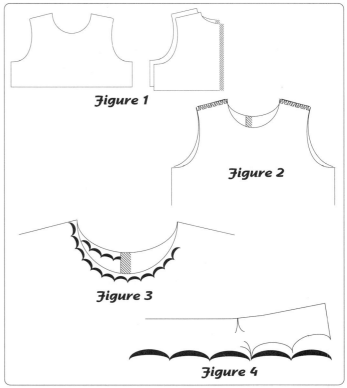

Figure 1

Figure 2

Figure 3

Figure 4

Note: *If your machine does not have scalloping capabilities, finish the edge with 3/8" edging (see A-line Slip-Step 3) or use this edge finishing method:*

a. Straight stitch 1/4" from the fabric edge **(fig. 5)**.

b. Turn the fabric edge to the inside along the stitching line, clipping the fabric as needed **(fig. 6)**.

c. Zigzag along the fold **(fig. 7)**.

d. Trim excess fabric from behind.

4. Place the sides of the bodice right sides together and stitch. **(fig. 8)**.

5. Cut one skirt piece to the following measurement (skirt lengths given are for use with 1-3/4" lace band of beading and edging lace):

17-1/2" dolls	6" by 45"
18-1/2" dolls	6-3/4" by 45"
19-1/2" dolls	7" by 45"
21-1/2" dolls	8-1/2" by 45"

6. Butt the beading to the edging lace and attach together with a zigzag. Refer to the "lace to lace" technique **(fig. 9)**.

7. Attach beading/edging lace along one edge of the skirt piece using the technique "lace to fabric". Press **(fig. 10)**.

8. Gather the top edge of the skirt piece to fit the bottom edge of the slip bodice. Stitch the skirt to the slip bodice, right sides together **(fig. 11)**.

9. Stitch the backs, right sides together, stopping 5" from the neck edge for the 17-1/2" doll and 6" from the neck edge for other sizes. This will create a placket **(fig. 12)**.

10. Press the seam allowances to the left side of the slip. Turn the slip to the right side and press the right side of the opening to the inside 1/4". Topstitch the seam allowance in place at the bottom of the opening **(figs. 13)**.

11. Close with small buttons, snaps or Velcro®.

12. Weave ribbon through the beading beginning and ending 6" from the right side seam. Tie the remaining ribbon into a bow.

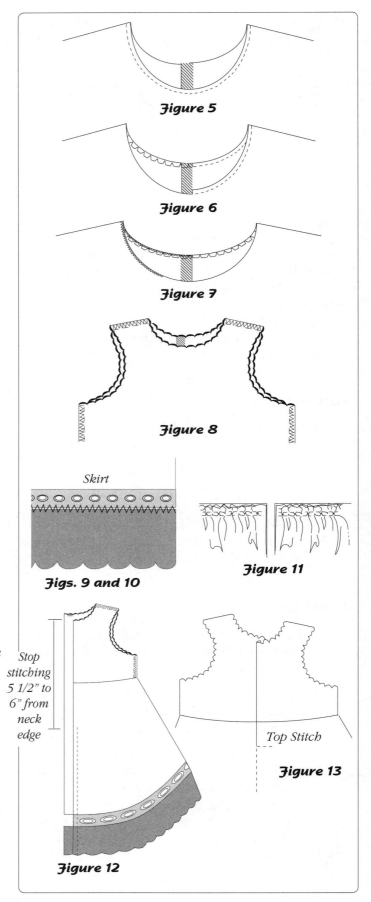

Figure 5

Figure 6

Figure 7

Figure 8

Skirt

Figs. 9 and 10

Figure 11

Stop stitching 5 1/2" to 6" from neck edge

Top Stitch

Figure 13

Figure 12

Peach Slip for Spoke Collar Cinderella Dress

Designed specifically to be worn under a white Swiss dotted dress, this peach slip serves as more than just an undergarment. It adds a hint of color to the total ensemble. The to-the-waist slip is made of peach Swiss batiste Nelona and the armhole and neck edge are finished with peach machine scallops. The back on the version pictured is closed with three tiny peach buttons and loops, however overlapping the placket and using Velcro® would be a suitable closure for a doll's slip. The bottom of the slip which peeks out from beneath the dress is finished with entredeux, beading run with peach ribbon, and wide gathered lace edging.

Supplies

Fabric	1/2 yd.
Lace Edging (2-1/4")	2-1/2 yds.
Lace Beading	1-1/4 yds.
Entredeux	1-1/4 yds.
Ribbon (to fit beading)	1-1/2 yds.

Notions: Lightweight sewing thread; snaps, buttons or Velcro®

Directions

1. Follow the directions given for the **Pink Slip for Victorian Dress** - Steps 1 through 4 (page 191).

2. Cut one skirt piece to the following measurement (skirt lengths given are for use with 3" lace band of entredeux, beading and gathered edging lace):

   17-1/2" 5" by 45"

   18-1/2" 5-3/4" by 45"

   19-1/2" 6" by 45"

   21-1/2" 7-1/2" by 45"

3. Attach the entredeux to the beading **(fig. 1)** using the technique "entredeux to lace". Gather the lace edging to fit the beading and attach **(fig. 2)** using the "lace to lace" technique.

4. Attach the entredeux/beading/edging lace band along one edge of the skirt piece using the technique "entredeux to fabric" **(fig. 3)**. Press.

5. Finish the slip construction using the directions given for the **Pink Slip for Victorian Dress - Steps 7 through 13.** (page 192).

- **All pattern pieces and templates found in the pattern section page 300-301.**
- **Color photograph on page 29**

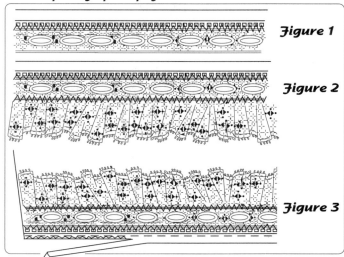

Figure 1

Figure 2

Figure 3

White Cancan Petticoat

When your dolly has a special occasion on her social calendar, she knows it's time to get out the cancan slip. Netting, straight stitched to the bottom of the simple design, kicks out a skirt for a party look. The slip is made of white batiste with the narrow bias binding around the neckline and armholes. The gathered skirt has a fullness of 29-1/2" and is finished with narrow lace edging stitched flat onto the bottom. A 3-1/2" wide double row of gathered stiff netting is stitched to the top of this petticoat for ultimate fullness. Buttons and loops close the back of the garment pictured, although Velcro® could certainly be used.

- *All pattern pieces and templates found in the pattern section page 300-301.*
- *Color photograph on page 30*

Supplies

Fabric	1/2 yd.
Lace Edging (1/2")	7/8 yd.
Netting	1/3 yd.

Notions: Lightweight sewing thread; snaps, buttons or Velcro®

Directions

1. Using the To-The-Waist Slip bodice pattern, cut one front from the fold and two backs from the selvage **(fig. 1)**.

2. Place the shoulders of the slip bodice, right sides together and stitch **(fig. 2)**.

3. Place the bodice front to the bodice back at the sides and stitch. See figure 2.

4. Measure around the neck with the back fold pressed to the inside of the bodice. Also measure around the arm openings. Cut one bias strip 1-1/8" wide by 1" more than the neck measurement. Cut two bias strips 1-1/8" wide by 1" more than the arm opening measurement. Press all strips in half lengthwise **(fig. 3)**. These folded strips will be used for the bindings.

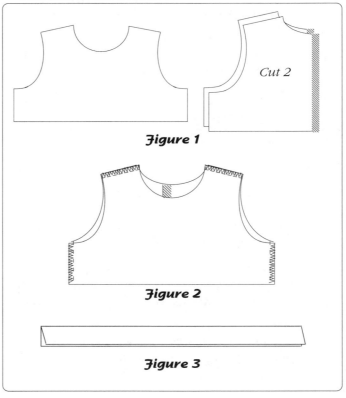

Cut 2

Figure 1

Figure 2

Figure 3

5. With the back facings folded in place, place the cut edges of the strip to the neck edge of the bodice allowing the excess strip to extend beyond the back folds **(fig. 4)** Stitch in place using a 1/4" seam. Trim the seam allowance to 1/8" **(fig. 5)**. Finger press the binding toward the seam allowance **(fig. 5a)**. Fold the extended tabs at the bodice back to the inside of the bodice, then fold the binding to enclosing the seam allowance **(fig. 5b)**. Stitch the fold of the binding to the inside of the bodice by hand or machine **(fig. 6)**.

6. Place the cut edges of the strip to the arm edge of the bodice starting the strip 1/4" past the side seam. Pin. Continue around the opening overlap ping the beginning of the strip by 1/2". Cut away any excess, if necessary. Working with the top binding piece only, fold the cut edge to the inside of the strip 1/4". Place the bottom strip inside the top folded strip, enclosing the bottom strip **(fig. 7)**. Pin. Stitch in place using a 1/4" seam. Trim the seam allowance to 1/8". Finger press the binding toward the seam allowance. Fold the binding to the inside of the bodice, enclosing the seam allowance. Stitch the fold of the binding to the inside of the bodice by hand or machine. Refer to figure 6.

7. Cut one skirt piece to the following measurement (skirt lengths given are for use with 1/2" lace edging):

17-1/2"   6-3/4" by 30"

18-1/2"   7-1/2" by 30"

19-1/2"   7-3/4" by 30"

21-1/2"   9-1/4" by 30"

8. Attach edging lace along one edge of the skirt piece **(fig. 8)** using the technique "lace to fabric". Press.

9. Complete the slip using steps 8-11, **Pink Slip for Victorian Dress,** page 192.

10. Cut one piece of netting to the following measurements: 17-1/2" dolls to 19-1/2" dolls cut to 8" by 45"; 21-1/2" dolls cut to 10" by 45". Stitch together along the short side creating a cylinder **(fig. 9)**.

11. Fold the netting in half and stitch a gathering row 1/4" from the fold. Gather to about 29-1/2" **(fig. 10)**. Distribute the gathers evenly and pin to the skirt slip with the cut edges of the netting even with the scalloped edge of the lace. Pin and stitch in place along the gathering row **(fig. 11)**.

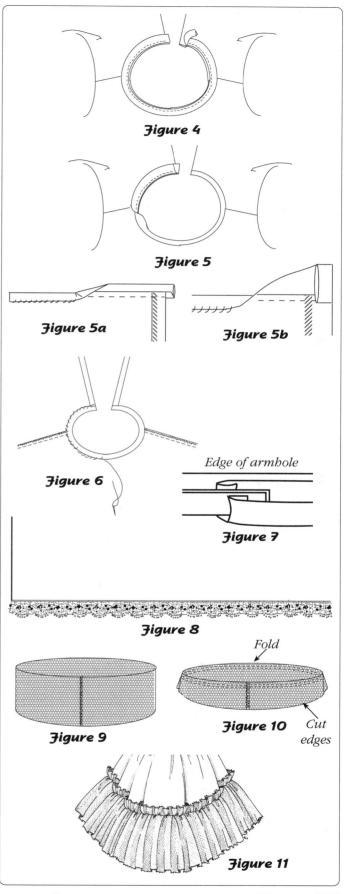

Figure 4

Figure 5

Figure 5a

Figure 5b

Figure 6

Edge of armhole

Figure 7

Figure 8

Fold

Figure 9

Figure 10   Cut edges

Figure 11

Triple-Tiered Petticoat

Three ruffles joined together give this petticoat added fullness. The version pictured was made of white Swiss batiste, trimmed on the lowest tier with flat lace edging. The waist is elastic. I can remember my Mama making me three-tiered skirts and trimming them with yards and yards of braid.

Supplies

Fabric	1/3 yd.
Lace Edging (3/4")	2 yds.
Elastic (1/8")	1/3 yd.

Notions: Lightweight sewing thread; snaps, buttons or Velcro®

• **Color photograph on page 31**

Directions

1. Cut strips of fabric to the following measurements to construct each tiar of the slip. The bottom will consist of two strips stitched together.

Doll Sizes	17-1/2"	18-1/2"	19-1/2"	21-1/2"
a. *Top strip 18" by*	2-5/8"	2-3/4"	3-1/8"	3-1/4"
b. *Middle strip 40" by*	2-3/8"	2-1/2"	2-7/8"	3-1/8"
c. *Bottom strip 45" by*	2-3/4"	3"	3-1/4"	3-1/2"
d. *Bottom strip 36" by* (cut two)	2-3/4"	3"	3-1/4"	3-1/2"

2. Run two gathering rows 1/8" and 1/4" in one long side of the middle ruffle strip and gather to fit the top strip. **(fig. 1)** Stitch together using a 1/4" seam. **(fig. 2)**.

3. Stitch the two bottom strips together creating one long strip. Attach edging lace to one long edge of the bottom strip using the technique "lace to fabric". Gather the other long edge to fit the lower edge of the middle ruffle. Stitch the bottom strip to the middle strip **(fig. 3)**.

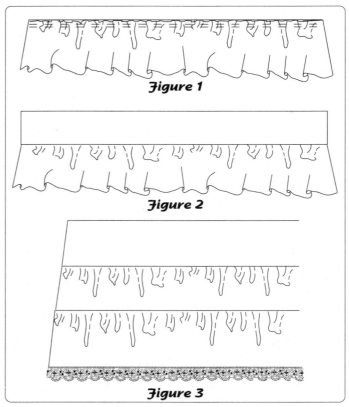

Figure 1

Figure 2

Figure 3

4. Place the back edges of the slip together matching each tier seam **(fig. 4)**. Stitch in place.

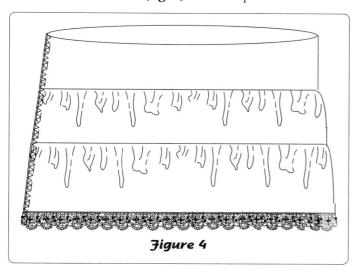

Figure 4

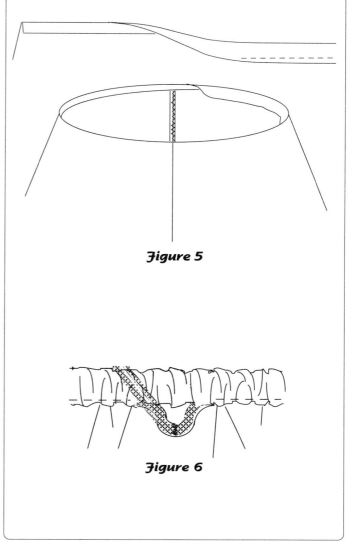

Figure 5

Figure 6

5. Turn the top edge of the slip to the inside 1/8" and then 1/4" **(fig. 5)**. Press. To create a casing, stitch along the folded edge leaving 1" open.

6. Cut one elastic piece to the following size:

17-1/2" doll	8-1/2"
18-1/2" doll	10"
19-1/2" doll	9-1/2"
21-1/2" doll	11-1/2"

7. Run elastic through the casing, overlapping the elastic 1/4". Stitch the ends of the elastic together with a small zigzag **(fig. 6)**.

8. Stitch the opening closed.

Peplum Camisole

White-on-white machine embroidery trims this peplum camisole down the center front. Four released tucks in graduating lengths line either side of the center embroidery. Narrow white edging finishes the neckline and the armholes, while a slightly gathered wider edging is zigzagged to the bottom. The peplum is cleverly created on the otherwise straight line garment by pulling the waistline in with elastic. Release tucks are the only embellishment added to the back, which is closed with Velcro®.

- **All pattern pieces and templates found in the pattern section page 298-299.**
- **Color photograph on page 29**

Supplies

Fabric	1/4 yd.
Lace Edging (3/8")	1 yd.
Lace Edging (3/4")	1 yd.

Notions: Lightweight sewing thread; snaps, buttons or Velcro®

Directions

1. Using the Peplum Camisole pattern, cut one camisole front from the fold and two camisole backs from the selvage. Using a fabric marker or fabric pencil mark the tuck/fold lines and the waistline along the camisole front and the waistline and the back fold lines of the camisole back **(fig.1)**.

2. Fold the camisole front along each tuck/fold line, wrong sides together. Stitch 1/8" from the fold stopping at the end of the line **(fig. 2)**. Backstitch. Continue stitching for all tucks. Press the tucks away from the center front. Optional: Stitch a decorative stitch along the center front of the camisole.

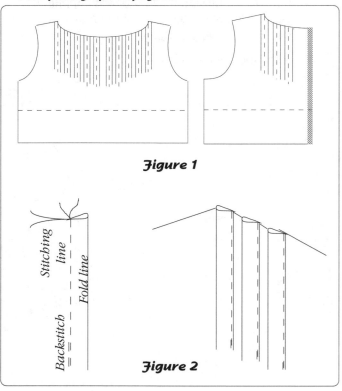

Figure 1

Figure 2

3. Place the shoulders of the slip right sides together and stitch **(fig. 3)**.

4. Attach 3/8" edging lace at the neck **(fig. 4)** and arm openings using the directions under the **A-line Slip**, Steps 3 and 4 (page 190).

5. Place the sides of the camisole, right sides together and stitch.

6. Attach lace edging to the lower edge of the camisole using the technique "lace to fabric".

7. Press the back edges to the inside of the camisole along the fold line.

8. Cut a strip of elastic to the following measurement:

17-1/2" doll	*8-1/2"*
18-1/2" doll	*10"*
19-1/2" doll	*9-1/2"*
21-1/2" doll	*11-1/2"*

9. The elastic will be held in place with a zigzag casing. Place the elastic along the waist line starting and stopping 1/2" from the back folds. When stitching the elastic in place start with a straight stitch, stitching about 1/8" along the center of the elastic, continue stitching with a zigzag wide enough to stitch over but not through the elastic **(fig. 5)**. End with a straight stitch.

10. Stitch the folded lace pieces at the top and bottom of the camisole in place with a zigzag. Close with small buttons, snaps or Velcro®.

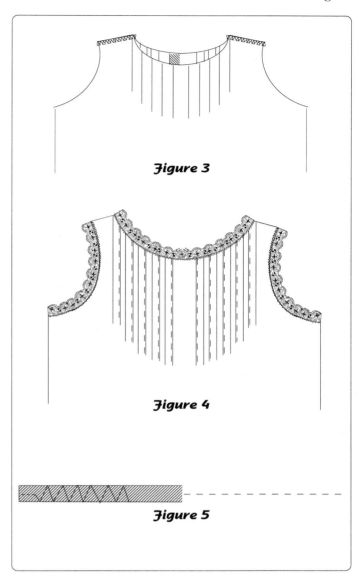

Figure 3

Figure 4

Figure 5

Fancy Puffed Camisole & Pantaloons

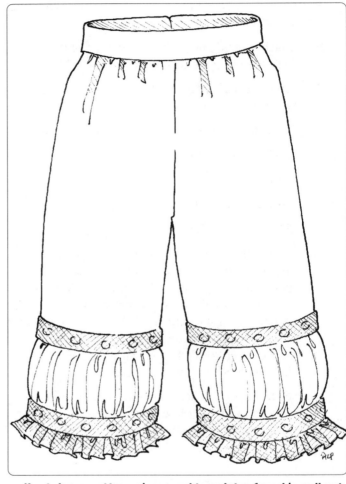

This precious puffed ensemble was specifically designed to be worn under Monet's Garden of Flowers Dress, which can be found in the dress section of this book. The lined camisole features a strip of puffing down the front with two strips of narrow French edging down each side. Entredeux and gathered lace trim the bottom. The back is closed with three snaps. Darts sewn into the back serve to make the camisole fit better underneath the to-the-waist dress. The waistband of the pantaloons closes with a snap. Decorative puffing on the bottom of each leg echoes the treatment on the camisole. Gathered lace edging finishes the bottom.

- **Pantaloons pattern pieces and templates found in pull-out section. Camisole pattern pieces found in pattern section page 300-301.**
- **Color photograph on page 17**

Supplies

Fabric	1/2 yd.
Lace Edging (1/2")	2 yds.
Insertion Lace	1-1/2 yds.
Entredeux	1/2 yd.

Notions: Lightweight sewing thread; snaps, buttons or Velcro™

Directions

1. Using the To-The-Waist camisole pattern, cut two camisole fronts from the fold (camisole and lining) and two camisole backs from the fold (camisole and lining) **(fig. 1)**. Using the Straight Leg Pantaloon pattern, cut two and set aside **(fig. 2)**.

2. Puffing strips - Cut two strips of fabric 2-1/4" wide by 45" long for the puffing. This will make enough puffing for the camisole and the pantaloons. Run gathering rows in each side of the strips at 1/4" and 1/2" or use a gathering foot with the seam at 1/2". Gather each piece to about 16" **(fig. 3)**.

3. Cut a piece of puffing
   5" *for the 17-1/2" doll*
   5-1/2" *for the 18-1/2" and 19-1/2" doll*
   6" *for the 21-1/2" doll*

4. Cut two pieces of lace insertion to the measurement given in Step 3.

5. Along each side of the puffing, place the edge of the lace over the 1/2" gathering line. Stitch the lace in place using a small, tight zigzag **(fig. 4)**. Trim the excess fabric from behind the lace.

6. Center the lace/puffing strip along the front of the camisole and stitch in place along the outer edges of the lace using a zigzag. Draw the neck opening on the lace/puffing strip using the camisole as a guide **(fig. 5)**. Trim the camisole fabric from behind the lace/puffing strip. Stay stitch the puffing/lace strip 1/8" inside the drawn neck line. Trim puffing/lace strip along the drawn line **(fig. 6)**.

7. Stitch the camisole front to the camisole backs at the shoulders and stitch the front lining to the back linings at the shoulders **(fig. 7)**.

8. Fold the lining to the camisole along the fold lines of the back, right sides together matching all edges. Stitch around the neck edge and arm openings with a 1/4" seam. Clip the curves **(fig. 8a)**. Turn to the right side by pulling each back through the corresponding shoulder "tunnel" (between the lining and camisole). Stitch the sides together, placing the front to the back and front lining to the back lining **(fig. 8b)**.

9. Fold the lower edge of the camisole and lining to the inside 1/4". Press. Pin the folded edges together **(fig. 9)**.

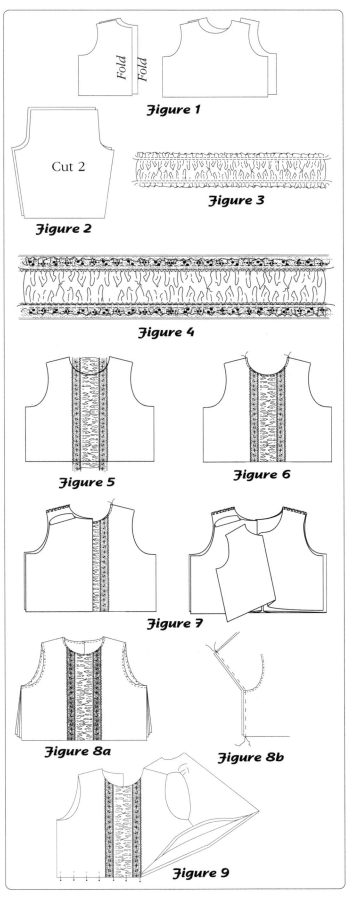

Figure 1

Figure 2

Cut 2

Figure 3

Figure 4

Figure 5

Figure 6

Figure 7

Figure 8a

Figure 8b

Figure 9

10. Cut a piece of entredeux to fit the lower edge of the camisole. Trim away one fabric edge of the entredeux. Butt the trimmed entredeux to the folded edges of the camisole. Zigzag in place. Trim the remaining fabric edge from the entredeux **(fig. 10)**.

11. Cut a 28" piece of edging lace. Turn each end of the lace under 1/2" and gather to fit the entredeux. Attach the lace to the entredeux using the technique entredeux to gathered lace **(fig. 11)**.

12. Close with small buttons, snaps or Velcro™.

13. For the straight leg pantaloons cut two puffing strips 10" long. Cut four insertion lace pieces 10" long. Place the insertion along each side of the puffing - refer to Step 5. Place the lace/puffing along the bottom edge of each pantaloon piece with the lower edge of the lace even with the edge of the pantaloons. Stitch along the upper edge of the top lace piece using a small tight zigzag. Trim the lace/puffing strip even with the sides of the pantaloons **(fig. 12)**. Trim excess fabric from behind the lace/puffing strip.

14. Cut two pieces of lace edging 20" long. Gather each piece to fit lower piece of lace insertion on each pantaloon leg. Stitch the insertion to the gathered lace with a zigzag **(fig. 13)**.

15. Place the pantaloons, right sides together. Stitch the center back from the placket mark to the inner leg **(fig. 14)**.

16. Cut a selvage strip 3/4" wide by 8" long. Note: A lace placket can be used if desired. Stitch the placket in the back of the pantaloons using the directions for continuous lap plackets used in a seam - c. Continuous Placket in a Seam (page 43) or b. Lace Placket (page 42), using a seam instead of a slit (refer to c. placket in a seam). Fold the right side of the placket to the inside of the pantaloons and pin in place.

17. Place the fronts of the pantaloons right sides together. Stitch the center front **(fig. 15)**.

18. Place the legs, right sides together, matching the laces and crotch seams. Stitch in place **(fig. 16)**.

19. Cut a waist band 1-1/2" wide by the following measurements:

17-1/2" dolls	*9-3/4"*
18-1/2" dolls	*11-1/4"*
19-1/2" dolls	*10-3/4"*
21-1/2" dolls	*12-3/4"*

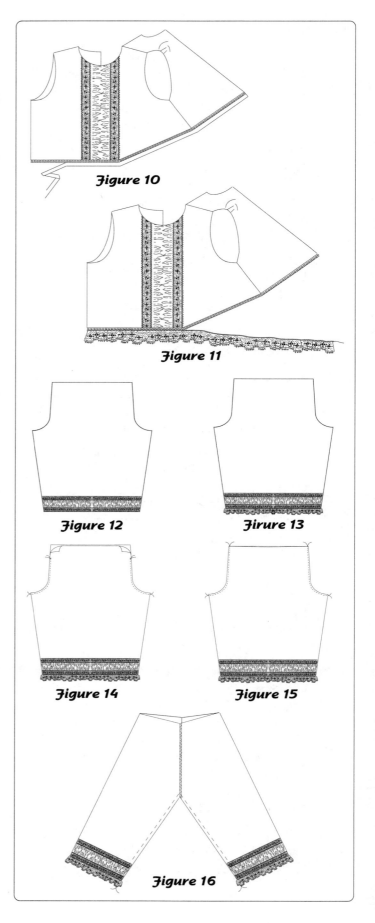

Figure 10

Figure 11

Figure 12

Firure 13

Figure 14

Figure 15

Figure 16

20. Stitch two gathering rows at 1/8" and 1/4" at the waist. Pin the waist band to the waist, right sides together, allowing the waistband to extend at the placket 1/4" **(fig. 17)**. Remember one side of the placket is folded to the inside and the other side is left extended. Gather the waist of the pantaloons to fit the waistband.

21. Stitch the waistband in place using a 1/4" seam. Press the waistband away from the pantaloons. Turn the top edge of the waistband to the inside 1/4" and press **(fig. 18)**.

22. Fold the waistband in half to the front side of the pantalets with the pressed 1/4" fold falling just past the stitching line. Stitch the short ends together being careful not to catch the placket **(fig. 19)**.

23 Flip the waistband so that the 1/4" fold falls just past the stitching line along the inside of the pantaloons. Stitch in place by hand or machine **(fig. 20)**.

24. Place a small piece of Velcro™ or a snap at the waistband to close.

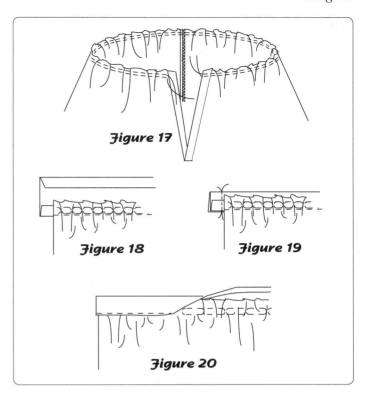

Figure 17

Figure 18

Figure 19

Figure 20

White Bloomers

Old-fashioned bloomers add a charming touch to just about any dress when they peek out from underneath. This pair is made of white Swiss batiste trimmed with Swiss embroidered trim on the bottom of the legs. The waistline and legs are elasticized, so they fit a myriad of doll sizes.

Supplies

Fabric	1/3 yd.
Eyelet (1-1/4")	2/3 yd.
Elastic (1/8")	1 yd.

Notions: Lightweight sewing thread; snaps, buttons or Velcro™

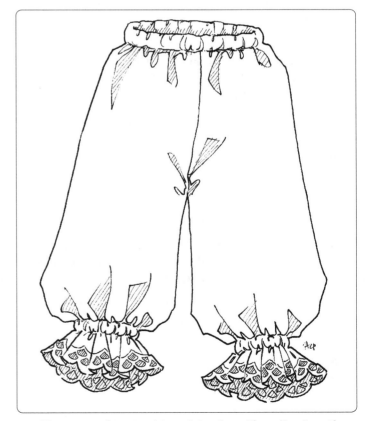

- **All pattern pieces and templates found in pull-out section**
- **Color photograph on page 29**

Directions

1. Using the Bloomer pattern, cut two.

2. Cut two pieces of eyelet to fit the lower edge of each bloomer piece. Place the eyelet to the bloomer, right sides together and stitch in place with a 1/4" seam **(fig. 1)**. Place the bloomers right sides together matching the center fronts. Stitch in place.

3. Place the bloomers right sides together matching the center backs. Stitch in place **(fig. 2)**.

4. Cut two pieces of elastic 7" long. Mark each piece 1" from the ends. Place the elastic over the seam of the bloomer and eyelet with the mark even with the edge of the bloomer **(fig. 3)**. Take several straight stitches on the elastic tacking the end in place. Refer to figure 3. Continue stitching with a zigzag **over** the elastic being careful not to catch the elastic **(fig. 4)**. About 1/4" from the other edge pull the elastic until the other mark is even with the edge of the bloomer, again take several straight stitches to tack the elastic in place. Trim the excess elastic. Repeat for the other leg.

5. Place the inner legs right sides together matching the crotch seam and the elastic. Stitch in place **(fig. 5)**.

6. Turn the top edge of the bloomers to the inside 1/8" and then 1/4" **(fig. 6)**. Press. To create a casing, stitch along the folded edge leaving 1" open **(fig. 7)**.

7. Cut one elastic piece to the following size:

17-1/2" doll	8-1/2"
18-1/2" doll	10"
19-1/2" doll	9-1/2"
21-1/2" doll	11-1/2"

8. Run elastic through the casing, overlapping the elastic 1/4". Stitch the ends of the elastic together with a small zigzag **(fig. 8)**.

9. Stitch the opening closed.

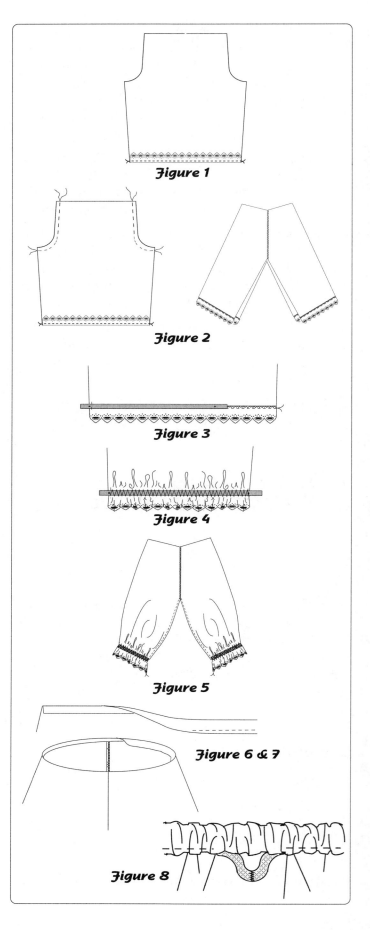

Figure 1

Figure 2

Figure 3

Figure 4

Figure 5

Figure 6 & 7

Figure 8

White Dropped Waist Slip

A dropped waist dress (of which there are several in this book) calls for a dropped waist slip, and this clean-line version is quick and easy to make. Like its A-line sister, this dropped waist design has limited embellishment. Narrow lace trims the neckline and arm openings; wider lace edges the skirt. The back closes at the top with one square of Velcro®.

Supplies

Requirements:

Fabric	1/2 yd.
Lace Edging (3/8")	1 yd.
Lace Edging (1")	1-1/4 yds.

Notions: Light-weight sewing thread; snaps, buttons or Velcro®

- **All pattern pieces and templates found in pattern section page 296-297.**
- **Color photograph on page 31**

Directions

1. Using the to the dropped waist slip bodice pattern, cut one front from the fold and two bodice backs from the selvage **(fig. 1)**.

2. Place the shoulders of the slip bodice right sides together and stitch. Starch and press the neck and arm openings **(fig. 2)**.

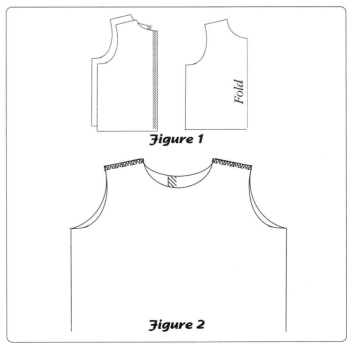

Fold

Figure 1

Figure 2

3. Place edging lace along the neck of the slip, allowing the scalloped edge of the lace to fall on the fabric edge and the lace to extend beyond the selvage edges 1/4". Stitch along the straight side of the lace using the technique for extra stable lace finishes (page 238)**(fig. 3)**.

4. Place lace around the armhole using the same technique (refer to fig. 3).

5. Place the sides of the slip right sides together and stitch **(fig. 4)**.

6. Cut one skirt piece 45" long by the following measurements:

Doll Sizes	17-1/2"	18-1/2"	19-1/2"	21-1/2"
Skirt	5-1/2"	6"	7"	7"

7. Place 1" edging lace along one long edge of the skirt piece using the technique lace to fabric. Press.

8. Run two gathering rows in the top of the skirt piece, 1/4" and 1/8" from the edge. Gather to fit the slip bodice **(fig. 5)**.

9. Stitch the skirt to the slip, right sides together.

10. Stitch the backs, right sides together, stopping 5" from the neck edge for the 17-1/2" doll and 6" from the neck edge for other sizes **(fig. 6)**. This will create a placket.

11. Press the seam allowances to the right side of the slip. Turn the slip to the right side and press the right side of the opening to the inside 1/4" **(fig. 7)**. Top stitch the seam allowance in place at the bottom of the opening.

12. Close with small buttons, snaps or Velcro®.

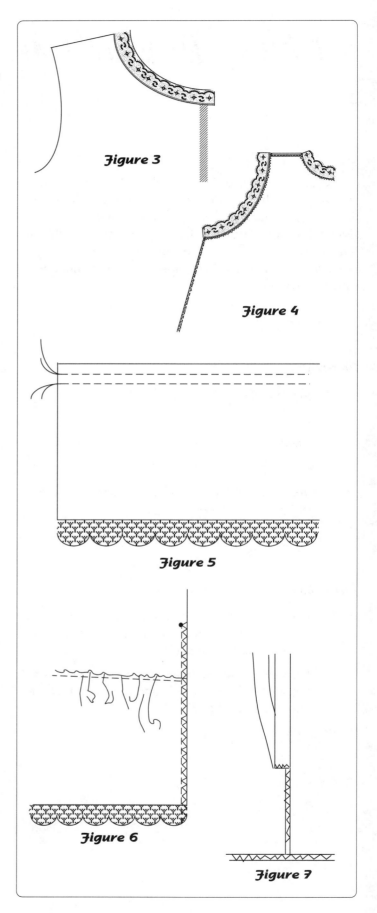

Figure 3

Figure 4

Figure 5

Figure 6

Figure 7

Techniques

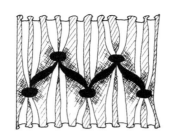

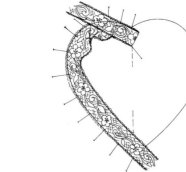

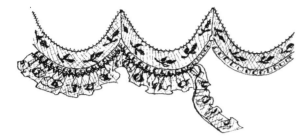

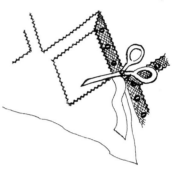

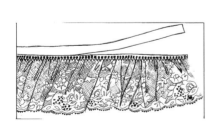

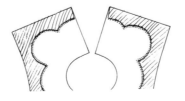

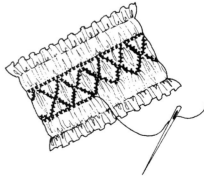

Preparing To Smock

Needles

Generally, a #8 crewel embroidery needle is used in smocking. Substitute a #6 or #7 crewel if threading three or four strands of floss through a #8 crewel poses a problem due to its smaller eye.

Some needles work better for certain fabrics. For example:

a. For fine batiste or batiste blend, use a #8 or #9 crewel needle. Use a smaller size when using fewer strands of floss.

b. For fine to medium fabrics, such as broadcloth or quilting fabric, use a #7 or #8 crewel needle.

Some smockers prefer to stitch with a milliner's needle. This needle is long and has a straight needle eye opening. Other smockers prefer to use #7 darners or #7 long darners.

Embroidery Floss

The general rule of thumb is to use three strands of embroidery floss when working with fine to medium fabrics. However, there are exceptions:

a. For a delicate look on fine fabric, try using two strands.

b. For picture smocking, most designers recommend four strands.

c. For some heavier fabrics, such as corduroy and velveteen, use up to five or six strands. Experiment with heavier fabrics to find the right weight of floss for the desired look.

d. It is perfectly acceptable to use pearl cotton #8 for smocking.

Preparing Floss

In order to prepare your embroidery floss for smocking, first make sure that it is put on grain properly. All thread has a grain. With DMC floss, it is easy to make sure the floss is on grain. Look at the two paper wraps on the embroidery floss. One has the round DMC symbol. The other has the color number and a picture of two hands pulling the floss out of the package. Follow these directions:

a. Grasp floss with the left hand on the side that pictures the hands.

b. Pull floss out of the package with the right hand from the opposite side.

c. Always knot the cut end. It is best to separate the six strands, then put three strands back together and knot those three strands

d. Put the other three strands back together, knot the end, and set aside.

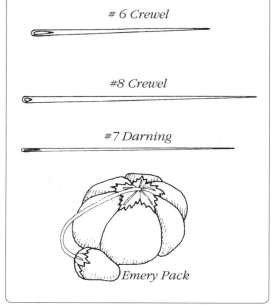

6 Crewel

#8 Crewel

#7 Darning

Emery Pack

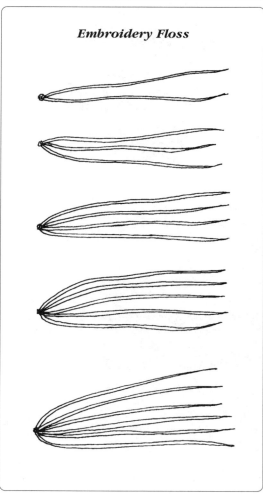

Embroidery Floss

It is easy to lose track of which end was cut from the skein. If for some reason this occurs, there is a simple solution. One end of the floss "blooms" more than the other. The cut end of the floss does not fuzz out as much. Knot the floss on the less fuzzy end.

Needles also have a right and wrong side. Think about sewing machine needles that only go in one way. If it is difficult to thread a needle from one direction, try flipping it to the other side. One side will usually thread more easily than the other.

Fabric

Popular fabrics to smock include blends of 65 percent polyester and 35 percent cotton. Sometimes, a higher polyester count does not pleat well. However, using all of the half spaces of the Pullen Pleater, 100 percent nylon pleats without a pucker. Ginghams, pima cottons, 100 percent cottons for quilting, challis, Swiss batiste, velveteen, soft corduroy, and silks are also good for smocking.

Fabrics, such as calico prints, which are 100 percent cotton, should be washed and dried before pleating. Fabrics with a polyester content generally do not shrink, and thus do not need to be washed prior to pleating. It is not necessary to preshrink Imperial batiste, Imperial broadcloth, 100 percent Swiss batiste (Nelona, Finella, Finissima), wool challis from Switzerland, and velveteen.

Note: *When a 45" piece for the front and one for the back of a yoke dress is necessary, it is easier to tear those skirt lengths first and preshrink them separately; smaller pieces of fabric can be pre shrunk and put "on grain" more easily. Then, preshrink the remaining fabric from which the bodice, sleeves, and collars will be cut.*

Putting Fabric On Grain

To put fabric on grain use one of two methods.

a. Tear both ends. Most fabric stores tear wovens **(fig. 1)**, or.

b. Pull a thread and clip across from selvage to selvage. This is the best technique for aligning fibers in Swiss batiste **(fig. 2)**.

Fabric may be preshrunk after having "torn" or "pulled a thread" and cut the fabric.

Tying Off Pleating Threads Before Smocking

Figure 3 An example of where the whole skirt will be used in the smocked garment.

Figure 4 A typical short yoke dress where a portion of the armhole curve must be cut away from the skirt. Do not smock that portion. Do not count that portion when figuring the 1" to 11/2" rule of tying off.

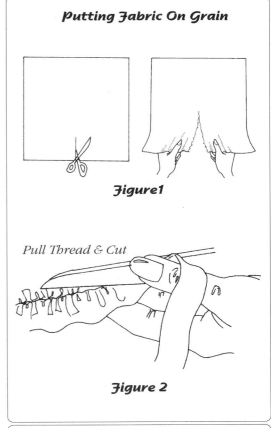

Putting Fabric On Grain

Figure 1

Pull Thread & Cut

Figure 2

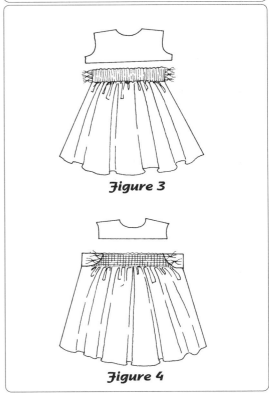

Figure 3

Figure 4

This rule is sometimes called "smocking to size." It is a must to size the smocking before beginning to smock. The smocking will have to be stretched too much to fit the dress if this rule is not followed. This often results in ripples and waves at the yoke after the dress is constructed. I suppose that the opposite could be true (smocking too loosely); however, rarely do beginning smockers smock too loosely.

The width of fabric before being pleated should be three times as wide as the finished smocked piece will be. A little more or a little less fullness is acceptable.

Right and Wrong Side of Pleated Fabric

Pleated fabric has a right and wrong side. The secret to figuring out which side of the fabric to smock, assuming that the fabric does not already have a designated right or wrong side, is easy to remember - Long is Wrong.

Stretch out the pleated fabric **(fig. 5)**. Look at the length of stitches on both sides. The flat stitches are longer on one side than they are on the other. This is the wrong side. The right side of the fabric, the side to be smocked, has the shorter stitches **(fig. 6)**. Hence, the rule - Long is Wrong.

Another way to determine the right and wrong side of the pleated fabric is by the height of the pleats. Flip the pleated fabric back and forth to see which side has the tallest pleats from the gathering row up to the top of the pleat. The right side of the pleated fabric has the tallest pleats.

When running fabric through the pleater, the right side of the fabric should face the floor or the bottom of the pleater. To smock a fabric with a designated right or wrong side (corduroy or printed fabric), run it through the pleater with the right side facing down to the floor.

Tying Off Gathering Threads Before Smocking

After opening the pleated fabric to the desired width, it is time to tie off the excess gathering threads **(fig. 7)**.

Tie off as many threads as is comfortable. The norm is three threads **(fig. 8)**.

It is not necessary to tie off gathering threads at all. Many smockers will work with them hanging long; however, these threads do tend to become tangled and caught in smocking. If this is a problem, tie them off and clip the excess.

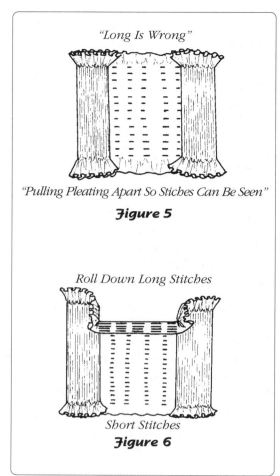

"Long Is Wrong"

"Pulling Pleating Apart So Stiches Can Be Seen"
Figure 5

Roll Down Long Stitches

Short Stitches
Figure 6

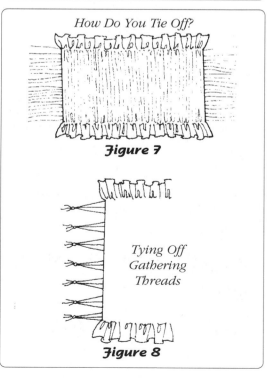

How Do You Tie Off?
Figure 7

Tying Off Gathering Threads

Figure 8

Tying A Surgical Knot

A surgical knot is best for securing sponge-like quilting thread, which tends to come untied.

1. Tie one knot. Do not take this first knot down to the fabric, but leave it about 1 inch away from the fabric edge **(fig. 9)**.

2. Hold the knot with your right hand. Wrap the left hand strings around the knot one more time **(figs. 10 and 11)**. Left handed smockers need to reverse this step.

3. Tie one more knot, just like the first one **(fig. 12)**. This last knot is pulled tightly for a very secure knot **(fig. 13)**.

4. Clip off the excess threads after tying each knot. Clip the threads to within 2" of the knot.

Centering Smocking Design

The easiest way to mark the center of the fabric is to fold it in half and mark. Counting the pleats to determine the center will also work. There are two methods of centering the smocking.

• Method 1

1. Begin smocking in the exact center of the skirt or dress. Tie knots at this point, as if this were the left-hand side of the smocking.

2. Knot the floss. Bring it in on the left-hand side of the middle pleat of the skirt. Smock half the skirt to the right side.

3. Turn the work upside down. Smock the other side, working from the middle to the other side.

• Method 2

This method avoids the two knots on the center pleats **(fig. 14)**.

1. Leave a long thread with the first stitch.

2. Take this first stitch from the front of the smocking. Do not bring the thread from the back. Leave the long, unknotted thread hanging on the front.

3. Smock all the way over to the right and tie off.

4. Turn the work upside down. Re-thread the long thread. Finish the first stitch. Smock the rest of the work to the other side.

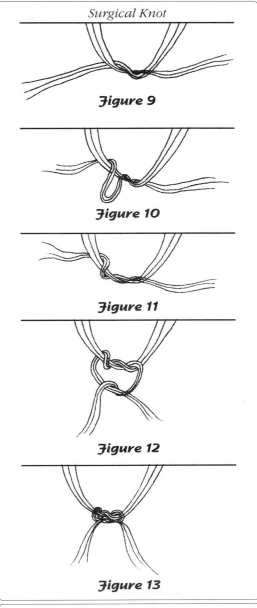

Surgical Knot

Figure 9

Figure 10

Figure 11

Figure 12

Figure 13

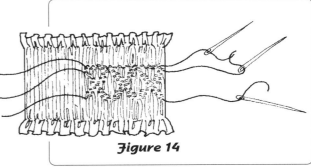

Figure 14

Smocking Stitches

Crazy Cat and The Courthouse Story

Many beginner smockers get frustrated with the rule: When you move up, the thread is down, when you move down, the thread is up. For a beginner, this is the most difficult concept to learn. I made up a simple, and very silly, story to help beginners remember this principle. I was a little embarrassed the first time I told the story, but several years and smockers later, I can honestly say this works.

- **Setting** - a courthouse with lots of tall steps leading to the door.

- **Characters** - A Tabby cat with a very long tail. Martha Pullen

- **Time** - During business hours.

Tabby Cat wants to drive a car and knows she must first have a driver's license. Martha Pullen drives Tabby Cat to the courthouse and parks at the side of the building to let Tabby Cat out. Tabby Cat climbs the long steps until she gets almost to the top. There, she remembers that you have to have money to pay for a license. Tabby Cat turns around, climbs down the long flight of steps and goes back to the car to get some money from her purse.

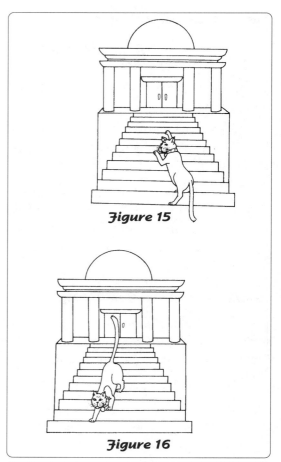

Figure 15

Important Points To This Story:

Point A. Tabby Cat's tail is the thread.

Point B. When Tabby Cat climbs stairs, her tail points downward **(fig. 15)**. In smocking, when the needle is moving up, the tail of the thread is down.

Point C. When Tabby Cat climbs down the stairs, her tail points upward **(fig. 16)**. In smocking, when you are moving to take a stitch downward, the tail of the thread is up.

Point D. When Tabby Cat turns around at the top of the stairs, at the landing, her tail swings around before she can begin to climb back down the stairs. This symbolizes a top cable before the wave or trellis moves downward. When Tabby Cat turns around at the bottom of the stairs to begin upward, this symbolizes a bottom cable before the climb back up.

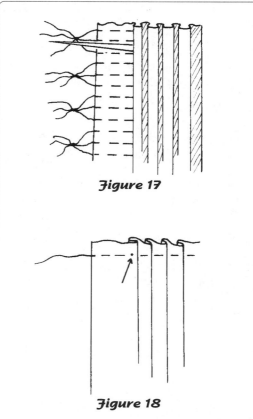

Figure 16

Bringing In The Needle To Begin Smocking

There are two schools of thought on where to make the first stitch.

• Method 1

1. Bring in the needle on the left hand side of the first pleat that begins your smocking **(fig. 17)**.

2. Bring in the needle just above the gathering thread **(fig. 18)**.

3. It is acceptable to bring in the needle in the same hole as the gathering thread, on this left side of the pleat.

4. This method leaves the knot of the floss hidden within the first pleat on the back of the smocking.

Figure 17

Figure 18

• Method 2

1. Bring in the needle on the left hand side of the second pleat, rather than on the left hand side of the first pleat **(fig. 19)**.

2. Go through the gathering holes of the first pleat to bring the needle out of the left hand side of the first pleat where smock ing begins. This hides the knot in the second pleat and is stronger and more secure. The knot will less likely pull out with wear and washing since it is one pleat over from the edge of the smocking **(fig. 20)**.

Stitch Bite

Nearly all smocking books advise picking up from 1/3 to 1/2 of the pleat above the gathering threads **(fig. 21)**.

I have tried my best to figure out how there is enough space using a #8 crewel embroidery needle to pick up 1/3 of the space above the gathering threads, when there is only about 1/16 of an inch in that distance. A #8 crewel needle is almost that wide.

I suggest picking up 5/8 to 7/8 of the distance from the gathering thread to the top of the pleat. Some people may pick up as little as half of the pleat above the gathering row.

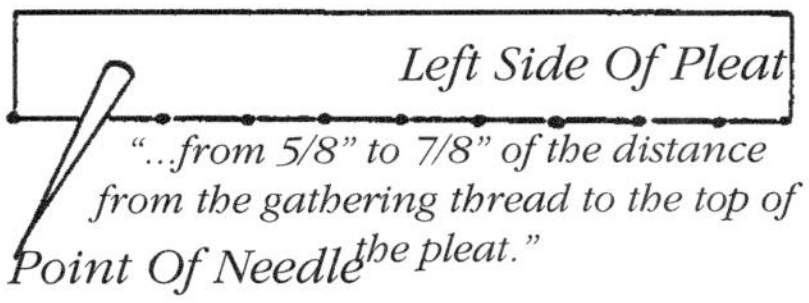

Tangled or Twisted Thread

Thread may become tangled after making consecutive smocking stitches. There are several ways to fix this. Hold the smocking up, with the threaded needle dangling below the smocking. Let the thread untangle by twirling around until it stops **(fig. 22)**.

With the needle still threaded, push the needle all the way down to the fabric. Separate the strands of floss, untangling them all the way down to the needle which is slipped all the way down to the fabric. After separating the strands, carefully rub them together again, slip the needle up and begin to smock again **(fig. 23)**.

Some people use beeswax for smocking. It does keep threads from tangling, somewhat. Be aware that beeswax may compress the threads resulting in less coverage **(fig. 24)**.

Some prefer to eliminate beeswax and simply run the threads (already threaded and knotted) over a dry bar of Ivory Soap. This gives a little lubrication **(fig. 25)**

Always remember to have floss running with the grain with the cut end knotted **(fig. 26)**. Always remember to separate the floss, strand by strand, before knotting.

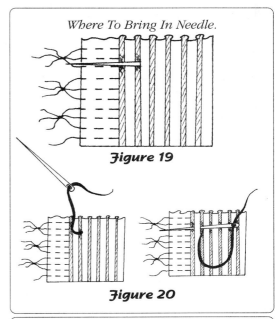

Where To Bring In Needle.

Figure 19

Figure 20

Point Of Needle
"…from 5/8" to 7/8" of the distance from the gathering thread to the top of the pleat."
Left Side Of Pleat

Figure 21

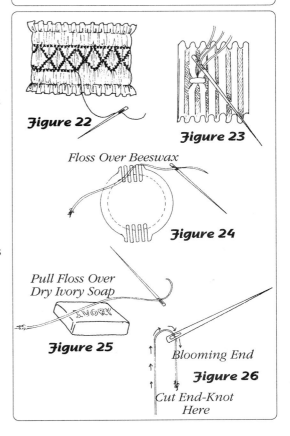

Figure 22

Figure 23

Floss Over Beeswax

Figure 24

Pull Floss Over Dry Ivory Soap

Figure 25

Blooming End

Figure 26

Cut End-Knot Here

Slip-Snail Knot

When thread runs out in the middle of a row, when it is necessary to change colors, or when a row of smocking comes to an end, the thread must be tied off properly. A slip snail knot serves this purpose well.

1. Take the thread to the back of the smocking.

2. Turn the work to the back and notice that the needle is in one pleat. This is the pleat on which you will want to put the knot.

3. Make a stitch in that one pleat **(fig. 27)**.

4. Tighten that stitch but leave a little loop **(fig. 28)**.

5. Take the needle and slip it through the loop **(fig. 29)**.

6. Pull the thread to form a little knot **(fig. 30)**. This is where the slip snail knot comes in. Slip the needle through the loop and slip a little knot in the thread. This knot should look like a snail.

7. For a second knot, follow the same instructions in the same pleat.

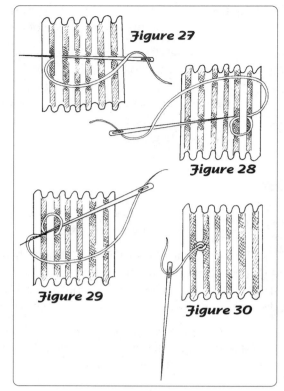

Figure 27

Figure 28

Figure 29

Figure 30

Tie-Off, Re-thread, and Begin Again In Middle

Since smocking is best worked with 15" to 20" lengths of thread, tie off and begin again in the middle of the row. It is easiest to tie off on a level stitch, using the following technique.

1. Take the smocking stitch, whatever that stitch may be.

2. Take the needle to the back by going between the last two pleats involved in that last stitch. Slip the needle down very close to the stitch before taking the thread straight back to the back **(fig. 31)**.

3. Tie a slip snail knot or two.

4. Re-thread. Tie a knot in the end of the thread.

5. Bring the new thread in on the left hand side of the last pleat that already has smocking on it. It may be difficult to do, since the stitch will already be secured and tied off **(fig. 32)**.

6. Try to bring the needle in at exactly the same place that the smocking thread has traveled in the left hand side of that last pleat. The thread will appear as if it were not tied off at all, coming through the same hole as described.

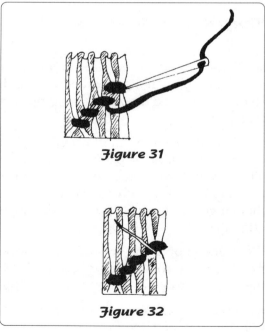

Figure 31

Figure 32

Note: *Try to bring the needle point in at exactly the same place that the smocking thread has already made a hole in the left hand side of that last pleat. The thread will appear as if it were not tied off at all.*

Specific Stitch Tie-Off Situations

Thread placement depends on whether the next stitch moves upward or downward.

- **Example A:** A two-step wave has just been completed and is coming down. The down cable has been made at the bottom. This is the turnaround stitch. Tie off the thread, and bring the new thread in the left-hand side of the last pleat of the down cable just completed. Bring the thread in on the top side of that down cable in order to go back up in the two-step wave **(fig. 33)**.

- **Example B:** A two-step wave has just been completed going up. The up cable at the top of the wave has been completed. Tie off the thread and bring the new thread in on the left-hand side of the last pleat of that up cable. Bring the thread in on the bottom side of that up cable in order to go back down in the two-step wave **(fig. 34)**.

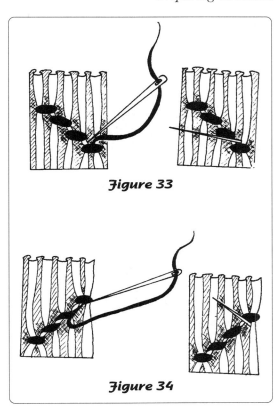

Figure 33

Figure 34

Blocking *(Smocking Completed)*

1. Always block smocking before constructing the garment. After smocking is completed, carefully remove all gathering row threads except the top gathering thread.

2. Set a steam iron on the lowest setting that still produces steam.

3. Pin the smocked piece to the board at the top, middle, and sides **(fig. 35)**. Gently stretch it out to the exact measurement of the yoke to which it will be attached. Consider pinning the smocking right side up to be sure the smocking design is straight.

4. Hold the steam iron at least 1" or 2" above the smocking. Do not touch the smocking with the iron. Steam the piece **(fig. 36)**. Allow it to dry thoroughly before unpinning the piece from board.

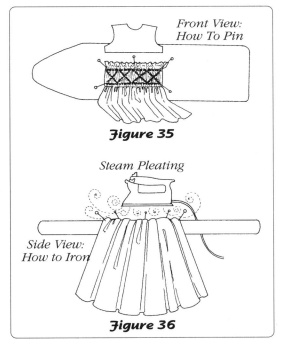

Front View: How To Pin

Figure 35

Steam Pleating

Side View: How to Iron

Figure 36

The Pleater

I have taught beginning smocking to more than 2,000 people, and I have found that the single largest problem for the beginners is guessing the location of the half spaces between the two rows of pleats. Many beginners end up with half-space smocking, which looks like a snake crawling through the rows. Needless to say, this can be frustrating. Here is some information, which can familiarize beginning smockers to the pleater.

Pleater Parts

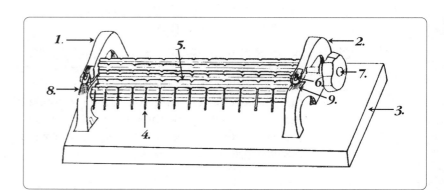

1. Left-hand end plate
2. Right-hand end plate
3. Base of the machine
4. Needles inserted into the grooves
5. Drop-in roller
6. Keeper and keeper screw
7. Knob
8. Left-hand groove for fabric to pass through
9. Right-hand groove for fabric to pass through certain pleating instances

Replacing Pleater Needles

1. Loosen the keeper screw. Complete removal of the keeper and the screws is not necessary; just slide the keeper forward on the loosened screw (**fig. 1**).

2. Tilt the machine back and prop it on a book. Tilting the pleater keeps the needles from falling out.

3. With the thumb, gently roll the small, drop-in roller up and off of the machine (**fig. 2**).

4. Reposition the needles according to the specific pleating needs (**fig. 3**).

5. Gently roll the drop-in roller back into place. Be sure to align the half spaces of the drop-in roller with the half-space grooves on the pleater.

6. Tighten the screw just until resistance is felt. Then turn just a tiny bit more. Do not over tighten. Loosen the screws when pleating heavier fabrics; tighten them for sheer fabrics.

   Note: *To hold your pleater in place during pleating, try this. Purchase a spool of 2-inch duck tape. Cut enough of this tape to put across the back of the pleater. Put the pleater on a flat surface with the duck tape across the back of the pleater and on the flat surface.*

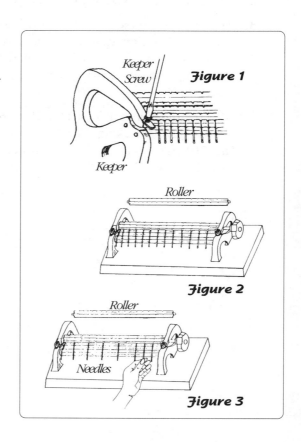

Figure 1

Keeper Screw

Keeper

Roller

Figure 2

Roller

Needles

Figure 3

Preparing To Pleat Fabric

1. Thread the required number of needles. I use a 36" long piece of quilting thread for each needle. Thread from the top. Pull 6" Let the long end hang **(fig. 4)**.

2. Do not cut off the armholes of the dress until after the fabric has been pleated.

3. The right side of the pleating should be downwards when going though the machine. The tallest pleats come from the bottom of the pleater **(fig. 5)**.

4. Lay the fabric flat right sides down, and roll onto a dowel stick. Run the fabric through the pleater, right side down **(fig. 6)**.

Note: *If you are using a bobbin continuous feed holder or system, your quilting thread may become spongy. This may help.*

Soak your spool of quilting thread in warm water. Place the spool in front of the refrigerator vent overnight to gently dry the thread. You may then wind it onto bobbins or put the spools into your smocking machine holder.

Dowel Sticks

Usually I use a 1/4", wooden, craft-type dowel stick, about 36" long. However, some people like small, thin, steel rods, which add weight when holding the fabric and dowel in place while pleating. Others like a café curtain rod, which opens or closes as much as needed for garments. The size of the dowel should suit the type of fabric used and be no larger than 1" in diameter **(fig. 7)**.

Directions

1. Put the dowel stick, covered with the rolled fabric, through the left-hand side of the pleater.

2. Line up the exact rows to pleat. Eyeball the groove that will serves as a guideline in order to run the pleating through evenly **(fig. 8)**.

3. Leave one whole pleater space for the guideline **(fig. 9)**.

4. Hold the fabric and begin to guide it through.

5. As the fabric runs through the pleater it is important to gently pull the fabric edge hanging out the left side. Gently pull parallel with the rollers. This will keep bumps from forming in the pleats. Let the rollers and the handle pull the fabric through **(fig. 10)**.

6. As the fabric comes onto the needles, stop and gently, gently, guide the fabric off of the needles. Do not force or jerk, since this could bend the needles.

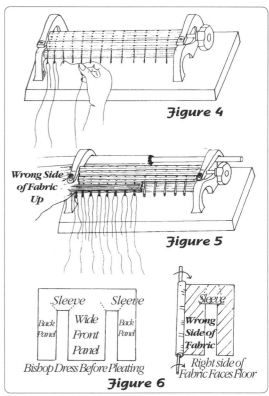

Figure 4

Wrong Side of Fabric Up

Figure 5

Sleeve   *Sleeve*

Back Panel   *Wide Front Panel*   *Back Panel*

Bishop Dress Before Pleating

Sleeve

Wrong Side of Fabric

Right side of Fabric Faces Floor

Figure 6

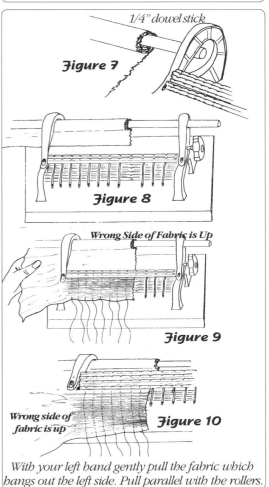

1/4" dowel stick

Figure 7

Figure 8

Wrong Side of Fabric is Up

Figure 9

Wrong side of fabric is up   **Figure 10**

With your left hand gently pull the fabric which hangs out the left side. Pull parallel with the rollers.

General Pleater Instructions

1. The fabric edge to be fed into the machine should be cut straight and started evenly to avoid a crooked pleat and for pleating with ease. Try gently "rocking" the fabric into the pleater.

2. Do not force or jam the fabric into the roller gears to get it started. Align the fabric straight into the gears and let the gears grab the fabric as they begin to rotate. Although unlikely, if the fabric should jam and some of the needle start moving wildly, the pleater may become very difficult to turn. Remove the drop-in roller gear and take out the needles and fabric. This will avoid having to cut out the pleating.

3. Always be sure to trim the selvage on heavier fabrics, such as corduroy and broadcloth. This is a good idea with any fabric, but especially with the heavier fabrics.

4. A strip of wax paper run through the pleater prior to pleating will lubricate the needles and allow the fabric to pass through fabric more freely. Do not pleat over French seams; the bulk of fabric can cause needles to break. Instead, serge the seams together using a rolled hem. If, however, it is unavoidable to pleat over French seams, rub a bar of soap on the seams before pleating them. Rubbing the bar of soap over the edge of heavier fabric edge works well also **(fig. 11)**.

5. Fabric may tend to pile up on the needles as it comes out of the pleater and makes the gears hard to turn. If this occurs, gently slide the fabric along the needles onto the thread as it accumulates **(fig. 12)**.

6. Replace bent and dull needles. Damaged needles can jam the cloth and break in the machine. A bent needle is easy to identify: it moves excessively while the pleater is turning, it has an unusual angle compared with the other needles, and it makes pleating more difficult.

7. Needles do need to be changed after excess usage because they will dull.

8. If the machine becomes stiff to operate, chances are that you have wound some threads into the machine or around the shaft of the roller. Pick these out carefully with a small needle and cut them.

9. Because the pleating needles will rust when exposed to moisture, keep the pleater in a dry place.

Rub a bar of Ivory soap over French seams before pleating them.

A strip of wax paper run through the pleater prior to pleating, will lubricate the needles and allow the fabric to pass more freely.

Figure 11

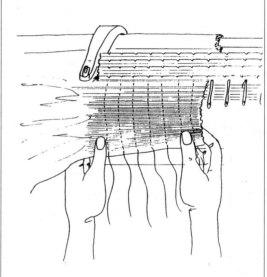

Fabric may tend to pile up on the needles as it comes out of the pleater and make it hard to turn. If this occurs, gently slide the fabric along the needles onto the thread as it accumulates on the needles.

Figure 12

Smocking Stitches

Cable Stitch

General Instructions

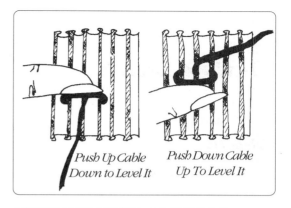

Push Up Cable
Down to Level It

Push Down Cable
Up To Level It

- This stitch is worked from left to right across pleats to form up and down cables. Start the thread on the left hand side of the pleat to smock.

- Take every stitch with the needle running parallel to the gathering line.

- Pierce or "bite" the pleats directly on top of the gathering row to ensure straight cables. It may appear that one stitch goes a tiny bit above (the up or top cable) the gathering thread and one stitch goes a tiny bit below (the down or bottom cable). To avoid crooked cable rows, stay focused on the gathering rows and not the optical effect created by the position of the stitches.

- A down cable is made by stitching into the pleat with the thread below the needle. An up cable is made by stitching into the pleat with the thread above the needle.

- Take one cable stitch in every pleat. Direct the thread to the bottom in one stitch, to the top in the next.

Directions

1. Bring in the thread on the left hand side of the first pleat.

2. Move to the second pleat and take a stitch there with the thread below the needle. This is a down cable **(fig. 1)**.

3. Move to the third pleat and take a stitch with the thread above the needle. This is an up cable **(fig. 2)**.

4. Move to the fourth pleat and take a stitch with the thread below the needle. This is another down cable.

5. Move to the fifth pleat and take a stitch with the thread above the needle. This is another up cable.

6. Every two to four stitches, with the needle or a fingernail, push the cable stitches together to be sure the fabric does not show through.

Note: *To make beautiful cable stitches, try this. After taking the stitch, begin to tighten by pulling upward on a down-cable and downward on an up-cable. Before actually pulling the final stitch to the fabric, place your thumbnail next to the stitch and guide the stitch into its exact position.*

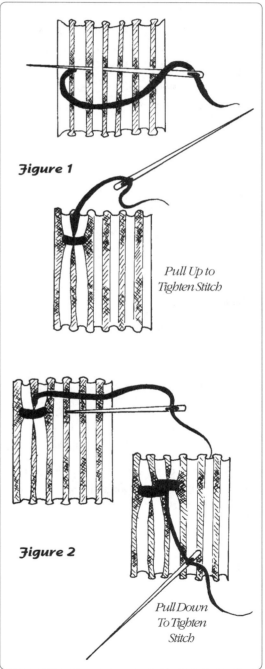

Figure 1

Pull Up to
Tighten Stitch

Figure 2

Pull Down
To Tighten
Stitch

Outline Stitch

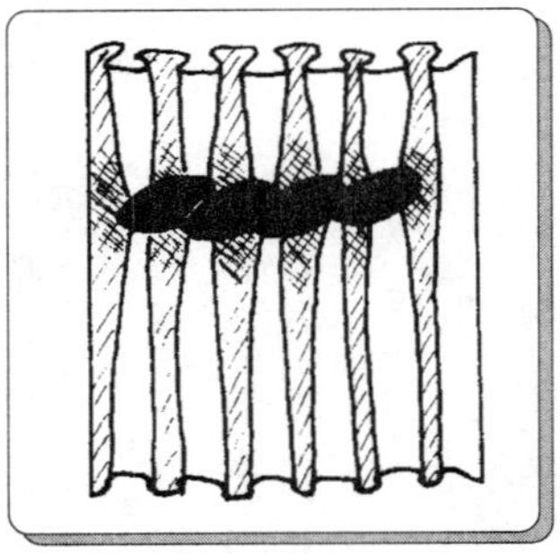

This stitch is worked from left to right.

Directions

1. Bring the thread in on the left-hand side of the first pleat **fig.1**.

2. The outline stitch is a continuous row of up cables. The thread remains above the needle for every stitch (**fig. 2**).

3. Pierce the pleat so that the needle is parallel to, and exactly on top of, the gathering row. Tighten each up cable by pulling down. Always tighten up cables in this manner (**fig. 3**).

4. After tightening each stitch, gently pull upward to align the whole row with the gathering row (**fig. 4**).

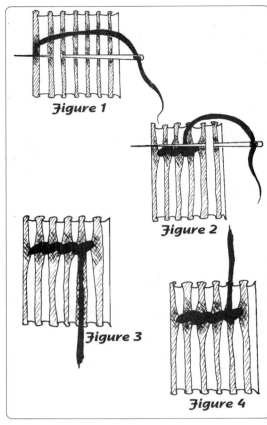

Figure 1

Figure 2

Figure 3

Figure 4

Stem Stitch

The stem stitch is worked from left to right.

Directions

1. Bring the thread in on the left-hand side of the first pleat (**fig.5**).

2. The outline stitch is a continuous row of down cables. The thread is thrown down below the needle for each stitch (**fig. 6**).

3. Take each stitch by running the needle in parallel to the gathering row on exactly the top of the gathering thread. Next, tighten each down cable by pulling up (**fig. 7**).

4. After completing the up tighten on each stitch, gently pull downward to align the whole row with the gathering row (**fig. 8**).

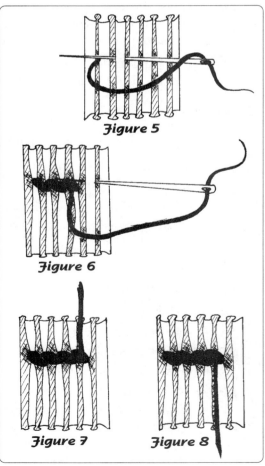

Figure 5

Figure 6

Figure 7

Figure 8

Wave/Chevron Stitch or Baby Wave

Directions

1. Bring the thread in on the left-hand side of the first pleat.

2. Move to the second pleat and make a down cable **(fig. l)**.

3. Make another down cable at the half-space line (marked with a gathering thread on the pleat). Remember the Cat and the Courthouse story. When the cat goes up the courthouse steps, the tail drops down **(fig. 2)**.

4. Make an up cable on the half-space line also **(fig. 3)**. It may look as if the second stitch went in between the bottom row and the half-space row. Looks are deceiving. The second bottom cable and the top cable (the turnaround stitch) are placed on exactly the same line - the half-space line.

5. Now move back down to the whole line. Make a top cable at the starting line **(fig. 5)**. Remember the Cat and the Courthousee.

6. At the same bottom row, make another down cable. This is the turnaround stitch **(fig. 6)**.

Note: *Half-space chevrons end at the half space on the smocking rows. Whole-space chevrons are taller and go all the way to another row.*

Half-space chevrons are easy if fabric has been pleated with a Pullen pleater because gathering threads are in the whole and half spaces. Half space indicates that the stitch only goes from the main row to the halfway point and back again to its main row.

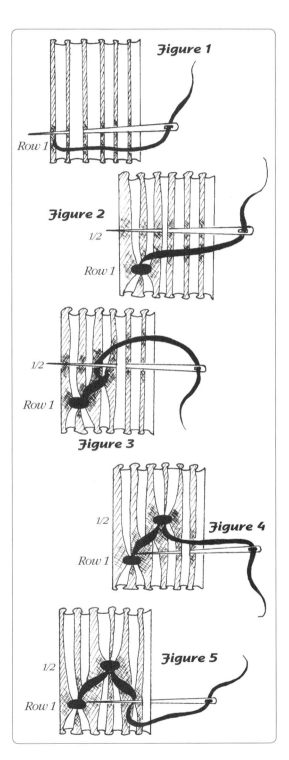

Figure 1
Row 1

Figure 2
1/2
Row 1

Figure 3
1/2
Row 1

Figure 4
1/2
Row 1

Figure 5
1/2
Row 1

Sitting in Martha's Smocking Class

"Bring the thread in on the left hand side of the first pleat, on Row 1. Move over one pleat and make a down cable. Move over to the next pleat at the same time moving up to the 1/2 space and make another down cable. At the same 1/2 space point, move over another pleat and make an up cable. This is your turn around stitch. Notice that two stitches were placed with your needle at the 1/2 space on your diagrams. Move over one pleat and make an up cable back at Row 1. Move over another pleat and make a down cable also at Row 1. That last stitch was your bottom turn around stitch".

Two, Three, or Four-Step Wave (Trellis)

When I was a beginner, just learning to smock, one thing always confused me about waves. So, let's try to clear this up first. When looking at a two-step wave, I counted four stitches going up on one side and three stitches coming down on the other. How could this stitch be called a two-step wave with all these stitches. Each wave must have a cable at the bottom and a cable at the top. These are "level" or "turn-around" stitches. Counting these as steps to the two-step wave is where I got confused. This stitch is called a wave or a trellis. Either is correct; I prefer wave.

Correct Way To Count A Two-Step Wave

Stitch 1 is a bottom cable serving as a turnaround stitch.
Stitch 2 is moving up as Step 1 in the two-step wave.
Stitch 3 is moving up as Step 1 in the two-step wave.
Stitch 4 is a top cable serving as a turnaround stitch.

Two-Step Wave (Trellis)

Directions

This stitch is worked from left to right. Smocking progresses one pleat at a time and moves up and down between the rows.

A two-step wave can have various heights, depending on the design. Example: A two-step wave which goes from Row 1 to Row 1/2 above it (technically called a half-space, two-step wave) is done like this:

1. Bring the needle in on the left side of the first pleat. Begin with a down cable on Row 1 **(fig. 1)**.

2. Move up halfway between Row 1 and Row 1/2 (a 1/4 space) for the next stitch, a down cable **(fig. 2)**.

3. Move up to the half space for the next stitch, another down cable **(fig. 3)**.

4. At this same half-space point, move over one pleat and work a top cable (turnaround stitch) **(fig. 4)**.

5. Move down 1/4 space, work a top cable.

6. Move down to Row 1 and work another top cable.

7. Complete the stitch sequence with another turnaround stitch (a bottom cable).

Note: *A common misunderstanding concerning two-step waves stems from the positioning of the stitches. I will try to clear this up. Look at the illustration showing a completed two-step wave. It appears that the two middle steps are stitched on the 1/3 and 2/3 points between the bottom cable and the top cable. That is only its appearance! In reality the two stitches are taken at the 1/4 point and at the 1/2 space itself.*

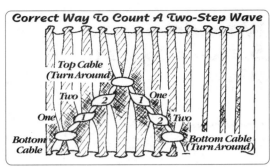

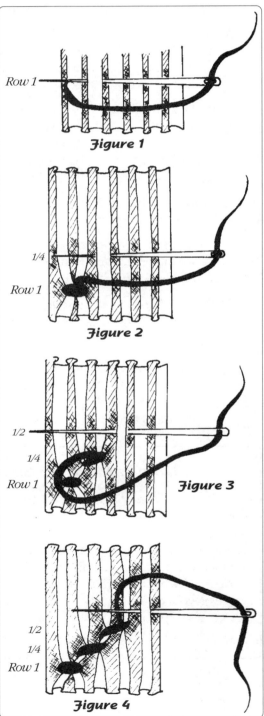

Three-Step Wave (Trellis)

Directions

A three-step wave or trellis is worked from left to right progressing one pleat at a time up and down between the rows.

A three-step wave can have various heights, depending on the design. **Example:** Work a three-step wave, which goes from one major gathering row to the next, for a distance of ³/8 inch (the usual distance between gathering rows on a pleater) in the following manner:

1. Begin row 1 with a down cable on the gathering row **(fig. 1)**.

2. Place the second stitch, a down cable, ¹/3 of the way up **(fig. 2)**.

3. Place the third stitch, a down cable, ²/3 of the way up **(fig. 3)**.

4. Place the fourth stitch, a down cable, on Row 2 the next gathering row line **(fig. 4)**.

5. Place the fifth stitch, an up cable on the same gathering row (Row 2) as the previous stitch **(fig. 5)**. Look at the finished work. The fourth and fifth stitches will appear to be at different levels, with the fourth stitch slightly below the gathering row. In reality, the last down cable moving up the row is placed at the same level as the turnaround stitch, the up cable at the top.

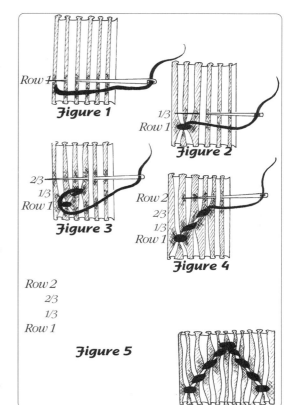

Figure 1 · Row 1
Figure 2 · Row 1 · 1/3
Figure 3 · 2/3 · 1/3 · Row 1
Figure 4 · Row 2 · 2/3 · 1/3 · Row 1
Figure 5 · Row 2 · 2/3 · 1/3 · Row 1

Sitting in Martha's Smocking Class

"One of the things I like to do when I count my three-step waves when going across a row is to say, "Bottom cable, 1, 2, 3, top cable, 1, 2, 3." Some people like to say, "Turn around, 1, 2, 3, turn-around, 1, 2, 3, turn around 1, 2, 3." Always count by realizing that the three steps are in the middle with a cable at the top and a cable at the bottom.

Four-Step Wave (Trellis)

Directions

This trellis is worked from left to right, progressing, one pleat at a time, as stitches are worked up and down between the rows.

A four-step wave can have various heights, depending on the design. It goes from one major gathering row (Row 1) to the next gathering row (Row 2).

1. Begin Row 1 with a down-cable on the gathering row **(fig. 6)**.
2. Place the second stitch, a down cable, ¹/4 of the way up **(fig. 7)**.
3. Place the third stitch, a down cable, on the half-space **(fig. 8)**.
4. Place the fourth stitch, a down cable, on the ¹/4 space **(fig. 9)**.
5. Place the fifth stitch, a down cable, on the top gathering row, Row 2 **(fig. 10)**.
6. Place the sixth stitch, an up cable, on the same gathering row (Row 2) as the fifth stitch **(fig. 11)**. Look at the finished work. The fifth and sixth stitches will appear to be at different levels, with the fifth slightly below the gathering row. However, the last down cable moving up the row is placed at the same level as the turnaround stitch, which is the up cable at the top.

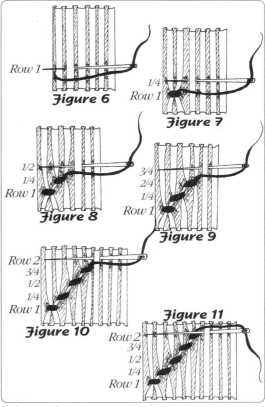

Figure 6 · Row 1
Figure 7 · Row 1 · 1/4
Figure 8 · Row 1 · 1/4 · 1/2
Figure 9 · Row 1 · 1/4 · 2/4 · 3/4
Figure 10 · Row 1 · 1/4 · 1/2 · 3/4 · Row 2
Figure 11 · Row 1 · 1/4 · 1/2 · 3/4 · Row 2

Double Wave or Diamond Stitch

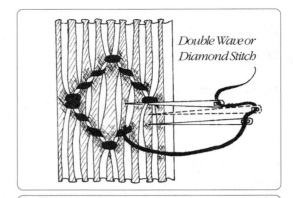

Double Wave or Diamond Stitch

Directions

A double wave means the second wave is worked in the opposite direction of the first, to form a diamond shape.

1. Begin the top portion of the diamond wave (one-, two-, three-, four-wave) with a down cable and work upward.

2. Begin the bottom portion of the diamond wave with an up cable and move downward.

3. Stack cables to meet in the middle.

Note: *A trick to matching the cables perfectly is to slip your needle between the pleats and slide it up. This will enable you to stitch very close to the first pleat.*

Six-Step Flowerette

Directions

A flowerette is worked from left to right.

1. Bring the needle up on the left side of pleat 1 or the left side of the first pleat to be involved in the flowerette.

2. With the thread below the needle, insert the needle on the right side of pleat 2 , picking up only pleat 2 **(fig. 1)**.

3. With the thread above the needle, insert the needle on the right side of pleat 3, picking up only pleat 3 **(fig. 2)**.

4. With the thread below the needle, insert the needle on the right side of pleat 4, picking up only pleat 4 **(fig. 3)**.

5. Carry the thread to the back of the fabric between the last two pleats (pleats 3 and pleat 4). Turn the work, as well as the illustration, upside down.

6. Bring the needle out on the left side of pleat 4, below the last down cable made **(fig. 4)**.

7. With the thread below the needle, insert the needle on the right side of pleat 3, picking up only pleat 3 **(fig. 5)**.

8. With the thread above the needle, insert the needle on the right side of pleat 2, picking up only pleat 2 (f**ig. 6)**.

9. With the thread below the needle, insert the needle on the right side of pleat 1, picking up only pleat 1 **(fig. 7)**.

10. Carry the thread to the wrong side of the fabric by inserting in between the last two pleats used, (pleats 1 and pleat 2), and tie off.

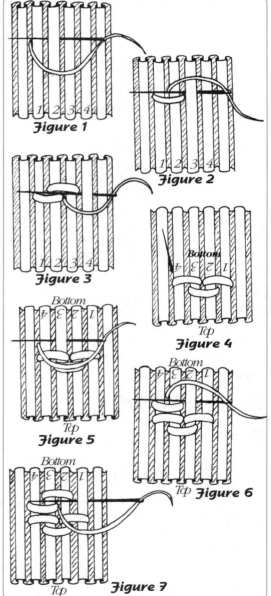

Double Wave or Diamond Stitch

Figure 1

Figure 2

Figure 3

Figure 4

Figure 5

Figure 6

Figure 7

Sitting in Martha's Smocking Class

"Just because we have stopped our instructions with a four-step wave doesn't mean that you can't make a five-step wave or a six-step wave or even more. Always remember that when you call a stitch a four-step wave, that you have a bottom cable at the top before you make four stitches downward. Don't forget to count the four-step wave as follows. Bottom cable 1, 2, 3, 4, top cable, 1, 2, 3, 4, bottom cable, 1, 2, 3, 4, top cable."

Picture Smocking

Thread

Good quality thread is essential to good picture smocking, and six-strand embroidery floss is not the only option. The notions market is brimming with suitable smocking products. Yarns, silk ribbon threads, pearl cotton, floche, or other fibers are perfectly acceptable as long as they can be stitched and pulled through the fabric. One word of caution, think about the care of the garments and try to match a like thread to it. In other words, use silk on silk or cotton on cotton.

When using DMC six-strand embroidery floss (the most common smocking thread), always remove floss from the wrapper by pulling from the end with the hands on the wrapper. Cut a piece of floss no more than 18-24" long. Anything longer has a tendency to fray, tangle, and wear, which in turn will cause problems with stitch coverage.

When cutting floss, notice the difference in the two ends. One end will unravel more easily than the other and thereby appear fuller. The fuller end of the floss should always be threaded in the eye of the needle and the cut end should always be knotted. In order to keep from getting confused when separating the six strands of floss, always knot the cut end.

Once floss has been cut to the correct length, separate each strand. Put the correct number of strands of floss back together. Then pull these strands of floss between the thumb and forefinger to strip them. This will give a more ribbon like appearance to the floss. Another method that is used frequently is to pull these strands through a fabric softener dryer sheet.

During smocking, the thread will eventually begin to twist, and stitches made with twisted threads will not lay flat. Flat stitches are desired for the ultimate coverage. The best method for untwisting the thread is to hold the end of the floss straight up and run the eye of the needle down the floss to the fabric and back up again. This can be done throughout the smocking process. Another popular method is to simply turn the pleated fabric upside down and allow the needle to dangle; the weight of the needle will untwist the floss.

Number of Strands

The following chart lists the recommended strands of floss to use when doing the various types of smocking.

- Three strands for all geometrics
- Four strands for stacking
- Two strands for backsmocking
- One to two strands for detail work

Heavier than the normal six strand embroidery floss, requires a smocker to adjust the recommended number of strands used. As with any type of smocking, always refer to the smocking plate for the suggested number of strands to use. Sometimes, it will be necessary to use more than the recommended number of threads, especially when using white floss. Consider testing a small area of smocking for coverage before starting each project; do so with each floss color. Caution, when dark floss colors are removed from some fabrics, they can often leave a permanent "fuzz" residue floss; never test floss overage on an area that will be seen in the finished smocked piece.

Stitches

When picture smocking, there will be times that the stitch will not lay as it should. To correct this problem, simply take the needle and lay it lengthwise on top of the stitch and press down toward the previous row. If all stitches are made correctly, there should be no problems in manipulating the stitches to lay properly.

If, at any time, an error in stitch placement is made or the stitch doesn't lay correctly, it is always best to remove that stitch. Even though it appears possible to "work around" the mistake, it will come back to cause problems later. To remove the unwanted stitch, unthread the needle and use the eye to pull out stitches one at a time. If there is a large number of stitches to remove, clip every fourth or fifth stitch with embroidery scissors and pull them out with the eye of the needle. Remember, since smocking relies on an accurate stitch count, it is always best to remove a mistake and rework a given area.

Tension

More often than not, the problem with picture smocking is tension. Tension is the most important thing in smocking. In order to achieve the desired finished look, stitches should not be tight nor should they be loose. Each stitch is critical and necessitates patience and accuracy. For the design to be correct, the tension should be equal throughout.

When completing a stitch, don't jerk the thread through the fabric. Gently pull the floss through the fabric by hand or with the needle. Carefully lay the stitch on the pleats making sure that the thread is not twisted. Any "open areas" between the stitches where the fabric shows or if pleats are distorted, indicates that the tension is too tight **(fig. 1)**, or pleats are too far apart. If the stitches have the appearance of "hanging off" the fabric, the tension is too loose **(fig. 2)**. Correct tension will allow the thread to gently "hug" the pleats **(fig. 3)**.

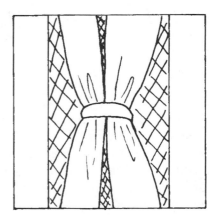

Figure 1

Fabric

Do not limit smocking projects to lightweight fabrics. Any fiber that is not tightly woven is generally smock-able. Linen, silk batiste, satin, 100 percent featherwale corduroy, some velvets and velveteen, cotton, poly-cotton blends, and lightweight challis are all good mediums. Any questionable fabrics should be tested first by running a sample piece through the pleater. If the fabric doesn't run easily through without having to tug or force it over the needles, smocking may not be the best choice of embellishments.

When pleating a tightly woven fabric such as Imperial broadcloth, it is always best to remove the selvage first. Broadcloth is often easier to pleat if it is first rinsed and dried to remove some of the sizing put in during manufacturing. After washing, try rubbing a bar of Ivory soap over the back of the fabric to make it easier to pleat, or run a sheet of waxed paper through the pleater before pleating.

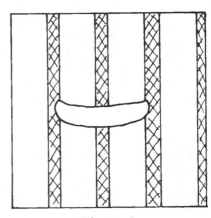

Figure 2

Seams

Avoid pleating fabric with French seams. When needles are forced to penetrate a bulk of fabric, such as a French seam, they will often skip stitches or break off in the fabric. When putting together a garment that calls for French seams, such as a bishop, simply serge the seam using a rolled hem or stitch the seam together by machine, press it open and then pleat the fabric.

Smocking Plates

Directions should be given on the back of each smocking plate. The directions give the order in which to work the geometric rows as well as the figures. Most smocking designs need to be centered, especially picture smocking. Smocking plates are designed for straight as well as round yokes. If making a garment with a round yoke, make sure the chosen plate was designed for a round yoke or includes round yoke variations.

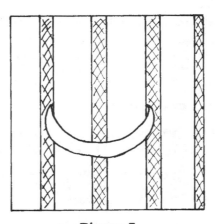

Figure 3

The most common problem caused by smocking plates is confusion with reading the rows of stitches. The confusion comes from reading the bottom stitches as one row and the top stitches as another. Remember, it takes both rows of stitches to make a single row of cables **(fig. 4)**.

In the beginning, many smockers find it easier to read the graph by taking a colored pencil and coloring every other row. This will make a complicated graph less confusing to read.

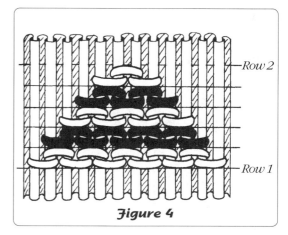

Figure 4

Changing Colors

The majority of picture smocking calls for more than one color of floss, therefore making it necessary to use more than one needle. To avoid continuous tying off of the threads, simply thread the different colors of floss in different needles before starting. When it becomes necessary to change colors, allow the needle being used prior to hang at the back of the smocked fabric or place it on the back side of the fabric so it will not get tangled with the floss in use. Smock the required number of stitches in the new floss color. This step is repeated for every color used in the graph.

Scissors and Needles

One of the most important tools needed for smocking is a good pair of embroidery scissors such as Gingher or Marks. The small, sharp, pointed scissors are a must when cutting the floss close to the fabric and for snipping unwanted threads close to the fabric for easy removal.

This author recommends using a size 7 or 8 crewel needle for smocking. The crewel needle is used because it will make holes large enough for four strands of floss to pull through easily.

Smockers who have trouble grasping a size 7 or 8 crewel needles for any reason, should substitute a size 7 or 8 long darner. This needle is wonderful for smockers who have arthritic hands and find it difficult to work with the short needles.

Directions For Picture Smocking

1. Bring the floss up on the left side of gathering Row 1, pleat 1, **(fig. 1)**.

2. With the thread below the needle, insert the needle on the right side of pleat 2, picking up only pleat 2 **(fig. 2)**.

   Notice that the first stitch of each row comes up on the side of the pleat to be worked, skips that pleat, and picks up the next one. In otherwords, the first stitch contains two pleats.

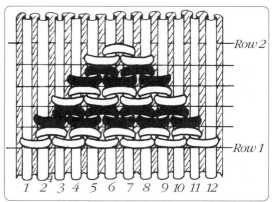

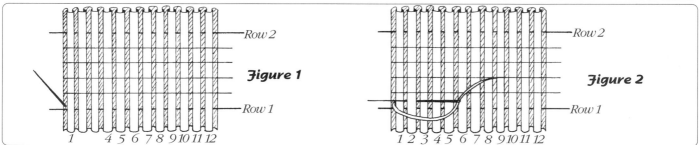

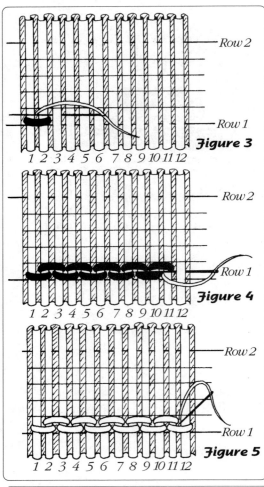

Figure 3

Figure 4

Figure 5

3. With the thread above the needle, insert the needle on the right side of pleat 3, picking up only pleat 3 (**fig. 3**).

4. Repeat Steps 2 and 3 totaling 11 cable stitches (**fig. 4**). This completes Row 1.

5. Take the thread to the back of the pleated fabric by sticking the needle between the two pleats (11 and 12) taken in by the last stitch. In other words, insert the needle back into the valley that the thread is coming out of (**fig. 5**).

6. For the purpose of this practice piece, allow the thread to travel across the wrong side of the fabric to begin Row 2. Do not pull it tight or it will distort the triangle.

7. Begin Row 2 by bringing the needle up on the left side of pleat 2 (**fig. 6**).

8. With the thread below the needle, insert the needle on the right side of pleat 3, picking up only pleat 3 (**fig. 7**).

9. With the thread above the needle, insert the needle on the right side of pleat 4, picking up only pleat 4 (**fig. 8**).

10. Continue across the row totaling nine cables. This completes Row 2 (**fig. 9**).

11. Carry the thread to the wrong side of the fabric as referred to in Step 5. Bring the needle up on the left side of pleat 3 (**fig. 10**).

12. With the thread below the needle, insert the needle on the right side of pleat 4, picking up only pleat 4 (**fig. 11**).

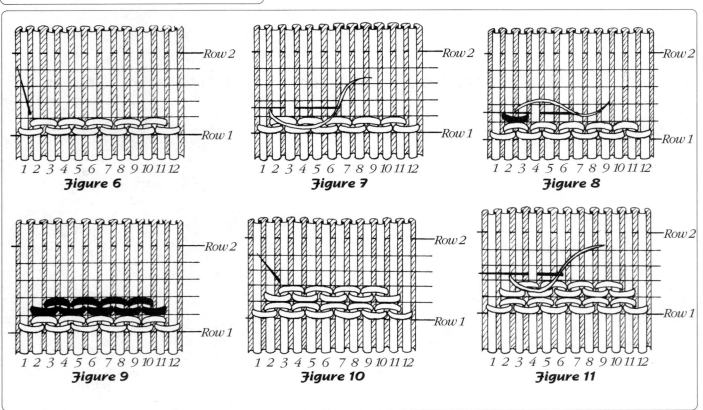

Figure 6

Figure 7

Figure 8

Figure 9

Figure 10

Figure 11

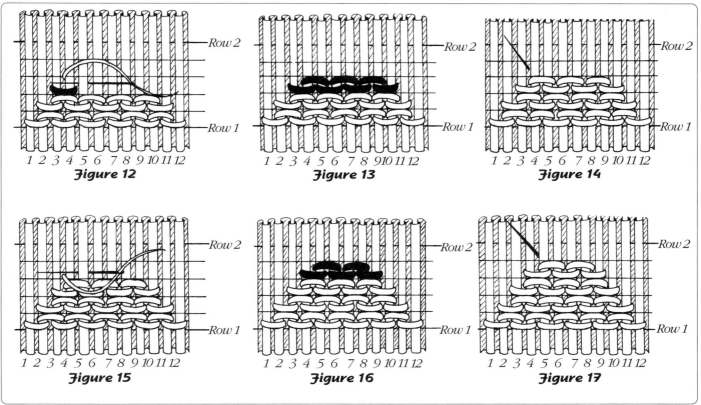

Figure 12

Figure 13

Figure 14

Figure 15

Figure 16

Figure 17

13. With the thread above the needle, insert the needle on the right side of pleat 5, picking up only pleat 5 **(fig. 12)**.

14. Continue across the row totaling seven cables **(fig. 13)**.

15. Carry the thread to the wrong side of the fabric as referred to in Step 5. Insert the needle on the left side of pleat 4 **(fig. 14)**.

16. With the thread below the needle, insert the needle on the right side of pleat 5, picking up only pleat 5 **(fig. 15).**

17. Continue across the row totaling five cables. This completes Row 4 **(fig. 16)**.

18. Carry the thread across the back of the fabric as instructed in Step 5. Bring the needle up on the left side of pleat 4 **(fig. 17)**.

19. With the thread below the needle, insert the needle on the right side of pleat 6, picking up only pleat 6 **(fig. 18)**.

20. With the thread above the needle, insert the needle on the right side of pleat 7, picking up only pleat 7 **(fig. 19)**.

21. Continue across the row totaling three cables. This completes Row 5 **(fig. 20)**.

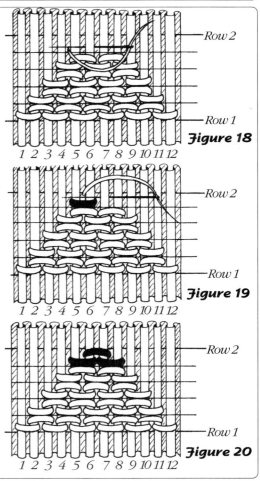

Figure 18

Figure 19

Figure 20

Beginning French Sewing Techniques

Lace Straight Edge To Lace Straight Edge

Use this technique when applying,

    (a.) lace insertion to lace insertion;

    (b.) lace insertion to lace beading;

    (c.) lace insertion or lace beading to non-gathered straight edge of lace edging;

    (d.) Swiss embroidered trims to entredeux edgings.

Directions

1. Spray starch and press each piece.

2. Place the two pieces, side-by-side, butting them together, but not overlapping. It is not important to match patterns in the lace **(fig. 1)**.

3. Begin 1/4 " or 3/8 " from the ends of the pieces to be joined. This keeps the ends from digging into the sewing machine **(fig. 2)**.

4. Zigzag the two edges together. Zigzag again if spaces are missed.

5. Stitch just widely enough to catch the two headings of the pieces of lace (or embroidery). Laces vary greatly in the widths of the headings. The stitch widths will vary according to the lace heading placement and preference.

6. Stitch the length as tightly or as loosely as desired. A satin stitch is too heavy; however, the stitch needs to be secure. Work with trims and the sewing machine to determine the best length and width.   Suggested stitch width and length:

Width=2 to 3 — I prefer 2-1/2

Length=1 to 1-1/2 — I prefer 1

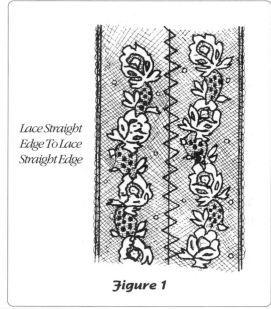

Lace Straight
Edge To Lace
Straight Edge

Figure 1

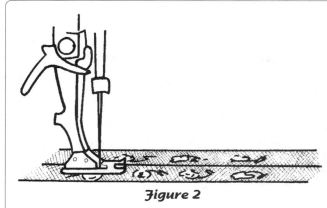

Figure 2

Lace Flat Edge To Fabric

Use this technique when applying,

    (a.) lace edging to ruffle or skirt;

    (b.) embroidered insertion to straight edge of lace;

    (c.) lace edging to sleeve edge, as on smocked sleeve or bottom of sleeve with elastic casing;

    (d.) Swiss edging (with scallops trimmed) to a flat surface to fabric edge, as on ruffles, sleeves, or collars.

Martha's Magic Directions

1. Spray starch and press both the lace and the fabric.

2. Place right sides to right sides.

3. Leave 1/8 " to 1/4 " of fabric edge before placing the lace to be joined **(fig. I)**.

4. Zigzag with a satin stitch, going into the heading of the lace and all the way off the fabric edge **(fig. 2)**.

   Suggested stitch width and length:

   Width=3-1/2 to 4

   Length=1/2 or as short as possible

Note: *1/8 " to 1/4 " of the fabric is exposed before the lace flat edge is put into place. The fabric edge will completely fold into the stitch when you are finished.*

5. Simply stitching together the edge of the lace and the edges of the fabric together will result in disaster. They will come apart. There is not enough strength in the edge of the fabric without the extra 1/8 " or 1/4 " folded into the zigzag.

6. Press the lace and fabric open. A common question is, "Which way do I press this roll?" Press the seam however it wants to lie. Naturally, it will fold toward the lace.

Topstitiching Lace

Directions

1. Work from the right side, after the lace has been pressed open.

2. Zigzag on top of the little roll, which is on the back of the garment. The width should be very narrow — just wide enough to go from one side of the roll to the other side. It should not be too short, but as invisible as possible **(fig. 3)**.

3. This zigzag holds the lace down and gives added strength to the seam. Its main purpose, however, is to hold the lace down.

   Suggested stitch width and length:

   Width=1/2 to 1-1/2

   Length=1 to 2

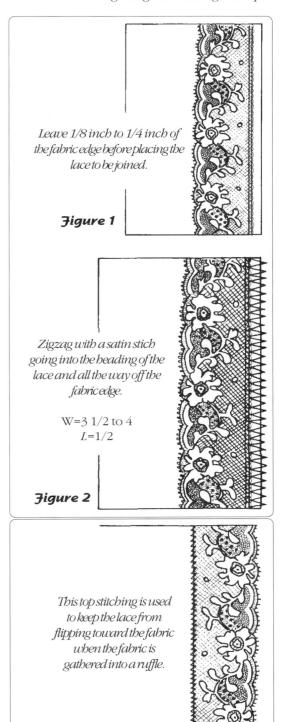

Leave 1/8 inch to 1/4 inch of the fabric edge before placing the lace to be joined.

Figure 1

Zigzag with a satin stich going into the heading of the lace and all the way off the fabric edge.

W=3 1/2 to 4
L=1/2

Figure 2

This top stitching is used to keep the lace from flipping toward the fabric when the fabric is gathered into a ruffle.

Figure 3

Cutting Fabric From Behind Lace That Has Been Shaped and Zigzagged

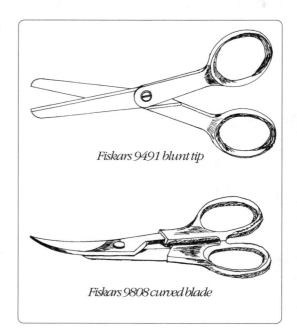

I absolutely love two pairs of Fiskars Scissors for the tricky job of cutting fabric from behind lace that has been shaped and stitched on. The first is Fiskars 9491, blunt tip 5" scissor. They look much like kindergarten scissors because of the blunt tips; however, they are very sharp. They cut fabric away from behind laces with ease. By the way, both of the scissors mentioned in this section are made for either right-handed or left-handed people.

Fiskars 9491 blunt tip

The second pair I recommend for this task is the Fiskars 9808 curved blade craft scissor. The curved blades are very easy to use when working in tricky, small areas of lace shaping. Fiskars are crafted of permanent stainless steel and are precision ground and hardened for a sharp, long-lasting edge.

Fiskars 9808 curved blade

Repairing Lace Holes Which You Didn't Mean To Cut!

Trimming fabric away from behind stitched-down lace can be difficult. It is not uncommon to slip, thus cutting a hole in lace work. How can this be repaired? It is really quite simple.

Directions

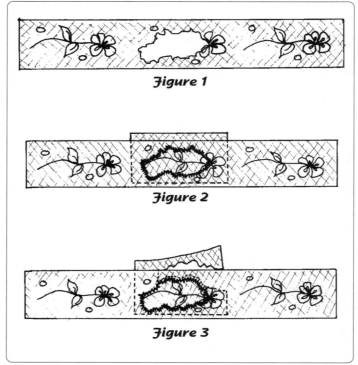

Figure 1

Figure 2

Figure 3

1. Look at the pattern in the lace where the hole was cut. Is it in a flower, in a dot series, or in the netting part of the lace (**fig. 1)?**

2. After identifying the pattern where the hole was cut, cut another piece of lace 1/4 " longer than each side of the hole in the lace.

3. On the bottom side of the lace in the garment, place the lace patch (**fig. 2**).

4. Match the design of the patch with the design of the lace around the hole where it was cut.

5. Zigzag around the cut edges of the lace hole, trying to catch the edges of the hole in the zigzag (**fig 3**).

6. Now, you have a patched and zigzagged pattern.

7. Trim away the leftover ends underneath the lace that has just been patched (**fig. 3**).

Note: *And don't worry about a piece of patched lace. As my grandmother used to say, "You'll never notice it on a galloping horse."*

Piecing Lace Not Long Enough For Your Needs

From my sewing experience, sometimes a longer piece of lace is needed than is available. Perhaps the lace was cut incorrectly or an insufficient amount was purchased. Whatever the reason, making a lace strip longer is easy to do.

Directions

1. Match the pattern with two strips that will be joined later **(figs. 1 and 3)**. Is the pattern a definite flower? Is it a definite diamond or some other pattern that is relatively large?

2. If working with a definite design in the pattern, join pieces by zigzagging around that design and then down through the heading of the lace **(fig. 2)**.

3. If the pattern is tiny, zigzag at an angle joining the two pieces **(fig. 2)**. Trim away excess laces close to the zigzagged seam **(fig. 4)**.

4. Forget that laces have been patched and complete the dress. Try to work the pieced section in an inconspicuous place.

5. If already halfway into making the garment when the short lace was discovered, simply join the laces and continue stitching as if nothing had happened.

If Your Fancy Band Is Too Short

Not to worry; cut down the width of the skirt. Always make the skirt adapt to the lace shapes, not the lace shapes to the skirt.

Making Diamonds, Hearts, Tear-Drops, Or Circles Fit Skirt Bottom

What is the best way to engineer diamonds, hearts, teardrops, or circles to exactly fit the width skirt planned? Precision here is not really important. Make the shapes any size Stitch them onto the skirt, front and back, and cut away the excess skirt width. Or, stitch up one side seam, and zigzag the shapes onto the skirt, and cut away the excess on the other side before completing the other side seam.

Ribbon To Lace Insertion

This is tricky! Lace has give and ribbon doesn't. For long bands of lace to ribbon, as in a skirt, it is better to place the lace on top of the ribbon and straight stitch (Length 2 to 2-1/2). For short strips of lace to ribbon, it is perfectly OK to butt together and zigzag.

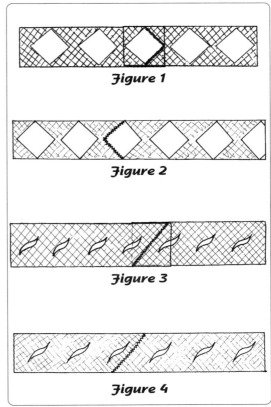

Figure 1

Figure 2

Figure 3

Figure 4

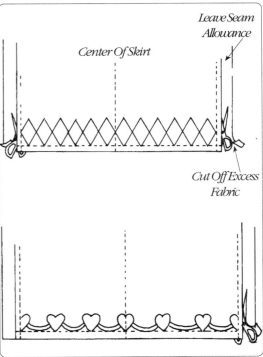

Leave Seam Allowance

Center Of Skirt

Cut Off Excess Fabric

Directions for Straight Stitch Attachment (fig. 1):

1. Press and starch the ribbon and lace.

2. Place the heading of the insertion just over the heading of the ribbon and straight stitch

   Suggested stitch:

   Length=2 to 2-1/2

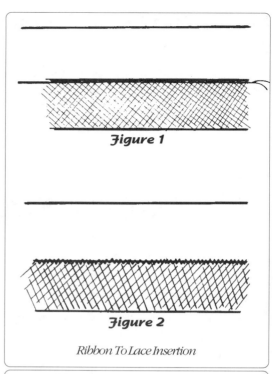

Figure 1

Directions for Zigzag Stitch Attachment (fig. 2):

1. Press and starch the ribbon and lace.

2. Place the two side-by-side and zigzag

   Suggested stitch width and length:

   Width=1-1/2 to 2-1/2

   Length=1 to 2

Figure 2

Ribbon To Lace Insertion

Directions for Flat Lace To Entredeux

1. Trim one batiste side of the entredeux.

2. Spray starch and press entredeux and lace.

3. Lay trimmed edge of entredeux beside the flat side of the lace. These should be right sides up. Butt them together; they should not overlap. In other words, zigzag, side-by-side, right sides up.

4. Zigzag them together, trying to make one stitch of the machine go into one hole of the entredeux and over, just catching the heading of the lace **(figs. 3 and 4)**

   Suggested stitch width and length:

   Width=21/2 to 3-1/2

   Length=2-1/2

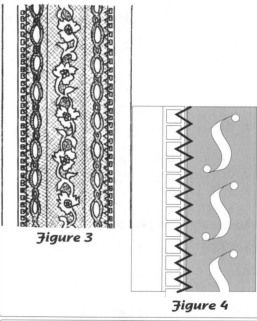

Figure 3

Figure 4

Entredeux To Flat Fabric

Method 1 - Stitch-In-The-Ditch

1. Do not trim entredeux.

2. Spray starch and press fabric and entredeux.

3. Place together batiste edge of untrimmed entredeux and edge of the fabric. (This is similar to the sewing of any two seams of a dress. Place the edges and sew the seam.)

4. Sew in straight, short stitches along the right-hand side of the entredeux (the side of the entredeux that is next to the body of the sewing machine.) This is called "stitch-in-the-ditch" because it is just that — the needle runs down the ditch of the entredeux (Length= 2-1/2) **(fig. l)**.

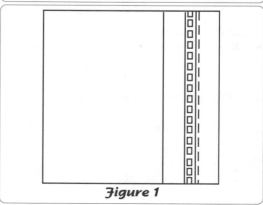

Figure 1

5. Trim the seam, leaving about a 1/8" seam allowance **(fig. 2)**.

6. Zigzag a tight stitch (not a satin) to go over the stitch-in-the-ditch and all the way off the edge of the fabric edge. This zigzag will completely encase the fabric left on the entredeux and the straight stitch just made (Width=2-1/2 to 3; Length=1) **(fig. 3)**.

7. Press the zigzagged seam toward the fabric. All of the holes of the entredeux should be showing perfectly.

8. This topstitching is not necessary if using entredeux to flat fabric, although it is acceptable. When topstitching, zigzag on top of the fabric. As close as possible, zigzag into one hole of the entredeux and into the fabric. Barely catch the fabric in this top zigzag stitch. Adjust the machine length and width to fit each situation **(fig. 4)**.

9. Suggested machine width and length:
   Width=l-1/2 to 2,
   Length=2

10. Consider topstitching from the back of the fabric. If working from the back, hold the seam down to see a little better. On entredeux to flat fabric, the choice of topstitching from the top or from the bottom is the stitcher's preference.

Entredeux To Gathered Fabric

Method 1

1. Press, don't spray starch the fabric.

2. Do not cut off the edges of the entredeux.

3. Run two rows of long gathering stitches on the fabric (Length=4). There are two methods for running these gathering stitches.

   a. Sew the first gathering row 1/4" from the edge of the fabric. Sew the second gathering row 3/4" from the edge of the fabric **(fig. 1)**.

   b. Sew the first gathering row 1/4" from the edge of the fabric. Sew the second gathering row 1/4" below the first row. This is the more traditional method of running two gathering rows **(fig. 2)**.

4. Gather by hand to adjust the gathers to fit the entredeux.

5. Lay right side of the entredeux to right side of the gathered fabric. This is similar to putting waistbands on very full gathered skirts and can certainly be considered basic dressmaking.

   a. If gathering with the first method (1/4" and 3/4" gathering rows), place the ditch of the entredeux below the first

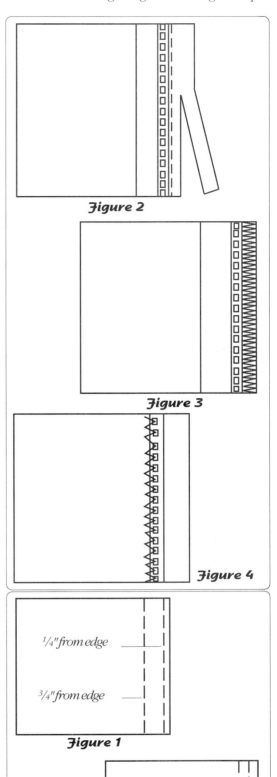

Figure 2

Figure 3

Figure 4

¹/₄" from edge

³/₄" from edge

Figure 1

¹/₄" from edge

¹/₂" from edge

Figure 2

gathering line. The ditch of the entredeux would be about 3/8 " from unfinished edge.

b. If using the second method (1/4" and 1/2" gathering rows), place the entredeux on or a little below the second gathering row.

6. Stitch in the ditch of the entredeux, using a short, straight stitch. This stitch is on the right side of the entredeux. This side is closest to the body of the sewing machine (Length=2) **(fig. 3)**.

7. Move over just a little and straight stitch the second time. This holds down the gathers under the entredeux **(fig. 4)**.

8. Trim away both layers as close to the straight stitch as possible **(fig. 5)**.

9. Zigzag to finish the process. This zigzag is not a satin stitch but close to a satin stitch. This zigzag stitch encloses the stitch-in-the-ditch seam, the second seam and goes off the side to catch the raw edges (Width=3; Length=3/4 to 1) **(fig. 6)**.

10. Press the satin stitched roll toward the fabric.

11. Topstitch on the wrong side of the fabric. Zigzag into one hole of the entredeux and off into the zigzagged seam. This should be as narrow a seam as possible (*Width*=1-1/2 to 2-1/2; *Length*=2) **(fig. 7)**.

12. This last can be zigzagged from the top also. It is easier to zigzag it from the bottom if it is "entredeux to gathered fabric" because of the bulk of the zigzagged seam. When zigzagging entredeux to flat edge (as given in the section just preceding this one) it seems easier to zigzag the final from the top.

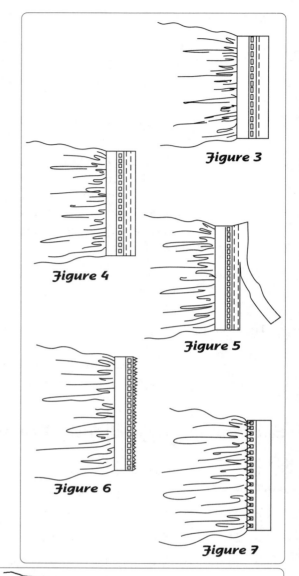

Figure 3

Figure 4

Figure 5

Figure 6

Figure 7

Method 2

1. Follow 1 through 6 of Method I **(fig. 1)**.

2. Trim to within 1/8" of the stitch-in-the-ditch **(fig. 2)**.

3. Zigzag, going into one hole of the entredeux and all the way off of the edge of the fabric. This will roll the fabric/entredeux border right into the entredeux (*Width*=3 to 4, *Length*=1-1/2) **(fig. 3)**.

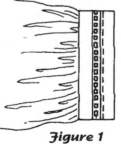

Figure 1

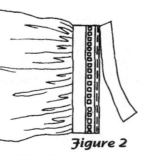

Figure 2

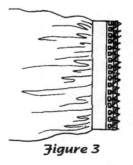

Figure 3

Serger Fever

Oh what a wonderful tool the serger is for French sewing by machine! I cannot say enough about how this machine has simplified the "Entredeux To Flat Fabric" technique and the "Entredeux To Gathered Fabric" technique. First of all, the serger does three things at once. It stitches in the ditch, zigzags, and trims. Secondly, the serger goes twice as fast as your conventional sewing machine. Kathy McMakin has written a how-to book, "French Sewing By Serger," which gives complete instructions and settings on how to do these wonderful French sewing techniques by serger. It is available from Martha Pullen Company.

Another way to use the serger is for French seams. I always did hate those little things. Now, I serge my French seams. I serge in my sleeves! I serge the sleeves in my smocked bishops; you will not believe the improvement in getting bishops through the pleater!

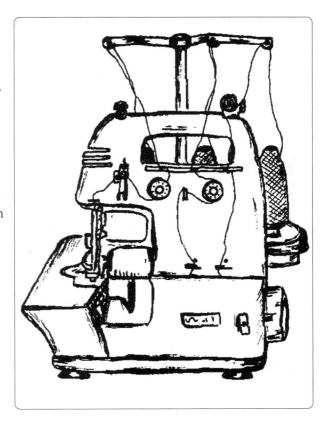

Holidays And Vacations

Holes in the seam of laces or between the laces and fabrics that have been joined are fairly comon. This occurs when both pieces of lace do not get sewn together in the zigzag or the laces do not get caught in the lace-to-fabric, zigzagged seam. This is not a mistake. I refer to this as a holiday or vacation. Sometimes we take long vacations (long holes) and sometimes we are only gone for a few hours (very tiny holes). These vacations and holidays are easily fixed by simply starting above the hole and zigzagging over it, being careful to catch both sides of lace or fabric to repair the opening. No backstitching is necessary. Clip the excess threads and no one will ever know about your vacation.

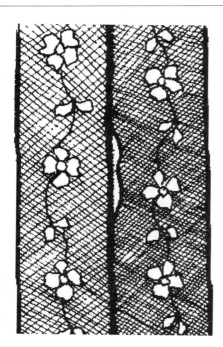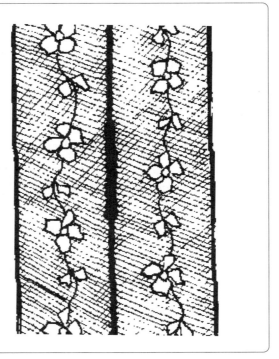

Extra-Stable Lace Finishing

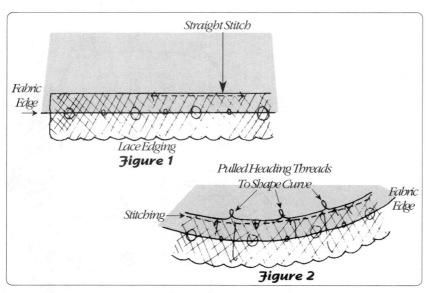

Figure 1

Figure 2

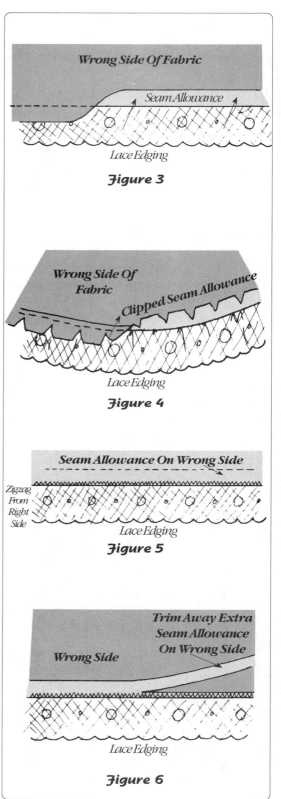

Figure 3

Figure 4

Figure 5

Figure 6

A. Extra-Stable Lace Finish for Fabric Edges

1. If the lace is being attached to a straight edge of fabric, pin the heading of the lace to the right side, ¹/4" or more from the cut edge, with the right side of the lace facing up and the outside edge of the lace extending over the edge of the fabric. Using a short, straight stitch, stitch the lace heading to the fabric **(fig. 1)**.

2. If the lace is being attached to a curved edge, shape the lace around the curve as you would for lace shaping; refer to "Lace Shaping" in the technique section of this book. Pull up the threads in the lace heading if necessary. Continue pinning and stitching the lace as directed in the previous step **(fig. 2)**.

3. Press the seam allowance away from the lace, toward the wrong side of the fabric **(fig. 3)**. If the edge is curved or pointed, you may need to clip the seam allowance in order to press it flat **(fig. 4)**.

4. On the right side, use a short, narrow zigzag to stitch over the lace heading, catching the fold of the pressed seam allowance **(fig. 5)**.

5. On the wrong side, trim the seam allowance close to the zigzag **(fig. 6)**.

B. Extra-Stable Lace Finish for Lace Shapes

1. Trace the lace design onto the fabric. Shape the lace according to the directions in the "Lace Shaping" section of this book **(fig. 7)**.

2. Using a short, straight stitch, stitch the lace heading to the fabric on both edges of the lace **(fig. 8)**.

3. After both sides of the lace have been stitched, carefully slit the fabric behind the lace, cutting in the middle between the two stitching lines. Be very careful not to cut through the lace **(fig. 9)**.

4. Press the seam allowance away from the lace, toward the wrong side of the fabric. If the edge is curved or has a corner, you may need to clip the seam allowance in order to press it flat **(fig. 10)**.

5. On the right side, use a short, narrow zigzag to stitch over the lace heading, catching the fold of the pressed seam allowance **(fig. 11)**.

6. On the wrong side, trim the seam allowance close to the zigzag **(fig. 12)**.

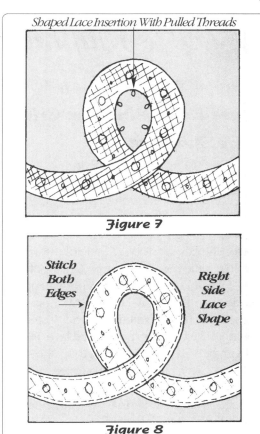

Shaped Lace Insertion With Pulled Threads

Figure 7

Stitch Both Edges → **Right Side Lace Shape**

Figure 8

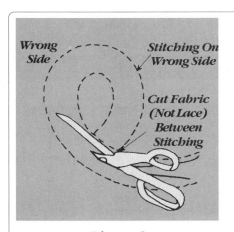

Wrong Side

Stitching On Wrong Side

Cut Fabric (Not Lace) Between Stitching

Figure 9

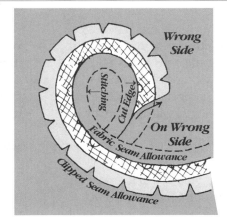

Wrong Side

Stitching

Cut Edges

On Wrong Side

Fabric Seam Allowance

Clipped Seam Allowance

Figure 10

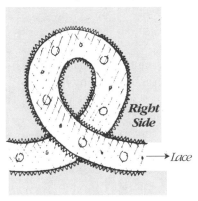

Right Side

→ Lace

Figure 11

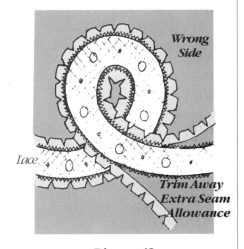

Wrong Side

Lace

Trim Away Extra Seam Allowance

Figure 12

Lace Shaping Techniques

Glass Head Pins Are Critical To Lace Shaping!

Purchasing glass head pins is one of the first and most critical steps to lace shaping. All of this type of work has to be spray starched and pressed right on top of the pins. Since plastic head pins melt, obviously they won't do. At one of my schools several years ago, I found I hadn't made myself clear enough about the importance of glass head pins. I thought I had told everybody in no uncertain terms never to use plastic, but apparently I hadn't. After one of my dear students had shaped a perfectly beautiful round portrait collar, she went to the ironing board to press her curved lace. In a few minutes she called to me with anxiety in her voice, "Martha," she said, "Something is wrong." Little pink, red, blue, orange, purple, and black circles emblazoned her French lace collar. I apologized profusely for not being clear in my instructions and my assistant quickly helped her begin another collar, minus the melted dots of color.

Metal pins such as the iris pins with skinny little metal heads can be used; however, after pinning hundreds of these pins into cardboard, you may find near as many holes poked into the ends of your fingers. Please purchase glass head pins and throw away any plastic ones. Once plastic and glass pins get mixed together, it's almost impossible to tell the difference between them until they're touched with an iron; by then, it's too late.

I also find that it is easier to pick up the pins one at a time if you use a wrist pin holder. Years ago when I lived in Charlotte, North Carolina, I used to sew for hours nearly every day. I went to the local grocery store so many times with my "fine wrist jewelry" in place, they called me the "pin lady."

Please don't work with pins by sticking your hands into a pin box. More than once, I have retrieved my hand with a pin protruding from one of my fingers. If you don't have a wrist holder, scatter some pins out on your fabric board so you can see them. This may seem trite, but until you've shaped lace, you can't imagine how many pins you will be working with.

Please Read This Before Learning Anything New!

I would like to share with you a life-changing philosophy of education borrowed from Dr. Bill Purkey, one of my mentors, while I was in graduate school at the University of Florida. I believe it applies to sewing as much as any form of education. He told me that he was going to blow the old adage, "When something is worth doing, it is worth doing right!" There is no truth to that statement, he claimed, and wondered if I was surprised. Consider the following. Think of one thing that you do extremely well! Raise your hand if you did this thing well the very first time you ever did it. Isn't that funny? I feel relatively sure that 99 percent of you didn't raise your hand, did you? Enlightened by my professor, I prefer to rephrase our old adage like this, "When something is worth doing, it is worth doing poorly, even awkwardly at first. Only then, will you ever have a chance of doing it over and over again to make it better and perhaps, eventually, as perfect as it can be."

Please have patience with yourself and your family when you or they begin something new. I wish every teacher in the world working with children, would share the same philosophy with their classes. I think self-concepts would be raised and little people would think that their first less-than-perfect work was just the beginning of something wonderful.

Drawing Shapes With Dots Rather Than A Solid Line

Margaret Boyles taught me years ago that it is simpler to draw shapes on fabric by making dots about 1/2" apart than it is to draw a solid line. This also means less pencil or marker to get out of the fabric after finishing the lace shaping **(fig. 1).**

Mark the turnaround areas, such as the center top and center bottom of the heart in a solid line. Also, make a solid line when marking the insides (bottom and top) of the heart for fold-back miters. When marking diamonds, make a solid line at the four angles of the diamonds. Make little dots around the straight sides. Make a solid line into the center of the diamonds where a pin will be placed at the top and at the bottom for the fold-back miter.

Shish Kebob Sticks or Skewers For Pushing And Holding Everything

When I teach in Australia, I learn so much from the women there who are expert seamstresses. Actually, I learn much of what I teach from students all over the world. I have always said that learning from my students is the most exciting part of my education no matter where I go. I first learned about using wooden shish kebob or skewer sticks from some of the technical school sewing teachers in Australia.

Nearly every woman in Australia uses a wooden skewer (about 5 or 6 inches long, not the super long ones) to push and to hold with her right hand as the sewing goes into the sewing machine. These sticks are used instead of the usual long pin or worse still, seam ripper that I have used so often. The sticks are wonderful for holding all fabrics, are inexpensive, have no sharp point to damage fabric or sewing machine needles and really are easy to hang on to. Also, it keeps fingers away from the actual needle. Although I have never run a needle through my hand, others have. Using this stick is a safe and efficient technique. I shudder to think what would happen if a sewing machine needle landed on a metal seam ripper. By the way, where do you get these wooden skewers? At the grocery store! If you can only find the long ones, just break them in half and use the end with the point.

Making A Fabric Board

Fabric boards are a must for lace shaping or any kind of working-in-the-round in heirloom sewing. They double as portable ironing boards also. At my School of Art Fashion in Huntsville, these boards are made in the double-wide version for collar classes and in the single-wide version for single lace shaping of hearts, diamonds, ovals, loops, and other shapes. Instructions for the double board follow, since it is the

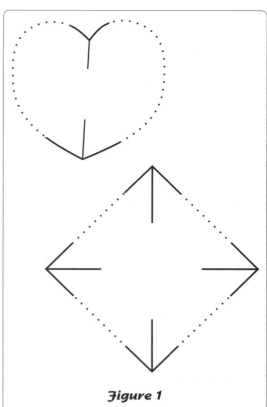

Figure 1

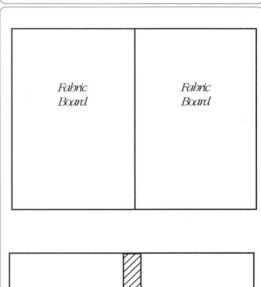

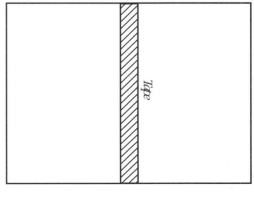

most convenient to have. Commercial boards like the June Taylor Quilting Board™ are also available. I recommend making a little "sheet" just like a fitted bed sheet to cover this type of quilting board when lace shaping. Since lace shaping calls for excessive starch, the sheet, which can be removed and washed, will protect the board's surface. A pillow-case will also suffice. Cardboard cake boards, covered with one layer of fabric or paper, also work well. You can also use just a sheet of card-board. Another alternative is to go to any store that has old shipping boxes to throw away and cut the side out of a cardboard box. Cover the cardboard with paper or fabric and use this as your fabric board. One of my favorite lace shaping boards is a child's bulletin board. Another good one is a ceiling tile. Just staple or pin white typing paper or butcher paper over the board before you start shaping lace.

One thing I don't particularly like in lace shaping is a padded board with a lot of spring. It is easier to shape properly without a lot of padding such as quilt batting under the chosen surface.

Shaping A Lace Scalloped Skirt

I have always loved scalloped skirts, but the first one I ever saw intimidated me so much that I didn't even try to make one for several years after that. The methods presented in this section are so easy that I'm sure you will be eager to try them. Scalloping lace can be a very simple way to finish the bottom of a smocked dress or can be a very elaborate way to put row after row of lace scallops with curved pintucks in-between. Plain or very elaborate, this is one of my favorite techniques in French sewing by machine. Enjoy!

Preparing The Skirt For Lace Scallops

Before diving into the actual process below, which is one technique for preparing scallops on a skirt, keep in mind that you can also follow the instructions found under the beginning lace techniques for scallops as well as diamonds, hearts, teardrops or circles. To use any size scallop for any width skirt, stitch or serge up one side seam of the whole skirt.

Directions

1. Pull a thread and cut or either tear the skirt.

   Note: *I usually put 88" in my skirt, two 44" widths - one for the front and one for the back. Make the skirt length the proper one for the given garment (fig. 1).*

2. Stitch a French seam (or serge) one side seam only for a flat skirt, which is approximately 88 inches wide **(fig. 1)**.

   Note: *By now you know that I rarely make French seams. I use the rolled hem finish on the serger. It is beautiful, strong, and prettier than most French seams.*

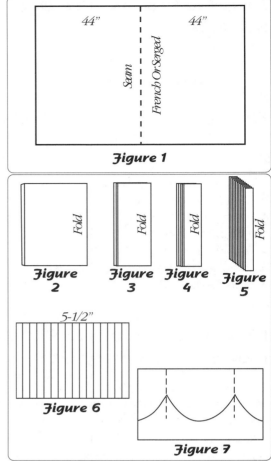

Figure 1

Figure 2 **Figure 3** **Figure 4** **Figure 5**

Figure 6

Figure 7

3. Fold the skirt in half at the seam line **(fig. 2)**. Press. Fold it again **(fig. 3)**. Press. Fold it again **(fig. 4)**. Press. Fold it again **(fig. 5)**. Press. Open up the skirt, to reveal 16 equal sections **(fig. 6)**. These sections serve as sidelines for the scallops. Each section 5-1/2" wide.

4. Make a template that fits between the folds by using a saucer, a dinner plate, an artist's Flex-i- curve® or whatever has a curved edge. Make one template which has only one full-sized scallop and the points of two more. Draw a straight line bisecting each top point of the scallop; make this line extend at least 2" above and below the point of the scallop **(fig. 7)**. Make this tem-plate on a piece of paper and move the bottom of the piece of paper along the bottom of the fabric to draw one scallop at a time. This is the simplest way to get those scallops drawn on the whole skirt.

5. Draw scallops between the folds or pressed-in creases **(fig. 8)**. Place the scallops anywhere on the skirt bottom. For maximum yardage, use the following guidelines when placing the scallops near the bottom of the skirt fabric. The bottom of the scallop (Line A to B) is at least 1-1/2" from the bottom of the skirt fabric **(fig. 9)**.

6. Draw a line at the top of each scallop, bisecting the top of the scallop, approximately 2" tall. On **figure 9,** the top of each scallop is point C; this 2" line extending above the scallop is point D **(fig. 9)**. These bisecting lines going extending from the top of each scallop are very important in the new fold-back method of miters which follow.

Placing Your Skirt On The Fabric Board

Directions

1. Purchase or make a fabric board approximately 23" wide, which generally fits four scallops at one time (depending, of course, on the size of scallops).

2. Working from the left side of the skirt, place the left side of the skirt on the fabric board, right side up **(fig. 8)**. Right-handers will want to work from left to right. The reverse is true for left-handers. Some stitchers prefer to start at the center seam and work one direction, then the other.

Pinning The Lace Insertion To The Skirt Portion On The Fabric Board

1. Cut enough lace insertion to go around all of the scallops on the skirt. Allow at least 16" more than the skirt width. Any excess lace insertion can be used in another area of the dress later. Shorter lace strips may be pieced as instructed in the section on piecing; try to piece laces so that the pieced area will be worked into a miter at the top of a scallop.

2. Pin the lace insertion to the skirt (one scallop at a time only) by poking pins all the way into the fabric board through the bottom lace heading and the fabric of the skirt. Notice on **(figure 10)** that the bottom of the lace is straight with the pins poked into the board. The top of the lace is rather "curvy" because it hasn't been shaped to lay flat yet.

3. When working the lace into the top of the first scallop, carefully place a pin into the lace and the board at points C and D. Pinning the D point is crucial to forming the miter **(fig. 10)**. Pin the B point at exactly the place where the flat lace crosses the line to bisect the scallop.

4. Fold back the whole piece of lace onto the other side **(fig. 11)**. Remove the pin at C and re-pin it to go through both layers of lace. Leave the pin at point D just as it is.

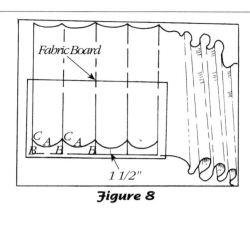

Figure 8

A = Bottom Curve Of Scall
B = Bottom Of Skirt Fabric
C = Top Of Scallop
D = Extended 2" Line Above Scallop

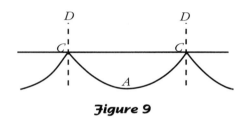

Figure 9

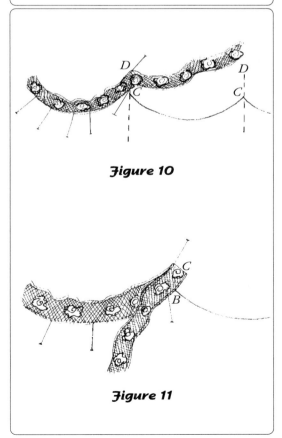

Figure 10

Figure 11

5. Then fold over the lace to place the next section of the lace to travel into the next part of the scallop **(fig. 12)**.

   Note: *If a little bit of that folded point is exposed after starting to form the lace into the next scallop, just push it underneath the miter until the miter looks perfect **(fig. 13)**. I lovingly call this "mushing" the miter into place.*

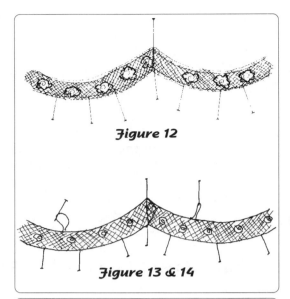

Figure 12

6. To shape the excess fullness of the top of the scallop, simply pull a gathering thread at the center point of each scallop until the lace becomes flat and pretty **(fig. 14)**.

7. Secure the thread loop pulled in the previous step with a pin just until the lace is spray starched and pressed flat. Remember, it is easier to pull the very top thread of the lace, the one which makes a prominent scallop on the top of the lace. If that thread breaks, pull another one. Many laces have as many as four or five total threads in the header. Don't worry about the pulled thread; it can be trimmed away after stitching the lace to the skirt. The heaviness of the zigzag or the entredeux stitch will secure the lace to the skirt.

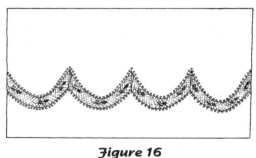

Figure 13 & 14

8. Spray starch and press each scallop and miter after finishing the shapes.

9. After finishing with the section of scallops on one length of board, pin the laces flat to the skirt, remove from the board and move over to another section of the skirt **(fig 15)**. Either zigzag each section of scallops to the skirt after it is finished, or wait until the entire skirt is ready to be stitched.

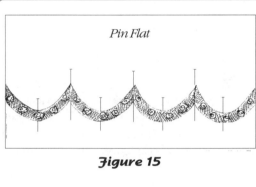

Pin Flat

Figure 15

10. If using a decorative sewing machine stitch (entredeux stitch with a wing needle) use a stabilizer underneath the skirt when stitching. Stitch 'n Tear™ is an excellent one. Tissue paper, wax paper, adding machine paper, or paper used to cover medical examining tables work for stabilizing lace and fabric when using a wing needle and heavy decorative stitching.

11. To secure lace with an entredeux sewing machine stitch, apply the stitch on both the top and bottom of the scalloped skirt **(fig. 16)** using either of two methods:

Figure 16

Method 1

a. After completing the entredeux/wing needle stitching on both the top and the bottom of the scalloped skirt, trim away the fabric from behind the lace scallop.

b. Carefully trim the fabric from the bottom of the skirt also, leaving just a "hair" of seam allowance **(fig. 17)**.

c. Now zigzag over the folded-in miters **(fig. 18)**. Use a regular needle for this zigzag.

d. Finish by zigzagging the gathered laces to the bottom of this machine-created entredeux.

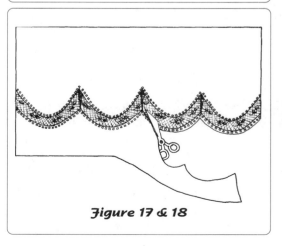

Figure 17 & 18

Method 2

    a. Machine entredeux the top only of the scallop **(fig. 19)**. Don't cut anything away.

    b. Butt the gathered lace edging, a few inches at a time, to the shaped bottom of the lace scallop. Machine entredeux stitch in-between the flat scalloped lace and the gathered edging lace, thus attaching both laces at the same time **(fig. 19)**. Be sure to put more fullness in at the points of the scallops.

    c. After the gathered lace edging is completely stitched to the bottom of the skirt with machine entredeux, cut away the bottom of the skirt fabric as closely to the stitching as possible **(fig. 20)**.

    d. Zigzag over the folded in miters **(fig. 20)**.

16. To attach the lace to the fabric with just a plain zigzag stitch, try a width of 1-1/2 to 2 and a length of 1 to 1-1/2. The zigzag must be wide enough to completely go over the heading of the laces and short enough to be strong. When zigzagging the laces to the skirt, zigzag the top only of the lace scallops **(fig. 21)**.

17. After zigzagging the top only of this skirt, carefully trim away the bottom portion of the fabric skirt, trimming all the way up to the stitches **(fig. 21)**.

18. With scallops complete, add entredeux and gathered lace or simply gathered lace to the bottom of the scalloped skirt. Just treat the bottom of this lace scallop as a finished edge; gather the lace edging and zigzag to the bottom **(fig. 22)**.

Finishing The Center Of The Miter After Attaching It To The Skirt and Trimming Away The Fabric From Behind the Scallops

I always zigzag down the center of this folded miter. Other options are to leave the folded lace portion in the miter to make the miter stronger or trim away the folded portion after zigzagging over the miter center **(fig. 22)**.

Shaping And Stitching Purchased Entredeux To Scallops

Directions

1. Completely trim off one side of the entredeux **(fig. 23)**.

2. Slash the other side of the entredeux **(fig. 23)**.

3. Pin, starch, and press the entredeux before sewing it to the scallops. It won't hang right, otherwise.

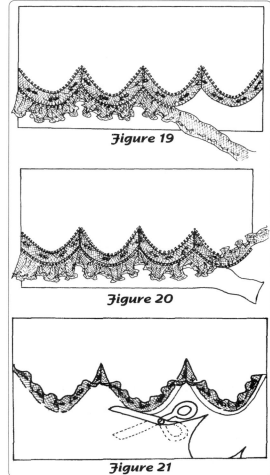

Figure 19

Figure 20

Figure 21

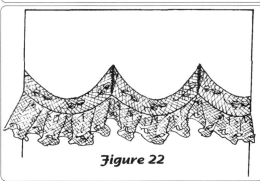

Figure 22

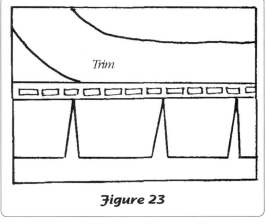

Trim

Figure 23

4. Here is a great trick. In order to pin the entredeux into the points of the scallops most effectively, trim entredeux about 1-1/2" on either side of the point. This allows a stitcher to see exactly where the entredeux will be placed **(fig. 24)**.

5. After pinning the entredeux into the points, starch, and press the entredeux into its shape.

6. Remove the pins from the skirt.

7. Zigzag the lace to the entredeux trying to go into one hole and off onto the lace (W=3; L=1-1/2).

8. Upon approaching the points with the entredeux, simply "mush" the entredeux into the point, stitch over it, and turn the corner **(fig. 25)**.

9. An optional method for sewing entredeux on to scallops is to put entredeux on the bottom of a lace-shaped skirt by using short pieces of entredeux. These go only from the top of the curve to top of the next curve **(fig. 26)**. Treat it exactly as instructed in Steps 1-6 in this section. Overlap the trimmed edges in each point. When attaching the gathered laces by zigzagging, these cut points will be zigzagged together.

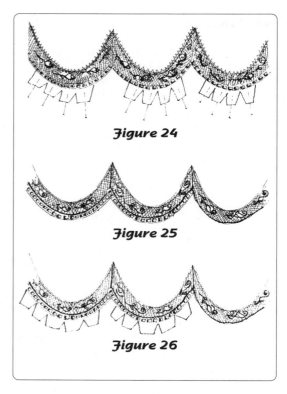

Figure 24

Figure 25

Figure 26

Adding Gathered Lace To The Entredeux At the Bottom of Scallops

Directions

1. Measure around the scalloped skirt to determine the measurement for gathered lace edging, which will finish the skirt bottom.

2. Double that measurement for a 2-to-1 fullness. Piece laces if edging is not long enough.

3. Cut the lace edging.

4. Using the technique "Sewing Hand-Gathered French Lace To Entredeux Edge" zigzag the gathered lace to the bottom of the entredeux **(fig. 27)**.

5. Or, use the method "Gathering French Lace By Machine, While Applying It To Trimmed Entredeux Edge" to attach this lace edging.

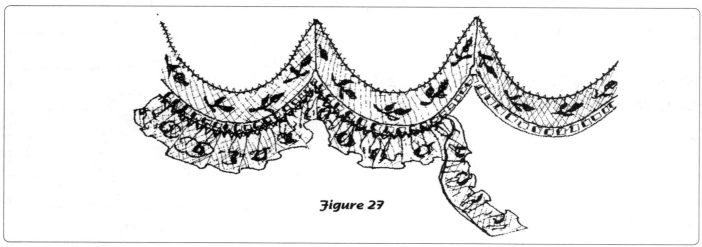

Figure 27

Gathering French Laces By Hand Pull Thread In the Heading of Laces

On the straight sides of French or English cotton laces are several threads called the "heading." These threads serve as pull threads for lace shaping. Some laces have better pull threads than others. Before beginning a dramatically-curved design, check to be sure the chosen lace has a good pull thread. The scallop on the top of most laces is the first pull thread to try. Most French and English laces have several good pull threads, so if the first breaks, pull another. If all the threads break, run a machine gathering thread in the top of the lace.

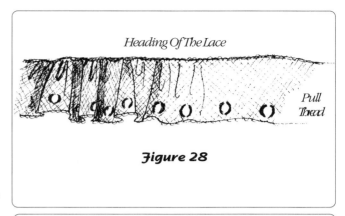

Heading Of The Lace

Pull Thread

Figure 28

Directions

1. Cut a length of lace 2-to-3 times the finished length; sufficient fullness to make a pretty lace ruffle.

2. To gather the lace, pull one of the heavy threads that runs along the straight edge or heading of the lace **(fig. 28)**.

3. Adjust gathers evenly before zigzagging.

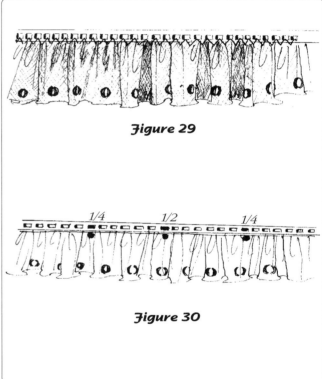

Figure 29

Sewing Hand-Gathered French Lace To Entredeux Edge

Directions

1. Gather lace by hand by pulling the thread in the heading of the lace.

   Note: *I use the scalloped outside thread of the heading first, since I think it gathers better than the inside threads. Distribute gathers evenly.*

2. Trim the side of the entredeux to which the gathered lace is to be attached. Side by side, right sides up, zigzag the gathered lace to the trimmed entredeux (Width=1-1/2; Length=2) **(fig. 29)**.

3. Using a wooden skewers, push the gathers evenly into the sewing machine while zigzagging.

1/4   1/2   1/4

Figure 30

Note: *To help distribute the gathers evenly, fold the entredeux in half and half again. Mark these points with a fabric marker. Before the lace is gathered, fold it in half and half again. Mark the folds with a fabric marker. Now gather the lace and match the marks on the entredeux and the marks on the lace (**fig. 30**).*

Gathering French Lace

Gathering French Lace While Applying To Trimmed Entredeux Edge

Note: *Allow for extra lace when using this method. It may require more than the pattern calls for. This method is easy and time saving. It can be used when attaching gathered lace around a collar that has entredeux at the bottom before the gathered lace. It is especially helpful when attaching gathered lace around a portrait collar. It is a great way to attach the gathered lace to an entredeux-trimmed neck edge. Actually, this technique can be used anytime gathered lace is attached to trimmed entredeux. It results in fairly even gathers, and eliminates the need to pin, distribute, and straighten-out twisted lace.*

Directions

1. Trim off the outside edge of the entredeux, after the other edge has been attached to the garment.

2. Press both the entredeux and the lace.

3. Side-by-side, right sides up, begin to zigzag with lace still straight (**fig. 1**).

4. About 6" out on the lace, pull one of the gathering threads. Using a little pick of some kind is effective. The same little pick that is used to pull a lace gathering thread, can also be used to push the gathers into the sewing machine. A pin will suffice if necessary (**fig. 2**).

5. In order to get the gathers to move in the right direction (toward the foot of the sewing machine), pull on the side of the thread loop closest to the sewing machine. Pulling on on the other side, will cause the gathers to go away from sewing machine. Pull the thread, and push the gathers toward the sewing machine (**fig. 2**).

6. Lift the pressure foot, and push a few gathers under it. Zigzag a few stitches (*Width*=3-1/2; *Length*=2). Notice that the width is a little wider than usual for zigzagging lace to entredeux. With gathered lace, it is necessary to make the width wider in order to catch all of the heading of the gathered lace. As always, adjust the width and length, according to the width of the entredeux and the lace heading. They vary so much it is hard to give one exact width and length. Lift the pressure foot again, and push a few more gathers under it. Continue, until all of the gathers on that one section have been stitched in (**fig. 3**).

7. Go out another 6" on the lace, and repeat the process. Continue, until all of the lace is gathered and stitched to the trimmed entredeux.

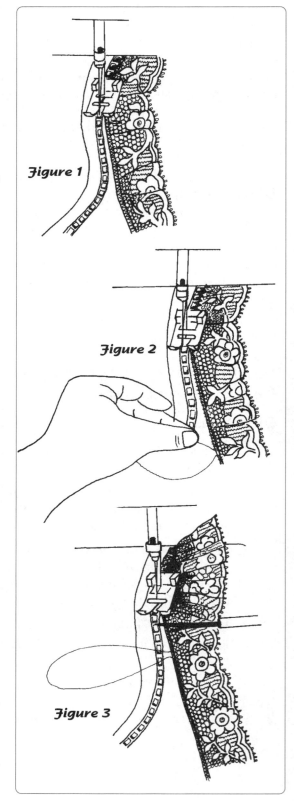

Figure 1

Figure 2

Figure 3

Making An Entredeux And Lace String

The method "Gathering French Lace A Little At A Time, While Applying It To Trimmed Entredeux Edge" is the perfect way to make an entredeux/gathered lace trim for the yoke of a French dress. This is the easy way to trim a yoke with entredeux and gathered lace. The hard way would be to apply your entredeux in the seams of the yokes and the sleeves.

Directions

1. Follow the techniques found in the technique "Gathering French Lace By Machine, While Applying It To Trimmed Entredeux Edge."

2. Make the entredeux and lace string as long as needed to travel around the entire yoke (front and back) and over the shoulders of the dress. After making this long strip of entredeux and gathered lace, simply trim the other side of the entredeux (**fig. 1**). Pin into place, around the yoke edges, and zigzag the entredeux and lace string right onto the finished dress (**fig. 2**).

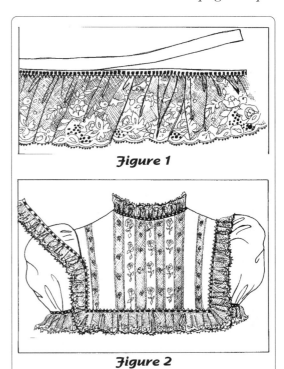

Figure 1

Figure 2

Finishing The Neckline With Entredeux/ Gathered Lace

So many times, French dresses have an entredeux/gathered lace neckline finish. Here is the technique I use.

Directions

1. Check the seam allowance on the neckline of the chosen pattern. This is important.

2. Check the seam allowance on the entredeux. It is usually 1/2"; however, this is not always the case. Measure the seam allowance of the entredeux.

3. If the seam allowance at the neck of the pattern and the seam allowance of the entredeux do not match, trim the seam allowance of the entredeux to match the seam allowance on the neckline of the specific garment.

4. Using the techniques "Entredeux to Flat Fabric," attach the entredeux to the neckline of the garment.

5. Stitch in the ditch (**fig. 3**). Trim, leaving a 1/8" to 1/4" seam allowance (**fig. 4**).

6. Zigzag the seam allowance to finish (**fig. 5**).

7. Trim the remaining clipped seam allowance. Press the seam toward the body of the dress.

8. Gather the lace edging. Butt it to the trimmed entredeux and zigzag (**fig. 6**).

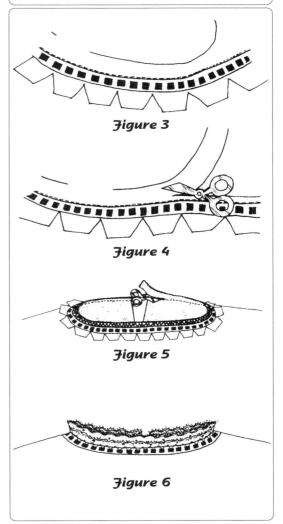

Figure 3

Figure 4

Figure 5

Figure 6

Shaping Lace Diamonds

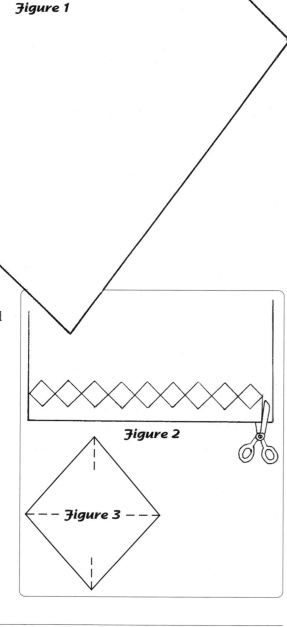

Lace diamonds can be used almost anywhere on heirloom garments. They are especially pretty at the point of a collar, on the skirt of a dress, at angles on the bodice of a garment, or all the way around a collar. The easiest way to make lace diamonds is to work on a fabric board with a diamond guide. Make these diamonds as large or as small as desired. The fold-back diamond method presented here is especially easy. There is no need to transfer the diamonds from the shaping board because they're shaped directly on your project fabric.

Making Lace Diamonds

Materials Needed

- Spray starch, iron, glass head pins, fabric board
- Lace insertion
- Diamond guide

Directions

1. Draw the diamond guide or template **(fig. 1)**.

2. Tear both skirt pieces. French seam or serge one side of the skirt only.

3. Working from the center seam completed in the previous step, draw diamonds all the way around the skirt. This technique accommodates any diamond size. Working from the center assures the same number of diamonds on both front and back skirts and the same amount of leftover fabric.

4. Simply trim the excess skirt away remembering to leave the necessary seam allowance on each side. The seam will be stitched after all the lace diamonds have been shaped and stitched to the skirt. This is the easy way to align any lace shaping design on a skirt; it will always fit perfectly **(fig. 2)**.

5. The guide or template drawn on the skirt, will serve as the outside of the diamond. Draw lines going into the diamond, bisecting each angle where the lace will be mitered. This is very important, since one of the critical pins will be placed exactly on this line. These bisecting lines need to be drawn about 2" long coming in from the angles of the diamonds **(fig. 3)**.

Figure 1

Figure 2

Figure 3

Note: *When making a diamond skirt, it is easier to draw the diamond larger and make the diamond shaping on the inside of the diamond. That way, the outside points of the diamond guidelines can touch.*

6. Place the skirt with the drawn diamonds on a fabric board.

7. Place the lace flat and guide it along the inside of the drawn template, put a pin at point A and one at Point B where the bisecting line goes to the inside **(fig. 4)**. The pin goes through both the lace and the fabric into the fabric board.

8. Guiding the edge of the lace along the drawn template line, place another pin into the fabric board through the lace (and the fabric skirt) at point C and another one at point D on the bisecting line **(fig. 4)**.

9. Fold back the lace right on top of itself. Remove the pin from the fabric board at point D, replacing it this time to go through both layers of lace rather than just one. Of course, the pin will not only go through both layers of lace but also through the skirt and into the fabric board **(fig. 5)**.

10. Take the lace piece and bring it around to once again following the outside line. Magically, a folded miter is already in place **(fig. 6)**.

11. Guiding further, the edge of the lace along the inside of the drawn template line, place another pin into the fabric board through the lace at point E and another at point F on the bisecting line **(fig. 6)**.

12. Fold the lace right back on top of itself. Remove the pin at point F, replacing it this time to go through both layers of lace rather than just one **(fig. 7)**.

13. Take the lace piece and bring it around to once again follow the outside line. Magically a folded miter is already in place **(fig. 8)**.

14. Guiding further, the edge of the lace along the inside of the drawn template line, place another pin into the lace at point G and another pin at point H on the bisecting line.

15. Fold the lace right back on top of itself. Remove the pin at point H, replace it this time to go through both layers of lace rather than just one.

16. Take the lace piece and bring it around to once again follow the outside line. Magically, a folded miter is already in place **(fig. 9)**.

17. At the bottom of the lace diamond, let the laces cross at the bottom. Remove the pin at point B and replace it into the fabric board through both pieces of lace. Remove the pin completely at point A **(fig. 10)**.

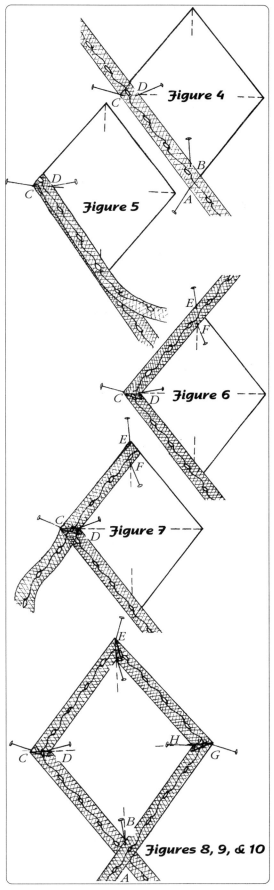

Figure 4

Figure 5

Figure 6

Figure 7

Figures 8, 9, & 10

18. Taking the top piece of lace, and leaving in the pin at point B only, fold under and back the lace where it lays on top of the other piece of lace. This process folds the miter for the bottom of the lace.

19. Put a pin in, now, at point B (**fig. 11**). Cut away this long tail of lace.

> **Note:** *I think the best time to cut is before you begin the final stitching to attach the diamonds to the garment. Although, it is perfectly fine to leave those tails of lace until the final stitching is done and then trim them.*

20. Spray starch and press the whole diamond shape. After spray starching and pressing the diamonds to the skirt, remove the pins from the fabric board and flat pin the lace shape to the skirt bottom. Zigzag the diamond or machine entredeux stitch the diamond to the garments (*Width*=2 to 3; *Length*=1 to 1-1/2).

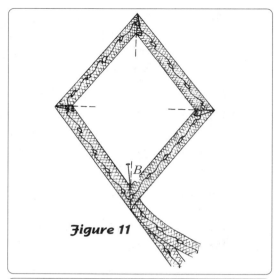

Figure 11

Finishing The Bottom Of The Skirt

These techniques are for finishing the bottom of a diamond skirt, a heart skirt, a bow skirt, or any other lace shaped skirt in which the figures travel all the way around the bottom touching each other.

Directions for Method 1

Using Plain Zigzag To Attach Diamonds (Or Other Shapes) To The Skirt.

1. First, zigzag across the top of the diamond pattern, stitching from point A to point B again to point A and finish the entire skirt (**fig. 12**). The lace is now attached to the skirt all the way across the skirt on the top. If the fabric and diamonds have been spray starched well, there is no need to use a stabilizer when zigzagging these lace shapes to the fabric. The width stitch will be wide enough to cover the heading of the lace and go off onto the fabric on the other side. The length will be from 1/2 to 1, depending on the preferred look.

2. Zigzag all the diamonds to the skirt, on the inside of the diamonds only (**fig. 13**).

3. Trim away the fabric of the skirt from behind the diamonds. Trim the fabric carefully from behind the lace shapes. The rest of the skirt fabric will now fall away leaving a diamond shaped bottom of the skirt (**fig. 14**). Fabric is removed from the top of the diamonds also.

4. If gathering lace and attaching it directly on to the shapes, zigzag it to the bottom of the lace diamonds being careful to put extra fullness in the points of the diamonds (**fig. 15**). If the lace isn't wide enough for a gathered ruffle, zigzag a couple of pieces of insertion or edging to extend the lace (**fig. 16**).

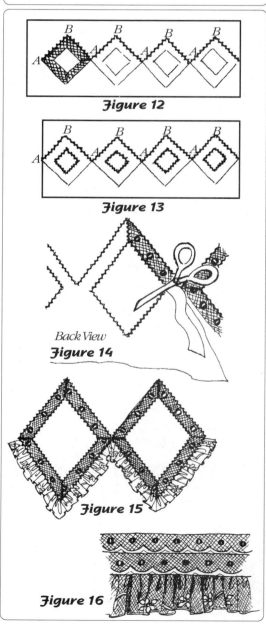

Figure 12

Figure 13

Back View
Figure 14

Figure 15

Figure 16

5. To finish the shapes first with entredeux then lace, follow the instructions on attaching entredeux to the bottom of a scalloped skirt given previously in this lace shaping section. Work with short pieces of entredeux stitching from the inside points of the diamonds to the lower points of the diamonds on the skirt.

Finishing The Bottom Of The Skirt Directions for Method 2

Using A Wing Needle Machine Entredeux Stitch To Attach Diamonds (Or Other Lace Shapes) To The Skirt

1. To use the wing needle and machine entredeux stitch to attach diamonds to a skirt, remember to use a stabilizer.

2. Place the stabilizer underneath the skirt, behind the shapes to be stitched. Use small pieces of stabilizer, which are placed underneath only a few shapes rather than having to re-adjust a long piece of stabilizer.

3. First, stitch the top side of the diamonds — entredeux stitching from point A to point B all the way around the skirt **(fig. 17)**.

4. Next, stitch the inside of the diamonds using the entredeux stitch **(fig. 18)**. Do not cut any fabric away at this point. Remember to continue using stabilizer for all entredeux/wing needle stitching.

5. Gather the lace edging and machine entredeux it to the bottom of the skirt joining the bottom of the diamonds at the same time the gathered lace is attached. An edge joining or edge stitching foot with a center blade for guiding, is helpful here.

6. Gather only a few inches of lace edging at a time. Butt the gathered lace edging to the flat bottom sides of the diamonds.

7. Machine entredeux right between the gathered lace edging and the flat side of the diamond. The stitching should be piercing the laces (which are butted together not overlapped), the fabric of the skirt and the stabilizer **(fig. 19)**. Put a little extra lace gathered fullness at the upper and lower points of the diamonds.

8. After stitching the machine entredeux all the way around the bottom of the skirt, the gathered lace edging should be securely attached to the bottom of the skirt by the entredeux stitch.

9. Trim the fabric from behind the lace diamonds. Trim the fabric from underneath the gathered lace edging on the bottom of the skirt **(fig. 20)**.

10. Either zigzag the folded in miters in the angles of the diamonds or simply leave them folded in.

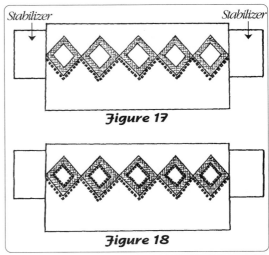

Stabilizer   Stabilizer

Figure 17

Figure 18

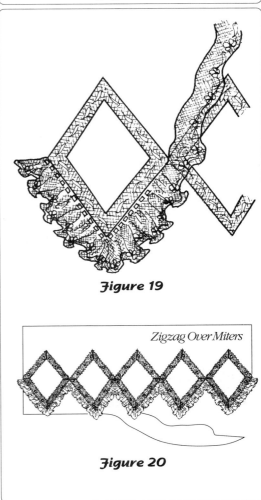

Figure 19

Zigzag Over Miters

Figure 20

Note: *I prefer to zigzag them* **(fig. 21)**. *You also have the choice of cutting away the little folded back portions of the miters or leaving them for strength.*

Shaping Flip-Flopped Lace Bows

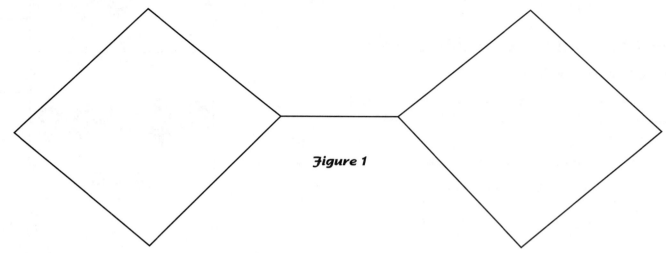

Figure 1

I make lace bows using a technique called "flip-flopping" lace — a relatively unsophisticated name for a lovely trim. I first saw this technique on an antique teddy I bought at a local antique store. Upon careful examination of this teddy's heirloom attire, I noticed the lace was simply folded over at the corners, then continued down forming the outline of a bow. The corners on the bow were somewhat square. Certainly this was easier than mitering or pulling a thread and curving. I found it not only looked easier, it was easier.

Follow the instructions for making a flip-flopped bow using a bow template. This technique works just as well for lace angles up and down on a skirt. Flip-flop any angle that traditionally would be mitered. It can be used to go around a square collar, around diamonds, and around any shape with an angle rather than a curve.

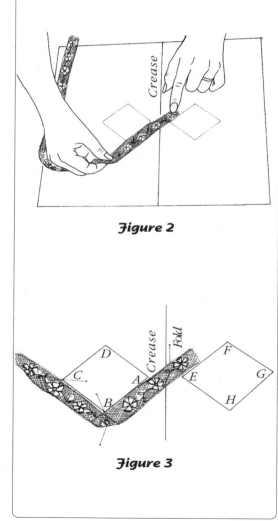

Figure 2

Figure 3

Directions

1. Trace the template onto the fabric where the bow will be placed **(fig. 1)**. Remember, the easy way to put bows around a skirt is to fold the fabric to make equal divisions of the skirt. To make a bow skirt, which has bows all the way around, follow previous directions for positioning diamonds starting at the skirt side seam.

2. Place the garment on a fabric board before beginning to shape bows. Beginning above the inside of one bow (above E), place the lace along the angle. The template should be treated as the inside guideline of the bow **(fig. 2)**.

3. At the first angle (B), simply fold the lace where it will follow along the next line (B-C) **(fig. 3)**. This is called flip-flopping

the lace.

4. Place pins sticking through the lace, the fabric, and into the shaping board. Place pins on both the inside edges and the outside edges. Remember to place pins where they lay as flat as possible.

5. The lines go as follows: A-B, B-C, C-D, D-A, A-E, E-F, F-G, G-H, H-E. Tuck the lace end under E, which is also where the first raw edge will end **(fig. 4)**.

6. Cut a short bow tab of lace that is long enough to go around the whole tie area of the bow **(fig. 4)**. This will be the bow tie!

7. Tuck in this lace tab to make the center of the bow **(fig. 5)**. Another way to attach this bow tie is to simply fold down a tab at the top and the bottom and place it right on top of the center of the bow. That is actually easier than tucking it under. Because the zigzagging will travel all the way around the bow "tie" it really won't matter whether it is tucked in or not.

8. Spray starch and press the bow, that is shaped with the pins still in the board, with its bow tie in place **(fig. 6)**. Remove pins from the board and pin the bow flat to the skirt or other garment. Attach the shaped bow to the garment.

9. This illustration provides ideas for making a bow two ways. First, the "A" side of the bow has just the garment fabric peeking through the center of the bow. Second, the "B" side of the bow illustrates what the bow will look like if adding a pintucked strip in the center. Both are beautiful **(fig. 7)**.

10. To make a bow as illustrated by side (A), zigzag around the total outside of the bow. Then, zigzag around the inside portions of both sides of the bow. Finally, zigzag around the finished bow "tie" portion **(fig. 8)**. The bows will be attached to the dress.

11. To make a bow as illustrated by side (B), follow the directions in this section, which apply to bows on areas other than the bottom of a skirt or sleeve or collar. For bows at the bottom of a design, refer to the skirt directions given in the diamond skirt section.

12. Zigzag the outside only of the bows all the way around. Notice that the bow "tie" will be partially stitched since part of it is on the outside edges.

13. Pintuck a larger piece of fabric and cut small sections, which are somewhat larger than the insides of the bows **(fig. 9)**.

14. Cut away fabric from behind both center sections of the bow.

15. Place the pintucked section behind the center of the lace bows. Zigzag around the inside of the bows which will now attach the pintucked section. From the back, trim away the excess pintucked section **(fig. 10)**.

16. Go back and stitch the sides of the bow "tie" down. After stitching all the way around the bow "tie," trim away excess laces, which crossed underneath the tie. This gives the bow tie a little neater look.

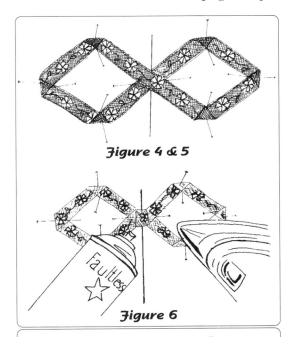

Figure 4 & 5

Figure 6

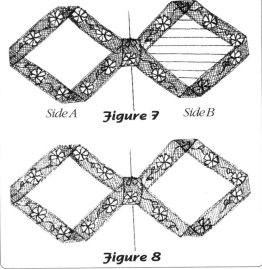

Side A   **Figure 7**   Side B

Figure 8

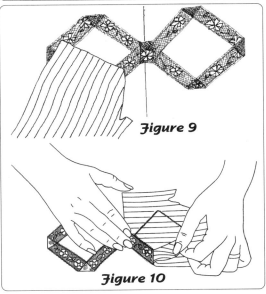

Figure 9

Figure 10

Tied Lace Bows

I saw this method for bow shaping for the first time in Australia several years ago. What makes it such a charming technique is that each flip-flop bow is a little different...like snowflakes, I suppose. Options on shaping the bow are as follows:

1. Flip-flop the bow, or

2. Curve the bow and pull a string to make it round, or

3. Flip-flop one side and curve the other side. Bows can be made of lace insertion, lace edging, or lace beading. When using a tied lace bow of lace edging, be sure to position the scalloped side of the lace edging on the outside of the bow and leave the string to pull on the inside.

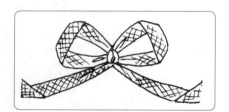

Materials Needed

- 1 yd. to 1-1/4 yds. lace insertion, edging or beading for one bow

Directions

1. Tie the lace into a bow leaving equal streamers on either side of the bow.

2. Using a lace board, shape the bow onto the garment using either the flip-flopped method or the pulled thread curved method.

3. Shape the streamers of the bow using either the flip-flopped method or the pulled thread method.

4. Shape the ends of the streamer into an angle.

5. Zigzag or machine entredeux stitch the shaped bow and streamers to the garment.

Lace Hearts,
The Fold Back Miter Method

Since many heirloom sewers are also incurable romantics, it's no wonder hearts are a popular lace shape. Hearts are the ultimate design for a wedding dress, wedding attendants' clothing, or on a ring bearer's pillow. As with the other lace shaping discussed in this chapter, begin with a template when making hearts. When using the heart template provided, shape the laces inside the heart design to achieve the same effect as pictured. Shaping along the outside of the heart design would result in a larger heart.

With the writing of the *Antique Clothing* book, I thought I had really figured out the easy way to make lace hearts. After four years of teaching heart making, I have totally revised my previous method. This new method is so very easy that I just couldn't wait to share it. After shaping the hearts, there is no need to remove them from the skirt to finish the heart. What a relief and an improvement! Enjoy this short-cut method of making hearts with the new fold back miters, it's ideal for doll clothing.

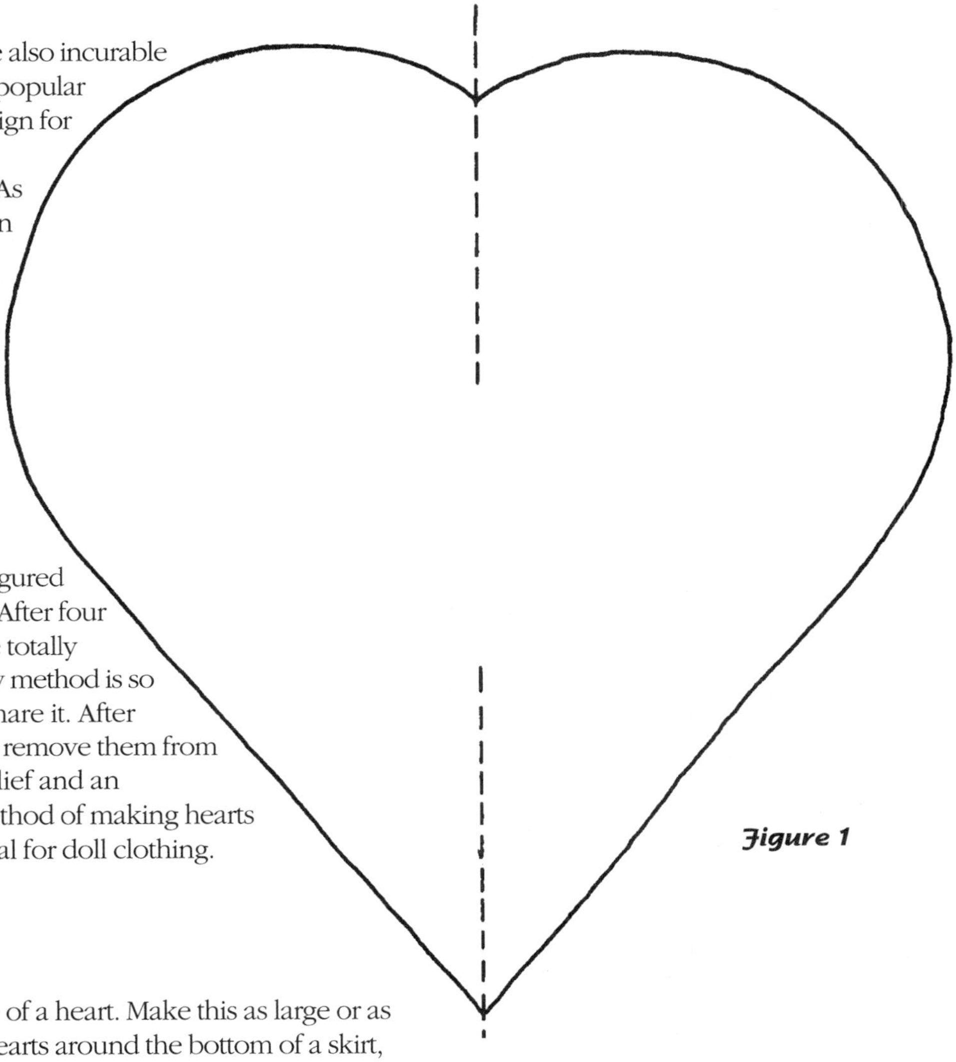

Figure 1

Directions

1. Draw a template in the shape of a heart. Make this as large or as small as desired. For equal hearts around the bottom of a skirt, fold the skirt into equal sections, and design the heart template to fit into one section of the skirt according to the chosen width of lace insertion.

2. Draw hearts all the way around the skirt. As always, when shaping lace, draw the hearts onto the fabric where the laces will be stitched.

3. Draw a 2" bisecting line at the top into the center and at the bottom of the heart into the center **(fig. 1)**.

Note: *I would like to refresh your memory on lace shaping along the bottom of a skirt at this time. Make the hearts (or other shape) above the skirt while the skirt still has a straight bottom. Later after stitching the given motif to the skirt, cut away to make the shaped skirt bottom.*

4. Lay the fabric with the hearts drawn on top, on top of the fabric board. As always, pin the lace shaping through the lace, the fabric and into the fabric board.

5. Cut one piece of lace, which will be large enough to go all the way around one heart with about 4" extra. Before beginning to shape the lace, leave about 2" of lace on the outside of the bottom line.

6. Place a pin at point A. Beginning at the bottom of the heart, pin the lace on the inside of the heart template. The pins will actually be on the outside of the lace insertion; however, all shaping is completed on the inside of the drawn heart template.

7. Work around the heart to point C, placing pins at 1/2" intervals. Notice that the outside will be pinned rather tightly and the inside **will be curvy.**

   > *Note:* *One of my students who is also a math teacher told me years ago, while I was teaching this lace shaping, a very important fact. She said, "Martha, did you know that a curved line is just a bunch of straight lines placed in a funny way?" Since I remembered as little about my math classes as possible, it certainly seemed like news to me. It also makes it a lot easier to explain how to take straight lace and make a curve out of it.*

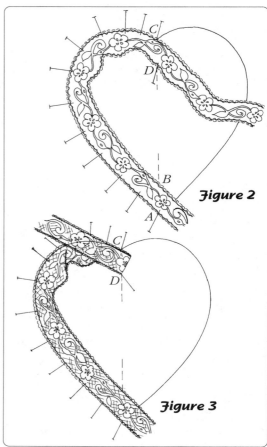

Figure 2

Figure 3

8. After finishing pinning around to the center of the heart, place another pin at point D **(fig. 2)**.

9. Lay the lace back on itself curving it into the curve that was just pinned **(fig. 3)**. Remove the pin from Point C, and re-pin it this time pinning through both layers of lace.

10. Wrap the lace to the other side and begin pinning around the other side of the heart. Where the lace was folded back on itself and re-pinned, there will be a miter which appears just like magic. This is the new fold-back miter which is just as wonderful on hearts as it is on diamonds and scalloped skirts.

11. Pin the second side of the lace just like the first one. At the bottom of the heart lay the laces one over the other and put a pin at point B **(fig. 4)**.

12. It is now time to pull the threads to make the curvy insides of the heart lay flat and become heart shaped. Pull threads either from the bottom of the heart or threads from the center of each side of the heart. Pull the threads and watch the heart lay down flat and pretty **(fig. 5)**.

   > *Note:* *After teaching literally hundreds of students to make hearts, I think it is better to pull the thread from the bottom of the heart. Thread must be pulled from the inside curve when shaping other lace shaped curves such as a scalloped skirt, loops, or ovals.*

13. Spray starch and press the curves into place.

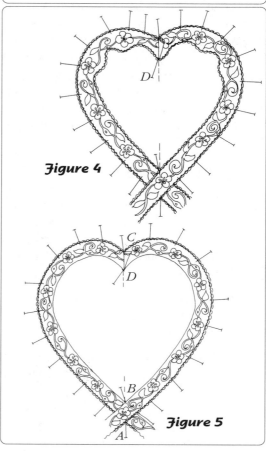

Figure 4

Figure 5

14. To make the magic miter at the bottom of the heart, remove the pin from Point A, fold back the lace so it lays on the other piece of lace, and re-pin Point A. This step completes the easy mitering on the heart **(fig. 6)**. Pin the hearts flat onto the garment and remove the shaping from the fabric board.

15. Trim these bottom "tails" of lace away before attaching the heart to the garment or after attaching the heart to the garment. It probably looks better to trim them before stitching **(fig. 7)**.

16. Attach the hearts just to the fabric or put something else such as pintucks inside the hearts. If hearts touch going all the way around a skirt, follow the directions for zigzagging which can be found in the diamond section

17. To work with a single heart on a collar or bodice of a dress, zigzag the outside first. To put something on the inside of each heart, cut away the fabric from behind the shape after zigzagging it to the garment. Then, insert the embellishment in the heart behind the heart shape and zigzag around the center or inside of the heart. Refer to the directions on inserting pintucks or other decorative work in the center of a lace shape in the flip-flopped bow section.

18. Entredeux/wing needle stitching may be used to attach the hearts. Follow the directions for machine entredeux on the lace shaped skirt found in the diamond section of this lace shaping chapter.

19. After cutting away the fabric from behind the hearts, go back and zigzag over each mitered point **(fig. 8)**. Therein remains the option of either leaving the folded-over section or of cutting it away.

> **Note:** *I usually leave the section because of the strength it adds to the miters.*

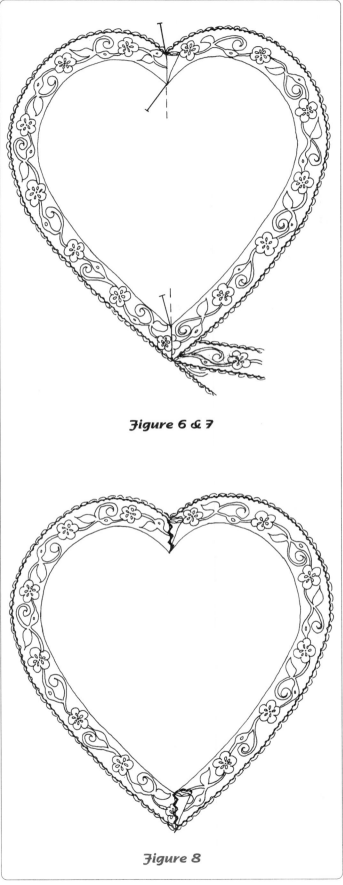

Figure 6 & 7

Figure 8

Round Portrait Collar

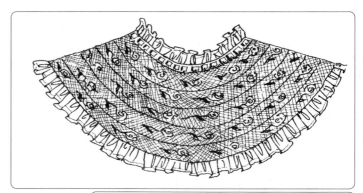

Materials Needed

- Sizes 4 and Under: 4 yards of 1/2" to 3/4" insertion; 2 yards of edging; 1-3/4 yards entredeux

- Sizes 5-12: 5 yards of 1/2" to 3/4" insertion; 2 yards of edging; 2 yards entredeux

- Adult: 6 or 7 yards of 1/2" to 3/4" insertion (This will depend on how wide the resulting collar, will be.); 3 yards of edging; 2-1/2 yards entredeux

    Note: *If you are using wider insertion, you need less yardage. If you are using narrow insertion, you need more yardage. You may want your collar wider than the shoulder/sleeve point. Get more lace. And vice versa. There is really no exact lace amount.*

- Glass head pins or Iris Super Fine Nickel-Plated Steel Pins.

    Note: *Do not use plastic head pins. They will melt when you press your laces into curves!*

- Iron

- Magic Sizing or Spray Starch.

- Make a double-wide fabric board using the directions given earlier in this chapter. You can ask your fabric store to save two for you.

- Threads to match your laces

- A large piece of tissue paper like you use to wrap gifts

- Scissors

Making A Fabric Board

Note: *Consult previous directions if necessary.*

Directions for Preparing The Paper Guide

1. Trace the collar guide onto a piece of tissue paper.

2. If the pattern doesn't have a collar guide, make one.

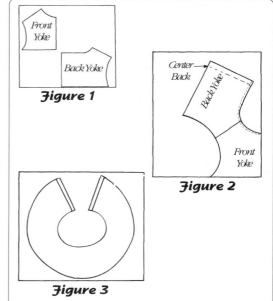

Figure 1

Figure 2

Figure 3

3. Cut out the front yoke and the back yoke of the paper pattern (**fig. 1**). Put the shoulder seams of the paper pattern together to form the neckline. Be sure to overlap the seam allowance to get a true seam line at the shoulder (**fig. 2**). Subtract the seam allowance around the neckline. This is the neck guide to use for the paper pattern. Trace the neckline off. Mark the center-back lines, which will be evident from the pattern pieces (**fig. 3**). Look at **figure 3**. Notice that a large circle is on the outside of this pattern piece. Draw this large circle on if it facilitates things; however, only draw the neckline shape and the center back. Draw the center back the length of the collar.

4. Mark the fold-back line. To get the fold-back line, measure the width of the gathered lace that will be used around the bottom of the collar and up the center back on both sides. Take that measurement off of the center-back point and mark the fold-back line (**fig 3**).

5. Notice that the neckline isn't really round, but oval shaped. That is the true neckline on any pattern, not an exact circle. Use that shaped neckline as the neckline guide.

6. This neckline guide and the center-back line on the pattern are the only lines that needed to shape the circular laces around the collar. Use the fold-back line after the lace shaping is done to finish the back of the collar. Only use the neckline guide for the first piece of lace. After that, use the previously-shaped piece of rounded lace as a guide.

Making The First Two Rows Of Insertion

Directions

1. Shape the neckline row first. Then work from the neckline down to complete the desired collar width.

2. Cut the lace for the neckline or first row of the collar.

   Note: *Cut extra. You will want to cut the laces longer than the center-back line of the marked collar. I suggest at least 3/4" to 1" longer than the exact center back.*

3. Place the tissue paper guide on the fabric board.

4. Using the fabric board as a work base and the tissue paper collar guide, begin shaping the collar.

5. Pin the outside of the lace where the inside will touch the neck guide when it is pressed down. The outside lace will have the pins jabbing through the lace and the tissue paper, right into the fabric board. This outside line is not gathered at all. The inside will be wavy. At this point, the inside has no pins in it (**fig. 4**).

6. After pinning the outside of the lace onto the fabric board, gently pull the gathering string in the heading of the INSIDE of the lace. The lace will pull flat (**fig. 5**). Gently distribute the gathers by holding the lace down. Be certain that it is flat on the fabric board. Pull the gathering rows from both ends. It is now time to put pins on the inside of the first row (**fig. 5**). Jab them into the fabric board. Spray starch lightly and steam.

7. Now that the first row is pretty and flat; begin a second row. Pin the OUTSIDE edge to the board by jabbing the pins, just like on the first row. Be sure the inside of the lace touches the first row when it is finger pressed down (**fig. 6**). After working all the way around with the second row of lace, pull from both ends to gather the inside row, just like on the first row (**fig. 7**).

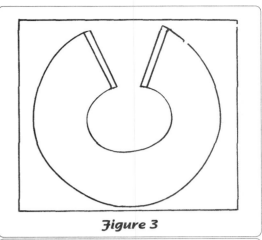

Figure 3

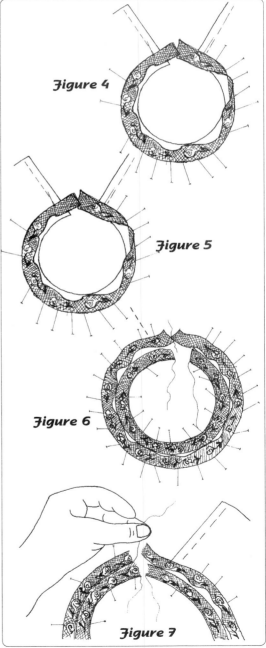

Figure 4

Figure 5

Figure 6

Figure 7

8. Remove the pins where the two rows butt (and where zigzagging will be stitched shortly) and leave pins on the two outside rows; his facilitates pressing.

9. Spray starch the two rows (**fig. 8**). Don't worry if spray starch gets on the tissue paper, this is expected. It may look a little soggy but, it will dry nicely with a hair dryer.

10. Using a hair dryer, dry the starch and the tissue paper where the starch made it wet. If the paper is not dried, it will tear easily. If the tissue paper does tear anytime during the process of making this collar, simply put another piece of tissue paper behind the whole collar and stitch through two pieces.

11. When dry, press and steam the laces right on the paper (**fig. 9**).

12. Remove the jabbed pins, one at a time, and flat pin the lace to the paper on both rows. Pin with the points toward the neck line. This makes it a lot easier when stitching the collar, because when the pins are in this position, they can be pulled during the zigzagging process. If they are pinned the other way, it is difficult to remove the pins during stitching. Never sew over pins, please! It is easier to remove the pin than it is to replace the needle (**fig. 10**).

13. (Stitch right through the tissue paper and the lace. The tissue paper will be torn away later. Move to a sewing machine, and zigzag (Width=1-1/2 to 2; Length=1-1/2 to 2) (**fig. 10**). This width and length are just suggestions. Actually, the width and length will depend on the width of the laces in the heading of the particular lace. The length stitch will depend upon personal preference. To achieve a heavier, closer together look, make the stitch length shorter. To achieve a looser, more delicate look, make the stitch length longer.

14. The first two rows should now be zigzagged together.

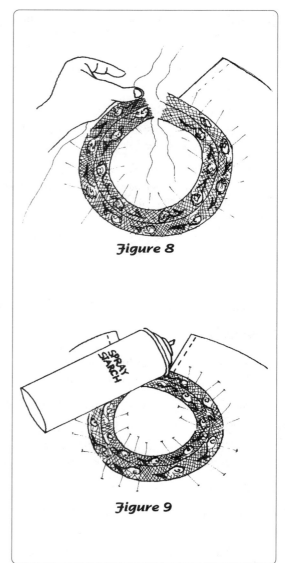

Figure 8

Figure 9

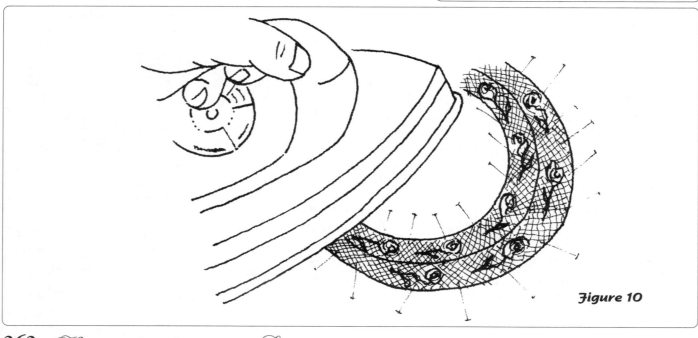

Figure 10

Making The Rest Of The Rows Of Insertion

Directions

1. Following the directions given for applying the second row, pin, and stitch the rest of the rows for the collar **(fig. 11)**.

2. Here is a little trick that I have learned through experience. After pinning, pressing, starching, pressing, and stitching the first two rows together, the remaining rows can be made on the paper pattern at the same time. Don't necessarily stitch each row of insertion right after shaping it **(fig. 11)**. The choice is yours.

3. Shape the laces on the rest of the collar by pinning, pressing, starching, pressing, and letting dry **(fig. 11)**.

4. After all the lace rows are shaped and the tissue paper is completely dry, pin them flat, remembering to place the pins with the points toward the neckline and the heads away from the neckline **(fig. 11)**. Zigzag the laces together.

5. Cut a piece of entredeux with enough length to go completely around the outside row of lace insertion, allowing for plenty of excess.

6. Trim off one side of the entredeux completely and slash the other row so it will curve easily **(fig. 11)**.

7. Pin the entredeux around the outside row of lace, jabbing pins into the holes of the entredeux about every 2" or so. After the entredeux is all the way around the curved lace collar, press, starch, press again, and allow to dry. Dry it with a hair dryer if desired to begin stitching immediately **(fig. 11)**.

8. Pin the entredeux to the tissue paper at several places. Begin stitching the first row of lace insertion that is not already stitched.

   Note: *Remember, if you have chosen to stitch each row of insertion after it was shaped, you might have already stitched all of your laces at this time.*

9. Stitch each row, starting with the unstitched one closest to the neckline. Move outward with each row of stitching. Remove the pins, one at a time, throughout the stitching process.

10. With each successive row, carefully remove the pins, and be sure to butt the lace edges exactly while stitching around the collar.

11. The entredeux to the last row of insertion may or may not be the last row that stitched, while the tissue paper is still on the collar. Choose whether to use Method I or Method II a little later on in the instructions.

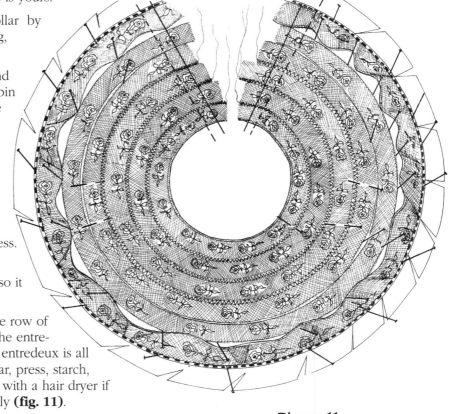

Figure 11

Using The Center Back Of The Collar

Check The Fold Back Line

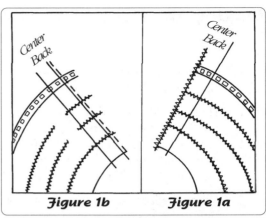

Figure 1b   **Figure 1a**

Directions

1. The center back of a garment is just that - where the backs meet. This collar will not end at the center back point unless the laces are positioned up the center back of the collar.

2. If choosing to put no laces and no entredeux up the center back, work on the center back line. The best way to finish the back of the collar, in this case, is to serge or overlock the collar just outside of the center-back line **(fig. 1a)**. Fold the serged seam to the back, and straight stitch it to the collar **(fig. 1b)**. That leaves just a finished lace edge as the center back.

3. If opting to add lace edging and entredeux up the back of the collar, use the fold-back line made in the beginning on the pattern. Laces don't need to overlap at the center back, but meet instead. Check to be sure that the fold-back line is as wide as the lace edging is from the center-back line on the pattern.

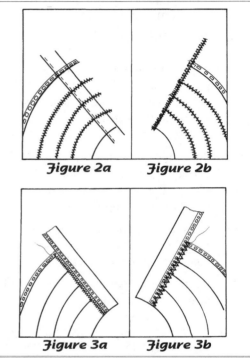

Figure 2a   **Figure 2b**

Figure 3a   **Figure 3b**

Adding Entredeux Method 1

Directions

1. Make a straight row of stitching on the fold-back line, still stitching through the tissue paper.

2. Trim away the laces, leaving about 1/8" of raw lace edge **(fig. 2a)**.

3. Zigzag very tightly (*Width*=1-1/2; *Length*=1/2) to finish the lace edge **(fig. 2b)**. Serge the back of the collar to finish it.

4. Butt the entredeux to the finished edge **(fig. 3a)** and zigzag, going into the holes of the entredeux and off **(fig. 3b)**.

Adding Entredeux Method 2

Directions

1. Using the technique "Entredeux To Flat Fabric," attach the entredeux to the back of the collar. Stitch in the ditch **(fig. 1)**, trim **(fig. 2)**, and zigzag **(fig. 3)**.

2. Consider either of two options when finishing this straight line of stitching. One, serge. Two, zigzag along this line. This decision applies to the next section. For right now, don't trim away any laces along the fold-back line; just leave the collar like it is.

3. Trim away the other side of the entredeux. It is now ready to trim with gathered lace.

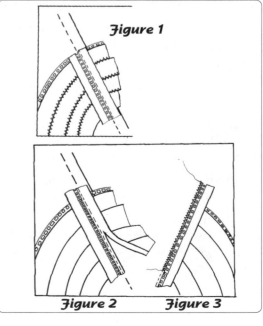

Figure 1

Figure 2   **Figure 3**

Round Lace Portrait Collar

Finishing The Collar Method 1

Attaching Gathered Lace To Entredeux On The Outside Edge of the Collar With Tissue Paper

Question: When would you use Method 1?

For some, this method is the easiest for distributing lace evenly because quarter points can be placed exactly where desired to control the fullness. If your machine isn't quite up to par, stitching laces on tissue paper is easier than working without it. So, for some people the method of stitching the gathered lace on while tissue paper is still attached is the easiest.

Directions

1. Cut lace edging to be gathered around the bottom and up the back of the collar. Use a 1-1/2-to-1 fullness or a 2-to-1 fullness, depending on the amount of lace desired.

2. After cutting the lace, (allow about 2" to turn each back corner and about 10" to gather and go up each back of the collar) fold the rest of the lace in half, and mark the center of the lace. Fold once again, and mark the quarter points. This will allow accurate distribution of the fullness.

3. Pull the gathering thread in the top of the edging. Pin the center of the lace to the center of the entredeux edge of the collar. Pin the quarter points of the lace to the approximate quarter points of the collar.

    Note: *You should have about 12" of lace on each end to go around the corner of the collar and to gather it up the back of the collar.*

4. After figuring out these measurements, begin to distribute and pin the gathered lace to the bottom of the collar entredeux. Distribute the gathers carefully. Pin all the way around.

5. Stitch the gathered lace (Width=1-1/2 to 2; Length=1/2) to the entredeux, still stitching through the tissue paper. Only stitch around the bottom of the collar. Leave the laces unattached at this point, coming up the center back.

6. Carefully tear away the tissue paper from the collar.

7. To use a serger, trim away the lace ends 1/4" from the fold-back line of the collar where it was stay stitched. This 1/4" provides a

seam allowance to zigzag to finish. To serge the outside of this line, do not trim away the lace since the serger does this while stitching.

8. Zigzag tightly over this stay-stitched line (*Width*=1 to 2; *Length*=1/2).

9. Serge this seam, if possible, rather than zigzagging over it.

10. If the seam has been serged, fold back the serged edge, and straight stitch it down.

11. To zigzag over this seam, use this rolled and whipped edge as the finished edge of this seam.

Finishing The Application Of Entredeux And Gathered Lace Edging

Directions

1. With the fold-back line complete, finish gathering the lace edging and zigzag it to the back of the collar.

2. Trim the other side of the entredeux up the back of the collar.

3. Put extra gathers in the lace edging when going around the corner. This will keep it from folding under.

4. After gathering the lace edging, butt the gathered laces to the trimmed entredeux and zigzag to the collar.

5. Fold down the top of the lace edging before completely zigzagging to the top of the collar. That way the finished lace edge is on the top of the collar.

Finishing the Collar Method 2

Attaching Gathered Lace To The Entredeux of the Collar Without Tissue Paper

Question: When would you use Method 2?

If the tension is good on your sewing machine, use Method II. If you don't mind the laces not being exactly the same gathering all the way around, use Method II. Frankly, the laces are never distributed perfectly, even when using Method I. I have yet to find a way to perfectly distribute and gather laces, including hand sewing! I will say, Method II is the easiest, however.

Directions

1. Tear away the tissue paper from the collar.

2. Cut the lace edging, which will be gathered around the bottom of the collar and up the back of the collar. Use a 1-1/2-to-1 fullness or a 2-to-1 fullness.

3. Now that the fold-back line is finished, gather the lace edging and zigzag it to the back of the collar.

4. Trim the other side of the entredeux.

5. Using the techniques found in "Gathering French Lace By Machine, While Applying It To Trimmed Entredeux Edge," attach the lace to the bottom of the collar and up the back edges.

Round Portrait Collar Variations

Adding A Fabric Neckline Piece

Portrait collars are lovely when they start with a fabric circular piece finished with entredeux at the bottom. After attaching entredeux, simply complete the portrait collar exactly as you would if the fabric weren't there. To add a fabric neckline piece, you must use the actual dress or blouse pattern to make a round portrait collar guide. To make a lace only portrait collar, use any general neckline guide since lace can be shaped to go into many shapes. For the fabric neckline, you must make an exact pattern to fit the neckline of the garment.

Materials Needed

- Laces and entredeux for portrait collar given in the portrait collar section

- 1/3 yard batiste for adult collar

- 1/4 yard for infant or small child's collar

- 1 extra yard of entredeux for use at the bottom of the fabric portion of the collar (Optional if you have a machine which makes machine entredeux with a wing needle.)

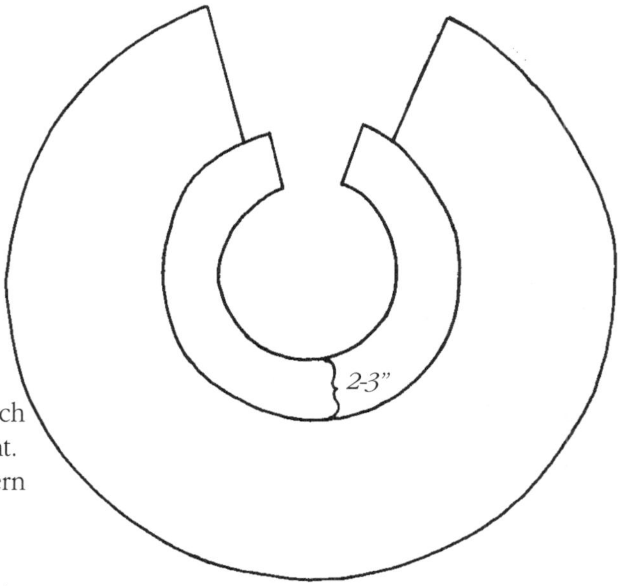

Directions

1. Refer to the directions for "Preparing The Paper Guide," which instructs how to get the neckline curve for an actual garment. To put in this fabric around the neckline, cut an actual pattern by the neckline of the garment to which it will be attached.

2. Be certain when cutting the collar fabric piece to mark in a seam allowance exactly like the one on the garment neck edge.

3. Cut out a circular neckline piece extending beyond the center back neck edge.

   Note: *You're not going to use this excess, it is only for security in case you want to make the center backs a little wider after trying on the collar! Also, after zigzagging entredeux and laces together, sometimes the fabric shrinks up just a little because of all of the heavy stitching (**fig. 1**).*

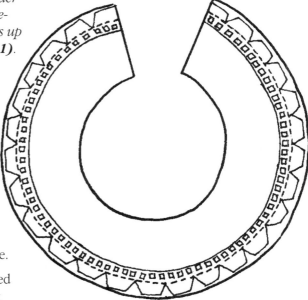

Figure 1

Method 1

Purchased Entredeux Added To Bottom Of Fabric Collar

Directions

1. Cut enough entredeux to go around this curve with a little excess on either side. Trim one side only of the entredeux. Slash the other side so it will curve around the neckline edge.

2. With the slashed side of the entredeux meeting the cut curved edge of the collar, pin, using the fabric board, the entredeux around the outside edge of this fabric neckline piece **(fig. 2)**.

3. Spray starch and press.

4. Using the method, entredeux to flat fabric (stitch in the ditch, trim and zigzag or serge the whole thing with a rolled hem), stitch the entredeux to the outside edge of the curve. The entredeux can also be serged to the collar. Before serging, however straight stitch in the ditch to be sure that it is perfectly placed. Then, using a rolled hem, serge it to the collar.

Figure 2

5. Press the entredeux down. The fabric circle with the trimmed entredeux already attached is complete. Attaching the first row of shaped laces comes next **(fig. 3)**.

6. Place this fabric/entredeux piece on the tissue paper, which should have been drawn to match this neckline edge. Shape the laces and finish the collar following all directions in the "Making A Round Lace Portrait Collar" section.

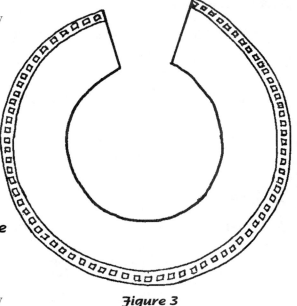

Figure 3

Method 2

Stitching The First Row of Laces To The Collar Using Machine Entredeux Stitch And Wing Needle

Directions

1. Skip the entredeux altogether. Shape the first row of laces overlapping the raw edge of the fabric portion of the collar by about 1/4"; opt to overlap more if desired **(fig. 4)**.

2. After pinning and shaping the first row of rounded laces to overlap this fabric collar, stitch a row of machine entredeux stitching at the seam line. It now appears as if the entredeux trims the collar and it was so much easier than actually applying entredeux. To remove excess fabric underneath the stitching, simply trim it away from the collar after the whole collar is finished **(fig. 5)**.

3. To finish the collar, simply follow all directions in the "Making A Round Lace Portrait Collar" section.

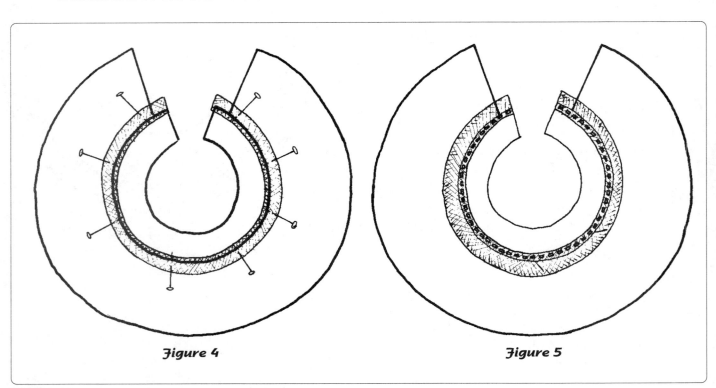

Figure 4 **Figure 5**

Puffing Techniques

Puffing Method 1

Gathering The Puffing Over A Quilting Thread Or Dental Floss

This method for making puffing simply rolls and whips the edges of the puffing strip by zigzagging over a quilting thread or dental floss. It has a finished edge, which can be butted up to lace and zigzagged together. Although this is a good method for making puffing to curve around in a round portrait collar, I really do not believe that it is the easiest. Read the following method which is Puffing Method I. Then, if your machine has a gathering foot, read Puffing Method II. Honestly, the latter is the easiest method. The choice is yours, of course.

Directions

1. Cut a puffing strip at least two times the length of the finished round portion of the collar to which it is to be attached.

2. A suggested puffing length is to cut two strips of 45" fabric about 2" wide.

3. Cut one of them in two pieces. Stitch these pieces to either end of the long strip. Consider a French seam or serge these seams together (**fig. 1**). Press the puffing strip if desired, but do not starch. Starching will affect the gathers of the puffing.

4. This puffing strip will probably be a little long for the collar.

    Note: *I like to have too much puffing and lace when I am working on portrait collars rather than too little. Since I like full puffing, I usually use the whole fullness. If it seems too full, then simply arrange the fullness as desired and cut off the back at both sides after having shaped the puffing.*

5. Mark the center of this puffing strip before rolling and whipping the edge. The two quarter points are already marked with the two side strips (**fig. 2**).

6. Roll and whip the edges using quilting thread or dental floss. To do this, simply place the quilting thread or the dental floss on the very edge of both sides and zigzag it into place. Be careful not to catch the quilting thread or dental floss in the stitching (**fig. 3**). Zigzag the edge of the fabric using approximately a 2-1/2 to 3-1/2 width and a 1 to 1-1/2 length. Zig going into the fabric and zag going all the way off of the fabric. The fabric will roll into a seam during stitching. The quilting thread will be rolled into that seam. Later use the very strong quilting thread to pull the gathers in the puffing (**fig. 4**).

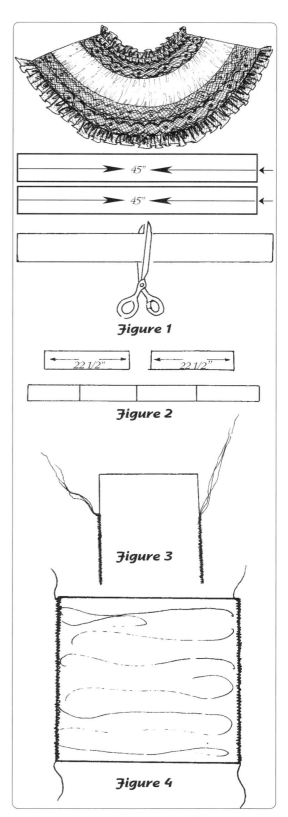

Figure 1

Figure 2

Figure 3

Figure 4

Note: *After zigzagging the quilting thread or dental floss into both sides of this puffing strip, notice a few fuzzies which may cause the work to look imperfect. This is normal because of the relatively loose stitch length (1 to 1-1/2) being used. Anything tighter tends to make the rolling and whipping too tight and makes the gathering of the puffing very difficult. Don't worry, the fuzzies disappear when the puffing is zigzagged to the lace.*

7. Some sewing machines have a foot with a little hole in the center of the foot. If the machine being used has this feature, put the quilting thread or dental floss in that little hole and the zigzagging will be perfectly in place. There will be no chance of zigzagging through the quilting thread in the process of stitching.

8. After finishing the rolling and whipping on both sides, pull the gathering threads on both sides from both ends until the fabric is gathered up to look like puffing **(fig. 4)**.

9. Pin the puffing to the fabric board right through the tissue paper to which the lace strips have been pinned. Match the center front of the collar with the center front of the puffing. Pin by "poking" the pins into the fabric board, on the bottom side of the puffing **(fig. 5)**.

10. Keep on playing with the gathers until they're evenly distributed. Then, pin the top side (the smaller side) of the puffing. Puffing should be treated just like laces. Pin the larger side first and then pin the smaller side **(fig. 6)**.

11. Press the puffing flat after spray starching it.

    Note: *On any garment which will be washed, it is necessary to press the puffing flat because you will have to do this after it is washed anyway. A puffing iron is perfect for this job, depending on how wide the puffing is. I love flat pressed puffing and there really isn't much choice in leaving it unpressed unless it will go into a pillow to put on the bed and not washed for a very long time.*

12. Playing with and distributing gathers carefully usually takes a long time. Don't become impatient. Just keep fiddling with the puffing to be sure they are distributed evenly. This is a good project to save for evening TV. After pinning the puffing where it looks beautiful, carefully remove the "poked" pins and pin it flat to the tissue paper where the edge of the puffing on the top exactly meets the bottom edge of the lace row above it **(fig. 7)**.

13. Now take the tissue paper with its rows of lace insertion and rows of puffing over to the sewing machine to zigzag the row of puffing to the top row of lace (*Width*=1-1/2 to 2-1/2: *Length*=1 to 2). Stitch right through the tissue paper. Leave the pins in the puffing after stitching around the top row because the next step is to shape the next piece of lace to the collar.

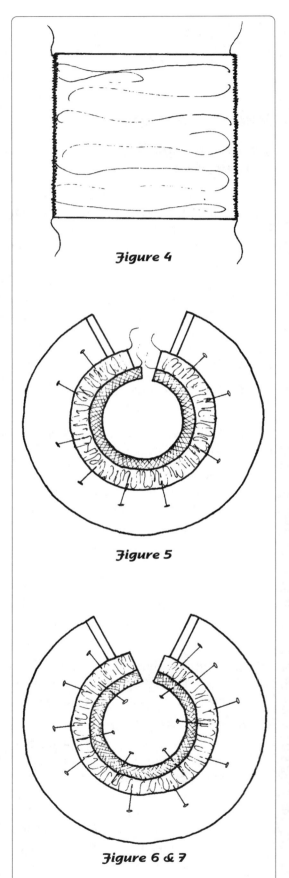

Figure 4

Figure 5

Figure 6 & 7

14. Continue adding lace rows to the portrait collar to make it as wide as desired.

15. Consider adding more puffing rows in-between the lace rows to put several puffing rows onto the collar.

Puffing Method 2

Gathering The Puffing Using The Gathering Foot On Your Machine

Two years ago, I wouldn't have told you that this was the easiest method of applying puffing into a round portrait collar. The reason being I didn't know how to make perfect puffing using the gathering foot on a sewing machine. I thought you used the edge of the gathering foot to guide the fabric underneath the gathering foot. This left about a 1/4" seam allowance. It also made the gathers imperfect in some places with little "humps" and unevenness on some portions. As a result, I wasn't happy with puffing made on the gathering foot. When I asked my friend, Sue Hausmann, what might be wrong, she explained to me that to make perfect gathering, I needed to move the fabric over so that I would have at least a 1/2" seam allowance. She further explained that there are two sides to the feed dogs; when using the side of the gathering foot, then the fabric only catches on one side of the feed dogs. It works like magic to move fabric over and guide it along one of the guide lines on the sewing machine. If the machine being used doesn't have these lines, simply put a piece of tape down to make a proper guideline.

Directions for Making Gathering Foot Puffing

1. The speed of the sewing needs to be consistent. Sew either fast or slow but do not sew fast then slow then fast again. Beginners should touch the "sew slow" button (if available). This will help to keep a constant speed.

2. The puffing strip should be gathered with a 1/2" seam allowance, with an approximate straight stitch length of 4, right side up **(fig. 1)**. Remember that to adjust the stitch length to make the puffing looser or fuller. Do not let the strings of the fabric wrap around the foot of the machine. This will cause the fabric to back up behind the foot causing an uneven seam allowance, as well as, uneven gathers. Leave the thread tails long in case adjustments are needed. One side of the gathering is now complete **(fig. 2)**.

3. Begin gathering the second side of the strip, right side up. This row of gathering will be made from the bottom of the strip to the top of the strip. In other words, bi-directional sewing (first side sewn from the top to the bottom, second side sewn from the bottom to the top) is allowed. Gently unfold the ruffle with the left hand allowing flat fabric to feed under the foot. Do not apply any pressure to the fabric **(fig. 3)**. The feeding must remain constant. Leave the thread tails long in case adjustments are needed. The puffing strip in now complete.

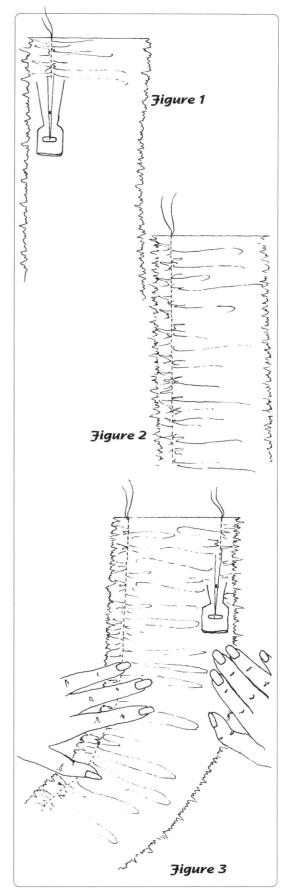

Figure 1

Figure 2

Figure 3

Placing Machine Gathered Puffing Into A Collar

Directions

1. Cut strips of fabric.

2. Gather both sides of the puffing running the fabric under the gathering foot. Be sure to leave at least a 1/2" seam allowance. When using a gathering foot, the give of the puffing isn't as great as when gathering it the other way.

3. Make note of the two raw edges on puffing which has been gathered with a gathering foot **(fig. 1)**.

4. Shape the puffing around the fabric board below the row of lace (or rows of lace) that have already been arranged into the rounded shape. Place the pins into the board through the outside edge of the puffing. Place the pins right into the place where the gathering row runs in the fabric **(fig. 2)**.

5. Pull the raw edge of the machine puffed strip up underneath the finished edge of the curved lace, so that zigzagging attaching the puffing will be on the machine gathering line. Put the rounded lace edge on top of the puffing. Pin the bottom edge of the puffing first so gathers can be "arranged" underneath the curved lace edge which is already in place (the top piece of lace) **(fig. 2)**.

6. It will be necessary to "sort of" arrange the machine gathered puffing, especially on the top edge which will be gathered the fullest on the collar, and pin it in place since the machine gathering thread doesn't give too much. After pinning and poking the gathering into place where it looks pretty on the top and the bottom, flat pin it to the tissue paper and zigzag the puffing strip to the lace stitching right on top of the lace.

   Note: *You will have an unfinished fabric edge underneath the place where you stitched the lace to the puffing. That is o.k. After zigzagging the puffing to the lace, trim away the excess fabric underneath the lace edge. Be careful, of course, when trimming this excess fabric, not to accidentally cut the lace.*

7. When using a machine with a machine entredeux/wing needle option consider using this stitch in place of the zigzagging. Since the fabric is gathered underneath the lace, be very careful stitching to get a pretty stitch.

8. Shape another piece of lace around the bottom of this puffing bringing the inside piece of curved lace exactly to fit on top of the gathering line in the puffing. Once again, there will be unfinished fabric underneath the place where the lace is being zigzagged to the puffing collar. After zigzagging the lace to the puffing collar, trim the excess fabric away.

9. Continue curving the rest of the laces to make the collar as wide as desired.

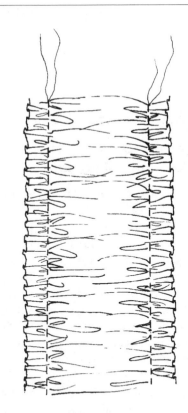

Figure 1

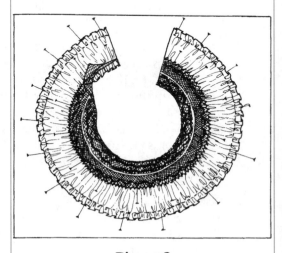

Figure 2

Hemstitching By Machine

Making Entredeux (Or Hemstitching) On Today's Computer Sewing Machines

About eight years ago, I was conned into purchasing a 1905 hemstitching machine for $1500. I was told that it had a perfect stitch and that stitch (about 2 inches) was demonstrated to me by the traveling salesman. I was very happy to finally have one of those wonderful machines. Guess how long that wonderful machine lasted before it broke down? I stitched about 10 inches more which looked great; at that point, the stitching was awful. I called several repairmen. It never made a decent hemstitch again.

The good news to follow this sad story is that today's new computer machines do an excellent job of making hemstitching and they work! I am going to give my favorite settings for my favorite sewing machines. Before buying a new sewing machine consider testing each of these machines at various dealerships to see if you love these stitches as much as we do.

Using A Stabilizer With Wing Needle Hemstitching Or Pin Stitching

Before hemstitching or doing any decorative work with a wing needle, which involves lots of stitching on these wonderful machines, first let me stress how important it is to use a stabilizer! Stitch-n-Tear™, computer paper, tissue paper (not quite strong enough but o.k. in certain situations), wax paper, physician's examining table paper, typing paper, adding machine paper or almost any other type of paper can be used, but use something. When doing heavy stitching such as a featherstitch, I recommend that type of paper which physicians spread out over their examining tables. It's available on a roll at any medical supply store. If using Stitch-n-Tear™ or adding machine paper in featherstitch type stitches, it is difficult to pull away all of the little pieces that remain when the paper is removed from the back of the garment. This physician's paper seems to tear away pretty easily.

I do not like the thin, plastic looking, wash-away stabilizers for heavy stitching with a wing needle because it doesn't have enough body. There is another type of wash-away stabilizer which is absolutely wonderful. It is the paint on, liquid kind. In this country it is called Perfect Sew™. Paint it on with a paint brush; let it dry, and stitch. There is no need to use and additional stabilizer underneath it. It washes out after stitching is complete It is available in this country from Pati Palmer, Palmer/Pletsch Publishing, Perfect Sew™, P.O. Box 12046, Portland, OR 97212, 1-800-728-3784.

Wash-away stabilizer can be made at home by using some water in a container and by dropping wash away plastic-looking sheet of stabilizer into the container. Some of the brand names are Solvy™ and Aqua Solve™. Stir with a wooden spoon; keep adding the plastic looking wash-away stabilizer sheets until it becomes the consistency of egg whites. Then, paint it on or brush it on with a sponge. Let it dry and then stitch. Both of the liquid, wash-out stabilizers make batiste-type fabrics about as stiff as organdy, which is wonderful for stitching. After stitching, simply wash the stabilizer away.

Preparing Fabric Before Beginning Hemstitching or Pin Stitching

Stiffen fabric with spray starch before lace shaping or decorative stitching with the hemstitches and wing needles. Use a hair dryer to dry the lace before ironing it if it has been spray starched too much. Also, if fabrics and laces have been excessively dampened too much with spray starch, place a piece of tissue paper on top of the work, and dry iron it dry. Hemstitching works best on natural fibers such as linen, cotton, cotton batiste, silk or cotton organdy. Avoid fabrics with a high polyester content. Polyester has a memory. When a hole is punched in polyester, it remembers the original positioning of the fibers, and wants to close up.

Threads To Use For Pin Stitching Or Hemstitching

Use all cotton thread, 50, 60, 70, 80 weight. If breaking thread is a problem, use a high-quality polyester thread or a cotton covered polyester thread, like the Coats and Clark for machine lingerie and embroidery. Personally, I like to press Needle Down on all of the entredeux and pin stitch settings.

Pin Stitching Or Point de Paris Stitch With A Sewing Machine

The pin stitch is another lovely "entredeux look" on my favorite machines. It is a little more delicate. Pin stitch looks similar to a ladder with one of the long sides of the ladder missing. Imagine the steps being fingers which reach over into the actual lace piece to grab the lace. The side of the ladder, the long side, will be stitched on the fabric right along side of the outside of the heading of the lace. The fingers reach into the lace to grab it. All of the settings given below require the use of a reverse image on one of the sides of lace so that the fingers will grab into the lace while the straight side goes on the outside of the lace heading.

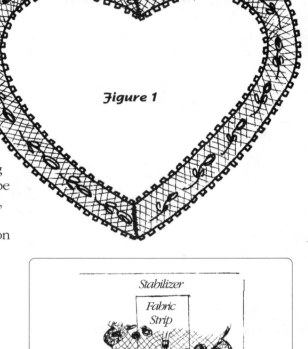

Figure 1

Attaching Shaped Lace To The Garment With Machine Entredeux Or Pin Stitching And A Wing Needle

Probably my favorite place to use the machine entredeux/wing needle hemstitching is to attach shaped laces to a garment. Simply shape the laces as desired into hearts, diamonds, ovals, loops, circles, or bows, and stitch. While forming the entredeux, this stitch also secures the shaped lace to the garment **(fig. 1)**. Always use stabilizer in conjunction with this type of heavy hemstitching.

Attaching Two Pieces Of Lace With Machine Entredeux

There is nothing prettier than a garment which has entredeux between each layer of fabric and lace. Unfortuately, it would to take forever to stitch with purchased entredeux, not to mention the cost. Here is how to use a hemstitch/machine entredeux stitch and wing needle to make laces look as if they had been joined with entredeux.

Directions

1. Butt two pieces of lace insertion together. Since entredeux/ hemstitching with a wing needle on a machine needs fabric underneath the stitching to hold the stitches perfectly, put a narrow strip of batiste or other fabric underneath the place where these two laces will be joined.

2. Put a strip of stabilizer underneath the butted laces and the fabric strip.

3. Stitch using a wing needle and a hemstitching stitch. If the machine has an edge joining or edge stitching foot this is a great time to use it. It's little blade guides in-between the two pieces of butted lace and makes it easy to stitch straight **(fig. 2)**. Note that the entredeux stitching not only stitches in one of the most beautiful stitches, it also attaches the laces.

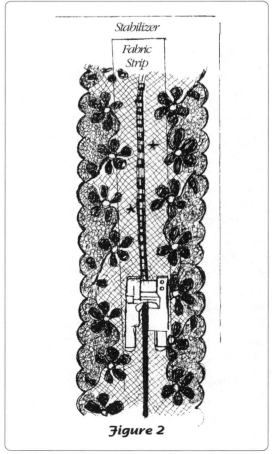

Figure 2

4. When stitching is finished, tear away the stabilizer and turn each side of the lace back to carefully trim away the excess fabric **(fig. 3)**.

5. Now it looks as if there are two pieces of lace with purchased entredeux stitched in between them **(fig. 4)**.

Making Machine Entredeux, Embroidery Designs Or Initials

Entredeux stitch can frame any larger, plain embroidery design. Often the design must be put into an embroidery hoop for maximum effectiveness. I have some old handkerchiefs and some old tablecloths which actually look as if hemstitching made the design. Place several rows of entredeux stitching together to form a honeycomb effect which might be used to fill in embroidery designs.

Some of the prettiest monograms are those with hemstitching around the letter. Once again, I think the liquid stabilizer and the embroidery hoop are wonderful assets in doing this kind of wing needle work. Let your imagination be your guide when thinking of new and elegant things to do with these wing needle/entredeux stitches **(fig. 5)**.

One of my favorite things to do with this entredeux stitch or pin stitch is simply to stitch it around cuffs, across yokes, around collars, down the center back or center front of a blouse. Stitched down both sides of the front placket of a very tailored woman's blouse turns an ordinary garment into a treasured heirloom. Decorative machine entredeux takes on a sudden sophistication when applied in black thread on black fabric. Machine entredeux is as effective standing alone as it is attaching laces.

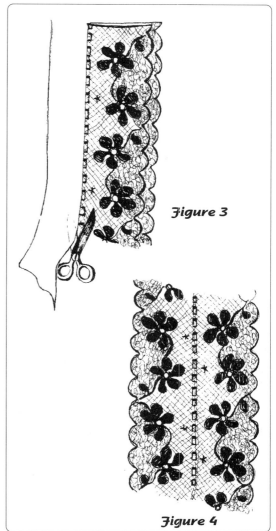

Figure 3

Figure 4

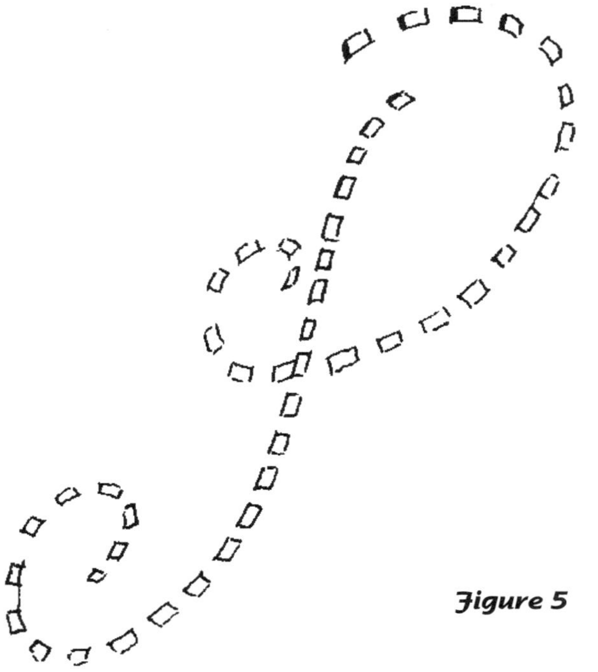

Figure 5

Basic Pintucking

Double Needles

Double needles come in different sizes. The first number on the double needle is the distance between the needles. The second number on the needle is the actual size of the needle. The chart below shows some of the double needle sizes. The size needle used will depend on the weight of the fabric that is being pintucked **(fig. 1)**.

Let me relate a little more information for any of you who haven't worked with a double needle before. The most common concern I hear when beginning a class on pintucking is that certain sewing machines only have an opening for one needle. Confusion about the term double needle is certainly understandable; many beginners assume that two separate needles are involved. And, indeed, they are; however, these two needles are attached to a single shaft or stem, which is inserted into a single needle slot on just about any model machine. When using a double needle, two spools of thread are required. If you don't have two spools of the fine thread, which I recommend for pintucking, run an extra bobbin and use it as a second spool. For most shaped pintucking on heirloom garments, I prefer either the 1.6/70, the 1.6/80 or the 2.0/80 size needle.

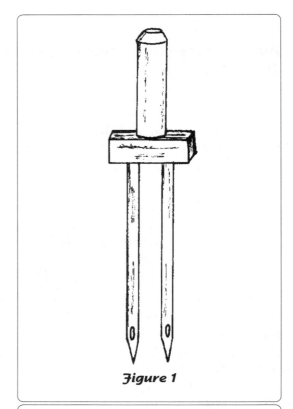

Figure 1

Needle Size	Fabric	Foot
a. 1.6/70 -	*Lightweight*	*9 Groove*
b. 1.6/80 -	*Lightweight*	*9 Groove*
c. 2.0/80 -	*Lightweight*	*7 Groove*
d. 2.5/80 -	*Lightweight*	*7 Groove*
e. 3.0/90 -	*Medium Weight*	3-5 Groove
f. 4.0/100 -	*Heavy Weight*	3-5 Groove

Note: *Needle size and foot may vary according to specific machines.*

Pintuck Feet

Pintuck feet are easy to use and because they serve to space straight pintucks perfectly, they shave hours off pintucking time . Some stitchers also prefer a pintuck foot when making curved and angled pintucks. Others like to use a regular zigzag sewing foot for curved pintucks. Pintuck feet correspond to the needle used with that pintuck foot; the needle used corresponds to the weight of fabric. The bottom of these feet have a certain number of grooves 3, 5, 7, or 9. The width of the groove matches the width between the two needles. The grooves position pintucks as close or as far away as the distance on the foot allows **(fig. 2)**.

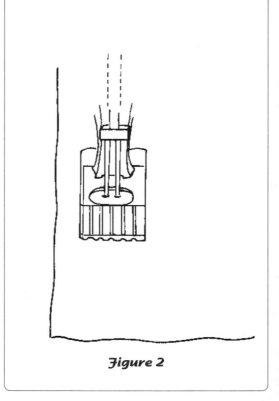

Figure 2

Preparing Fabric For Pintucking

Pintuck a small piece of chosen fabric that has been spray starched and one without starch, to decide, which gives the best results. In most cases, spray starched fabric results in flatter pintucks, which is not the desired effect. Always press all-cotton fabric. A polyester/cotton blend won't need to be pressed unless it is very wrinkled.

Straight Pintucking With A Pintuck Foot

Two of the most common places pintucks are used is on a high yoke dress bodice and down sleeves. Straight pintucks applied vertically also offers a less frilly embellishment for a woman's blouse. Another tailored option is to place straight pintucks horizontally across the back yoke of a blouse and carry the look through by pintucking around the cuffs.

Directions

1. Insert a double needle. Thread machine with two spools of thread. Thread one spool at a time (including the needle). This will help keep the threads from becoming twisted while stitching the tucks. This would be a good time to look in the guide book, which came with the sewing machine, for directions on using pintuck feet and double needles. Some sewing machines have a special way of threading for use with double needles.

2. The first tuck must be straight. To make this first tuck straight, do one of three things:

    a. Pull a thread all the way across the fabric and follow along that pulled line.

    b. Using a measuring stick, mark a straight line along the fabric. Stitch on that line.

    c. Fold the fabric in half and press that fold. Stitch along that folded line.

3. Place the fabric under the foot for the first tuck and straight stitch the desired length of pintuck. (Length=1 to 2-1/2; Needle position is center) **(fig. 1)**.

4. Place the first completed tuck into one of the grooves in the pintuck foot. The space between each successive pintuck depends on which groove this first pintuck is placed into **(fig. 2)**.

5. Continue pintucking by placing the last pintuck made into the chosen groove in the foot.

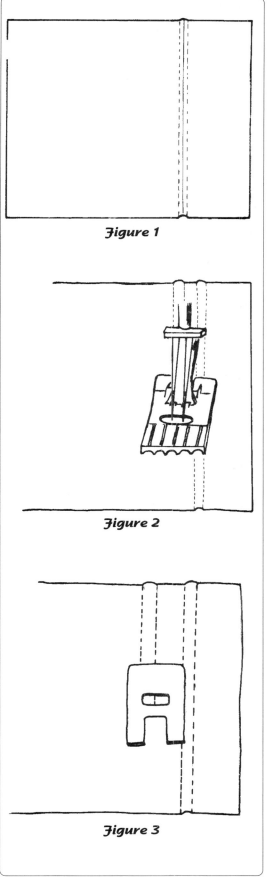

Figure 1

Figure 2

Figure 3

Straight Pintucking Without A Pintuck Foot

1. Use a double needle. Use a regular zigzag foot.

2. Thread the double needles.

3. Draw the first line of pintucking. Pintuck along that line. At this point use the edge of the presser foot as a guide **(fig. 3)**.

   Note: *A "generic" pintuck foot for your particular brand of machine may be available. Consult your instruction book or dealer.*

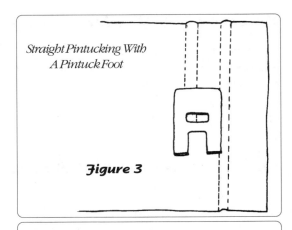

Straight Pintucking With A Pintuck Foot

Figure 3

Properly Tying Off Released Pintucks

A released pintuck is usually used to give fullness to a skirt. It is a perfectly elegant way to add detail to a garment. Again, a pintuck foot can facilitate the pintucking process, A double needle is essential.

Straight pintucks that are made on a piece of fabric, cut out, and stitched into the seams of a garment, do not have to be tied off. Why? When sewing the seam of the garment, the pintucks will be secured within that seam. Released pintucks stop at a designated point in the fabric. They are not caught in a seam and, therefore, have to be tied off. Effective released pintucks must be tied off properly.

For a short cut, either backstitch by machine or use the tie off feature that some of the modern machines offer. Please do not use a clear glue sold for tying off seams in sewing. One of my friends had a disastrous experience when making a Susan York pattern featured in *Sew Beautiful* several years ago, which required over a hundred gorgeous released pintucks. She dabbed a little of this glue product at the end of each pintuck; when she washed and pressed the dress, each place on the Swiss batiste garment where that product had touched, turned brown. The dress with all of the money in Swiss batiste and French laces, had to be thrown away.

Properly tying off released pintucks is a lot of trouble. Remember, you can backstitch and cut the threads close to the fabric. The result isn't as pretty but it does save time.

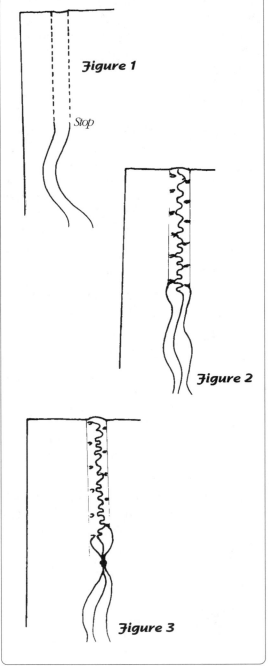

Figure 1

Stop

Figure 2

Figure 3

Directions.

1. End stitching at the designated stopping point **(fig. 1)**.

2. Pull out a reasonable length of thread before cutting the threads for this pintuck to go to the next pintuck. Five inches should be ample.

3. Pull the threads to the back of the fabric **(fig. 2)**. Tie off each individual pintuck **(fig. 3)**.

Bi-Directional Stitching Of Pintucks

The general consensus, when stitching pintucks, is to stitch down one side and back up the other side instead of stitching pintucks all in the same direction.

To prevent pintucks from being lopsided, stitch down the length of one pintuck, pull the sewing machine threads several inches, and stitch back up in the opposite direction **(fig. 4)**.

Making Waffle Pintucks

1. Stitch pintucks all in the same direction to the desired width.

2. Stitch pintucks in the opposite direction **(fig. 1)**.

Cording Pintucks And Raised Pintucks

Cords make pintucks more prominent. Use Mettler gimp or #8 pearl cotton. Cording comes in handy when pintucks are being shaped. When pintucking across a bias with a double needle, distortion may result. The cord acts as a filler and will keep the fabric from distorting. Consider cording in order to add color to your pintucks. If I were asked, "Martha, do you usually cord pintucks?" My answer would be, "No." However, just because I don't usually cord pintucks, doesn't mean that you won't prefer to cord them.

Some machines have a small device which sits in the base of the machine and sticks up just a little bit. That device tends to make the pintucks stand up a little more for a raised effect. Some people wouldn't pintuck without this feature.

Directions

1. If the machine being used has a hole in the throat plate, run the cord up through that hole and it will be properly placed without another thought **(fig. 2)**.

2. If the machine being used does not have a hole in the throat plate, put the gimp or pearl cotton underneath the fabric, lining it up with the pintuck groove. Once cording is lined up under the proper groove, it will follow along for the whole pintuck.

3. Corded pintucks can be stitched without a pintuck foot. Some sewing machines have a foot with a little hole right in the middle of the foot underneath the foot. That is a perfectly proper place to align the cord for shadow pintucks. Remember, if using a regular foot for pintucking, use the side of the foot for guiding this next pintuck.

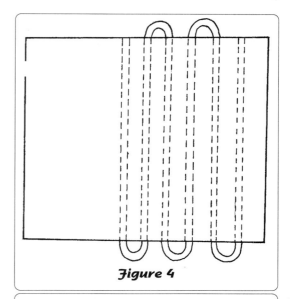

Figure 4

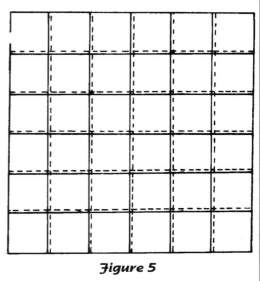

Figure 5

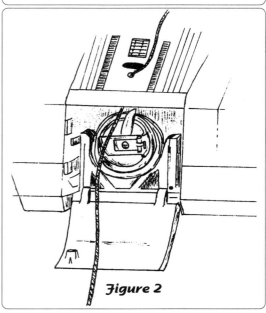

Figure 2

Pintucking Questions & Answers

Q. What is a shadow pintuck?

A. Shadow pintucks are pintucks with a touch of color showing through. Some people simply put a colored thread in the bobbin. You might want to try this to see if you like the effect. To properly shadow pintuck, you must use sheer fabric — batiste, organdy, or pastel silk.

1. Using the cording techniques found in this section, choose #8 pearl cotton in a color you would like to see peek through the batiste or silk.

2. Pintuck, using thread that matches your batiste in the regular sewing machine hook-up, and colored pearl cotton for the shadow. However, I have seen pintucks with colored thread for the regular sewing machine thread and color for the cording. The choice is certainly yours.

Q. What do I do about puckering when I pintuck straight strips of fabric?

A. There are several things that you can try. Sewing machine pintucks tend to pucker slightly. You can shorten your stitch length. You can pull the fabric from the front and back as you sew. You can lightly starch your fabric before you pintuck. You can loosen your bobbin tension. If you do any or all of these things, you may prevent your fabric from puckering, but you will also change the look of the pintuck. Try various techniques on your particular sewing machine. Actually, I don't mind the tiny puckers. They add texture to the garment and make the pintucks stand out.

Q. Would I ever want to use a cord enclosed in my pintucks?

A. Cords will keep the fabric from puckering so much. They also keep the pintuck from smashing flat when you press it. Some people absolutely love cords in their pintucks. In fact, all of the students I met while teaching in Australia use cords within their pintucks.

Cords are also used decoratively with a darker color of cord under white or ecru batiste. One of the dresses in the first *Sew Beautiful* Sweepstakes, had dark peach cording under ecru batiste pintucks; it was fabulous.

Q. Can pintucks be run any way on your fabric, or do they have to run vertically or parallel with the straight of grain?

A. Pintucks can be run in any direction. Consider scalloped pintucks. The ease or difficulty of making pintucks depends on the fabric you use. When making straight pintucks, I prefer to make them on the straight of the grain, parallel to the selvage.

Q. Are there any fabrics to completely avoid for pintucking?

A. Yes. Dotted Swiss is terrible. Printed fabrics, on which the design has been stamped, does not pintuck well. Resulting pintucks are uneven. Stiff fabrics do not machine pintuck well. You will end up with parallel stitching lines with no fabric pulled up between the stitching lines.

Q. What happens when I put a pintuck in the wrong place or my pintuck is crooked? Can I take it out?

A. Yes. Pintucks are easy to take out. Turn your fabric to the wrong side, and slide your seam ripper underneath the bobbin thread, which looks like a zigzag on the underside. The parallel topstitching lines will just come right out after you slice the underside stitching.

Q. How do I press pintucks?

A. I prefer to spray starch a series of tucks before pressing it. Don't be afraid to starch and press pintucks. You might want to pin the edges of the pintucked fabric to the ironing board, stretching it out as far as you can. (This is nothing more than blocking your pintucked fabric.) Slide the iron in one direction to make all the pintucks lay in that one direction. Starch and press again. This will take out most of the puckers. Then, remove the pins from the ironing board. Flip over the pintucked piece you have just blocked and pressed, and press again. Not everyone prefers pintucks that lay in the same direction. For a less stringent appearance, lay your pintucked fabric piece face down on a terry cloth towel for the first and last pressing.

Shaping Curves & Angles With Pintucks

Pintucks are inexpensive to make. They add texture and dimension without adding cost to the dress. They're rarely found on store-bought clothing. One of my favorite things in the whole world to do is to follow pintucked shapes with lace insertion or decorative stitches on your machine for an enchanting finish. Simply use a template and pintuck, then apply insertion like a Swiss handloom. For threads, use white-on-white, ecru-on-ecru, or any pastel color on white or ecru.

The effect of shaped pintucks is so fabulous. Yet virtually everybody is afraid to try them the first time. It is so easy that I just can't wait to share the tricks. I promise, nobody in my schools all over the world ever believes me when I tell them there is an easy way. Then, everybody, virtually everybody, has completed these curved and angled pintucks to absolute perfection. I've heard, "This is really magic!" more than once.

The big question here is, "What foot do I use for scalloped pintucks?" For straight pintucks, I use a pintuck foot with the grooves. That foot is fine for curved or scalloped pintucks also, but I prefer either the regular zigzag foot or the clear appliqué foot, which is plastic and allows easy "see through" of the turning points. Try the pintuck foot, a regular sewing foot, and a clear appliqué foot to see which one you like the best. Like all aspects of heirloom sewing, the "best" foot is really personal preference. Listed below are my absolute recommendations for curved and angled pintucks.

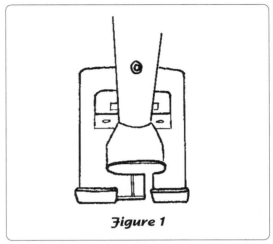

Figure 1

Martha's General Rules Of Curving And Angling Pintucks

Directions

1. Use a regular zigzag foot, or a pintuck foot **(fig. 1)**.

2. Either draw on the pintuck shape, or zigzag lace insertion to the garment. Either draw on pintuck shapes or follow the lace shaping.

   Note: *My favorite way to make lots of pintucks is to follow lace shaping, which has already been stitched to the garment.*

3. Using a ruler, draw straight lines with a fabric marker or washable pencil, bisecting each point where a turnaround with the pintuck must be made. In other words, draw a line at all angles where a turn is necessary to continue stitching. This is the most important point to make with curved and angled pintucks. A bisecting point is not necessary around curves where stops and pivots do not apply. Straight lines must be drawn at every stop and pivot point **(fig. 2)**.

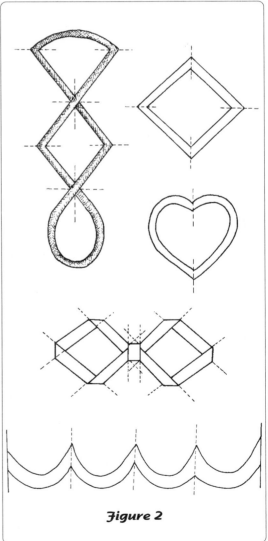

Figure 2

4. Use a 1.6 or a 2.0 double needle. Any wider doesn't curve or turn well!

5. Set the machine for straight sewing, (Width=1.5). Notice this is a very short stitch. This short stitch is necessary for pretty turns at angles.

6. Press Needle Down if the machine has this feature. This means that the needle will remain in the fabric whenever the sewing process stops.

7. Stitch, using either the first line drawn or following around the lace shaping which was stitched previously. The edge of the presser foot will guide along the outside of the lace shape. To continue around curves, turn the fabric and keep stitching; do not pick up the presser foot and pivot. This makes the curves jumpy, not smooth **(fig. 3)**.

8. When approaching a pivot point, let the foot continue to travel to a position that enables a clear view into the hole of the foot. The double needles need to straddle the perpendicular line which was drawn on the fabric. Remember the needles should be in the fabric **(fig. 4)**.

9. Sometimes, the needles won't exactly straddle the line exactly the way they straddled the line on the last turnaround. In this case, lift the presser foot. (Needles are still in the fabric.) Turn the fabric where the edge of the presser foot properly begins in a new direction following the insertion lace shaping or the drawn line, lower the presser foot, and begin sewing again **(fig. 5)**.

Note: *Wait A Minute! Most of you are now thinking, "Martha You Are Crazy. There are two major problems with what you just said. You said to leave the double needles in the fabric, lift the presser foot, turn the fabric, lower the presser foot, and begin sewing again. If I do that, I will probably break my double needles, and there will be a big wad or hump of fabric where I twisted the fabric to turn around to go in a new direction. That will never work!" I know you are thinking these two things because everybody does. Neither one of these things will happen! It is really just like magic. The only way you'll truly believe it is to try it.*

11. After completing one row of double needle pintucks, use the edge of a regular zigzag sewing machine foot guiding along the just stitched pintuck row, as the guide point for more rows. The only thing to remember, is to have made long enough lines to bisect each angle at each turning point. Without the turnaround lines there is no way to know when to stop sewing, where to leave the needles in the fabric, turn around, and begin stitching again. The lines are the real key.

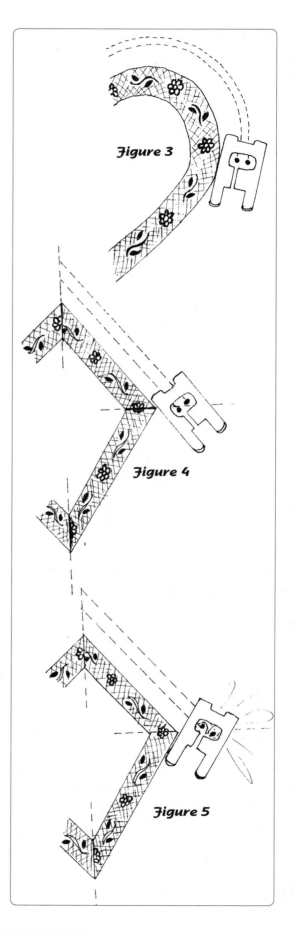

Figure 3

Figure 4

Figure 5

Making A Skirt For Curved Pintuck Scallops Or Other Fancy Design

I always like to give the easiest way to do anything. To divide any garment piece (skirt, bodice, collar or whatever) into equal parts, fold it in half. This marks the halfway point. Continue to fold in halves until the piece is divided as desired. If marking the bottom of a skirt, seam (French seam, flat lock or rolled serger hem) one side first in order to work pintucks across the entire skirt bottom **(fig. 1)**.

To use drawn scallops to make a scalloped piece of lace insertion, guide a regular zigzag sewing machine foot with the double needles along the scalloped lace insertion later for curved pintucks. Remember, those bisecting straight lines are the most significant part of making pintucks turn around properly at angles.

1. Take the skirt, sleeve, bodice, or pattern part and fold it in half. Press **(fig. 2)**.

2. Fold that in half again. Press. When working on a skirt with the front and back already stitched together on one side, fold in quarters. The seam will be on one side. Press on that seam line.

3. Fold in half again. Press. The piece is now divided into eighths **(fig. 3)**.

4. Repeat this process as many times as necessary in order to achieve the desired divisions.

5. Open up the garment part. Use these fold lines as measuring points and guide points **(fig. 4)**.

6. It is now time to make one template, which will fit between the scallops. Using this illustration, make one template, only, with partial scallops on either side of this template. Use a piece of typing paper or notebook paper **(fig. 5)**. It is perfectly accept able to use a dinner plate, a saucer, or a coffee can or whatever to draw the scallop that fits between the folds. Measure up evenly on each side of the scallop before making this one pattern. Where the curve of the scallop meets the folded line of the skirt must be evenly placed on either side. After completing one pattern, trace the first row of scallops on the skirt.

7. Make the template pattern so that the bottom of the piece of paper lines up with the bottom of the skirt. When moving the paper over to mark a new scallop line up the bottom of this template with the bottom of the skirt. Draw the scallops and the dotted A-B lines also.

8. Draw dotted lines to bisect the tops and bottoms of the scallops **(fig. 5)**. Make these lines as tall as the planned scallops will be. These lines serve as the turnaround points for all of the pintucks. They are absolutely necessary for correct turning around at the angles. These lines are the real keys to perfect sets of pintucks traveling in any angle and turning around at the proper point.

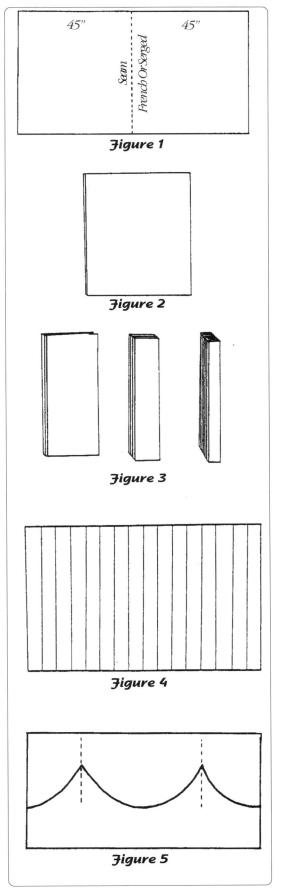

Figure 1

Figure 2

Figure 3

Figure 4

Figure 5

9. Trace with a fabric marker the scallops between the fold lines (**fig. 6**). Move the template from fold to fold, marking the whole scallop and a part of the next one. Mark the straight up-and- down lines bisecting each scallop. These lines will be along the fold lines. When moving the template over to the next fold to mark the next scallop, line up three things: the last piece of the scallop which overlaps, the straight lines, and the bottom of the template along the bottom of the skirt.

10. Use the curved lines for making only the first row of machine pintucks. After that use the edge of the sewing machine foot for guiding the next row of scallops.

11. Follow directions from "Martha's General Rules Of Curving And Angling Pintucks.".

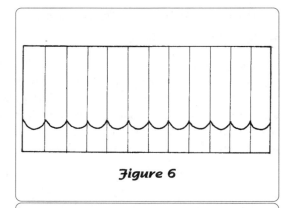

Figure 6

Making Strips Of Pintucking To Insert In Center Of Lace Shapes

One of the prettiest things to do in lace shaping is to make a strip of double needle pintucks and insert these pintucks behind the center of a heart, a diamond, a bow, or an oval. There are several methods of inserting this pintucked strip behind a lace shape. I think the one below is the easiest.

Direction

1. Complete the heart, diamond, or bow and zigzag or machine entredeux stitch (outside only) to the garment skirt, collar, bodice, or whatever. In other words, first make all of the shapes needed to complete a design and zigzag the outside only to the garment (**fig. 1**).

   Note: *If you are making a heart, diamond, oval or bow skirt, go ahead and stitch all the hearts around the skirt (outside stitching only) (**fig. 2**). Trim away the inside fabric of the diamonds, several at a time. Stitch the pin stitching in each of those trimmed hearts before trimming the inside fabric of the next hearts.*

2. Make a straight strip of machine pintucks longer than the actual insides of the shapes, and a little bit taller also (**fig. 3**).

3. After zigzagging or machine entredeux stitching the outside only, of the lace shape (diamond, heart, bow, loop or whatever) to the garment, cut away the whole fabric inside of the lace shape. It is alright to cut almost to the stitching since the heavy stitching of a heavy zigzag or the machine entredeux stitching has hundreds of stitches holding the shape to the garment (**fig. 3**).

   Note: *If you are making a heart, diamond, oval or bow skirt, go ahead and stitch all the hearts around the skirt (outside stitching only). Trim away the inside of the hearts several at a time. Stitch the pin stitching in each of those trimmed hearts before trimming the inside fabric of the next hearts.*

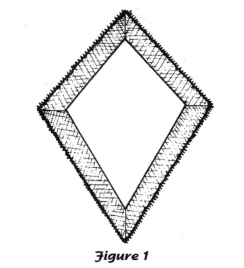

Figure 1

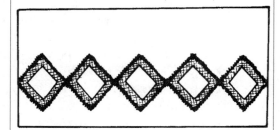

Figure 2

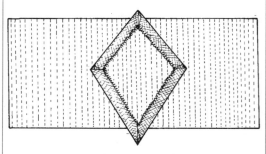

Figure 3 & 4

4. Place the pintucked strip behind one shape at a time. Stitch around the inside of the shape attaching a portion of the pintucked strip **(fig. 4)**. Either zigzag , machine entredeux stitch, or machine pin stitch.

5. Trim away the pintucked strip very close to the zigzag extending from behind the lace heart, diamond, bow or oval.

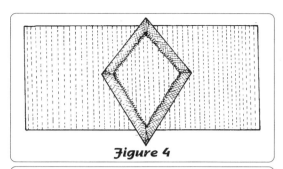

Figure 4

Stitching One Or Two Rows Of Pintucks Inside A Fancy Lace Shape

Unlike inserting a strip of pintucks into a lace shape, when stitching only one or two rows of pintucks following the shape within a heart, bow, diamond, oval or whatever, there is no need to cut away the fabric. Use the double needles, a regular zigzag foot and the drawn lines bisecting each turnaround point.

Directions

1. Make the desired lace shape such as a heart, bow, diamond, oval or whatever. Attach to garment.

2. After shaping the desired lace shape, simply draw the bisecting lines to intersect the turn-around points. Draw the lines only to the inside of the shape if pintucks are only going to be placed inside of the shape **(fig. 1)**.

3. Using the regular zigzag foot and a 1.6 or 2.0 pintuck double needle, travel around the inside of the lace shape using the edge of the zigzag foot to guide along the lace shapes. Use a Needle Down position and a straight stitch with a length of 1.5.

4. Using the directions for making curved and angled pintucks, stitch within the figure.

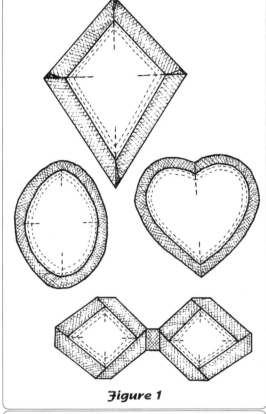

Figure 1

Making Double Needle Shadow Embroidery Designs

When I was in Australia, one of my students who is a sewing teacher in New Zealand asked me if I had ever made shadow embroidered double needle designs. I replied that I hadn't but that I was certainly interested. She then painted on liquid stabilizer, let it dry and placed this piece of fabric in an embroidery hoop. She drew a shadow embroidery design, put in 2.0 double needles, white thread, and proceeded to stitch all the away around that shadow embroidered bow simply straight stitching with a short stitch (1.5 length) and made a perfectly acceptable looking shadow embroidered bow. She used a regular zigzag sewing foot not a pintuck foot with her double needles. Now, shadow work embroidery, it isn't; however, it is very lovely and very quick. You might want to try it **(fig. 2)**.

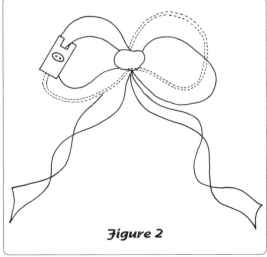

Figure 2

Shadow Appliqué

Different colored fabrics can be applied to the wrong side of a sheer fabric to give a shadow effect. This simple technique adds elegance to collars, blouse fronts, cuffs, and skirt hems. An open zigzag, blanket stitch or other decorative stitch best secures the colored fabrics to the base fabrics.

Supplies

- Sheer base fabric (blouse, collar, etc.)
- Bright or dark appliqué Fabric
- Open toe appliqué foot
- Machine embroidery thread
- Size 70 to 80 needle
- 6" to 8" hoop (wooden machine embroidery or spring tension)
- Marking pens or pencils, water or air soluble
- Small, sharp pointed scissors
- Appliqué scissors

Shadow Appliqué Fabrics

A. Base Fabric

The base fabric should be a sheer fabric so that the fabric appliqué will show through from the wrong side. If a fabric other than white is used, experiment to see how it will change the color of the appliqué fabric. The appliqué will show more distinctly after it is lined.

B. Appliqué Fabric

The appliqué color should be bright enough to show through base fabric. Some colors will look "muddy" under the base fabric. Always test appearance of color by placing a single layer of appliqué fabric between two layers of the base fabric.

General Shadow Appliqué

Directions

1. To determine the size of base fabric to be shadow appliquéed, consider the position of the appliqué. The fabric should extend beyond the appliqué design in all directions, so that it may be placed in the hoop. For example, when doing shadow appliqué on a pocket edge, even though the pocket pattern itself is small, start with a piece of fabric large enough to fit in the hoop (**fig. 1**). Another example would be when placing shadow appliqué near the edge of a collar, the base fabric must be large enough to contain the whole collar pattern plus enough fabric on the edges to hold in the hoop (**fig. 2**).

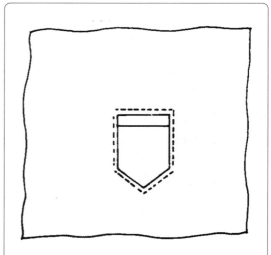

Figure 1

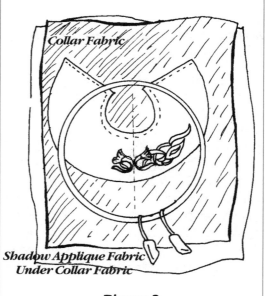

Collar Fabric

**Shadow Applique Fabric
Under Collar Fabric**

Figure 2

2. Press and starch the pre-treated fabric to remove all of the wrinkles and give the fabric some body. Several applications of starch can be used.

3. Trace the pattern piece (cutting lines, seam lines and centerfront line and all other necessary markings) **(fig. 3)**. Trace the design, within the pattern stitching lines, to the base fabric in the desired position **(fig. 4)**. When tracing, especially the design for the appliqué, maintain as fine a line as possible since stitching will follow along directly ON this line. A washable marking pencil with a sharp point is helpful. To trace the design, place the base fabric in a hoop large enough to encompass the design. This will help to hold the fabric flat and keep it from shifting while tracing. Don't pull fabric too tight in the hoop.

4. To determine the thread color to use, place a piece of each of the appliqué fabrics between two layers of base fabric. Match the thread to the color that shows through the base fabric. It will be lighter than the actual appliqué fabric. Use this color for the top thread. White or base fabric color thread can be used in the bobbin throughout the project.

The upper thread tension should be loosened so that the bobbin thread will pull the top thread to the wrong side. It should not be so loose that the bobbin thread forms a straight line on the wrong side. Test to make correct adjustments.

5. Decide what stitch to use to attach the appliqué fabric to the base fabric. There are several choices.

    a. A narrow open zigzag can be used, a stitch width of about 1 mm and a length of 1 mm **(fig. 5)**. This is not a satin stitch, but a short, narrow zigzag stitch.

    b. A pin stitch or blanket stitch can also be used if available **(fig. 6)**. The pin stitch generally has a heavier look than the blanket stitch. The stitch width should be narrowed to about 1 mm and the length may also need to be adjusted. Test on a sample to make adjustments.

6. With machine shadow appliqué, the appliqué fabric is placed to the wrong side of the base fabric and the design worked from foreground to background (opposite from regular machine appliqué). Place both fabrics in a hoop, layered with the right side of the appliqué fabric to the wrong side of the base fabric. When learning to do shadow appliqué by machine, use appliqué fabric large enough to be placed in the hoop with the base fabric. For those who are adept at this technique, it is not necessary to place the fabrics in a hoop **(fig. 7)**. When the stitching is done, care should be taken to keep the appliqué fabric from shifting or wrinkles being stitched in. Pin in place if necessary or use a touch of water-soluble glue stick to hold the fabric in place. Spray starching the appliqué fabric again will help it to remain flat.

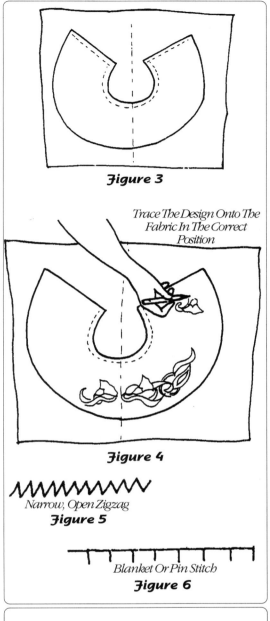

Figure 3

Trace The Design Onto The Fabric In The Correct Position

Figure 4

Narrow, Open Zigzag
Figure 5

Blanket Or Pin Stitch
Figure 6

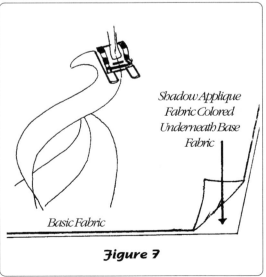

Shadow Applique Fabric Colored Underneath Base Fabric

Basic Fabric

Figure 7

7. Decide on the starting point, generally not a corner or a point. Pull up bobbin thread and tie on by taking several tiny straight stitches on the drawn line of the appliqué pattern. Stitch on the design line to completely enclose the area in that color **(fig. 8)**. When using the pin stitch or blanket stitch, the straight part of the stitch should be on the design line and the "fingers" part or "ladder steps" of the stitch should be piercing the appliqué **(fig. 9)**. Engage "mirror image" if available or stitch in the opposite direction to position the stitch correctly.

8. Trim the appliqué fabric close to the stitching lines, being careful not to cut the stitches **(fig. 10)**. If both the base fabric and the appliqué fabric are in the hoop, remove the hoop, and re-hoop just the base fabric. Trimming will be easier if the base fabric remains in the hoop.

9. Working foreground to background, place the next color to be appliquéed under the base fabric as above and stitch. For areas that touch each other, the stitching must be done on BOTH sides of the appliqué **(fig. 11)** Allow the regular zigzag stitches to just touch each other (not overlap) or the straight part of the pin or blanket stitch to be beside each other **(fig. 12)**.

10. Continue in this manner until all of the appliqué pieces are attached and trimmed.

11. Wash fabric to remove all of the markings.

12. Press with the right side down on a towel.

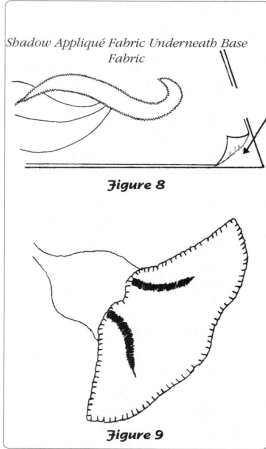

Shadow Appliqué Fabric Underneath Base Fabric

Figure 8

Figure 9

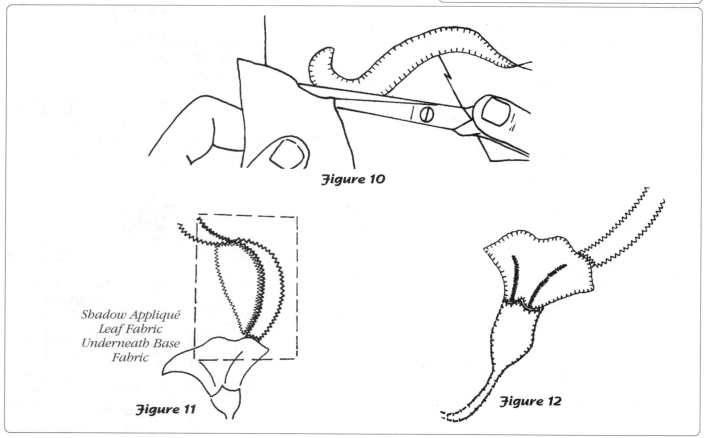

Figure 10

Shadow Appliqué Leaf Fabric Underneath Base Fabric

Figure 11

Figure 12

French Waterfall Technique

Supplies:

- Fabric - Color #1
- Fabric - Color #2
- Insertion Lace
- Wing Needle and Tear-Away Stabilizer - If using a wing needle, a hemstitch should be used to stitch lace to fabric.

Directions

1. Trace the waterfall template on the center fabric (color #1). If a waterfall template is not available a template can be made by tracing two rows of identical scallops, mirror imaged from each other and an equal distance apart.

2. Shape the lace along the template lines using the directions for lace scallops found on page 242.

3. Pin in place and stitch along the inside edge of the lace using a zigzag or wing needle hemstitch **(fig. 1)**.

4. Trim the fabric from behind the lace creating a scalloped lace panel **(fig. 2)**.

5. Place the scalloped lace panel on the base fabric (color #2). Pin in place and stitch along the outer edges of the lace scallops using a zigzag or wing needle hemstitch **(fig. 3)**.

6. Trim the fabric from behind the lace panel.

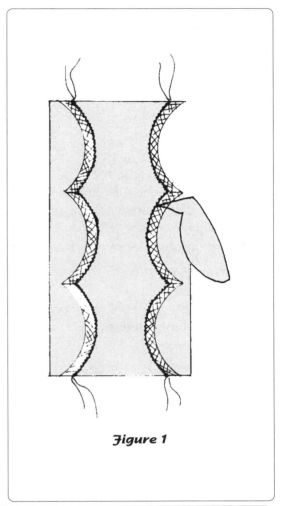

Figure 1

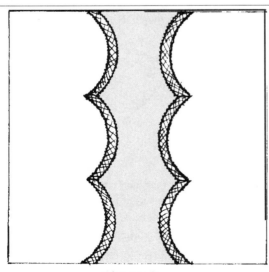

Figure 2

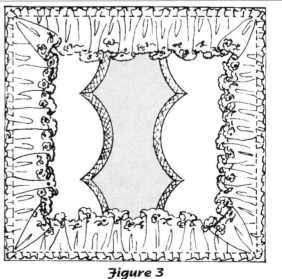

Figure 3

Maderia Appliqué Techniques

Madeira appliqué originated on the island of Madeira in Portugal. It involves stitching a fabric onto another fabric. By hand, the raw edges are turned under and the folded edge is stitched down using the Point de Paris stitch. Here, we have changed it so that it can be done on the sewing machine. This technique can be used for applying borders ir shapes to collars, cuffs, etc.

Supplies

Base fabric
Appliqué fabric
Water soluble stabilizer
Fine weight machine embroidery thread
Water and/or air soluble marking pens
Trimming scissors
Wing or large size needle for entredeux or pin stitch

Optional Supplies:

Light box
Temporary water-soluble, spray-on adhesive (KK-200)
Water soluble glue stick
Point turner

General Madeira Appliqué

Directions

1. Pretreat all fabric since WSS will need to be rinsed away when finished.

2. Trace the appliqué pattern to the right side of a block of the appliqué fabric or on the WSS.

3. Layer the WSS to the right side of the appliqué fabric.

4. Stitch completely around the design with a short, straight stitch (1 to 1.5 mm) **(fig. 1)**.

5. Trim the seam allowance to 1/8 inch. Clip and notch curves as needed.

6. Press flat on the fabric side.

7. Slit the WSS in the center **(fig. 2)**

8. Turn the WSS to the wrong side of the appliqué, which turns the seam allowance to the wrong side.

9. Press to form a sharp crease at the stitching line **(fig. 3)**.

10. Place the appliqué piece with the turned under seam allowance in position on the base fabric. Pin or glue stick in place **(fig. 4)**.

11. Use an entredeux, pin stitch or other desired stitch to stitch the edge of the appliqué to the base fabric **(fig. 5)**. Adjustments in width and/or length may be required to achieve the desired look. Use of a wing or large size needle will create a more

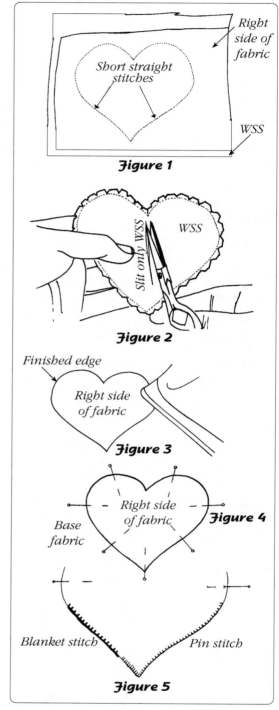

Figure 1

Figure 2

Figure 3

Figure 4

Figure 5

obvious hole for the entredeux or pin stitch. Always test on excess fabrics to achieve the desired effect.

12. Rinse to remove the WSS that is under the appliqué.

Madeira Appliqué Collar and Hem

Supplies

Base fabric
Appliqué fabric for border
Water soluble stabilizer (WSS)
Fine weight machine embroidery thread
Water and/or air soluble marking pens
Trimming scissors
Wing or large size needle for entredeux or pin stitch

Optional Supplies:
Paper stabilizer (if dark appliqué fabric is used)

I. Madeira Appliqué Collar

1. Trace the collar pattern and the Madeira template on a square of appliqué fabric. If the appliqué fabric is dark and the pattern can not be traced easily, layer the collar in the following manner to transfer the pattern and ready the appliqué fabric for application: appliqué fabric (right side up), water soluble stabilizer, and paper stabilizer with the traced pattern **(fig. 1)**. Pin together. If the pattern can be traced on the appliqué fabric omit the paper stabilizer layer using just the water soluble stabilizer. The traced pattern should be seen through the water soluble stabilizer.

2. Stitch, with short straight stitches, around the outer edge, back edges and neck edge of the collar and the Madeira template lines.

3. Carefully tear away the paper stabilizer, if used. The Madeira fabric square and water soluble stabilizer will be left **(fig. 2)**.

4. Place the collar fabric square and the appliqué fabric/WSS square together, with the wrong side of the collar fabric and the water soluble stabilizer side together. Pin in place.

5. With the appliqué fabric side up, stitch 1/4" inside the cutting line (stitching line sewn in step 2) **(fig. 3)**.

6. Trim all layers along the outer stitching line, up the back and around the neck **(fig. 4)**.

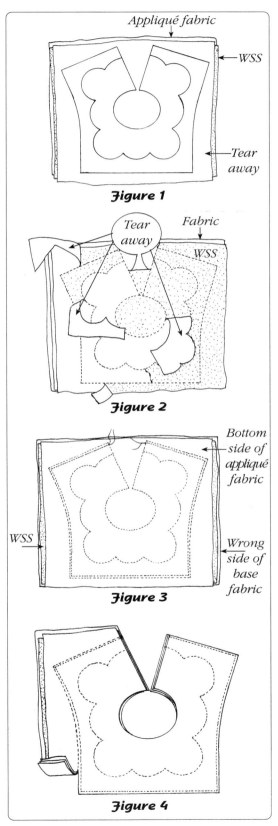

Figure 1

Figure 2

Figure 3

Figure 4

7. Trim appliqué fabric and WSS only, 1/8" away from the Madeira template stitching lines. Clip and/or notch the curves corners and points **(fig. 5)**.

8. Turn the appliqué border fabric to the right side of the collar fabric. The WSS will now be on the outside **(fig. 6)**. Use a point turner to ensure sharp points. Pull or trim the WSS from the outer stitching and turn the WSS to the inside of the appliqué fabric. The WSS will now be between the appliqué fabric and the collar fabric (see fig. 6). The WSS will act as a facing for the appliqué border, making the inside edges easy to turn under. Use a point turner to ensure sharp points. Press well.

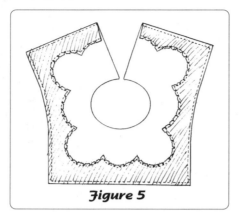

Figure 5

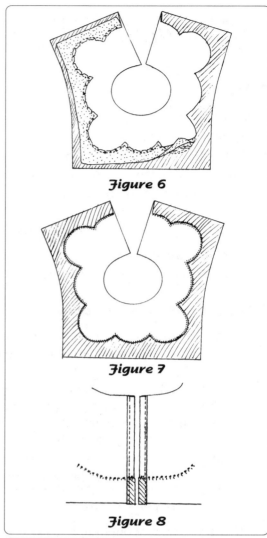

Figure 6

Figure 7

Figure 8

9. Pin in place. Use a pinstitch or other desired stitch to attach the top edge of the appliqué fabric to the collar **(fig. 7)**.

10. Fold the back edges of the collar to the inside 1/8" and 1/8" again. Stitch in place **(fig. 8)**.

11. Place the collar on the dress and finish as directed in the dress directions. If the collar is to be detachable, finish the neck with a bias facing or bias binding.

II. Madeira Appliqué Hem

1. Stitch the skirt together to form a cylinder **(fig. 9)**. Set aside.

2. Stitch the border strips together to form a cylinder. Make sure the circumference of the border and the skirt are the same. Trace the border template along the right side of the border fabric **(fig. 10)**.

3. Cut WSS strips to fit the circumference of the border. The width of the WSS strips should be about 1" less than the width of the border. Pin the WSS to the right side of the border fabric covering the template lines.

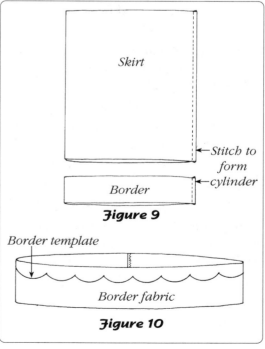

Skirt

←Stitch to form
←cylinder

Border

Figure 9

Border template

Border fabric

Figure 10

4. Stitch the WSS to the border fabric using short straight stitches along the template lines **(fig. 11)**.

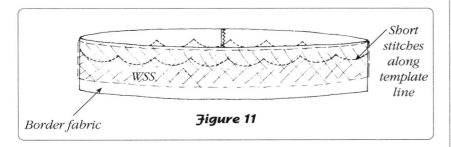

Border fabric

WSS

Short stitches along template line

Figure 11

5. Place the right side (the side with the WSS) of the border fabric to the wrong side of the skirt fabric. Stitch the skirt to the border fabric along the lower edge using a 1/4" seam.

6. Trim top edge of the border fabric and WSS only, 1/8" away from the template stitching lines. Clip and/or notch the curves corners and points **(fig. 12)**.

7. Turn the appliqué border fabric to the right side of the skirt fabric. The WSS will now be on the outside **(fig. 13)**. Turn the WSS to the inside of the border fabric. The WSS will now be between the border fabric and the skirt fabric. The WSS will act as a facing for the border making the inside edges easy to turn under. Use a point turner to ensure sharp points. Press well **(fig. 14)**.

8. Pin in place. Use a pinstitch or other desired stitch to attach the top edge of the appliqué border fabric to the skirt. Press well **(fig. 15)**.

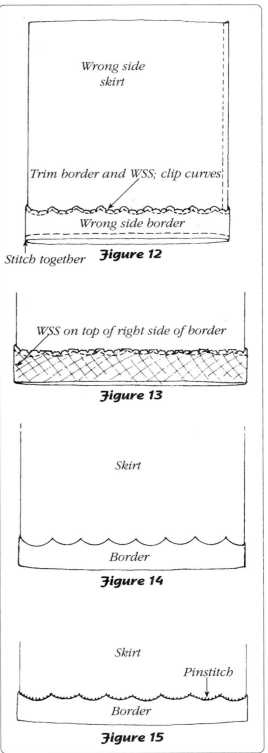

Wrong side skirt

Trim border and WSS; clip curves

Wrong side border

Stitch together **Figure 12**

WSS on top of right side of border

Figure 13

Skirt

Border

Figure 14

Skirt

Pinstitch

Border

Figure 15

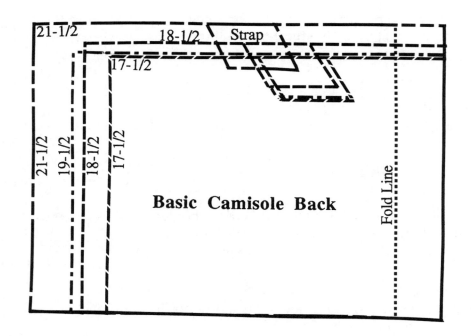

21-1/2
18-1/2   Strap
17-1/2

21-1/2 19-1/2 18-1/2 17-1/2

Basic Camisole Back

Fold Line

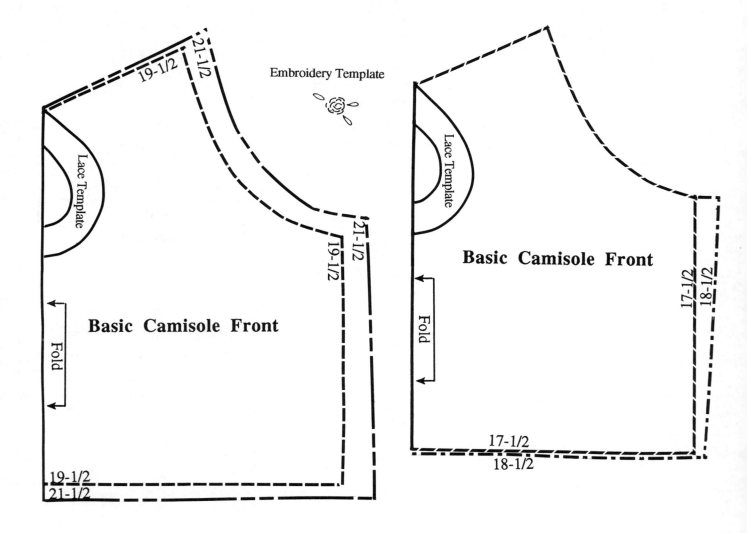

21-1/2 19-1/2

Embroidery Template

Lace Template

21-1/2 19-1/2

Basic Camisole Front

Fold

19-1/2
21-1/2

Lace Template

Basic Camisole Front

Fold

17-1/2 18-1/2

17-1/2
18-1/2

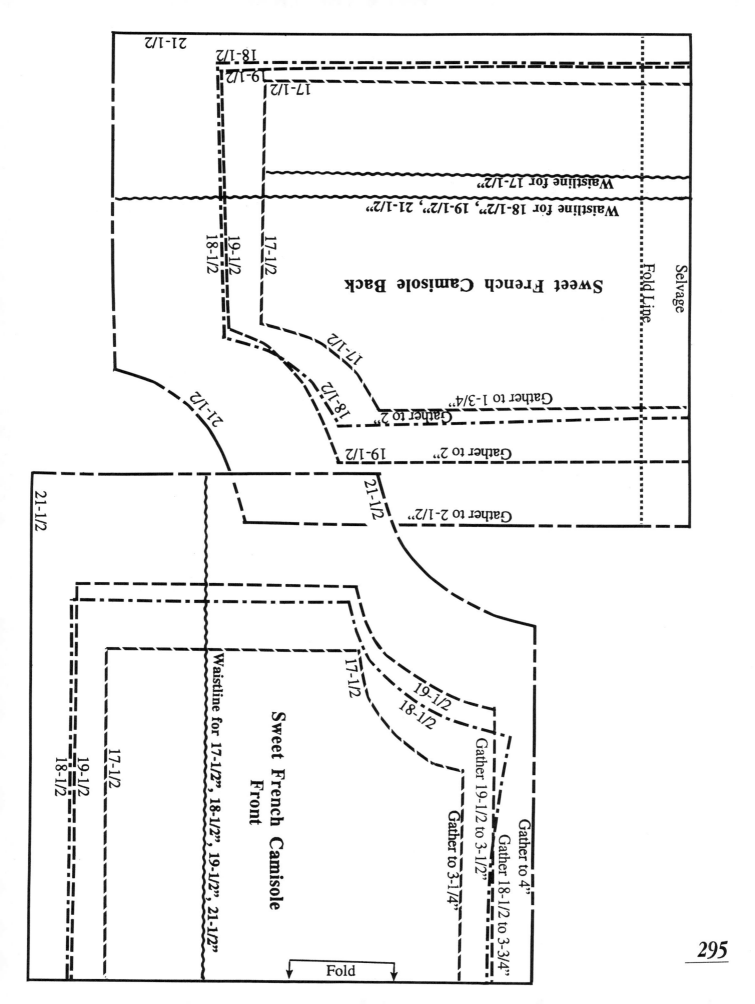

Sweet French Camisole Back

21-1/2

18-1/2
19-1/2

17-1/2

Waistline for 17-1/2"

Waistline for 18-1/2", 19-1/2", 21-1/2"

Fold Line

Selvage

17-1/2

18-1/2

Gather to 1-3/4"

Gather to 2"

19-1/2

Gather to 2"

21-1/2

Gather to 2-1/2"

21-1/2

17-1/2

19-1/2
18-1/2

Gather 19-1/2 to 3-1/2"

Gather 18-1/2 to 3-3/4"

Gather to 4"

Gather to 3-1/4"

Sweet French Camisole
Front

Waistline for 17-1/2", 18-1/2", 19-1/2", 21-1/2"

17-1/2

19-1/2
18-1/2

Fold

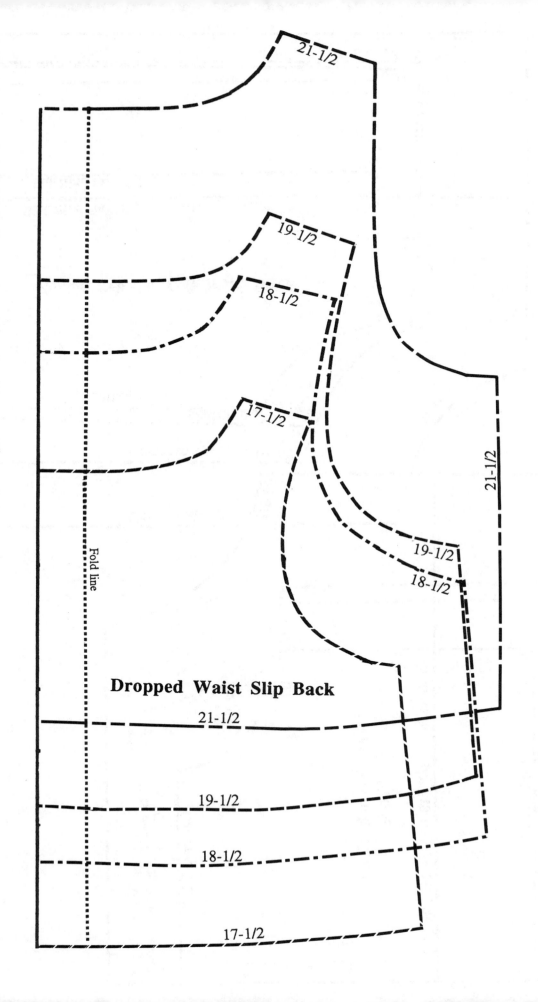

21-1/2

19-1/2

18-1/2

17-1/2

Fold line

21-1/2

19-1/2

18-1/2

Dropped Waist Slip Back

21-1/2

19-1/2

18-1/2

17-1/2

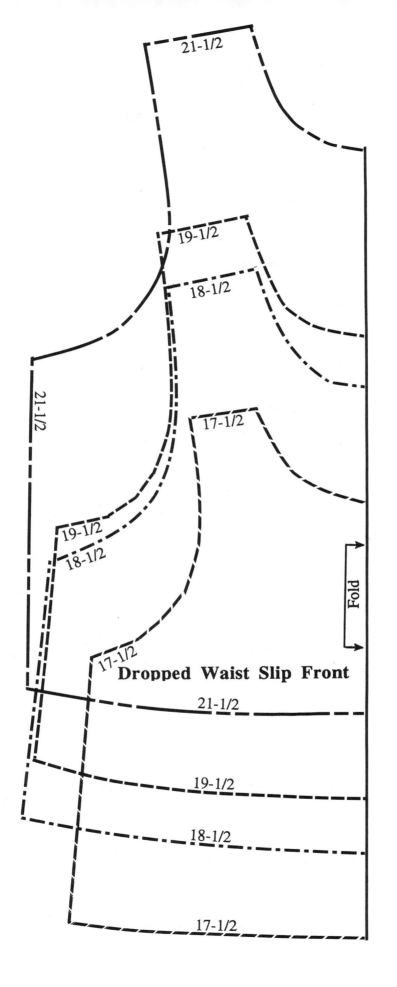

21-1/2

19-1/2

18-1/2

21-1/2

17-1/2

19-1/2

18-1/2

Fold

17-1/2

Dropped Waist Slip Front

21-1/2

19-1/2

18-1/2

17-1/2

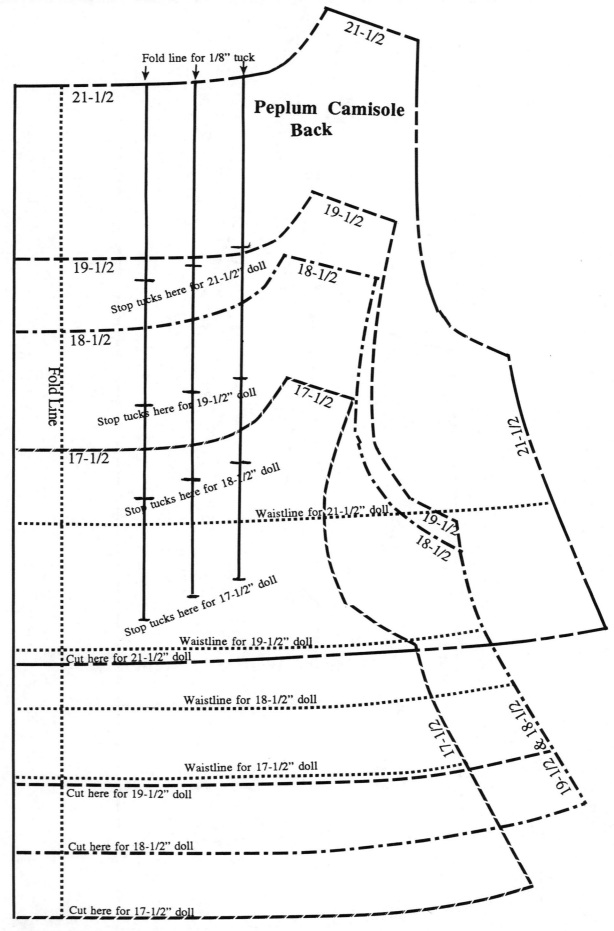

Fold line for 1/8" tuck

21-1/2

21-1/2

**Peplum Camisole
Back**

19-1/2

18-1/2

19-1/2

Stop tucks here for 21-1/2" doll

18-1/2

Fold Line

17-1/2

Stop tucks here for 19-1/2" doll

17-1/2

21-1/2

Stop tucks here for 18-1/2" doll

Waistline for 21-1/2" doll

19-1/2

18-1/2

Stop tucks here for 17-1/2" doll

Waistline for 19-1/2" doll

Cut here for 21-1/2" doll

Waistline for 18-1/2" doll

17-1/2

19-1/2 & 18-1/2

Waistline for 17-1/2" doll

Cut here for 19-1/2" doll

Cut here for 18-1/2" doll

Cut here for 17-1/2" doll

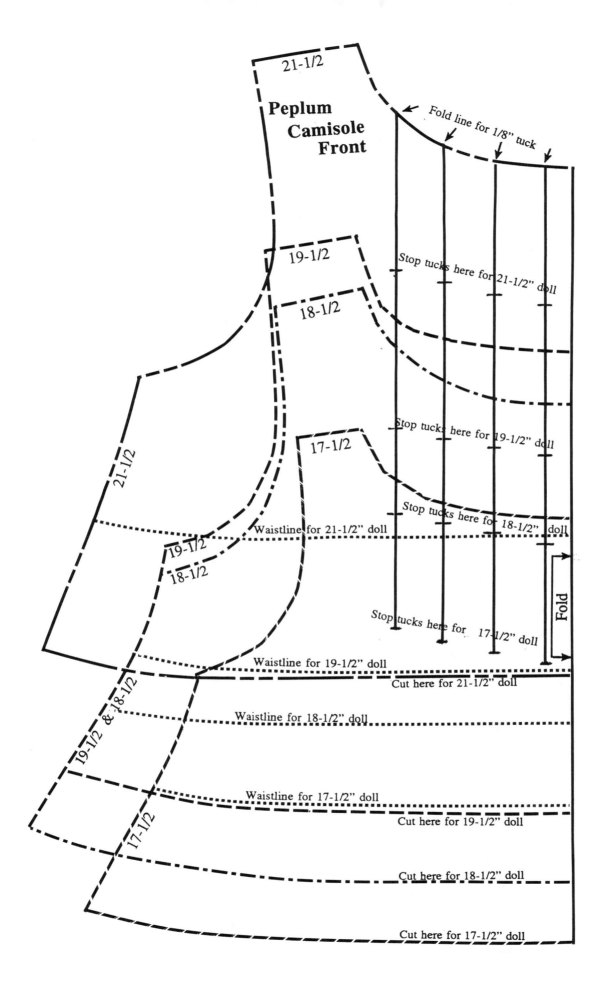

Peplum
Camisole
Front

21-1/2

Fold line for 1/8" tuck

19-1/2

18-1/2

Stop tucks here for 21-1/2" doll

21-1/2

17-1/2

Stop tucks here for 19-1/2" doll

19-1/2

18-1/2

Stop tucks here for 18-1/2" doll

Waistline for 21-1/2" doll

Fold

Stop tucks here for 17-1/2" doll

Waistline for 19-1/2" doll

Cut here for 21-1/2" doll

19-1/2 & 18-1/2

Waistline for 18-1/2" doll

Waistline for 17-1/2" doll

17-1/2

Cut here for 19-1/2" doll

Cut here for 18-1/2" doll

Cut here for 17-1/2" doll

299

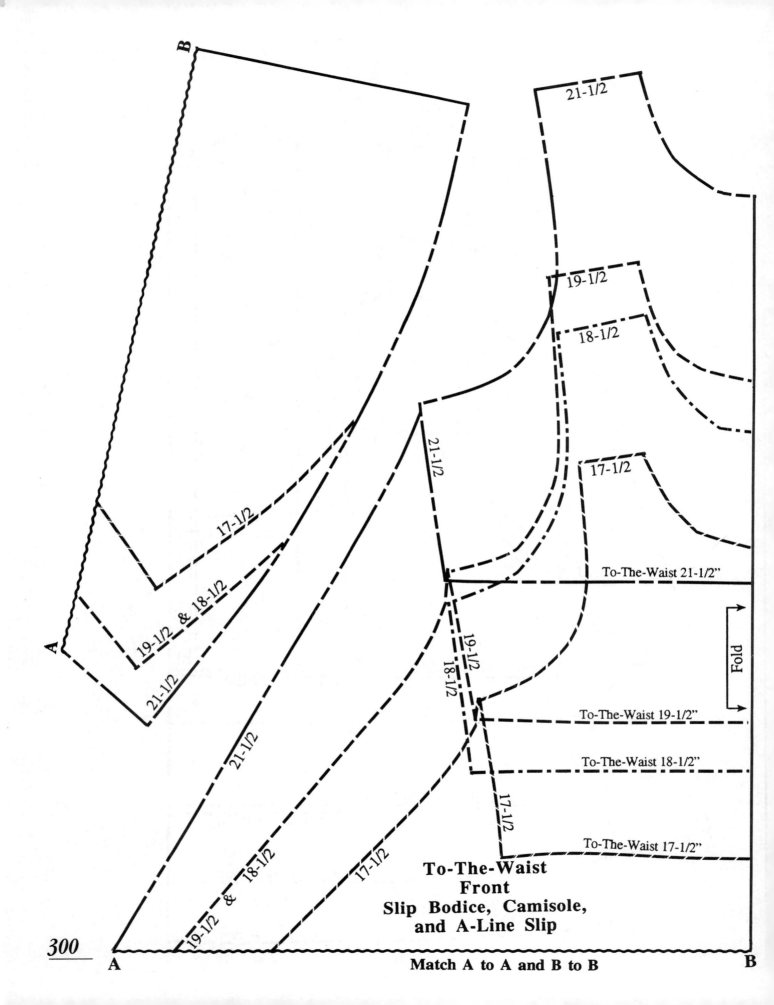

B

A

21-1/2

19-1/2

18-1/2

17-1/2

21-1/2

17-1/2

19-1/2 & 18-1/2

21-1/2

21-1/2

19-1/2 & 18-1/2

17-1/2

To-The-Waist 21-1/2"

19-1/2

18-1/2

17-1/2

Fold

To-The-Waist 19-1/2"

To-The-Waist 18-1/2"

To-The-Waist 17-1/2"

**To-The-Waist
Front
Slip Bodice, Camisole,
and A-Line Slip**

A

Match A to A and B to B

B

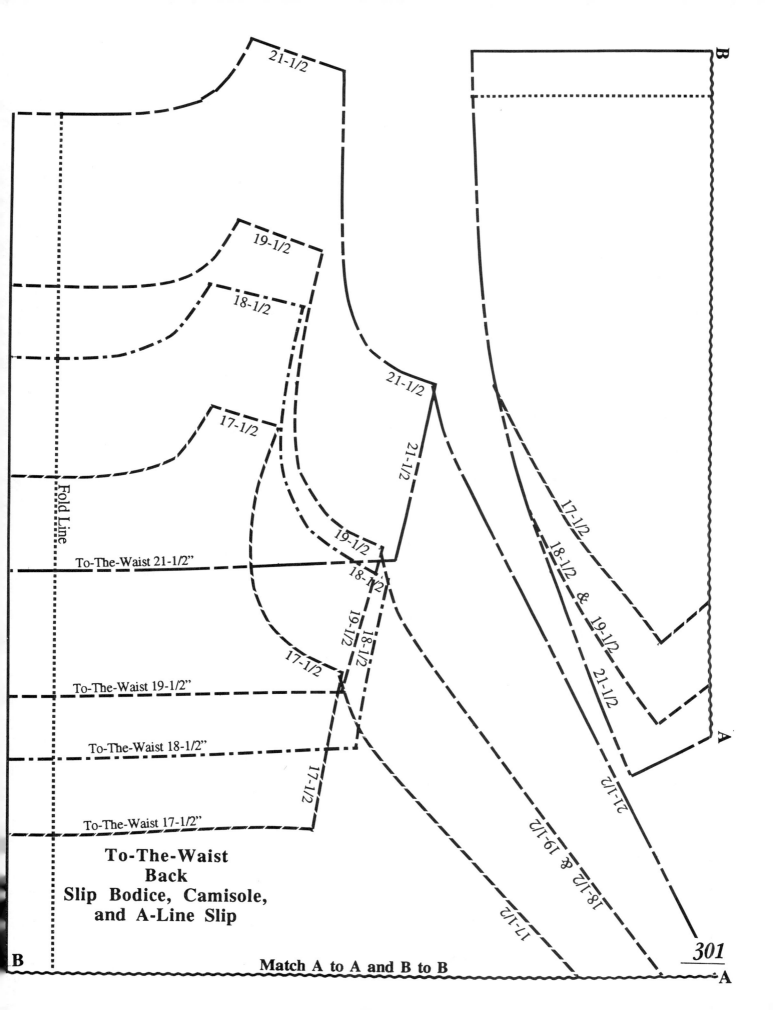

21-1/2

19-1/2

18-1/2

17-1/2

21-1/2

21-1/2

19-1/2

18-1/2

Fold Line

To-The-Waist 21-1/2"

19-1/2
18-1/2

17-1/2

17-1/2
18-1/2 & 19-1/2

21-1/2

To-The-Waist 19-1/2"

To-The-Waist 18-1/2"

To-The-Waist 17-1/2"

17-1/2

**To-The-Waist
Back
Slip Bodice, Camisole,
and A-Line Slip**

17-1/2

18-1/2 & 19-1/2

21-1/2

B

A

B

A

301

Match A to A and B to B

Index